INTERNATIONAL STUDENT SECURITY

More than three million students globally are on the move each year, crossing borders for their tertiary education. Many travel from Asia and Africa to English speaking countries, led by the United States. The provider countries include the UK, Australia and New Zealand, where students pay tuition fees at commercial rates and prop up an education export sector that has become lucrative for the host nations. But the 'no frills' commercial form of tertiary education for international students, designed to minimise costs and maximise revenues, leaves many students feeling under-protected and disenfranchised.

International Student Security, which draws on a close study of international students in Australia, exposes opportunity, difficulty, danger and courage on a massive scale in the global student market. It works through many unresolved issues confronting students and their families, including personal safety, language proficiency, finances, abuses at work, sub-standard housing, dealings with immigration authorities and universities, student networks and personal support, and issues of loneliness, racism and segregation. It calls for closer and more student-centred forms of regulation and support, and for an education that brings international and local students closer together. The authors' underlying purpose is ambitious and far-sighted. It is nothing less than to extend liberal humanism beyond national borders to globally mobile populations; and to support a cosmopolitan international education that facilitates intercultural exchange on equal terms between the West, emerging Asia and the developing world, foreshadowing the future global society.

Simon Marginson is Professor of Higher Education at the Centre for the Study of Higher Education at the University of Melbourne, Australia.

Christopher Nyland is Professor of International Business in the Faculty of Business and Economics at Monash University in Melbourne, Australia.

Erlenawati Sawir is Research Fellow at the International Education Research Centre at Central Queensland University in Melbourne, Australia.

Helen Forbes-Mewett is Research Fellow/Lecturer in Sociology in the School of Social Sciences at La Trobe University in Melbourne, Australia.

SIMON MARGINSON,
CHRISTOPHER NYLAND,
ERLENAWATI SAWIR AND
HELEN FORBES-MEWETT

WITH THE ASSISTANCE OF GABY RAMIA AND
SHARON SMITH

INTERNATIONAL STUDENT SECURITY

CAMBRIDGE
UNIVERSITY PRESS

CAMBRIDGE UNIVERSITY PRESS
Cambridge, New York, Melbourne, Madrid, Cape Town, Singapore,
São Paulo, Delhi, Dubai, Tokyo

Cambridge University Press
477 Williamstown Road, Port Melbourne, VIC 3207, Australia

Published in the United States of America by Cambridge University Press, New York

www.cambridge.org
Information on this title: www.cambridge.org/9780521138055

First published 2010

Cover design by David Thomas
Typeset by Aptara
Printed in China by Printplus

A catalogue record for this publication is available from the British Library

National Library of Australia Cataloguing in Publication data
Marginson, Simon.
International student security / Simon Marginson . . . [et al].
9780521138055 (pbk.)
Includes index.
Students, Foreign – Australia – Protection.
Students, Foreign – Australia – Economic Conditions.
Students, Foreign – Australia – Social Conditions.
Foreign study – Australia.
Nyland, Christopher.
Sawir, Erlenawati.
Forbes-Mewett, Helen.
378.19820994

ISBN 978-0-521-13805-5 paperback

CONTENTS

FIGURES

TABLES

ABOUT THE AUTHORS

Simon Marginson is a Professor of Higher Education at the Centre for the Study of Higher Education in the Graduate School of Education at the University of Melbourne in Melbourne. He works on globalisation and higher education, knowledge economy policy and issues of freedom and creativity, comparative and international education, and university rankings with emphasis on the Asia–Pacific region. His previous books include *Markets in Education* (1997), *The Enterprise University: Power, governance and reinvention in Australia* (2000) with Mark Considine, *Creativity and the Global Knowledge Economy* (2009) and *Global Creation: Space, mobility and synchrony in the age of the knowledge economy* (2010), the last two books with Peter Murphy and Michael Peters.

Christopher Nyland is a Professor of International Business in the Faculty of Business and Economics at Monash University in Melbourne. He works on human security and international business, including foreign investment and employee security, enterprise flexibility and worker security in transition societies, the new economics of the lifecycle, international students and crime, and the history of business thought. His previous books include *Reduced Worktime and the Management of Production* (1999), *Globalisation in the Asian Region* (2004) and the *Status of Women in Classical Economic Thought* (2006).

Erlenawati Sawir is Research Fellow at the International Education Research Centre of Central Queensland University in Melbourne. Previously, she worked as Research Fellow at Monash University and the University of Melbourne, and prior to 2000 as a Senior Lecturer at the University of Jambi in Sumatra, Indonesia. A 2003 Monash PhD graduate in sociolinguistics and education, and specialist in international education, she has contributed to *Asian EFL Journal*, *Australian Journal of Education*, *International Education Journal*, *Higher Education*, *Journal of Studies in International Education*, *Journal of Asia Pacific Education*, *Higher Education Policy* and *Global Social Policy*.

Helen Forbes-Mewett is Research Fellow/Lecturer in Sociology in the School of Social Sciences at La Trobe University. She graduated with a PhD on international student security from Monash University in Melbourne in 2009. She is currently working on international student safety from crime. Her scholarly contributions include articles in *Journal of Education and Work*, *Labour and Industry*, *Journal of Studies in International Education* and *Higher Education Policy*. Her work is in the sociology of organisations, social inclusion and human security.

PREFACE

The journey of a thousand miles begins beneath one's feet.
~ attributed to Chinese philosopher Lao-tzu, 614–531 BCE.

International Student Security has been built on a full engagement with its topic. It has been nurtured by four research projects, a commissioned literature review and much reading and discussion. It is the product of planning sessions, research data collection, conference papers, policy interventions and participation in media and public debate in several Asia–Pacific countries. Often it has been controversial. The $16 billion international education industry in Australia is good at market research and image management but uncomfortable when critical research findings are discussed. Researchers not owned by the industry create a strategic dilemma for it. In the process of the research we, the authors, have been alternatively abused, invited, enticed and ignored. None of this blocked the research or changed our findings. Nor did the industry assist. None of our efforts to raise research money from industry sources worked, though we do sense there is now more interest in our research than there was before, and it might be contributing to industry reassessment. We are deeply grateful to the Australian Research Council whose unstinting support for critically minded scholarly research made this book possible.

From 2003–6 the research was carried out from Monash University. We sincerely thank the Monash Institute for Global Movements, which supported the first two projects in Australia and New Zealand in which perspectives and methods were developed. An Australian Research Council Discovery Grant (Nyland, Marginson, Ramia, with Michael Gallagher) underpinned the empirical work. Simon Marginson was supported by an ARC Professorial Fellowship, which provided invaluable scholarship time. The Queensland government funded a 2007 literature review on student safety. The Centre for the Study of Higher Education at the University of Melbourne hosted meetings of the project group in 2006–9.

Above all, the research, book preparation and forays into the public and policy arenas were sustained by involvement with our subjects, the international students we interviewed. Research on international education rarely foregrounds the voices of the students themselves. It should. They have much to say. We are deeply grateful to the 200 voluntary student interviewees from 35 nations. We trust the book is worthy of them. (Of course none are responsible for its interpretations.) Each of us has been changed by our encounter with the thoughts, ideas and feelings of the interviewees. International students in Australia are engaged in a challenging project of self-formation. We are in awe of what they achieve. We know that if the circumstances were more favourable to them they could achieve more. In preparing *International Student Security* we have been conscious that they deserve more respect and that their self-determining freedoms should be advanced.

The work program was developed in productive research program meetings attended by the authors, Gaby Ramia and Sharon Smith. Gaby was at the core of the work. His ideas on policy and regulation helped shaped the book. Sharon joined us for the second half of the work. Her knowledge of policy and regulation and forensic research assistance on housing, employment and safety were invaluable. Joint grant holder Ana Deumert provided early wisdom before moving to South Africa. Felicity Rawlings-Sanaei was joint grant holder for the research in New Zealand. Ly Tran, who is researching internationalisation in vocational education, provided valued research assistance on student safety.

Simon Marginson prepared first drafts of chapters 1–4, 8, 10, 11, 13, 15 and 16, as well as the introductions to parts 2 and 3; he also edited the manuscript. Chris Nyland provided first drafts of chapters 6, 7 and 9. Erlenawati Sawir provided first drafts of chapters 12 and 14. Helen Forbes-Mewett drafted chapter 5 and assisted with the final edits. Chris led the focus on human security across a larger program of research on global markets and assembled the research team. Erlenawati conducted all the interviews with international students and managed most of the project administration. Other interviews were conducted by Gaby and Felicity in Australia and New Zealand, and Chris and Helen in China. Helen provided access to her PhD study of international student security at Monash, now completed.

In preparation of the book Simon drew on work on globalisation and international education prepared for the Organisation for Economic Cooperation and Development (OECD), the European Commission and the Australian government, and data from other ARC-supported research, including a 1998–2000 Large Grant project with Fazal Rizvi on the internationalisation of Australian higher education. He would also like to thank Professor Yamamoto Shinichi and the staff of the Research Institute for Higher Education at Hiroshima University, a generous scholarly setting for completion of the last four chapters.

In this total body of work, there is a further book by Simon Marginson and Erlenawati Sawir, *Intercultural Education and Self-formation*, which focuses on intercultural relations in international education, including teaching and learning. That book was prepared simultaneously with the present volume. Gaby Ramia is anchoring another jointly authored volume on student security and national and global governance, drawing on the empirical work in Australia and New Zealand.

We are most grateful to our publisher, Debbie Lee at Cambridge University Press. Debbie's wisdom and enthusiasm have been essential. We also thank Sandra Goldbloom Zurbo for splendid editing, and David Thomas for the cover design.

We also sincerely thank for their help at different times and in various ways Phil Altbach, Sophie Arkoudis, Catherine Armitage, Melissa Banks, Fiona Buffinton, Shanton Chang, Tony Crooks, Sushi Das, Paula Dunstan, Julie Hare, Jeroen Huisman, Richard James, Jane Kenway, Jenny Lee, Allan Luke, Joanne Mather, Grant McBurnie, Dennis Murray, Rajani Naidoo, Tony Pollock, Field Rickards, Fazal Rizvi, Luke Slattery, Sue Willis, Hans de Wit, Adrian Wong and Christopher Ziguras. None are responsible for the contents of the book.

Earlier and different drafts of several chapters were published as follows.

- Finances (chapter 5): Forbes-Mewett, H., Marginson, S., Nyland, C., Ramia, G. & Sawir, E., 'Australian University *International* Student Finances', *Higher Education Policy*, 22 (2), 141–61 (2009).
- Work (chapter 6): Nyland, C., Forbes-Mewett, H., Marginson, S., Ramia, G., Sawir, L. & Smith, S., International student-workers

in Australia: a new vulnerable workforce, *Journal of Education and Work*, 22 (1), 47–60 (2008).
- Loneliness (chapter 14): Sawir, E., Marginson, S., Deumert, A., Nyland, C. & Ramia, G., 'Loneliness and international students – an Australian study', *Journal of Studies in International Education,* 12 (2), 148–80 (2008).
- Intercultural relations (chapter 15): Marginson, S., 'Sojourning students and creative cosmopolitans', in M. Peters, S. Marginson and P. Murphy, *Creativity and the Global Knowledge Economy*. New York: Peter Lang, 217–56 (2009).

PART 1 STUDENTS IN THE GLOBAL MARKET

1 THE STUDENTS

There's hell a lot of differences between living there and living here. The advantage of living out here is it teaches you how to be independent, the survival of the fittest. How to do things, manage your entire life. Back home, you have your parents to support you, back up. Out here, there is no back up; you're on your own. There are crucial decisions, and the decisions have to be taken by you, not by your parents. You learn a lot.

~ male, 27, business, India

INTRODUCTION: HAPPY DAYS

It is early December in Melbourne, Australia, and a pleasant 24°C. Summer has just begun. Those hot dry north winds that make life difficult in southern Australia and drive everyone to the beach, are still weeks away. We are on a large university campus where people are gathering for the graduation ceremony. The string quartet is tuning up to welcome them. The baroque musicians would be out of place in other student settings but today they seem to be exactly right, hinting at something special, at that reservoir of ineffable culture, the mediaeval mystery of deep learning, that the university represents. Graduation is about rites of passage and the journey into work and profession, about long years of investment of family money and economic benefits received, but it is also about something scholastic and timeless and the ceremony will reflect that. Altogether 415 students today will be invested as bachelors, masters and doctoral degree holders. Among the students and their families entering the university hall are many Asian faces. Almost half of the soon-to-be graduates are international students, mostly from China, Malaysia, Singapore, Indonesia and India.

Excited students greet each other and their voices echo between the buildings. The atmosphere is upbeat and joyful as if Christmas, which is celebrated by most but not all of the people who are accumulating here, has come early. Many parents and siblings, beautifully dressed in dominant blacks and whites as if they are attending a wedding, seem to glow. Some of the soon-to-be graduates have also made the effort. Others have stuck to their principles, draping the black academic gowns and newly won degree colours supplied by the university over blue jeans with frayed edges above white trainers. Some graduands wear their black mortarboards perched on top of their heads, some carry them a little awkwardly at their sides and others are making as if to throw them in the air in celebration as in the classic graduation photographs. Digital cameras are everywhere. Compact knots of people form, smile in unison and disperse.

It is a great day, one of those truly happy occasions without a cloud in the sky that come along a few times in life and are always remembered. For the families who have journeyed en masse from east and southeast Asia at much expense for this special 90 minutes, the day is especially poignant. Often it has been a great struggle to sustain full cost fee payments and there have been years of constant worry about their children. Were they getting enough to eat? What would happen if they were sick? Was their job stopping them from studying? Who were their friends? Were they getting into trouble? Why hadn't they rung? Now it has all been worthwhile. They have made it, they have finished their degrees. They have learnt to speak good English. The future is bright. They can stay in Australia, seek a professional job and apply for permanent residence. Or they can come home to marry and take a respected place in the community, contribute to the family business and the nation and help to pay for the overseas education of their brothers and sisters.

For the Australian university, also, today is nothing but positive. University leaders and professors watch the families enter the hall as they have done so often before, feeding off the atmosphere around them. The long procession past the chancellor is tedious, but no matter how many graduation ceremonies you attend there is always something warm and fulfilling about them. The happiness of the participants, and the respect parents and families show for the university and its process, ground the university on its own terms and declare its moral worth. Graduation makes up for the indifference many of the soon-to-be graduates showed towards their teachers. The university invests new hopes in its charges; once they leave (the university hopes) they will become increasingly sentimental and wealthy alumni. Especially, every batch of international graduates, with its clutch of younger brothers and sisters who will attend in future years, is like gold. Without those international graduates and their families, without the continuing growth year by year in their numbers, the university simply could not stay afloat. Their tuition fees, which are carefully pushed up when feasible, finance many of the new buildings and facilities and part of the research that maintain the university's facade of modernity (which is as important as its facade of tradition) and keep it abreast of its competitors. Graduation day is an expensive show, but the ceremony, in all its seductive dignity and glory, is crucial to the consumer equation.

Yes, international education is a winner for everyone: for the players in string quartets who would otherwise be underemployed, for the families, whose long and patient struggle has paid off, for the university, which needs the revenue but still wants to retain its tradition and purpose, for the home countries, which gain skilled human capital generated abroad at the citizen's own expense, for Australia, which gains some of that human capital as immigrants and $15.5 billion per year (2008) in export revenue[1] by educating over half a million foreign students per year, almost 300 000 of them in higher education. And above all for the graduates themselves.

Yes, full fee international education certainly is a winner all round.

Or is it?

NOT FOR EVERYONE

Incident 1

One night in 2002 officers from the federal Department of Immigration, Multicultural and Indigenous Affairs (DIAC) entered the home of Muhabab Alam, a 22 year old international student from Bangladesh. The DIAC officers found another student they were looking for was absent and, without a search warrant, searched Alam's room and

1 ABS, 2009.

belongings. They found payslips that they interpreted to mean the student had worked for 22 and a quarter hours in a particular week, so breaching his visa conditions, which specified he should work for no more than 20 hours per week during study semester. The mandatory penalty is loss of the student visa and expulsion from Australia. The student's payslips were removed as evidence and he was taken away for interrogation. While being removed Alam asked if he could put on a shirt, but the request was refused. After interrogation he was told that he would lose his visa and would be imprisoned in Villawood Detention Centre unless he could pay bond of $10 000. He could not raise the money on the spot and was forbidden to telephone his sister for assistance; no reason was given.[2] He was held in prison conditions for three weeks.[3]

When the case was finally resolved in the Federal Court three years later on 23 July 2005 Alam was successful on appeal, securing the reinstatement of his visa. The judge was highly critical of the treatment Alam had received. In March 2006 the Senate Legal and Constitutional References Committee of the Australian parliament completed an inquiry into the administration of the *Migration Act 1958* (Clth). Its report noted that from 2002–3 to 2004–5 there had been 17 134 raids or 'compliance operations' involving DIAC officers with 24 567 student visas cancelled. While some students left immediately others appealed to the Migration Review Tribunal (MRT), the Federal Court and the High Court. As a result of these appeals more than one-third of the cancellations had been set aside.[4]

Incident 2

In early 2005 police in Canberra, Australia's capital, were called to Chandler Street in Belconnen near the University of Canberra, after neighbours complained of a smell coming from an apartment. Inside was a badly decomposed body identified as 25 year old Chinese student Hong Jie Zhang, also known as Steffi Zhang, an international student at the University of Canberra. Her boyfriend, Zhang Long, who was not in Australia at the time Hong's body was found, was

2 Senate Committee, 2005, 316–17.
3 ABC Radio, *PM*, 27 July 2005; see also Rost, 2005, 18.
4 Senate Committee, 2005.

suspected of the killing. Forensic analysts estimated that Hong had been killed in June 2004. Her body had been lying in the flat for seven months before her death was discovered.[5] The *Australian* interviewed the University of Canberra vice-chancellor after the discovery was made known:

> Professor Dean was cautious in response to questions about whether the university should shoulder any responsibility for the failure to notice Zhang's absence. He cited the failure of social networks. 'The idea that nobody would have noticed her missing from that peer group or from the flat for so long is quite amazing and very worrying', he said.[6]

Incident 3

Late in the evening on 22 January 2008 lecturer and researcher Cao Zhongjun, 41 years, married with one daughter, was walking home in Empire Street, Footscray, from his job at Victoria University when he was attacked by eight youths and men of varying ages. Cao's attackers had met a few minutes before at a nearby McDonald's store and decided to go 'curry bashing', meaning assault and rob a foreign student. The term 'curry bashing' originated because of the large number of Indian students in the western suburbs of Melbourne. The fact that Cao was from China rather than India made no difference. After bashing him so viciously that his body was sent several metres through the air and he landed on his head, the attackers stole his wallet and phone; they moved on to assault and rob another victim in neighbouring Sunshine. Cao never regained consciousness and died in hospital four days later. Ironically, Cao Zhongjun began working as an academic in Sydney in 1997 because he deemed Australia a safe place to live. In 2004, he completed a PhD at Monash University where he was friends with one of the authors of this book. At the time of his death Cao was investigating how Chinese international students were coping with Australia. He was popular at the university; Professor Roger Gabb described him as 'quiet, kind and gentle'. People appreciated

5 Green and Rood, 2005; Australian Federal Police, 2005.
6 Illing, 2005.

his willingness to join in. 'He was universally loved', Gabb said.[7] Cao was close to his wife Zhou Jingfang and daughter Cao Qing. 'We had a good family', Zhou said. 'A very happy family.'[8]

A year later two of his attackers pleaded guilty in the Supreme Court to manslaughter. One, who had suggested the 'curry bashing' expedition, received three years detention in a youth justice centre for manslaughter and two months for robbery. He looked at his father and 'smiled broadly'[9] when he heard that he had avoided adult jail. The other received less than two years detention.[10]

Incident 4

In relation to questions of student safety, the customary stance of Australian universities, and government officials with responsibility for the export industry, had always been to lie low and say nothing, and to rely on Australia's reputation as being a safer place than the USA to work in their favour. But in August and September 2008 diplomatic representatives of the People's Republic of China began to speak out in public about what they saw as inadequate attention to the safety of international students from China who were resident in Australia. Zhou Bo, China's education consul in Sydney, quoted a survey of 100 Chinese students that found that 'more than one in four had been a victim of crime, 20 had been burgled at home and six had been robbed, several at knifepoint'.[11] China supplies much the largest number of international students to Australia and the intervention by its consular officials was too important to ignore, especially as China's recent withdrawal of support for New Zealand as a destination on grounds of student safety had sent the number of Chinese students in New Zealand plummeting downward. The Australian government decided to instigate a workshop on international education, to be held on 28 October in Shanghai. The underlying purpose of the workshop was for Australian officials to persuade their Chinese counterparts that the threats to student safety had been exaggerated, and, to the

7 Rout, 2008a.
8 Anderson, 2008a.
9 Ross, 2008b.
10 Rennie, 2008; Anderson, 2008a, 2008b.
11 Levett, 2008.

extent that safety was a problem, the Australian industry had it well in hand. In other words the workshop was an exercise not in student safety but in policy spin.

Back in Sydney on the day the Shanghai workshop was held, an intruder forced his way into the apartment of four international students and raped them in turn at knife point. Two of the students, a woman of 18 and a man of 19, jumped naked from the balcony of the apartment in a desperate bid to escape their tormentor. The young woman died and the young man suffered permanent spinal injuries. The media were soon onto the disaster and within 24 hours it had been reported in hundreds of newspapers, on radio and television stations and on internet sites around the world, thoroughly overturning the Australian government's strategy in Shanghai of talking down the safety problem. When the mother of the young female student came to Sydney to attend her daughter's funeral, her lawyer announced that the family believed inadequate attention was being given by Australian authorities to the security of international students. The family intended to establish a fund to provide for the instruction of newly arrived students in matters of safety, the lawyer said. They wanted 'all overseas students and the public to know that safety issues for overseas students are very, very important'.[12]

INTERNATIONAL STUDENTS AS WITNESSES

Some might say that these incidents are selective, sensationalised, cases of tabloid research. Comparative data show that Australia is safer and more tolerant than most English-speaking countries. Statistically, 99.99 per cent of Australia's half a million international students survive their sojourn and most graduate after a largely happy experience living and studying in Australia. Surveys of international students in Australia and the UK record satisfaction rates of above 80 per cent (though it can be less for students from specific nations or in particular localities).

All of that is true. But the above incidents are also true and there are other cases like them. International education is not always the

12 Cited in Tibbits and Robinson, 2008.

win–win that happy graduation days suggest. Nor is it easy. Nor are its problems always transparent.

International education involves wonderful opportunities, exciting freedoms, disabling changes, and real difficulties and dangers. It does not affect everyone in the same way. Many of the issues are felt differently and involve different cultural interpretations. There is a dark side: international students do not always enjoy full security and non-white students, especially, experience exclusions in the foreign land. This dark side affects most students to some degree. Yet those who benefit from the burgeoning global industry want nothing but good news stories, and policy makers, regulators and researchers rarely seek advice from the international students themselves.

In the last two decades, in the era of global convergence via the internet and the reduced cost of air travel, international education has become a great export industry that has financial flows estimated at $40 billion worldwide. Each year three million people cross national borders for at least 12 months for education; many more travel for shorter periods. Cross-border migration, whether permanent or temporary, for work or study, is always challenging for those undertaking it. Mobile people move from familiar rules, conventions, supports and citizenship rights, to another, less familiar, country where they have less support, lack citizen rights and where the rules may be unknown. Global mobility demands adjustment by mobile people and by the institutions they encounter. Social science and market research suggest that for some international students the issues are not successfully resolved, that the experience could be better for almost all students, and that the experience is also unsatisfactory for some of those who educate them.

The commercial character of international education in Australia, the UK, New Zealand and some other countries and programs, in which international education is a revenue-raising business and its students are seen as consumers with needs and rights understood in terms of a bargain struck in the marketplace, creates further challenges. Part of the dynamism of international education derives from its commercial character but this can generate limits, frustrations and abuses. Are the supports and protections part of a consumer bargain adequate to the needs of international students as they see it? Do these supports and protections deliver a common entitlement to human rights? What kind of international student security regime is consistent with the healthy functioning of the global education market and the human needs and rights of the students themselves? More generally, what are the implications of human security regimes, national in nature, for moving cross-border populations in a globally convergent world?

These are important questions. They have been little explored or settled, yet they have much to tell us about the fast-changing times in which we live. They are the questions that have brought *International Student Security* to life.

The focus of the book is the human security of mobile students. We set out to clarify what human security means, and the strengths and weaknesses of existing practice in the context of the global education market. These matters are addressed in terms of international students as a globally mobile population, and international students as people mostly engaged in an intercultural educational and social experience.

For the purposes of *International Student Security*, the social and economic security of cross-border students is defined to include personal safety, financial issues and work experiences, housing, health and welfare services, language problems, students' personal and social networks, including family, community and affinity groups, and experiences with government and university authorities.[13] We investigate not only the formal legal framework governing international education and the institutional educational practices fostered within it, but also the non-government, informal and private organisations and life worlds that also contribute to student security as broadly understood. Here we develop the idea of a regime of international student security, that is constituted on the one hand by the formal domain of policy and regulation (part 2), on the other hand by the informal and private domain (part 3), and examine the implications for formal governance of the security gaps in the informal and private domain.

The underlying objective of *International Student Security* is to improve the human security of international students. At the same time we are aware that to understand and advocate things as they should be, we first must understand things as they are. This book is grounded in four research projects that were designed to map and monitor international student security, principally, an Australian Research Council (ARC) funded study that involved intensive interviews with 200

13 Chapter 4 explains the rationale for this broad definition of student security.

individual students from 34 nations. These interviews are quoted throughout the book. *International Student Security* is one of the few studies in this field that examines the issues in the words of the international students themselves.

International students are our best witnesses of the exciting potentials and real problems of cross-border education. It is their lives that are shaped, for better or worse, by the student security regime in place. At the same time, they are active agents, in part they make their own security and they all have something special to tell. As one researcher on international education, Michael Singh, notes, each has a 'different and particular transnational educational history'. International students are not simply units of revenue, or sites of deficits in the English language or academic practice, or 'empty vessels' waiting to be filled with Western wisdoms. They are 'media' of global or local connectedness.[14] They are self-creators. They are remaking themselves in international education, and in the process creating a more convergent and complex world.

We will now look briefly at the underlying research study that has shaped this book and how it utilises insights generated directly by international students.

THE STUDY

Most of the interviews with 200 international students took place in 2005, at nine Australian public universities as follows: Ballarat, Deakin, Melbourne, RMIT, Swinburne and Victoria Universities in the city of Melbourne, Deakin in Geelong, Ballarat in the city of Ballarat, University of New South Wales and Sydney University in Sydney, and Central Queensland University in Rockhampton. The student interviews were voluntary and were arranged through emails advertising the study or with the help of university international offices. Interview data suggest there were differences between the universities in the provision of human security but those differences are not discussed here. When negotiating to set up the interviews it was promised that there would be no performance monitoring or quality comparison on an institutional basis, and the interviews would form a single

14 Singh, 2005, 10.

pool for the purpose of data analysis. Otherwise the study would not have occurred.

The study was qualitative. Most studies involving international students are sample surveys that are structured to represent the source population. Surveys generate an impressive amount of information but are limited to preset questions and so confined by the researchers' prior assumptions. There is no opportunity for those under study to put things in their own words or to explore new issues arising. Instead, we opted for intensive semi-structured interviews, based on a group of 63 stem questions on all aspects of international student security, to gain depth of insight and provide the students with space in which to shape the enquiry. This is not to say that this book is nothing but the students' voices, that the interviewees define its assumptions and methods of analysis. The authors are responsible for the data interpretation, drawing on the framework set out in chapter 4. But there is no doubt that the encounter with the interviewees augmented this framework. It strengthened our understanding of the students as self-determining agents.

Semi-structured interviews are like a conversation. The researcher asks a stem question on a topic and follows with impromptu questions based on the answers. Depending on the answers some later stem questions are omitted. The interviewer in our study was a former international student, author Erlenawati Sawir, which helped to create trust and empathy in relation to sensitive topics. This has been a primary factor in the success of the study.[15] Interviews took 30–60 minutes. The process was resource intensive, which limited the potential participants, but 200 interviews is a large number in a qualitative study and we are confident our methods have generated more and deeper insights than most research in the field. In reporting the interviews we have tidied up the students' words, straightened out the tenses and removed the 'umms' and ubiquitous 'like' common to all students, local and international, but the nuances of the answers are preserved unchanged.

The study covered one-quarter of all Australian universities, mostly those with very large international student numbers. The profile of the

15 In a study by Jenny Lee and Charles Rice (2005) at the University of Arizona, the non-Anglo interviewer was able to secure more free and frank interview data than the Anglo interviewer; personal communication with Jenny Lee (2009).

Table 1.1 Nations of origin of 200 students interviewed in this study

Nation of origin	Number of interviewees	Proportion of all interviewees (n = 200) %	Proportion of all international students* 2005 %
Southeast Asia and the Pacific			
Indonesia	49	24.5	4.4
Malaysia	18	9.0	11.7
Singapore	11	5.5	10.9
Vietnam, Laos, Cambodia	6	3.0	1.9
Other	6	3.0	4.5
Northeast Asia			
China	28	14.0	19.3
Hong Kong China	5	2.5	10.4
Other (Japan, Korea, Taiwan, Macao)	9	4.5	5.8
South Asia			
India	21	10.5	8.7
Other	19	9.5	3.8
North Africa and the Middle East	7	3.5	2.7
Sub-Saharan Africa	7	3.5	3.1
Europe and the UK	8	4.0	5.5
USA and Canada	3	1.5	5.6
Latin America	3	1.5	0.9
Others	0	0	0.8
Total	200	100.0	100.0

* Country of permanent residence
Source: DEEWR, 2009.

interviewees broadly resembles the source population but is closer in some respects than others. In terms of gender 51 per cent of interviewees were female compared to 47 per cent of all cross-border students in Australia in 2005. The survey is least representative in terms of age because the selection process encouraged experienced students who could provide more insightful answers: 53 per cent of interviewees were over 25; 37 per cent were at Bachelor level, 41 per cent at Masters level and 23 per cent in PhD programs, compared to 56 per cent Bachelor, 31 per cent Masters and 3 per cent doctoral in the source population. In terms of fields of study the largest groups were from Business, Management, Administration and Economics (henceforth Business) with 33 per cent, Society and Culture

12 per cent and Information Technology 11 per cent. This compared to 48 per cent Business, 8 per cent Society and Culture and 13 per cent Information Technology in the source population. Arts, Science and Education students were overweighted; Engineering and Health sciences were about right (DEEWR, 2009).

WHY *INTERNATIONAL* STUDENT SECURITY?

Some may ask: Why focus on *international* student security? Don't all students have issues of financial support, working life, accommodation, health, academic progress? The parents of international students, aware of unique challenges and dangers, will not need to be convinced of the purpose of the book. The economic importance of the student market and the cost of international student fees – twice as high as local tuition charges – are obvious. But looking beyond utilitarian arguments, at the contribution *International Student Security* makes to knowledge, international students do represent a special population in some ways, and the study has much to tell us about the human side of globalisation.

Three factors distinguish international and local students. First, international education entails cross-border mobility and temporary residential status. It confers on participants outsider non-citizen status and an information gap. These factors affect all internationals, regardless of cultural background though the effects reduce over time. The second factor is cultural difference, the contrast between cultural practices in the country of origin and the country of education. This may include politeness and interpersonal relations, religion and the cultures of bureaucracies and institutions. Communication is a key divide. In Australia most international students experience cultural difference. Most are from homes where a language other than English is spoken. International students share the experience of cultural difference with some local students, almost a-third of whom are from non-English-speaking homes. But these students were largely educated in English at school and are used to living in a dual cultural setting. Note that for international students the two sets of factors – mobility and outsider status, and relations of cultural difference – can reinforce each other. 'Not only do international students need to adapt to a foreign education system and a foreign language and culture, like migrants, they also need to adjust to being part of a social minority; that is, they encounter difficulties associated with being different.'[16]

The third factor, in the commercially minded countries, is the positioning of the international student as consumer with consumer rights. There is talk about the customer-centred education of locals too, but local students are not regulated via consumer protection law and benefit from conventions about citizen rights to education. It is noted by the Australian government that 'Overseas students differ from domestic students in that they are subject to migration controls and face different needs for consumer protection'.[17] Mobility and consumption impose on the international students a strange combination of top down Weberian bureaucracy and formal bargaining rights.

How are these differences manifest in student security? They are more obvious in some aspects of security than others, and more obvious for students from certain backgrounds. Differences between international and local students become especially clear when outsider status, cultural identity, communication problems and lack of local knowledge are all at play. Student satisfaction surveys find that differences between local and international students are most apparent in areas where cultural identity is central.[18] The differences can be less obvious in areas like finances, work, housing and health. However, even where the statistical incidence of problems is similar for international and local students, the experience of those problems, and their solutions, is often different. Students from both groups experience ultra exploitation and other problems at work (chapter 6). What makes the international student experience distinct (aside from less knowledge of labour markets and a smaller list of potential employers) is immigration status. In Australia, international student visas include a condition limiting the holder to no more than 20 hours work per week during academic semester. Internationals often work longer to make ends meet, which leaves them more vulnerable to low rates of pay, demands to work excessive hours and sexual harassment.

16 Forbes-Mewett and Nyland, 2008, 185.

17 Australian Government, DEEWR, National Code, 2007, section 6.1.

18 AEI, 2007a, 2007b.

Students working outside their visa conditions cannot complain to the authorities. Local students are not constrained in this way.

Table 1.2 compares the formal rights and entitlements enjoyed by citizen local students with those of non-citizen international students in 2007. It shows that international students are bearers of inferior rights and a lesser set of entitlements.

The differences have direct implications for security. In 2007 nearly all public financial support, including welfare and housing, were inaccessible to international students. In New South Wales and Victoria, international students paid full fares on public transport while locals paid concession rates. Schooling was compulsory for children up to the age of 15 years but while public schooling was free for local families most international students paid for it in full. International students had less financial support from universities though paying much higher tuition.

Both groups had access to health cover but international students were not included in the Medicare scheme and had to take out private insurance, which is more costly than the Medicare levy paid by local students through taxation. The right to work was restricted only for international students, who also experienced unique government intervention and surveillance, including address tracking and requirements that course changes must be approved by government.

Some international students had implied restrictions on potential political activity. These were the students whose visas include condition 8303: 'You must not become involved in any activities that are disruptive to, or in violence threaten harm to, the Australian community or a group within the Australian community'. This condition was routinely applied to the visas of students from certain countries.

To further test the distinctive character of the international student experience, in 2008 we conducted parallel interviews with two groups of students at one university, 20 internationals and 20 locals, using the study questionnaire. The international students were from nine countries, mostly in southeast Asia. Most students in both groups were female. The local group was younger with a majority aged less than 25. Fields of study were similar except that more international than local students were studying education. Table 1.3 compares the student responses to certain interview questions of a yes/no character.

Table 1.2 Rights and entitlements of non-citizen international students compared to those of local students, Australia 2007

Field	Student citizen or PR	International student visa	Comments
Taxation			
Obligation to pay tax	Yes	Yes	Higher if < six months in Australia
Medicare (health) tax levy	Yes	No	Ineligible for Medicare benefits
Public financial support			
Student income support	Yes*	No	
Rent assistance	Yes*	No	
Family tax benefit	Yes*	No	
Childcare benefit	Yes*	No for most	Yes, with Australian scholarship
Child support collection	Yes	Yes, some	No, if the child leaves Australia
Bank services			
Savings accounts	Yes	Yes	
Personal loans	Yes	One bank	
Education loans	Yes	One bank	
Credit cards	Yes	Two banks	
Work			
Right to work	Unrestricted	Restricted, V	20 hours weekly during semester
Superannuation			
Compulsory employer levy	Yes	Yes	
When benefits received	Retirement	On exit from Australia	
Student-specific finances			
Direct tuition charges	No for most	Yes	Most local postgraduates pay
Deferred repayment (HECS)	Yes for most	No	No local postgraduates and PR
Student services fee	Voluntary	Compulsory	Included in tuition charge
University non-tuition loans**	Yes all	Yes some	Varies by institution
Scholarships	Yes all***	Yes some	Ineligible for some postgraduate
Public transport concession			
Pay concession fare levels	Yes	Some	No in NSW and Victoria
Health benefits			
Medicare program benefits	Yes	No	Unless bilateral arrangements

(cont.)

Table 1.2 *(cont.)*

Field	Student citizen or PR	International student visa	Comments
Private health insurance	Voluntary	Compulsory V	Delivers Medicare benefits plus
Private extras (e.g., dental)	Voluntary	Voluntary	Same costs and benefits
Pharmacy prescription benefits	Yes*	Yes	In health insurance, dollar limits
Child and maternal health free	Yes	Yes	
Immunisation free	Yes	Yes	Doctors may charge for referrals
Education and benefits			
Education of children <16	Compulsory	Compulsory V	If residence exceeds three months
Public school for children free	Yes	Mostly no****	Yes for some scholarship holders
Community learning programs	Yes	Yes	Concession rates for some locals
Welfare benefits			
Payment for disability carers	Yes	No	Payments are from Centrelink
Funding HEI disabled support	Yes	No	Universities not entitled to claim
Drug/alcohol/gambling rehab	Yes	Yes	Same services, eligibility, costs
Housing			
First home owner grant	Yes	No	
Public housing eligibility	Yes*	No	
Loans for bond payments	Some	No	New South Wales and Victoria only
Rent assistance	Yes*	No	
Emergency temporary housing	Yes	No	Except New South Wales DV cases, three months
Tenants' Union assistance	Yes	Yes	
Legal services			
Legal aid by state government	Yes*	Yes*	
Immigration law advice	Yes*****	Yes*	Immigration legal centres
Immigration law representation	Yes*****	No	Use private migration agents

(cont.)

Table 1.2 *(cont.)*

Field	Student citizen or PR	International student visa	Comments
Crime and police protection			
Multicultural liaison support	Yes	Yes	Specific to Victoria
Police-provided interpreters	Yes	Yes	Specific to Victoria
Domestic violence help	Yes	Yes	Specific to Victoria
CASA counselling service	Yes	Yes	Specific to Victoria
Surveillance and control			
Notify change of address	Unregulated	Compulsory V	Tell education provider in seven days
Notify course or thesis change	Unregulated	Compulsory V	Requires departmental approval
Political activity	Unrestricted	Controls V	Condition of some visas only
Public language services			
Translation/interpreting service	Yes	Some	Less in health-related areas
Translation of documents	Yes	Some	Mostly not available to students
AMEP English language tuition	Some*	No	
University help with English	Yes	Yes	Some extra for internationals

Note: PR = permanent resident, AMEP = Adult Migrant Education Program, HEI = higher education institutions, DV = domestic violence, V = condition of student visa

* Subject to eligibility requirements such as income tests or particular residency status

** Maximum amounts vary, often lower for international students

*** Except for specific international scholarships

**** In some states children of international students pay full cost fees, in other states they pay less than international school students. Special additional charges can apply for students with disabilities

***** Humanitarian and protection visa holders

Source: Compiled by Sharon Smith, Monash University, 2007.

In quantitative terms the small group of international students was less likely than local students to have worked and less likely to be exposed to risk in the labour market. There was little difference between the groups in the incidence of financial difficulties. In interview more local students talked about financial hardship while several international students talked about tuition fee levels and increases. Most local students were subject to deferred tuition supported by income contingent repayment and did not experience direct tuition charges.

Table 1.3 Experiences of international students compared to local students, sample of 40 students (20:20), one Australian university, 2008

	Local students ~ n = 20)		International students ~ n = 20)	
	Yes	No	Yes	No
Are you experiencing or have you experienced financial difficulties at any stage?	7	13	5	15
Are you working or have you worked while studying in Australia?	17	3	10	10
Are you aware of student services provided to assist you, e.g. counselling, health, financial?	19	1	12	8
Talking about the situation now, does English create difficulties for you in your academic work?	2	18	9	11
Have you experienced periods of loneliness or isolation in Australia?	7	13	12	8
Have you been able to make friends with people from other culture(s)?	17	3	20	0
Have you been able to make friends with local students? (question asked only of international students)	–	–	7	13
Are there significant barriers in making friends across cultures?	14	6	15	5
Have you experienced discrimination or bad treatment while in Australia?	4	16	8	12
Looking at it overall, have you had problems in Australia that you did not expect before you came?	–	–	13	7
Should there be better or different information for prospective students, about risks and problems of studying and living here?	14	6	12	8
Did you know that in Australia there are rules and guidelines specifying how universities look after international students?	–	–	2	18

Erlenawati Sawir, University of Melbourne, 2008.

The international students were much less likely to know about the student services designed to protect them, thus reducing their comparative security in areas such as physical and mental health. It is significant that almost none knew that in Australia there are rules and guidelines specifying how universities should look after international students, such as the National Code (see part 2). The international students were much more likely to face difficulties related to the use of the English language and more likely to be lonely. Some students from both groups were or had been lonely, but only international students mentioned isolation from kin outside the country. In the interviews, international students were more likely to mention difficulties in dealing with government, specifically, immigration authorities. All international students and most local students had made intercultural friends but most of the international students made these with people other than local students. In quantitative terms both groups were about equally aware of intercultural barriers but in interview international students expressed themselves more strongly and at greater length on this, and were more likely to say they had experienced discrimination. The answers on intercultural relations and on language underline the point that cultural issues are often central to the differences between international student security and local student security.

THE BOOK

The remainder of part 1 of *International Student Security* provides background on Australia and the Australian higher education where the research interviews were conducted, and considers the relevance of the Australian case for the USA, the UK and other nations that house cross-border students (chapter 2), the global student market and the remarkable growth of Australian international education within it (chapter 3) and the nature of human security and its regulation in international education in the formal and informal domains (chapter 4).

These chapters are the foundations for parts 2 and 3, which provide the main findings of our book in the different zones of human security. Each chapter reflects on the research literature in its topic, elucidates data from the 200 student interviews in the topic area, and draws out conceptual and practical conclusions.

Part 2 (chapters 5–10) discusses the formal side of student security, those aspects seen as the province of governmental and educational regulation and provision, and subject to the shifting three-way split of responsibility between government, institution and individual where the politics of social policy are played out. It covers student expectations and experiences with finances (chapter 5), employment (chapter 6), international student housing (chapter 7), physical and mental health (chapter 8), the safety of the person, including background to the incidents that were described at the beginning of this chapter

(chapter 9), and relations with government, especially in relation to immigration (chapter 10).

Part 3 (chapters 11–15) discusses the more informal social, private and emotional dimensions of security as they affect international students, including students' relations with authority in universities and government (chapter 11), language use and problems (chapter 12), bonding and networks with family and friends (chapter 13), loneliness and isolation (chapter 14) and intercultural relations between international students and local students and communities, including the problems of Othering and discrimination that affected many interviewed for the study (chapter 15).

Chapter 16 draws out implications and conclusions.

2 THE SETTING: AUSTRALIA

I've heard patients say stuff to me, but nothing in a racist sort of way. More like 'Don't Asians have blue eyes?' A woman actually asked me that. Like, what planet are you from? (laughs) Blue eyes! . . . So yeah, I do get some remarks that make you stand out. People have preconceptions when they see me. And they immediately stereotype . . . often white people are surprised when I open my mouth and start speaking English to them. They can't believe I can speak English. And I say to them, do you believe I just got here six months ago (laughs) . . . I think I'm more Australian than some Australians.

~ female, 26, medicine, Malaysia

INTRODUCTION: THE NATIONAL FACTOR

International students in Australia have similar experiences to their counterparts in other English-speaking countries – the USA, the UK, New Zealand and Canada – especially those who are non-white students from countries where English is a foreign language. This will show in the research literature and the interview findings in parts 2 and 3. All non-citizen students who cross borders for study face common issues and problems, including those who go to China, Japan, Malaysia, Singapore and India. For students crossing borders within the European Higher Education Area the experience is not as foreign as it once was. Nevertheless all students away from home, studying in unfamiliar institutions and daily using a new language, face challenges, the more so if they arrange their own accommodation and must work part time to survive.

These common elements are always manifested locally, and each nation is distinctive. Nations do not educate international students according to global rules. They have their own frameworks of law and policy for education and immigration, histories, institutions and modes of government, regimes of public and private regulation, ways of teaching, learning and administering education, conventions about human behaviour and patterns of intercultural relations. All these domains have implications for human security.

In relation to Australia much will emerge in the chapters to follow, but an advance overview of the nation may help. It also provides a basis for reflecting on the relevance of this book elsewhere. The chapter passes across Australia, its history and economy, and its higher education institutions. It then looks at relations with neighbouring Asian countries, where international education has long played a significant role, and discusses the foundations of commercial export (for Australia's current positioning in the global market see chapter 3). In its conclusion the chapter returns to the question of the relevance of student security in Australia for international education in the UK, the USA and elsewhere.

AUSTRALIA

The population of Australia was 21.4 million in 2008, with average life expectancy at birth of 81 years and population growth of 1.7 per cent per annum (2007).[1] This population, modest by Asian regional standards, occupies a continent of 7.7 million square kilometres, roughly the size of China or the USA. The Australian economy is relatively large. In 2008 its gross domestic product (GDP) was $1015.2 billion, 14th in the world. Gross national income per head was $34 040, just below that of France. Australia is largely a primary production and services economy; manufacturing plays a lesser role. In 2008 the top three exports were coal, iron ore and education. Unemployment rates are low in world terms. With a nationally regulated and stable banking system the economy weathered the 2008–9 global financial crisis better than most other economies, with just one three month period of negative growth. For the last two decades exports of minerals and energy to China have sustained the Australia economy. Australia–China relations have been more sympathetic than

1 World Bank, 2009.

those between China and most other Western-origin nations. This relationship has also underpinned the flow of students from China (chapter 3).

Geographically, Australia is next to southeast Asia in the southern hemisphere of the western Pacific. Its nearest neighbour is Indonesia. It is close to the time zones of the dynamic economies of China, Taiwan, Singapore and Korea, and to Japan, still second largest in GDP terms. It is also fairly proximate in time and space to India. Thus six of the world's 10 most populous nations are within Australia's vicinity: China, India, Indonesia, Pakistan, Bangladesh and Japan.[2] At the same time Australia is a European heritage settler state. It began as a clutch of colonies founded by Great Britain from 1788 onwards, located in the opposite side of the world to the north Atlantic zone. Britain was then the world's dominant naval power and its first interest was geostrategic. Later Australian became a place where surplus population could be sent and a mass producer of agriculture and minerals for British manufacturing and consumption. (This began the depletion of the fragile Australian landscape by technologically intensive primary industries, a process that continues unabated.) Systems and habits remain closely affected by British origins. The one official language is English. Australia uses British common law. Government and business still closely resembles UK practice, especially government. Australian policy makers often follow UK initiatives in education and other sectors. Sometimes the reverse imitation occurs.

Like the USA, Australia was an English colony but unlike the USA there was no rebellion, never a moment when Australians were absolutely determined to be different. Independence was handed down by the colonial mother in 1901 in a ceremony that took place not in Australia but in London. From the start Anglo-Celtic Australians were more democratic than the mother country, with a pronounced scepticism about British hierarchies. They were proud of the achievements of the settler state and saw themselves as a new beginning, and there was always a sense of separation (the geographical distance helped). But it took a long time to begin to feel comfortable on the edge of Asia, and longer to start to see the region in local Australian rather than British ways.

2 *ibid.*

Australia still carries the British union jack on the top left corner of its national flag. Remarkably, it has failed to adopt the brilliant Indigenous flag with its geologically apposite black, yellow and red. The upside of the British heritage is that successful state building produced a stable and accessible polity and economy, and a functional and peaceful civil order that attracts visitors and immigrants. Social opportunities are more open than in the UK, class divisions are less entrenched and tradition runs less deep.

The UK is also a long way away and the old economic ties of the empire have weakened. Australia's trade is now mostly with China, Japan and southeast Asia. Australians who consider the UK home are now mostly in their 60s and older. The nation's foreign policy has been regional in orientation since World War Two.

The forbears of Indigenous Australians crossed from Asia during the ice ages, when sea levels were lower. They achieved a successful symbiosis with the land amid the difficult climactic conditions, characterised by long, erratic episodes of low rainfall that make intensive agriculture impossible across half the land. For them the British colonies and the consolidation of the nation have been a disaster. As in North America, and in New Zealand, Indigenous communities were economically and socially displaced, and were devastated by European diseases, habitat loss and frontier militias. By 1901 the population had dropped to about 100 000. Many government officials pursued policies designed to demographically assimilate Indigenous peoples, including the removal of children from their birth families and districts. Numbers have recovered but, by developed nation standards, Indigenous health, education and employment indicators remain very poor. This is a failure of inclusive nation-building and a serious continuing problem for modern Australia. Australia has been much more successful in constructing relations between its 230 years of immigrants than in reconciling Indigenous peoples within a common polity and society. Indigenous students participate in higher education at half the rate of Australians as a whole, and participation and completion rates have declined since the mid 1990s.

HIGHER EDUCATION

The foundations of Australian higher education were British. It now finds itself influenced by US higher education, and a large minority of its students are from Asia via temporary or permanent immigration. Australian higher education is also nationally distinctive in its financing, organisation and ethos, though less so in teaching and research.

The first universities began in the colonial 19th century in the British redbrick tradition, less gothic and more modernist than Oxford and Cambridge. They also had a utilitarian settler state bent that focused on solving problems not abstractions for their own sake. This became a defining characteristic. Research emerged slower than teaching, with the first local doctoral degrees awarded in 1946. From 1957 the federal government exercised a strong leadership role, building institutions in the 1960s and 1970s that lifted the age participation rates for students well above the OECD country average and achieved critical mass in research in most disciplines. Australia produces 2 per cent of the world's scientific papers and has distinctive strengths in parts of medicine and life sciences, engineering, astrophysics and mathematics. Government expenditure thinned after the mid 1980s but government maintained a centralising role in shaping university behaviour. In this respect Australian higher education is more like that of the UK than the USA. Australia has devised its own effective system of income-contingent tuition loans for local students, repayable through the tax system only when graduates have the capacity to pay, which enables students from poorer families to continue to access higher education, despite high tuition. Australia is also distinctive in its level of international education enrolments.

Australia spends 1.6 per cent of GDP on tertiary education compared to an OECD average of 1.3 per cent, putting it above the UK but well below the 2.9 per cent in the USA. Investment in tertiary education from public sources (0.8 per cent) is below the OECD average but investment from private sources (also 0.8 per cent), mostly local and international student tuition, is well above average.[3] In total 45 per cent of all institutional income in 2007 was provided by government and 36 per cent by students. Philanthropic income is much lower than in the leading US institutions though similar to that for most UK and European institutions. In 2007 there were 1.03 million students in higher education, nearly all in 39 legally designated public

3 OECD, 2008a.

universities that conduct research and provide degrees up to doctoral level. This included 42 704 doctoral students, about one-fifth of whom were international. All but two universities are governed by state or territory Acts of parliament but the federal government is the main source of public funding and policy influence. Public universities are self-accrediting and governed by independent councils, most of which have a majority of members from outside the university. Governing bodies appoint the chief officer, mostly now designated as vice-chancellor and president, which is emblematic of the dual British–American orientation. Australian higher education is notable for the level of strategic initiative, entrepreneurship and budgetary control exercised by executive leaders,[4] a factor that has quickened the growth of the export industry. All institutions are subject to external quality assurance every five years and must comply with various federal laws, including the Educational Services for Overseas Students (ESOS) Act (see part 2).

Australian public universities are comprehensive in their roles and large in size by international standards. All are expected to be active in research, in teaching across most of the primary fields of study and professions, in the international student market and in servicing local and regional needs. The largest institution in 2007 was Monash University with 55 765 students. Perhaps the closest American parallel is the midwest public universities, or universities in Canada such as Toronto or British Columbia. In research terms the leading Australian institutions are not quite as strong as those two Canadians. Australia has three universities in the Shanghai Jiao Tong University ranking of the world's top 100 research universities: the Australian National University in Canberra and the Universities of Melbourne and Sydney. A further three universities are in the top 200 group. Of the 37 522 academic staff, in 2007 a majority had doctoral degrees and 97.5 per cent of academic positions were classified as 'teaching and research'.[5]

There are 67 private providers of higher education, three of which are designated universities. The private sector is growing, but institutions are small and 95 per cent of all students are in the public sector. There are no liberal arts colleges of the American type. Outside

4 Marginson and Considine, 2000.
5 DEEWR, 2009.

the formal boundaries of the higher education sector are 1.67 million students in vocational education and training (VET) programs, mostly at one and two year level, though three year degrees in VET is a growth area. Like the specialist English language (ELICOS) colleges the VET sector enrols a significant number of international students. Cross-border enrolments in these two sectors are more volatile than in higher education but reached a majority of all international students in Australia in 2008. Many of these students undertake relatively short courses and do not experience the full range of issues dealt with in this book. The research study reported here was confined to university students, but VET and ELICOS are important sites for future research on student security.

AUSTRALIA AND ASIA

A notable feature of Australia that it shares with the USA, Canada, New Zealand and the UK, and one that has helped to carry the great growth in international student numbers, is that it is a high immigration country. Human development has been powered by successive waves of settlers from Britain and Ireland, from northwestern, eastern and southern Europe (especially Greece and Italy), Turkey and Lebanon, and from the Asia–Pacific, beginning with arrivals from Vietnam in the second half of the 1970s and now including many people from China, Hong Kong China, the Philippines, Malaysia, India, Indonesia and elsewhere. Although there were significant arrivals from China during the goldrush period in the 19th century, for much of its history Australia pursued the notorious White Australia policy, which excluded people from the region. Though the policy was officially abolished in 1973, its residue lingered longer in the immigration department. But in recent years half the new arrivals have been from Asia. Over 10 per cent of people in the two largest cities, Sydney and Melbourne, are Asian born. As in the other English-speaking countries, but unlike most of western Europe where there is wariness about non-European entry, a primary objective of Australian immigration policy is to build productive 'human capital' through mass high skill immigration.[6] In recent years almost half of the high skill migrants

6 Tremblay, 2005.

have been international student graduates from Australian education institutions. The potential for immigration has become one of the chief drivers of education export.

Australian official policies of multiculturalism normalise immigration and respect for founding identities within a larger emphasis on integration. A monolingual approach prevails in official dealings, business and commerce and the education system. These policies have contributed to social harmony under the Anglo-Australian blanket; though specific cultural needs are underplayed, and some locals (especially outside the main cities) remain ill at ease with non-white people. Episodic social tensions break out that can affect international students (see chapters 9 and 15). Nevertheless, Australia, along with Canada, is one of the two most Asian-friendly nations in the English-speaking group.

The double claim of British history and Asian geography remains unresolved in the Anglo-Australian psyche. National identity is also complicated by the impact of American examples. These are profoundly felt in Australia, as they are all over the world, more so because Australia shares the American experience of being an Anglo-integrated settler state, and because there is an ease of mutual recognition between the two peoples. But Australians have not borrowed the American sense of national exceptionalism and imperial destiny. If such generalisations are possible, compared with Americans, Anglo-Australians are more direct[7] and egalitarian, though they can be less meritocratic. A sense of cultural superiority and a tendency to identify with the coloniser not the colonised is a stumbling block to regional relations.[8] The flaw is British rather than American. A serious obstacle here is Anglo-lingualism. In 2007 less than 1 per cent of Year 12 school students studied Indonesian language, a declining figure. It was reported that only 85 students were enrolled in south-east Asian languages at degree level.[9] The numbers learning French greatly exceeded those acquiring Putonghua (Mandarin), the Chinese national language. Australia is still facilitating weekend school trips across the British Channel. A prime minister (Kevin Rudd) who speaks fluent Putonghua, and the creation of Confucius Institutes supported

7 Murphy, forthcoming.

8 Grant, 2009.

9 Lindsey, 2009.

by China, may change this. In 2009 a report by the Griffith University Asia Institute arising from the prime minister's 2020 Summit called for investment in Asian language learning that would enable two-thirds of Australians aged under 40 to become proficient in a second language.[10]

In his *The Clash of Civilisations and the Remaking of World Order* Samuel P. Huntington unkindly called Australia a 'torn country'[11] pulled between 'the West' and Asia. It is more a case of evolving agenda than of crisis. The two markers of identity, Anglo-American institutions and the regional setting, could become a productive antinomy (as happens in a different way in Singapore) once the old notion of Australia as regional sheriff for Britain or the USA is completely banished. The trend towards a regionally attuned identity seems irreversible and will be advanced by the next generation of Asian-Australians as they take their share of leadership roles. The long-term solution is a confident hybrid nation that is rooted decisively in Australia, its ecological limits, its successful social institutions and its emerging cosmopolitanism, its plural population and its Asian regional potentials. Australia's demography and history will be increasingly shaped by its geography.

INTERNATIONAL EDUCATION

A handful of students from Asia entered Australian universities prior to World War Two; in 1947 there were about 300 non-European students in the universities.[12] At the same time the Australian government began more systematically to engage with neighbouring countries. But for the next two decades it was believed that 'White Australia could forge meaningful links with the region while maintaining a separate, racially exclusive national identity centred on British heritage and traditions'. It was not until the 1960s that the British presence in Asia faded and 'the Australian government's national interest was no longer viewed through the prism of a British Australia',[13] which paved the way for the dismantling of the White Australia policy.

10 Wesley, 2009.
11 Huntington, 1996.
12 Megarrity, 2007a, 90.
13 *ibid*, 88.

Here international education moved ahead of the trend. In 1951, with Australia playing a strong initiating role, the British Commonwealth established the Colombo Plan aid program, which offered economic and technical assistance, including university scholarships, to emerging Asian nations.[14] The Plan was part of a strategy for containing communism and creating Western friendly elites; Australia also deployed it to counter criticism of the White Australia policy in Asia, but there were unforseen consequences. The quality of Colombo Plan students was high. Graduates were required to return home and many became national leaders in government, the professions, business and the universities. The Plan did much to build goodwill and render Australia an educational pathway for Asian students. Unsponsored private international students grew in number and by 1964 constituted 84 per cent of all international students.[15] They received little policy attention, aside from recurring concerns that they might block local student entry. Private overseas students, who paid the same fees as local students, had separate quotas on numbers. After White Australia was abolished it became easier for these students to secure immigration status and three-quarters did so. In 1979, however, specific additional tuition charges were introduced and immigration was restricted.[16]

In 1984 a major change occurred. Following the creation of full price tuition for international students in the UK, the Australian government decided that adoption of a similar policy could enhance exports and reduce the cost of public funding of the universities. Full fee places began on 1 January 1986, and from 1990 no more subsidised places were offered. Subsidised student numbers fell from 20 000 in 1986 to 6000 in 1991 while full fee students rose from 2000 to 48 000.[17] At the same time the number of scholarships were whittled down. The new policy was defined as a shift 'from aid to trade'. Growth was assisted by government coordination of recruitment in southeast Asia, which restricted the tendency of institutions to market against each other and enhanced a generic brand Australia. The immigration regime for student visas was relatively permissive and

14 Meiras, 2004.
15 Megarrity, 2007a, 97.
16 Megarrity, 2007b, 40.
17 Bradley, 2008, 90.

economic incentives were carefully crafted by government to kick start entrepreneurial behaviour. Institutions had to provide international places on a full fee basis with no cross-subsidisation from funding for local education. They could enrol as many students as they wished; after initial charges were set at full cost levels, price was deregulated. Places for international students did not conflict with opportunities for locals, which were fixed separately and continued to be subsidised by government. Meanwhile, in 1988, average federal funding per student was reduced by 10–15 per cent in real terms.[18] International student fees were the substitute and numbers jumped. The capitalist dynamic had been installed. Chapter 3 will take that story further.

CONCLUSIONS

Some may ask why Australian international education should be singled out for specific attention. The answers are that the researchers are based in Australia, the growth of the commercial student market there has been very dynamic and the Australian case has much to tell. This does not mean there is a special problem of student security in Australia in that international students are worse off there than in other countries. On the contrary, our impression is that internationals are better off in Australia than in most places. In our approach to the subject matter we aim to treat all nations without fear or favour. But if we could put on our national hats for a moment, we would hope that *International Student Security* helps Australian international education to develop the most advanced student security in the world, and become a shining example to other nations.

International education in Australia closely resembles that of the UK and New Zealand in many respects. All three nations have large scale commercial export with many students from Asia. In contrast with the UK, in Australia and New Zealand there are fewer scholarships for graduate research. In all three countries there are recurring problems of discrimination and abuse in the community. All three nations regulate international education as consumer protection. New Zealand, with its code of practice for pastoral care, and the UK, with an attentive Home Office, may do more for student security

18 The reductions varied by institutional type; Burke, 1988.

than does Australia. How much more is debatable. It seems that similarities considerably outweigh the differences. The differences are mostly in scale. Some Australian institutions have over 10 000 international students. Here Australia is ahead of the UK on the same trend line.

In the USA and Canada the approach is less commercial and numbers are less than in Australia, except in Toronto. International education is not regulated in a holistic fashion, as it is in Australia. It is marginal to local education in the USA and has difficult gaining regulators' attention. Perhaps there is more space for intercultural approaches in the classroom but little evidence that they happen. In the USA almost one-third of internationals in doctoral universities are doctoral students, an essential source of labour for research and teaching. They receive better scholarship opportunities and oncampus job opportunities than do internationals in Australia. But most of the sharp issues facing international students are common to all English-speaking countries: community hostility, difficulties of integrating with local students, monoculture in class, some hostile administration of student visas and a lack of entitlements that are taken for granted by local students. Our American colleagues tell us that the bulk of the evidence in this book will resonate in North America.

The book is also very relevant in China, Hong Kong China, India, Malaysia, Singapore, Indonesia, Thailand, Taiwan and other Asian nations. These nations send large numbers of students to Australia and to the other English-language nations that provide international education as a commercial industry. Beyond the English-speaking world the problems continue to fall under the same headings, while the manifestations and policy solutions diverge more. But lack of equal respect, problems of intercultural mixing, language barriers, difficulties with finances, work, housing, health care, safety, immigration, university bureaucracies and loneliness are endemic to the international student experience everywhere. For these reasons this book will speak to all the exporting and importing countries.

The next chapter will look more closely at the global student market, its remarkable growth in Australia and the nature of the Australian industry.

3 THE GLOBAL STUDENT MARKET

Everything is painted so rosy when they are marketing.
~ female, 29, PhD in education, India

INTRODUCTION: STUDENTS ON THE MOVE

In 2006, 2.9 million tertiary students enrolled outside their countries of citizenship, almost five times the 0.6 million in 1975. Since 2000 foreign tertiary students have increased at 7.5 per cent per annum,[1] twice the rate of increase of tertiary students as a whole. Tertiary campuses are 'more cosmopolitan thereby intensifying the intercultural aspect of internationalisation at home in host countries', says the OECD, though the effects are uneven across the world.[2] Australia has seen very rapid growth of international students coupled with modest growth in local students, an extreme version of the overall pattern. The degree of intercultural education is less clear.

This chapter describes the patterns of global student mobility, including the expanding commercial market in foreign degrees, with some focus on Australia.

ROOTS OF GLOBAL MOBILITY

Cross-border mobility has roots in globalisation, policy and market forces:

1 OECD, 2008a, 352.
2 OECD, 2008b, 61.

> During the early years, public policies aimed at promoting and nurturing academic, cultural, social and political ties between countries played a key role, especially in the context of the European construction in which building mutual understanding between young Europeans was a major policy objective. Similar rationales motivated North American policies of academic co-operation. Over time, however, driving factors of a more economic nature played an increasing role. Indeed, decreasing transportation costs, the spread of new technologies, and faster, cheaper communication resulted in a growing interdependence of economies and societies in the 1980s and even more so in the 1990s. This tendency was particularly strong in the high technology sector and labour market. The growing internationalisation of labour markets for the highly-skilled fostered individuals' incentives to gain an international experience as part of their studies . . . the spread of Information and Communication Technology (ICT) lowered information and transaction costs of study abroad and boosted the demand for international education.[3]

Mobility has been facilitated by partial convergence around the world in the structures of degree programs, qualification systems and doctoral education. Further, 'the rise of the knowledge economy and global competition for skills provided a new driver for the internationalisation of education systems in many OECD countries, whereby the recruitment of foreign students is part of a broader strategy to recruit highly skilled immigrants'.[4] International education supplements revenues in nations looking to contain domestic educational costs, and 'at the institutional level, drivers of international education derive from the additional revenues that foreign students may generate – either through differentiated tuition fees or public subsidies'.[5] The World Bank and the OECD also see commercial international education as a means of expanding supply to importing nations where domestic provision cannot meet all needs or is inadequate in quality.[6]

For many students and their families, foreign education is a major financial commitment, an investment in upward social mobility

3 OECD, 2007a, 302–3.
4 *ibid.*
5 *ibid.*
6 OECD, 2007; World Bank, 2007; Bashir, 2007.

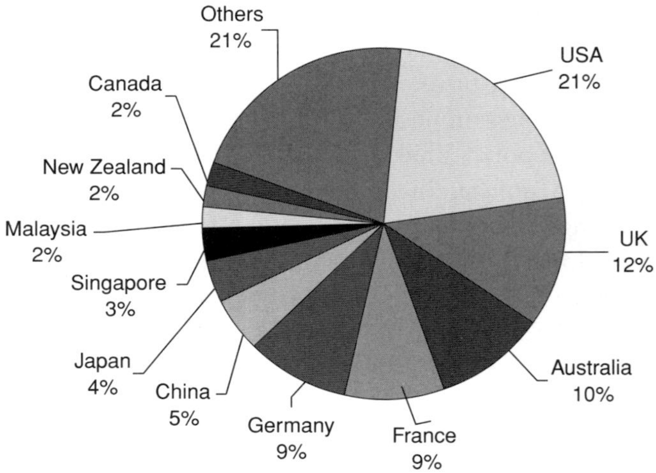

Figure 3.1 Shares of cross-border students, by export nation
Source: Verbik and Lasanowski, 2007.

designed to progress a career at home or transfer abroad to migration-friendly English speaking nations. Half of all cross-border students move out of Asia to English-speaking nations and OECD Europe. There is also movement within Asia. Figure 3.1 shows students who cross into provider (export) nations.[7] In education an exporting nation has institutions providing educational services to citizens of other nations. Most such services take place in the exporting nation itself, the institutions stay put and the students come to them. Services are exported while foreign students are temporarily 'imported'. Some countries like Australia also provide transnational educational services in importing countries. Service and institutions are exported, students stay put. Transnational education is not part of the present study.

Half the exports are by English-speaking countries, led by the USA (21 per cent), the UK (12 per cent) and Australia (10 per cent). Singapore, Canada and New Zealand total 7 per cent. Most students are from non-English-speaking countries.

7 These data, sourced originally from UNESCO, include the English language colleges excluded from the OECD data on international students in tertiary education. In the OBHE–UNESCO data Australia constitutes 10 per cent of the global market (figure 1.1), in the OECD data 6 per cent, behind Germany and France. Both collections exclude transnational enrolments; see Verbik and Lasanowski, 2007; Bashir, 2007; OECD, 2007a, 304.

China is the largest importer of education and the sixth largest exporter. It takes in 5 per cent of all international students, having increased from 52 150 in 2000 to 162 695 in 2006, 212.0 per cent, while Australian exports grew by 103.5 per cent and the UK's by 46.9 per cent.[8] Japan enrols more than 4 per cent of the world's mobile students, Malaysia 2 per cent. Malaysian college provision for foreign students, and some programs in China and western Europe, particularly at postgraduate level, use English.[9] With English now the dominant language of international business and the professions, to acquire good English language skills can be as useful as acquiring the degree certificate and the academic learning.

DIFFERENTIATION OF THE MARKET

Products in a market are unequal in cost and value (qualities that can diverge from each other). International education is no exception. The global market is segmented by nation, by category of institution and by hierarchy of value within each category. In size and power of attraction the USA is the leading exporter, though international students are less than 4 per cent of American enrolments and, except in research, are marginal in most institutions. The USA focuses primarily on international student quality, not quantity: 30 per cent of all internationals in American doctoral universities are PhD students, most with scholarships. These students serve as graduate research and teaching assistants and often immigrate later to the USA, swelling its knowledge economy. Despite the fact that American doctoral universities do not set out to maximise revenues from foreign students the nation is the largest export earner with US$14.1 billion in 2005, well ahead of the UK with $6.1 billion and Australia with $5.6 billion in the same currency (table 3.1). Bashir notes that global trade in education was 3 per cent of world trade in services at the end of the 1990s, and that in 2000 global education exports were almost three times the value of health service exports. In 2004 people in China spent $5.1 billion in American dollars on importing education, with $0.8 billion allocated by Hong Kong China. India spent $3.1 billion,

8 Verbik and Lasanowski, 2007, 37.
9 *ibid.*

Table 3.1 Exports of education services, English-speaking nations excluding Singapore, 2000–5 (US dollars)

	2000 US$ million	2001 US$ million	2002 US$ million	2003 US$ million	2004 US$ million	2005 US$ million	growth 2000–5 %
USA	10 350	11 480	12 630	13 310	13 640	14 120	36.4
UK	3766	3921	3891	4709	5627	6064	61.0
Australia	2259	2528	2897	3925	4872	5563	146.3
Canada	615	699	784	1014	1268	1573	155.8
New Zealand	257	343	632	925	998	1000	289.1
Total of above	*17 247*	*18 971*	*20 834*	*23 883*	*26 405*	*28 320*	*64.2*

Source: Bashir, 2007, 19.

Malaysia $0.9 billion, and Indonesia and Singapore each about $0.5 billion.[10]

In relation to type of institution, research universities with high global prestige are largely concentrated in the USA, to a lesser extent the UK, and a handful elsewhere. There are also medium prestige research institutions in the UK, Australia, Japan and parts of Europe, polytechnic and vocational education and training institutions in many countries and for-profit teaching only institutions such as the University of Phoenix, Malaysian private colleges and online providers.

The global market is also diversified in terms of the economics of student places. On the one hand are national systems and institutions where international education at first degree and Masters level is a commercial business, the word 'industry' is used as a descriptor, students pay for full cost tuition, there is global competition for market share and the number of places expands dynamically over time to build revenues. Here government often sees international education as a means of reducing public funding.[11] On the other hand are systems and institutions in which places are subsidised by government or institutions, and in some cases are free, are mostly subject to quotas and may be seen as a form of foreign aid. In those nations growth of international education is largely regulated and has been less dramatic.

10 Bashir, 2007, 19–20.

11 See discussion in OECD, 2004, 2007a, 2008a; Naidoo, 2006.

Doctoral education is a competitive global market in talent but places in research universities are scarce and subsidised by scholarships.

Roughly half of all international students pay full cost tuition. The commercial approach is endorsed by the World Trade Organization whose General Agreement on Trade in Services is designed to facilitate the opening up of national systems to cross-border trade in education. In English-speaking countries outside North America the commercial mode is dominant. It was pioneered by the UK in the early 1980s, and followed by Australia, New Zealand, Singapore and Malaysia. Malaysia created full fee private colleges in the 1990s, partly to profit from foreign students. In the international market nearly all Australian institutions, including non-profit public and private institutions, are commercial providers. They set their own tuition prices and can expand international places without limit. Public universities use a business structure to organise international education, while full fee international students mostly study alongside the subsidised local students; both groups access common student services. Some nations offer a mixture of modes. The USA sustains a commercial approach by its institutions when located abroad, mostly subsidises the foreign students educated at home and largely protects the domestic system from the entry of foreign providers. The subsidised approach dominates in the doctoral universities. Some lesser status institutions take a largely commercial approach.[12]

Within Europe there is no discrimination between nationals and other European students. Some non-Europeans pay full fees, mostly at Masters level. Germany provides free places to many international students. In French public institutions fees are low: French and foreign students face similar admission requirements and have equal access to student benefits. Japan subsidises international education to encourage the internationalisation of Japanese universities and society, and as foreign aid mostly within Asia. The annual value of exports of higher education services from the five main exporting nations exceeds their annual bilateral and multilateral aid for post-secondary education by a factor of 10. There has been significant decline in such aid in the UK and Australia.[13] France, Germany and Japan between them

12 In future some US public institutions may take a more commercial approach given continuing reductions in state government funding.

13 OECD, 2004, 284–6; Bashir, 2007, 11, 21.

contributed almost 80 per cent of aid in 2004; China receives 65.0 per cent of Japanese educational aid.[14]

DRIVERS OF STUDENT CHOICE

Although revenues are a primary motive in only some nations, it seems that almost all conceive a single global market in which market share is a common measure of national prestige, and 'tertiary education institutions . . . have academic incentives to engage in international activities to build or maintain their reputation in the context of academic competition on an increasingly global scale'.[15] Much research is focused on determinants of student choice. According to a 2001 Edu-World survey of 1000 undergraduate students who travelled abroad from 10 Asian countries, 'mobile students' key choice factors' are 'country (54 per cent), course (18 per cent), institution (17 per cent) and city (10 per cent)'. The desire to access education of higher quality than available at home was as strong a motive as the desire for foreign education and experience for their own sakes.[16]

Comparative student costs are affected by tuition, living expenses and work opportunities, as well as by fluctuating exchange rates. Base level tuition in the US doctoral sector tends to be relatively expensive, though this may be offset by scholarships and oncampus employment. The cost of living is especially high in London but the UK provides free health cover for international students and their dependents, while in the USA and Australia students must take out private health cover (see chapter 8). On average Australia, New Zealand and Canada provide international education more cheaply than the two leading countries. But cost factors are not always primary. In a study of students from eight cities in China studying abroad, Mazzarol and colleagues found that ease of obtaining information about the host country and courses is the primary determinant of location, followed in order by the social and cultural environment, including safety, crime and tolerance, climate, quality of education and portability of qualifications and availability of part-time work. Other factors include the presence of an established population of foreign students, government guarantees of the quality of education, the cost of travel to the country and prior

14 *ibid*, 21–5.

15 OECD 2007a, 303.

16 OECD 2004, 172–3, 266.

family experience. The students separated the English-language countries into two tiers: the first, the USA and the UK , was associated with institutions of high reputation. Australia, Canada and New Zealand constituted the second tier, offering cheaper English-language education and attractive environments. Australia also benefited from proximity to Asia. Selection of the USA, especially at postgraduate level, was strongly affected by reputation, despite perceptions that living there was not fully safe. But a safe environment was the most significant predictor of Chinese students' intentions to choose Australia in preference to Australia's competitors.[17] Similarly, focus groups in Indonesia and Taiwan indicated that many parents send their children to Australia rather than the USA because Australia was deemed safer.[18]

UK research suggests that internet-informed students are becoming more discerning.[19] Recent studies of student choice place growing emphasis on the standing of nations and institutions in the annual global university rankings first issued in 2003,[20] and on student security as safety (chapter 9). Safety became more important after the 2001 attack on the World Trade Centre and Pentagon, which enhanced its potential to differentiate the English-language countries. In the UK studies report that safety is the most important of the hygiene factors that determine international student choice and that the UK has a reputation for being 'one of the safest places in the world to study'.[21] The studies also reported that safety is 'the most important element of the lived experience in the UK'.[22] The 2007 international student survey conducted by Australian Education International (AEI) confirms safety as a very important 'influencing factor in deciding to study in Australia'.[23]

AUSTRALIA IN THE GLOBAL MARKET

Chapter 2 described how the commercial market in education exports was established in Australia. Full fee-paying international student enrolments grew quickly. It became apparent to university leaders

17 Mazzarol et al., 2001.
18 Mazzarol and Soutar, 2002.
19 Davidson, 2008.
20 SJTUIHE, 2008; Times Higher, 2008.
21 i-Graduate 2008, 4.
22 CUBO, 2008, 7.
23 AEI, 2007b.

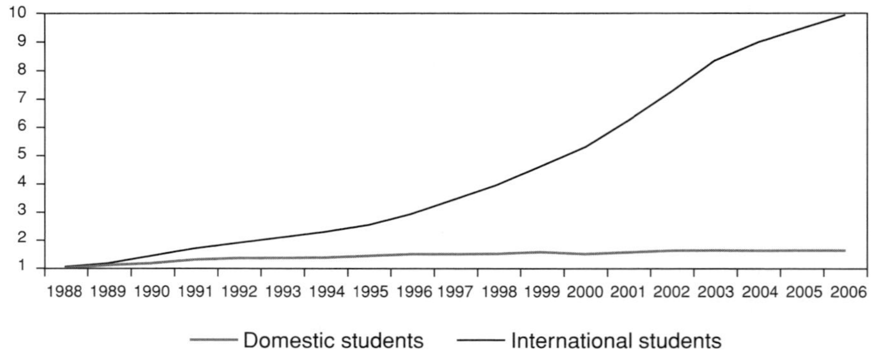

Figure 3.2 Rates of growth of domestic and international students, Australia 1988–2006 (1988 = 1.00)
Source: DEEWR, 2009.

that numbers could be expanded at will and the global market was the most effective way to increase income. Meanwhile, financial needs increased. As noted, in 1988 public funding per local student was reduced by 10–15 per cent in real terms. In 1995 the government abolished full indexation adjustment of grants for local student places, so that each year more private revenues were needed to fill the gap. Further, federally funded research was at an average 70 per cent of real costs. Then the 1996 federal budget announced further annual reductions in government grants for 1997–2000.

From 1995 to 2005 Australia was the only OECD nation to reduce public spending on tertiary education. Public funding per student fell by 28 per cent in real terms.[24] Between them, these factors spurred more rapid growth of international education.

From 1985–2005 the number of international students multiplied three times at world level but 12 times in Australia. Australia's local student growth was much slower (figure 3.2). Between 1990 and 2007 the number of international students grew from 25 000 to 254 414, to reach 26.0 per cent of enrolments, including transnationals,[25] the highest level in the developed world. OECD data for 2006 found that onshore international students were 19.7 per cent of degree-level students in Australia compared to 15.2 per cent in the UK,

24 OECD, 2008a.
25 DEEWR, 2009.

15.1 per cent in New Zealand and 13.4 per cent in Switzerland. The OECD country average was 7.3 per cent.[26]

SCALE OF EDUCATION EXPORTS

Aside from the Australian National University, which receives special research funding, Australian institutions have a common incentive to generate international student revenues en masse. In many institutions the number of students is very large by world standards. In 2006 the American university with the largest complement of foreign students (7115) was the University of Southern California in Los Angeles; in Australia 13 Australian universities, led by RMIT University with 17 894, had more international students (table 3.2). Institutional dependence on international fees (figure 3.3) was a high 14.9 per cent of total revenues in 2006 and close to 50 per cent at Central Queensland University (table 3.2).[27]

Since 1982, education services exports have grown at 14 per cent per year in volume terms, compared to 6 per cent for each of total exports and service exports. In 2007 education exports, including spending by onshore students on tuition, housing, food, transport, living and entertainment, were A$12.6 billion, 39 per cent from tuition. As noted in chapter 2 education was the third largest export (5.6 per cent) behind coal (9.5 per cent), iron ore (7.5 per cent) and ahead of tourism (5.4 per cent).[28] In 2008 education exports reached A$15.5 billion, up from $8.6 billion in 2004.[29] Education exports were at the level of 1.2 per cent of GDP. Commercial exporter nations have achieved something that intrigues treasury departments elsewhere. They have devised a way to mobilise education, a part public good,[30] subject to market failure in general education and research, in the direct creation of economic value at scale. International education also provides skilled migrants. According to an Australian Education International survey, 'in 2007 78 per cent of international respondents

26 OECD, 2008a, 366.
27 DEEWR, 2009.
28 Reserve Bank, 2008.
29 ABS, 2009.
30 Samuelson, 1954.

Table 3.2 International student enrolments and tuition revenues at the 20 institutions with the largest number of international students, Australia, 2006

	Enrolled international students (higher education only)			Tuition revenues from international students	
Institution		**Proportion of all students %**	**Onshore students only**	**$ *million***	**Proportion of all income %**
Royal Melbourne Institute of Technology University*	17 894	43.2	7457	125.9	27.5
Monash University	17 087	31.2	11 080	190.7	18.1
Curtin University of Technology	16 501	41.8	8005	115.8	23.3
Central Queensland University*	13 899	54.9	12 579	145.0	49.6
Macquarie University	10 468	33.6	9709	111.4	28.0
University of South Australia	10 422	31.2	4598	63.0	16.4
University of Melbourne*	10 376	23.9	10 277	191.6	16.1
University of Sydney*	9680	21.1	9060	148.1	12.2
University of Technology, Sydney	8954	27.4	6688	95.0	23.9
University of Southern Queensland	8895	35.2	8895	25.4	15.9
University of Wollongong	8620	39.4	4900	55.1	18.4
University of New South Wales*	8618	22.2	8546	119.6	14.4
Griffith University	8358	23.7	7850	96.4	20.1
Deakin University*	6715	20.2	5633	67.5	15.3
University of Queensland	6607	17.6	6607	107.7	11.5
Charles Sturt University	5817	17.0	2448	13.0	5.1
Swinburne University of Technology*	5815	33.4	4704	54.9	17.2
University of Ballarat*	5798	55.6	4249	48.2	26.4
La Trobe University	5619	19.8	4091	47.1	12.2
Victoria University*	5547	27.5	2889	40.5	12.4
All other institutions	59 104	17.7	42 354	513.5	9.7
All institutions	250 794	25.5	182 619	2375.4	14.9

Note: In the present study interviews were conducted at nine of these institutions; marked thus [*].
Source: DEEWR, 2009.

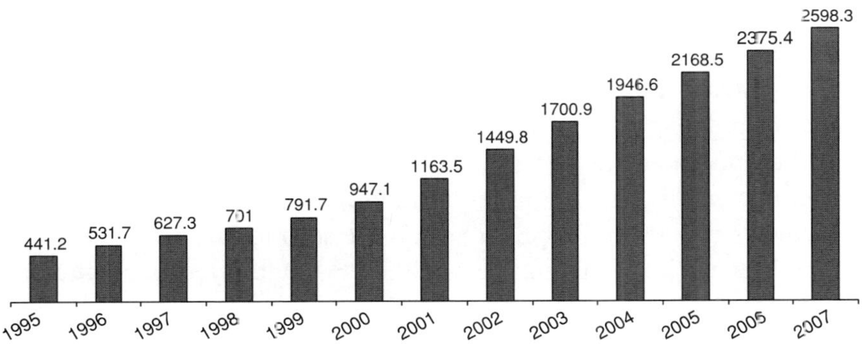

Figure 3.3 Annual revenues from international student fees, higher education, Australia 1995–2007 ($ million)
Source: DEEWR, 2009.

either had applied for (30 per cent) or planned to apply (48 per cent) for permanent resident status in Australia'.[31]

IMBALANCES

It is important to emphasise that the hyperindustry in Australia is an artifice of the policy settings. The government's objective has been to build student volume and thereby maximise export revenue and maximise fiscal savings in the education budget. International education has also been used to drive efficiency, entrepreneurship, competitiveness and a limited global engagement of universities. Exports have grown rapidly in Australia not because of superior quality, or cheaper price and growing demand in Asia, though the latter factors have helped. It has been driven by scarcity induced by deliberately underfunding teaching and research. It is not surprising that distortions have resulted.

In focusing on export revenues Australia has neglected the material conditions of educational quality and downplayed the public good benefits. General education (advanced literacy) and non-commercial research generate long-term benefits in economic growth, social cohesion and the quality of life. Since the mid 1990s the average student:staff ratio in higher education has risen from 15 to one to

31 AEI, 2008a, 9.

20 to one,[32] and the share of basic research in total research has fallen sharply. Revenues from international education are funnelled into specialised business costs such as marketing, buildings and services, not public goods in teaching and research. Australia is a leading export earner but a weaker global competitor in research and doctoral education, which rest on public funding. It has three universities in the world's top 100 but they are all in the second 50.[33] Two of these universities are forced to enrol more than 9000 international students to balance their books.

In striving for maximum growth the industry has opened itself to the shaping effects of market forces, which are indifferent to balances between disciplines, between levels of study and between nations of origin (figure 3.4). In 2007, 216 842 students (79.4 per cent) were from Asia, consistent with Australia's geographic position, demography and Colombo Plan history; but the industry was increasingly dependent on China (58 079) and India (23 491), which had generated nearly all growth since 2002. China, together with Hong Kong China (22 775) provided 29.6 per cent of students in 2007.[34] Malaysia (29 538) and Singapore (29 345) remained important but in the 10 years to 2007 enrolments from Indonesia, Malaysia and Singapore, where Australia was traditionally the strongest English-language provider, fell from 32.6 to 11.7 per cent.[35] In trade monopsonistic importers are in a position to influence exporters. China's government has come to appreciate that it can influence international education policy within host nations by threatening to limit the number of Chinese students studying in them, as happened to the New Zealand industry with devastating consequences.[36]

In terms of field of study, as in all English-language countries, business education is dominant. More specific to Australia and New Zealand is the strong concentration on first degrees and short coursework Masters and the weakness of international doctoral education. In 2007 there were 76 654 coursework Masters foreign students in Australia, 28.1 per cent of all international enrolments, but only

32 DEEWR, 2009.
33 SJTUIHE, 2008.
34 DEEWR, 2009.
35 AEI, 2008b.
36 In New Zealand the number of international students in higher education fell by 28.4 per cent between 2002 and 2007 (see chapter 9); Education New Zealand, 2007.

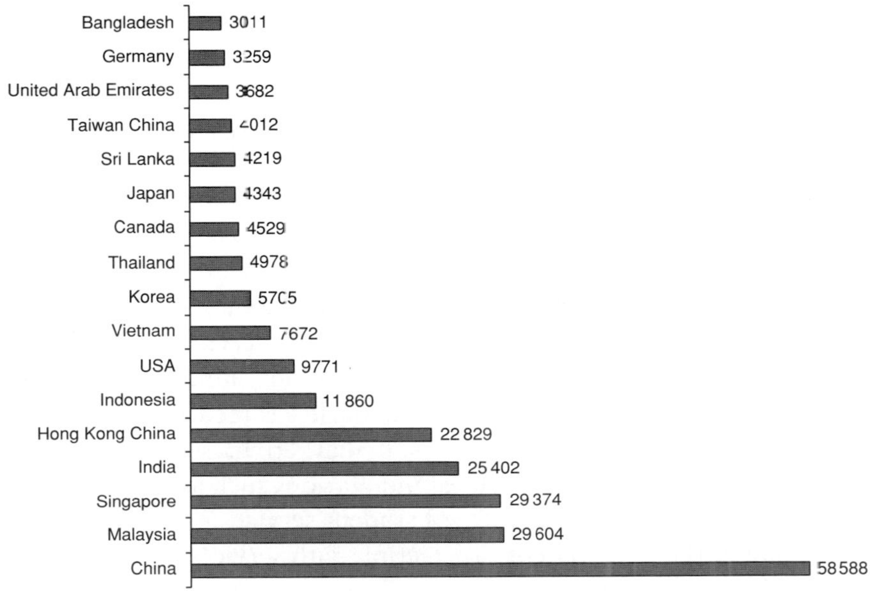

Figure 3.4 Countries supplying more than 3000 international students to Australian universities, 2007
Source: DEEWR, 2009.

8513 doctoral students (3.1 per cent).[37] In 2003 research students constituted a much higher proportion of cross-border enrolments in several European nations, including Switzerland (18.4 per cent), Finland (17.8 per cent), Sweden (12.7 per cent), and the UK (9.4 per cent);[38] they were 30 per cent of international enrolments in US doctoral universities.[39] Like Australia, the UK has a commercial international education program but in 2004 there were 34 533 international doctoral students, compared to 6594 in Australia, though UK higher education was just three times as big as Australia's.[40] Australia offers few doctoral scholarships with living allowances, though there are more places with just fee remission, or funding for students but not dependents. Inevitably, bright students with other global options go elsewhere. Some Australian institutions attempt to subsidise doctoral scholarships from fee revenues, but the

37 DEEWR, 2009.
38 OECD, 2005, 272.
39 IIE, 2007.
40 OECD, 2007b.

system settings draw the surplus into other purposes and these strategies are too small scale to solve the problem.

AUSTRALIA'S POSITION IN THE GLOBAL MARKET

Consistent with the commercial paradigm and systems of quality assurance, the Australian industry is locked into service improvement and customer satisfaction, not product (teaching and learning) improvement. It differentiates itself from the USA and the UK not by educational and cultural content but also by services, price, proximity, climate and tourist benefit, and generic claims about safety and excellence. Its quantity edge in the market is secured by national coordination, executive acumen, good marketing, recruitment and non-academic services, and business innovations such as transnational delivery. Surveys suggest that use of student services is higher in Australia than in the UK; student satisfaction with services is also higher. Satisfaction with academic quality is lower,[41] and Australia has failed to use the period of growth to develop substantial innovations and improvements in the academic product. Because every possible dollar is siphoned out of international education, the students fail to secure full value and academic innovations are a luxury. Academic cultures remain surprisingly unchanged. Key problems, such as poor English preparation and support, are yet to be effectively tackled (chapter 12), though progress there would strengthen Australia's market position. The pedagogical and curricular potentials of intercultural education are little explored. It has been difficult to synergise the academic capacities of universities with their business strengths or to utilise the growing engagement with Asia to evolve a strong set of cross-border research linkages.[42] But there is limited scope to bring research cultures to bear on the high volume course work programs for middle-level business students that are the industry staple and cheaper and easier to slot these programs into standardising marketing cultures that are regulated by quality assurance.[43]

The drive to minimise costs so as to maximise surplus pushes international education into a one size fits all mould that reduces or

41 UKCOSA, 2004; AEI, 2007a; AEI, 2007b.

42 Quiddington, 2008.

43 Sidhu, 2006.

eliminates the potential for depth, nuancing, customised programs, learning strategies and pastoral care. There is an inherent temptation to cut corners on international student security, especially by devolving functions from government and institution to informal peer networks and self-management by the students. But as the case of Hong Jie Zhang in Canberra shows, devolving security blind to the informal and private domain, without monitoring each individual student's situation, leaves security and safety incomplete. There is an inherent conflict between the commercial character of the market and comprehensive student security. It can only be overcome by a policy that factors into the regime of student security, for each individual student, full welfare, pastoral care and human rights. Inescapably, this adds to unit costs.

Tensions between the commercial character of the program and the educational, cultural and security objectives that it espouses but does not always achieve, has led to growing criticism and debate within Australia, particularly in Melbourne, some generated by our own research.[44] 'Don't treat them like cash cows' says the *Herald-Sun*.[45] In the *Age* Das refers to

> a growing perception that Australia's international students have been exploited on one hand, and neglected on the other . . . Many of Australia's foreign students have happy experiences, but a sizeable and vocal minority are furious about what they say is an appalling and callous lack of welfare support for students navigating their way through a crippling lack of affordable housing, workplace exploitation, cultural roadblocks and threats to personal safety.[46]

Das notes that 'fears among education experts that negative publicity overseas and within Australia about the plight of international students could start a reputational bushfire' with 'serious ramifications for the international market'.[47] At the same time the head of Australian Education International declared that it was time to move from growth to consolidation and 'sustainability'.[48]

44 Ross, 2008a.
45 Nyland, 2008, 19.
46 Das, 2008a.
47 *ibid.*
48 *ibid.*

CONCLUSIONS

In the last decade the worldwide number of cross-border international students has grown by 7 per cent per year, but over the last two decades Australia's rate of growth has been double that. This has accumulated what the American *Chronicle of Higher Education* referred to in August 2008 as a 'dangerous dependence' on the international market.[49] In September 2008 the Victorian government established a taskforce on international students that focused on security issues. In December 2008 the federal government's review of higher education called for a broader international education program with more emphasis on doctoral education and a wider range of countries prominent in the intake.[50] But fundamental change was impossible as long as the same drivers of export growth remained in place.

The next chapter looks at human security in the global education market.

---

49 Slattery, 2008.
50 Bradley, 2008.

4 STUDENT SECURITY AND REGULATION

We're basically seen as cash cows and that's something that should change.

~ male, 33, PhD in medicine, Spain

INTRODUCTION: STUDENTS CHANGING THEMSELVES

Human beings are complex creatures. Amartya Sen points out that 'We all have multiple identities, and . . . each of these identities can yield concerns and demands that can significantly supplement, or seriously compete with, other concerns and demands arising from other identities'.[1] Each person must navigate these multiple identities. For those who cross borders the complexities and tensions are greater. The transitional character of the study experience, and the large communities in which it plays out, opens all international students to changing associations and new kinds of self, rendering their human security more chancy and unstable.

As Pedersen puts it, 'the multicultural person is always recreating an identity as roles are learned, modified or discarded in each discontinuous situation'.[2] While not many international students change their basic values, objectives or commitment to their country, most tend to adopt attitudes 'favouring greater open-mindedness, the value of knowledge, and greater freedom in the relationship between sexes'.[3] This response is almost inevitable. It is difficult to accommodate the new environment without becoming more flexible. But becoming more open and flexible sets into

1 Sen, 1999, 120.
2 Pedersen, 1991, 18.
3 *ibid*, 22.

being a process of self-transformation that cannot be fully anticipated and sometimes feels uncontrolled. Hayes and Lin, confirming Sen, comment that international students not only belong to several networks, but many also experience 'a profound sense of loss'[4] that opens them to the new. When the linguistic context changes many of the old markers of self are stripped away. Proficiency in host country language often determines the ease with which students move between old sites and new[5] while controlling their evolving sense of self. Appadurai remarks that this kind of diasporic bi-location, where the proximate site constitutes a powerful experiential significance while an older site retains emotional and imaginative significance, lends itself to the interpolation and self-creation of hybrid[6] or divided identities.

In the interviews for this study students reflected on the effects of mobility on themselves. Students in the foreign environment were more isolated than they had been at home. They had to be responsible for themselves. This had attractions. Many talked of a new sense of freedom. Family, custom and the social world pressed on the student less incessantly in Australia than at home. For others, the removal of kinship obligations and social hierarchies and expectations left them disturbed or bereft. There was a strain of nostalgia, longing and partial disconnectedness in some interviews.

> I love it here, I'm comfortable. You see the thing is, I fit in over here. I don't fit in, in India. I'm a feminist. OK, I'm a strong minded woman and in the India subcontinent it is very difficult. [Here] I have the freedom to lead my own life and I am not expected to come home and . . . I don't have all the social pressures to deal with. I have my life.
>
> ~ female, 19, arts, India

> It is a lot more individualistic here. It's really difficult if you don't have friends because you don't have many people that care about you.
>
> ~ male, 27, computing, Indonesia

4 Hayes and Lin, 1994, 7.
5 *ibid*, 8–11.
6 Appadurai, 1996.

Students found themselves positioned between old and new, determining who they wanted to become, or unsure and in tension. They were asked if there were risks and problems they did not know about, or underestimated before they came to Australia.

> Maybe the principle of life. Because in Indonesia freedom is not really encouraged. What is right, what is wrong, [that is what] is really respected. But here I learn that freedom is really appreciated. As I experience it, I change a little bit of my values into Australian. My parents, they are pretty shocked actually. But it's hard for me, because I can't jump to Australian culture, and I can't really be Indonesian anymore . . . I have become more individualistic. It's normal here, but I can't be that, you know, because I am still Indonesian . . . Home sweet home . . . still, I like Indonesia. Melbourne is a good place to study, [there's] no pollution at all, the system is really beautiful; in Indonesia we don't have that. Still, in Indonesia has all the cultural friendliness, the warmth of the family. I still can't get it here.
>
> ~ male, 18, engineering, Indonesia

For the mobile student in transition, change is happening on all fronts. The formal institutional setting and rules are only partly known in the early months but it is already clear they are dramatically different from those at home. The student's relationships, which are crucial to a continuous sense of self and provide resources for survival and resettlement, are stretched and fragmented, and must be created and recreated in the new setting. Changes in individual identity are conditioned by changes in formal roles, personal ties and social networks, and vice versa. In these circumstances, in which self and situation are shifting with an often bewildering speed, international student security is always incomplete. Indeed, it is scarcely adequate to the challenge. It must be continually constructed.

HUMAN SECURITY IN THE GLOBAL SETTING

In this more global era students are not the only category for whom mobility has increased. Other kinds of people also move across borders: travellers for business and work, tourism, long-term migrants, people displaced by war or natural disaster. For settled populations in some countries human mobility can engender tensions, especially mobility associated with migration and refugee settlement. Nations differ in their receptiveness to entrants, in their openness and willingness to share, in their tolerance for difference and in the opportunities they provide. For people crossing the border, whether temporarily or permanently, their first concern is normally to achieve social and economic security for their families and themselves.

Security is an elemental human need. Clements notes that it is paramount that the need for security is satisfied because without security 'social life would be both meaningless and relatively dangerous'.[7] But what do we mean here by 'security'? The term is variously discussed in political theory, sociology and cultural studies, and in international relations, which examines the joint and several security of states.[8] Baldwin defines security generically as 'a low probability of damage to acquired values'. This can apply to individuals and also to states.[9] However, when considering human security, including that of international students, it might be more useful to use a specific definition, especially as state-centred security can be in tension with the security of individuals, groups and particular communities within nation-states. Also, Baldwin's definition might be unduly defensive.[10] Protection is a key element in security, and the definition is useful where it focuses on avoiding damage. At the same time human agents, and especially international students, change their values without necessarily impairing agency itself. Not all such changes are forced on them. Nor, when one must adjust quickly and effectively to new requirements, does security always reside in maintaining tradition unchanged. A low level of change in acquired values might signify the absence of security, not its presence. For mobile students affected by globalisation (and perhaps all people in the era of modernity) security is likely to lie in a viable combination of tradition and change.

Identity, values and location all affect variations in the meaning of human security. 'Together they present a combination of cultural elements that interact to shape understanding of what constitutes insecurity and who has responsibility for ensuring communities and

7 Clements, 1990, 2.
8 Forbes-Mewett, 2008; Forbes-Mewett and Nyland, 2008.
9 Baldwin, 1997, 13.
10 Forbes-Mewett, 2008, 5–6.

individuals are secure.'[11] Religions have differing understandings of security. Islam balances individual motivation with cooperation and mutual responsibility, social justice and the equitable distribution of wealth. Liberal Christianity calls on the goodwill and charity of individuals, especially leaders, to provide what is needed for security. These traditions also exhibit diversity in terms of family and gender relations.[12] State security practices take on different meanings according to the traditions and attitudes that prevail. These same state practices also shape popular attitudes in a reciprocal effect. As Bénabou and Tirole[13] note, dominant views on this question differ across nations. In English-speaking countries influenced by neoliberal values (see below) personal effort is the maker of security. In the USA individuals tend to be held responsible for their own security, whereas Europeans are more inclined to see the community as a primary source of security. The USA spends significantly less than Europeans on the security needs of citizens, though more than Europeans on the security of the state itself. Chinese people maintain a relatively strong belief in the need for the state to provide social protection.

> The significance of the fact that different cultures have divergent understandings of what security entails comes to the surface when individuals relocate to a foreign environment. People relocating are confronted with a new set of complex cultural issues that affect their security. Likewise, the host country is also confronted with a new set of complex cultural issues that may appear to be threatening.[14]

Contemporary notions of human security are partly shaped by global agencies with responsibility for peace, refugees and poverty relief. In the United Nations tradition 'human security' suggests the individual 'is to be made secure from two basic kinds of threats: freedom from fear and freedom from want'.[15] The *1994 Human Development Report* of the United Nations Development Programme formalises human security as 'protection from sudden and hurtful

11 Forbes-Mewett and Nyland, 2008, 183.
12 *ibid.*
13 Bénabou and Tirole, 2005.
14 Forbes-Mewett and Nyland, 2008, 183–4.
15 Nesadurai, 2005, 9.

disruptions in the patterns of daily life; whether in homes, jobs or in communities'; and 'safety from chronic threats such as hunger, disease and repression'.[16] This definition encompasses security relating to food, health, safety of the person, and the economic and political order. The notion of security is defensive in relation to risk but proactive in economic development. Economic prosperity is often seen as a precondition of human security, though as Forbes-Mewett remarks, the economic security of individuals can conflict with national (and global) economic security.[17] But there is more to the conditions necessary for human security than this.

AGENCY AND SECURITY

In *Development as Freedom* (2000) Sen reworks the intersection of human agency, human security and social and economic development. In contrast with the argument that economic development is a prior condition of individual security and self-realisation, Sen regards free self-responsible human agents, in charge of their own identity and values, as a prior condition of economic and social evolution.[18] The self-responsible individual is at the core of modern societies. 'Any affirmation of social responsibility that *replaces* individual responsibility cannot but be, to varying extents, counterproductive.'[19] Nevertheless, the capacity to exercise individual responsibility cannot be taken for granted. 'Responsibility requires freedom', and individual capabilities are formed not inherent. 'The substantive freedoms that we respectively enjoy to exercise our responsibilities are extremely contingent on personal, social and environmental circumstances',[20] including social policies, education, democratic political participation and human rights.

> Responsible adults must be in charge of their own wellbeing; it is for them to decide how to use their capabilities. But the capabilities that a person does actually have (and not merely theoretically enjoys)

16 UNDP, 1994, 23.
17 Forbes-Mewett, 2008, 5–6.
18 Sen, 2000, 287–8; emphasis in original.
19 *ibid*, 283; emphasis in original.
20 *ibid*, 284.

> depend on the nature of social arrangements, which can be crucial for individual freedoms. And there the state and the society cannot escape responsibility.[21]

State policies are in turn shaped by individual freedoms. For Sen free agency embodies three elements. First, an active human will and conscious identity, the seat of self-directed activity. Sen calls this 'agency freedom'. Second, freedom from external threat or constraint, which Sen calls 'control freedom' and many call negative freedom. Third, freedom as the capacity to act, which Sen calls 'effective freedom' or 'freedom as power', and many call positive freedom.[22] Control freedom and effective freedom are the defensive and proactive moments of agency.

Sen's approach fosters a broad understanding of human security, which is shaped by individual freedoms and by the social relations and arrangements. Once we admit human agency as constructive of social practices, *and* vice versa, we circumvent the barren either/or argument of individual responsibility versus social responsibility, though the individual–society balance can be fixed in differing ways.

Hence, in *International Student Security*, human security rests on the economic, policy, social and cultural conditions, including the prevailing social values, and on the scope for self-determining human agency itself. Human agency is both product and producer of human security. To adapt Marx, international students make their own security, in circumstances that they do not entirely control, including the scope for agency itself. This does not mean that individual international students sink or swim solely by their own efforts. Others share responsibility because they affect the conditions in which the students make their security. State policy and regulation, institutional management, the civil and private sphere: all influence the practices of security and the potentials of students as self-propelled agents. At the same time, the students can also affect the wider setting. The more they are empowered to do so, the more their security is advanced. 'Basic civil rights and political freedoms are indispensable for the emergence of social values', says Sen. 'The freedom to participate in critical

21 *ibid*, 288.
22 Sen, 1985, 1992.

evaluation and the process of value formation is among the most crucial freedoms of social existence.'[23]

Thus the present study defines human security as *maintenance of a stable capacity for self-determining human agency*. This can be understood in either individual or group terms but the main focus here is individual security. The terms 'maintenance' and 'stable capacity' capture the defensive and protective element that is one component of security. Here protection is not seen as an end in itself but one of the conditions essential to active human agency, its expression in all zones and its self-managed evolution or self-formation. The term 'self-determining human agency', which expands on the adjective 'human' in the term 'human security', provides scope for variation in identity and values and for the subjective element of self-defined needs that must be part of any humanist construct of human security.

Once agency is placed at the centre of the problem, then subjective variation in security becomes inevitable. We must ask: 'Security for whom, for what and under what circumstances or conditions?' (Clement).[24] One of the achievements of post-Enlightenment evolution, alongside the rise of the self-responsible individual, is the enhanced scope for this subjective element. 'There is a general moral consensus that suggests that people's need-satisfaction should be fulfilled to the extent that enables them to participate in their culture and develop their individuality.'[25]

The definition of human security as 'maintenance of a stable capacity for self-determining human agency' has a number of implications for the study. First, maintenance of a stable capacity is problematic for students who move from one location, personal circle and cultural environment to another, though the break from the previous setting is rarely complete. Mobility is two sided in its implications for human agency. Life forms first learnt to move with their own power and to search for food, prey on others and escape their predators in the Cambrian era more than 500 million years ago. Evolution leapt forward. The fossil record shows there was an explosion of new species. Ever since then mobility has brought with it the double experience of opportunity and danger. It also means change and self-change.

23 Sen, 2000, 287.
24 Forbes-Mewett, 2008, 13.
25 *ibid*, 13.

On the move we face new problems and acquire new characteristics. Mobility destabilises agency, while at the same time it draws on the capacity of agency to remake itself. It calls on powers of self-determination in a new situation that confronts the student as other-determination. The agency of some students is weakened, while many others exhibit a robust, conscious, flexible and growing sense of self. Studies suggest that this kind of active human agency, that is open to change and manages self-change, is integral to academic success, emotional happiness and intercultural relations in the country of study (see chapter 15).

Second, the multiple character of international student life also undermines stable capacity. Old linkages and identity survive in the new period. International students live in more than one security setting with more than one set of networks in more than one nation. Each student's individualised human security combines the different elements but the mosaic is a mixture of styles and often incomplete. As noted in chapter 1, this is one of the definitive elements of international education, the reason it creates an unsolved problem of global governance and a driving force in the work that led to this book. The student lives under two different sets of governmental rules and regimes of citizenship and informal supports. At the same time the student lives under neither regime. Absent from the home country, the student cannot access all its protections and entitlements. At the same time the student has less than equal rights in the country of education and the informal networks are attenuated. Both sets of arrangements affect the student. Neither is complete. Each has the potential to destabilise the other.

Third, for non-English-speaking students from non-Anglo cultural environments, human security is affected by cultural issues. Equal cultural respect is hard to secure in a country such as Australia in which formal systems are monolingual and education and public policy are monocultural. Cultural difference is mostly accepted and tolerated in Australia but not officially endorsed or expressed.

Fourth, because international students are, for the most part, from a non-English-speaking environment and also unfamiliar with Australia, they begin from a notable information asymmetry in their relationship with education institutions. Access to knowledge, access to information and access to communicative resources are crucial to self-determining agency, and can be vital to personal security.

Finally, given Sen's point about the social setting, the question of international student security brings into sharp relief the role of government, public policy, law and regulation, which, as a rule, means the nation-state. One dimension of the nation-state is the material benefits and protections it provides and government is often discussed in those terms. But Sen's point about self-determining agency – and its corollary, the subjective definition of needs – draws our attention also to the effects of governance and regulation for human agency itself. Here the role of state is two sided. As we shall see, government empowers international students in some respects and disempowers them in others. Likewise governments provide benefits and protections in some areas and deny them in others. The precise mix is crucial. And cross-border populations create special challenges for national governments. The next section will consider the governance and regulation of student security.

GOVERNANCE AND REGULATION

Polanyi remarks that 'in order to be sustainable, markets should be underpinned by the twin forces of self-regulation and outside regulation typically by public authorities'.[26] Governments set conditions for economic production and exchange and may supplement economic markets in areas of market failure, that is, by meeting social objectives underprovided by market forces. Governments also regulate the non-market provision of state sector education in the public interest.

Put simply, the distinction between governance and regulation is a distinction between macro and micro levels of relations of power. 'Governance' concerns the broad approaches, ideologies and rationales used in systems of power. The term was once confined to the sovereign realm of nation-states. Governance or 'government' are now seen as including civil society and private life, taking in not only state regulation but also the forms of self-regulation explored by Foucault under the heading of 'governmentality'.[27] The shift in the literature corresponds to a change in governance in the real world. More indirect and sophisticated modalities of power have developed, theorised as 'steering from a distance' and 'government by self-regulation'.

26 Polanyi, 1944.
27 Foucault, 1991.

In *Powers of Freedom* Rose discusses 'responsibilization', the downward transfer of responsibility for outcomes and government by 'the conduct of conduct'.[28] Governance shades into the core social sites of family, workplace, school, churches and consumption and absorbs some of their logics. Regulation invokes and enables a plurality of legal and policy domains.[29] It is a double movement in which nation-states become less coercive and more respectful of freedom as control, while spreading their influence via the civil and private realms, deploying the self-determining freedoms of institutions and individuals as mediums through which state agencies achieve their policy objectives. Citizen-subjects are nudged onto preferred pathways where they move forward with their own volition.

In *International Student Security* we are interested in governance as it affects international students. Much of this is enacted at the level of regulation. Following Baldwin and Cave,[30] 'regulation' refers to the rules and mechanisms used to operationalise the approach to governance. This includes state systems of allocating resources, framing institutions and determining individual conduct; it also extends to the conventions that govern social behaviour in civil society. In fact regulation encompasses 'all forms of social control and influence'.[31] Here we are interested in the regulatory mechanisms and rules affecting international students.

CHANGES IN GOVERNANCE

In the last 30 years in English-speaking nations such as Australia, and to some extent in all countries, there have been three main changes at the level of governance with implications for the regulation of international students.

The first change in governance has already been suggested. Consistent with the growing role of individual agency and self-responsibility in modern societies, and with steering from a distance, there is reduced use of systems based on top-down control and ordering, and growing reliance on systems based on devolution and delegation to

28 Giddens, 1990; Rose, 1999, and others.
29 Parker et al., 2004; Arup et al., 2006.
30 Baldwin and Cave, 1999.
31 *ibid*, 2.

choice-making individuals and institutions. Governments make a virtue out of sending functions of social order, mutuality and welfare to a plethora of non-government organisations, institutions such as universities, and households and individuals. Devolution and informal systems lower the expectations on formal state agencies, shift the basis of social programs from universal entitlement to individual choice, save money that would otherwise be spent in public programs and reduce political pressure on nation-states, all in the name of enhanced popular powers and freedoms.[32] The passage from paternalistic state bureaucracy to self-managed social policy is incomplete. Paternalism survives. Coercion also survives. But there is widespread use of self-regulation and informal mechanisms and this is one key to the governance and regulation of international education.

The second change in governance is the passage from the welfare states established after World War Two in western Europe and the English-speaking world to more attenuated policies influenced by neoliberalism, which privileges economic markets above social objectives. In this process there has been a partial retreat from the goal of universal access to high quality public services. Certain organisational forms and cultures of the business firm have been installed in social services such as education.[33] In turn this has determined the direction taken by systems of devolution and steering from a distance. The use of partial market mechanisms and contractual bargains for allocating and ordering public services, the notion of student-as-consumer and the emphasis on trade objectives rather than foreign aid in international education are signs of this change in governance. International education in Australia is a good example of neoliberal governance. The central notion of student-as-consumer is explored immediately below.

The third change in governance is the impact of globalisation on the agendas and methods of nation-states. Here the term 'globalisation' refers to the partial convergence of systems and practices across national borders and the growth of worldwide systems and structures as in finance and trade, transport and communications, ideas and knowledge.[34] Some scholars argue that devolution and globalisation

32 Le Grand and Bartlett, 1993; Powell, 2007.

33 Marginson, 1997.

34 Marginson and van der Wende, 2007.

together constitute a reduction in the authority and materiality of the nation-state. We are not persuaded of this. As we see it, nation-state government has been changed, but in overall terms has not been reduced. It has new tasks. It is increasingly affected by global flows of people, trade, capital, technologies, communications, knowledge and ideas; and more focused on global comparisons and competitiveness. The growing global movement of people and the global trade in education provide new opportunities and imperatives for nation-state governance and regulation.

International education is at one and the same time local and institutional, national and global. Globalisation invokes the challenge of regulating activities such as education when they cross more than one national space. Sometimes two national governments, those of the home and the host country, are in play, as in China's interventions in international education in Australia and New Zealand. It is inefficient to sort all global matters through bilateral negotiation, and developments in international law place in question the traditional assumption that limits of national territory are also limits of governance.[35] But global governance and regulation are underdeveloped and do not necessarily synchronise with the national dimension. Decisions about the global movement of people across and between nations continue to be made by national governments whose formal authority stops at the territorial border. The rights and lives of mobile individuals are regulated through the prism of national policy on aliens, rather than global citizenship. In this context, the term 'security' often refers to the vulnerability of nation-states and their quasimilitary self-protection through border controls, rather than the rights and needs of international students and other cross-border people. Governments struggle to manage global people flows they can never fully control. Here governance and regulation can appear arbitrary and unstable. At times nations respond to global pressures with greater flexibility, as, for example in Australia, which introduced systems of dual citizenship and facilitated the inward flow of skilled immigrants, including international graduates. Yet nations can also be coercive (see chapter 10). In Australia, the regulation of student visas by immigration authorities epitomises this more heavy-handed form of governance. The failure

35 Vaughan-Williams, 2008, for example 323.

of humanism in this domain may seem puzzling, but it points to the long deep connections between borders, law and fear, the customary use of preemptive violence by nation-states to protect themselves from potential external threats and the unnatural character of national borders. Having been imposed by force in the past, and continually placed in question by globalisation, borders could always be different. They must be continually remade.[36] Borders are places where security and liberty are not combined as they should be, but are often in tension.[37] State interests are powerful interests and have more than economic objectives.

Thus international education is a cross-border market in which the student-as-consumer is nominally sovereign and devolution and responsibilisation are the order of the day. But international education also triggers border anxiety, old style bureaucratic regulation and state force. National government wants to build the international market and skilled migration and invite student entry, and stretches categories such as identity and residency to accommodate globalisation. But government is also concerned with border threats, trusts no one but itself, uses exclusive categories and is not fully persuaded that it wants the alien at all. International student security is simultaneously shaped by these two different cultures of governance and regulation, and the tensions between them.

THE STUDENT-AS-CONSUMER

As discussed, in countries providing international education on a commercial basis, such as the UK, Australia and New Zealand, the student is imagined and regulated as a consumer in a contractual relationship with the provider of educational services. The neoliberal student-as-consumer has also entered the policy rhetoric and quality assurance mechanisms used in educating local students, but it takes legal form only in international education. Interestingly, though government shapes this market via law, regulation, policy and funding (chapter 3) there is no contract between students and government. Responsibility is devolved from government to educational provider. Through the consumption relationship, the provider

36 *ibid*, 326–8.

37 Basaran, 2008, 339.

devolves much of the responsibility for the success and happiness of students to the students themselves. The ethos of self-responsibility built into the academic process provides favourable conditions for the devolution-based approach, though it also implies more than consumption.

Much follows from the notion of student-as-consumer. It is two sided in its implications for human security: it is a regression from universal human rights and provides less security than some forms of national citizenship, yet it also augments agency and security in certain ways, compared to the notion of international students as aliens without rights regulated only by coercive border regimes and when compared with national citizenship itself.

The Australian government is formally committed to universal human rights, which would imply that it sees international students as more than consumers.

> Human rights policy in Australia is based on the principle that human rights are inherent, inalienable, indivisible and universal. They are the birthright of all human beings, cannot be lost or taken away, are all of equal importance and apply to all people irrespective of race, sex, disability, language, religion, political or other opinion, national or social origin, age, property or other status.[38]

This could be seen as an overarching framework for Australia's dealings with international students and a comprehensive security regime. But the practice of international student security is radically different. Universal humanism plays no part in the legal framework. Rights are seen as nation-bound and Australian citizens are superior on their own soil, as shown by the comparison of rights and entitlements (chapter 1). International students are imagined as aliens with no rights other than consumer rights donated by the host nation. There is genuine cross-border equality only in the trading relationship. It is as if only when thinking about trade can nation-states readily imagine a world without borders in which government stands back from control. The way through the potential tension between bordered nation-state and open global market is to position the international student as

38 Commonwealth Government, Attorney-General's Department, 2005, 5.

an abstract consumer, as a purely economic subject, while preserving national control over cross-border movements via the immigration regime.

The notion of international student-as-consumer ensures that the claims students make on authority are primarily legal and economic in character, or possibly they can make claims for pastoral care and educational quality to the extent these are consumer rights protected by a spare legal contract. Questions of social, industrial, civil and political rights, ultimately claims on governments rather than merely claims on providers, are off the agenda. The student-as-consumer is a regression from the broader notions of self-determining democratic agency that have evolved since the French revolution. The business transaction metaphor is a slippage from the stronger notion of knowledge producers shaping their own development that higher education entails. It is also a slippage from the welfare state notion of high quality services as a universal citizen right without regard to capacity to pay. The welfare regime was paternalistic and underplayed individual responsibility, but it was more generous and equitable. In many nations this approach was extended to selected international students. In some, it still is (chapter 1), though it is difficult to see how one nation could extend it universally to all potential students.

Nevertheless, the notion of international student-as-consumer does not eliminate student agency altogether. It gives foreign students subordinate powers, albeit further limited by the provider–consumer information asymmetry typical of education. And it makes one vital move towards student security as a global right. The market is universal: it cuts across differences of nation, culture, gender, age and social position and offers students from anywhere a common presence. Though nested within a national legal regime, and partly compromised by the immigration policy of that same nation-state, it decisively extends beyond national borders. This move is a minimum essential that enables the global student market to operate. At the same time, as a global form of agency it suggests larger potentials.

THE REGIME OF INTERNATIONAL STUDENT SECURITY

In formal terms international education, including student security, is structured by a three-way division of responsibility between government, educational institution ('provider') and student. In the formal domain of student security governance and regulation are constituted by the legal relations between government and provider, and the financial or contractual relation between provider and student. However, as we noted, there is a fourth element in student security, beyond the formal domain.

Much of life is lived beyond state regulation and market contracts and the recognised public side of civil society. This life beyond eludes precise definition. Husserl and Habermas refer to the 'life-world', which they define respectively in terms of intersubjective consciousness and intersubjective communication.[39] In Japanese the term 'seikatsu' is used to refer to everyday life, or to a wide range of human activities independent of the powers of state and market. Sugimoto notes that 'the agents of *seikatsu* are *seikatsusha*, the ordinary, nameless and common men and women who actively construct their living conditions . . . not simply as passive and submissive consumers'.[40] We are sympathetic to this notion, which draws attention to the manner in which people are not solely determined by law, polity and economy but also make their own conditions of life. This accords with the international student experience, in which it is more than normally obvious that people make their own conditions of life, and in doing so make themselves. In the informal and private domain the student is more than a consumer. This is not to say that the informal and private domain is wholly unaffected by state and market. *Seikatsu* is shaped partly by government, in defining, for example, the mix of rights and entitlements of citizens and non-citizens, and influencing the resources each person has at their disposal. For international students, the informal and private domain is also partly structured by the semi-formal relations between educational provider and student inside and outside the classroom. At the same time it is also affected by non-government organisations, by family, friendship and same-culture networks and by the private, inner world largely invisible to government and provider. The informal domain does not figure in policy. Nor is it essential to legal contracts. But it matters. Though government makes the rules, and the provider is central to them, the care of students falls partly in the informal and private domain.

39 Husserl, 1970; Habermas, 1987.
40 Sugimoto, 2009, 7.

One way to expand the scope of international student security is to strengthen the entitlements and protections that are provided in the public and formal domain. That is where most of the discussion falls. But it is not the only way to enhance security. The formal domain of government, policy and politics, the world of sovereignty, laws, open decisions, budgets, policies, administered programs, meetings and records rarely acknowledge the informal and private domain in clear-cut fashion. A distinctive move made by this book is to acknowledge that student security is both enhanced and reduced in the informal and private domain.

The formal and informal domain plays a role in the constituting of international students as agents. Human beings are governed subjects and the mechanisms of law, regulation and official programs continually shape their active mentalities. These are not the only influences at play. The spheres of the family, of economic production and transactions, of religious institutions and cultural traditions, also make people what they are and what they can become. There are some tensions between top-down formal systems, and bottom-up institutions and private life. Nevertheless, it needs to be repeated that in contemporary systems of government the domain of the informal and private is by no means necessarily opposed to the formal domain. Often the contrary is the case. The relationship between formal and informal domains is more one of symbiosis than opposition. In international education the role of the informal domain is deliberately fostered – or tolerated and encouraged – by the domain of formal policy, regulation and the agencies of the nation-state. Thus in Australia under the Education Services for Overseas Students (ESOS) Act the primary practical responsibility for student security and care is devolved downwards from government to the institutions that provide the education, and through them to the students themselves.

We use the term 'regime of international student security' to refer to the whole constellation of the formal and informal domains, the sum of the practices of government, institution, civil and private life, and students themselves. Each nation has its own regime of student security. There is scope for variation between the elements. 'Ideas relating to the provision of security are influenced by who is believed to have responsibility for ensuring individuals are secure.'[41]

41 Forbes-Mewett and Nyland, 2008, 2.

The different international student security regimes around the world can be distinguished in four ways:

1 how the international student is imagined, whether as consumer, pastoral subject, welfare subject, or rounded self-determining agent
2 the type and level of rights, entitlements and protections
3 how self-determined student needs are defined, expressed and met
4 the manner in which the formal and informal dimensions of security are constituted in relation to each other.

The Australian regime of international student security is not seamless. It has gaps, overlaps and inner tensions, which are explored in part 2, which focuses on the formal domain, and part 3, which focuses on the informal domain, beginning with chapter 11 on student relations with the universities which focuses primarily on the informal side. But the point is that as experienced by the student, the formal and informal domains form a whole. Each part of student security can only be understood as part of the larger regime and in conjunction with the other parts.

The Australian industry is formally regulated in the ESOS Act, which installs the student-as-consumer. Under the Act the *National Code of Practice for Registration Authorities and Providers of Education and Training to Overseas Students* specifies the obligations of providers to government and students, defines provider–student contracts and establishes student rights of redress. Students have the right to fair dealings and the fulfilment of all signed obligations. If the provider goes bankrupt or disappears students are entitled to the return of their tuition fees. They are entitled to enrol in and study for the program they have purchased, protection from misleading advertising in some areas (though this is hard to enforce) and a specified minimum of services. In New Zealand the structure is similar but a little more generous. When students believe that providers have failed to fulfil their obligations under the code, they can take their case to an independent appeals authority. In both nations there is sparse acknowledgement of welfare rights, little notion of educational rights and no mention of industrial rights despite documented cases of exploitation of international students in the workplace. Civil and political rights are largely absent. A consumer's rights are nothing more than that. The introduction to part 2 examines the National Code in more detail.

Students have spare definition in the formal domain and a rich full presence in the informal domain. Government is the leading (though not the most active) player in the formal domain and a shadowy presence in the informal domain, where it leaves traces in the minds of students but does not intervene directly. Provider institutions are active in both domains. Their role in student security is central but ambiguous. The provider carries a spare set of formal responsibilities under the ESOS Act to which it is accountable. It is central to the economic contract with the student. Beyond that it has complex, largely uncodified and partly informal relations with the student, particularly inside the classroom, which is little regulated. Institutions deal with international students in several ways at the same time. They relate to students as contractors in a marketplace on the basis of nominal buyer–seller equality. They relate to students bureaucratically like a government department, hierarchical and authoritarian. They also relate to students in a pastoral manner in the classroom and in services such as meet and greet, orientation, structured intercultural mixing, counselling, welfare and housing assistance.

This thickness in the ambiguous relations between institutions and students is instrumental to the commercial industry. For its viability the industry depends on institutions providing more in practice than they are formally mandated to provide under the Act and the signed contracts with students, in, for example, pastoral care and services. From time to time (but not all the time, as we shall see), the institutions monitor students' accommodation, networks and level of personal support. No doubt this heads off many possible problems. Here institutions find themselves connecting directly to the private domain. Yet in that domain the provider's role in student security is not comprehensive. Likewise some academic staff, some of the time, expend great effort to assist individual students, particularly those in difficulty with English. The unspoken assumptions in the regulatory framework are that market competition drives providers to offer a more generous service than the minimum provision in the Act, while the spare character of mandatory requirements protects the providers from student claims. Consumers cannot hold institutions to account for more than a bare minimum of provision.

This is unsatisfactory for students. Competition does not always deliver high quality services and security. But what can consumers do? The only sanction is to exit, but most institutions have more applications than places and switching institutions carries with it costs of a time, financial and educational kind. It also requires permission from the immigration authorities, and few international students feel comfortable about that process. Complainants have a narrow basis for claim. In a 2004 submission to the review of the ESOS Act, the National Liaison Committee (NLC), an organisation of international students, argued that the legal framework did not provide adequately for consumer rights. 'The ability of international students to address consumer complaints while in Australia is extremely limited.' There was no external ombusperson and 'many factors prevent students from seeking advice and help in such areas, the most prevalent being fear of visa cancellation'.[42] Students had little redress in matters of educational quality. 'Language support departments are usually understaffed and not adequately resourced to cope with demand from students (especially international students)', and 'the code does not give enough detail with regard to extremely important learning support services . . . Resourcing of such services is not covered by the code nor is continuation of learning support access or staff ratio per student'.[43]

The 200 interviews for the present study suggest that in any case, most students have little awareness of their rights as consumers. None had detailed knowledge of the ESOS Act and the National Code despite the mandatory provision of information. Further, some were critical of the consumer relationship. One concern was a perceived gap between marketing claims and service delivery:

> They are promoting their education and they are making huge money . . . [but] the impression that we got back home was altogether different. Once we arrived here then slowly we realised that we are not getting all the facilities that we were promised back home at the educational fair.
>
> ~ male, 26, computing, India

Others stated that universities treated international students as cash cows without giving them the same rights as local students, for example, the opportunity to compete for postgraduate scholarships or enter work experience programs. Two students stated that institutions exploited students with poor English skills.

42 NLC, 2004, 5.
43 *ibid*, 7–8.

> The universities in Australia, they want to make money, they are profit-making . . . but it's not the way to make money, out of students that can't even speak English . . . it just drags the whole educational level down.
>
> ~ female, 21, business, Malaysia

Interviewees were less critical of the government than of the universities, pointing to the effectiveness of the devolution framework. One stated:

> There is no point of coming here if government is not helping international students. Because they are charging us double the amount that they are charging with Australian students and if they are charging us more then they should give us something for that. They should give attention to our problems.
>
> ~ male, 22, business, India

From the industry's viewpoint a relatively passive and disengaged (albeit partly cynical) student body might be considered a sign of success. But the regulatory framework can be disadvantageous for providers. They, not government, must meet student expectations, though the industry settings are beyond their control. An ambiguous, many-sided role multiplies expectations. It seems the institution must deliver service quality, student security, teaching, academic assistance and intercultural relations while maximising numbers and surplus and minimising unit costs. Institutions can cut corners only some of the time. It is difficult to achieve all these objectives without blemish. The sparseness of contractual duty is never a complete defence against student needs.

CONCLUSIONS

There is more than one possible regime of international student security and more than one normative basis for judging current provision. In this the closing section of part 1, we set down our preferred approach, which underpins our critical assessment of international student security in Australia in parts 2 and 3.

International students make their own security in that they define themselves and they define what they choose to protect and advance. International student security is a function of their freedoms, in combination with social arrangements. Government, institutions and civil and private agents all contribute to security. All in some manner are accountable. This approach to student security differs from that implied by the model of the student solely as market consumer. Neoliberal services never imagine that education could be provided on the basis of self-determination, while standards and security are comprehensively guaranteed by provider and nation-state. Neoliberalism always imagines the choice as either self-determination and individual decision or state bureaucracy, either freedom or social protection. Zero sum. We disagree. This dualism creates a contradiction that undermines the freedom promised by self-responsibility. When educational standards are guaranteed and comprehensive individual protections are provided the scope for choices and freedoms are enhanced. But when social protections are reduced and security and quality devolved to the consumer, when negative freedom (freedom from coercion) is sustained, for many positive freedom (the capacity to act on one's own behalf, which includes having the resources to do so) has been reduced; the power of the consumer is emptied out. It is true that the international student is a consumer. But the student is much more than this. We believe that international (and domestic) students should receive high quality services, *and* exercise comprehensive security and protections *and* self-determining freedoms.

This comprehensive approach to student security has three implications. First, because we see international students as self-determining people capable of managing their own identity and life trajectory and defining their own needs and values, security is held to embrace the full range of acknowledged human rights, not just consumer rights but industrial rights, legal rights, rights to welfare, health care and other essential public services, rights to safe and affordable housing, to quality education, to assistance in crisis, civil and, more controversially, political rights. These rights include the right of students to differ from each other and from ourselves in the precise exercise of freedom. Once the self-determining agent is placed at the heart of the problem this admits variations in needs. No two self-definitions of human security are exactly alike. At the same time there is the irreducible common element in all security, which is defined by rights. Thus at any given time human security appears to all of us as a combination of objective rights with variable subjective needs. Needs are defined by individuals and groups, while rights are socially defined. Taking Sen's argument, over time the social and policy dimension of rights is accessible to intervention by individuals acting in concert. Ultimately, the bedrock of common rights is also agent-defined but so defined through collective social processes not simply through individual choices.

Second, as discussed above, human security is affected by more than the conventional staples of policy and regulation in those zones normally seen as accessible to public regulation, such as housing, the workplace and the health system. Much of life takes place in the informal and private domain. This domain is not subject to direct legal regulation. Nor should it be. But the informal and private domain of life interacts with the formal domain, and what happens in the informal and private domain affects overall human security. The regulation of international education should take what happens there into account, more so as much of the practical responsibility for student security has been devolved to this domain.

Third, by extending comprehensive human security to non-citizens as well as citizens, we adopt the premise of universal humanism rather than national particularism.[44] Charles Taylor argues that it is 'utterly wrong and unfounded to draw the boundaries' of our respect and concern for people 'any narrower than the whole human race'.[45] We agree. We start from the assumption that non-citizens should be able to exercise the same rights as citizens, and then consider if any rights might to be subtracted because of temporary residence. The prima facie obligation should be placed not on us to justify universal humanism, but on those who model international students as the bearers of restricted rights to justify their position. We emphasise again that this treatment of international students differs from most of the literature. As non-citizens and temporary immigrants, cross-border students are usually imagined as aliens with no rights other than those conferred on them at the whim of the country of education in order to maintain its market share. Thus educational institutions in all countries supply a measure of pastoral care. Typically, pastoral care is conferred by grace and favour. Premised on unequal capability, like all deficit models it is accompanied by a paternalism inconsistent

44 Sen, 1999.
45 Taylor, 1988, 6–7.

with the treatment of international students as self-determining adult people. At the same time, in defining international students as worthy of equal respect with local students we are not thereby arguing that specified care as such disappears, that the student 'stands alone on their transition pathway', as Prescott and Hellsten put it.[46] Undergoing a challenging cross-border experience, international students are entitled to full professional support in learning, counselling, housing and other services.

It is one of the marks of a civilised society that it treats the human security of every person as an elemental human right. It is the mark of a civilised and cosmopolitan society that it regulates security in a manner sensitive to differences in needs and values between individuals and between groups, always providing, to adapt the famous argument of J. S. Mill in *On Liberty*,[47] that the security of the one should never be sustained at the expense of the security of another. When applied to international student security the Millian argument cuts both ways. Cross-border mobility has implications for the maintenance of a stable capacity for human agency in the receiving populations. Though there is less transformation among residents than sojourners, the former experience a more complex cultural map and changes to traditional institutions. Though these issues are not our primary concern here we note that to achieve consensus on the rights of globally mobile students it is essential to endorse the rights of residents within a framework in which tolerance and multiple affiliation are human rights. When absolute priority is given to the human security of residents above the human security of sojourners, Mill's requirement is violated. For example, one month after the attack on the Pentagon and the World Trade Centre on 11 September 2001 the American Patriot Act created a new regime of surveillance governing international students in the USA. Under this regime of surveillance international students are positioned as potentially dangerous aliens and, as such, are subjected to blanket monitoring and tracking. The implications will be discussed in chapter 9.

Regulation that limits the rights of non-citizens is in any case inconsistent with the global character of the market. This tension is at the core of the governance and regulation of international education,

46 Prescott and Hellsten, 2005, 82.
47 Mill, 1947.

which opens national borders in the national interest but in a suspicious fashion. As noted, in global trade the notion of consumer rights establishes a global right independent of citizenship. Here the regulations and ideologies associated with the market have moved ahead of the nation-bound framework that still confines our political imaginations. The limitation in this notion of student-as-global-consumer is that it constructs student and global relations in limited and solely economic terms. The present study extends this notion of common global rights to the full range of possible global rights. For the purposes of the study we exclude rights seen as wholly exclusive to national citizens, such as the right to vote. (Even so, it could be argued that because temporary immigrants pay taxes and are affected by governance they have a stake in the political system and should be able to exercise a temporary right to vote.)

If we admit the notion of human agency that freely crosses national borders and we acknowledge that issues of human security are rendered problematic by the nation-bound character of citizenship, this suggests the need for some form of global citizenship with concomitant rights and protections. The United Nations Declaration of Human Rights[48] is a pointer in this direction, though fundamentally handicapped by the absence of any machinery of enforcement. Such global citizenship would need to be regulated by a global agency, whether multilaterally composed or originating from beyond the nation-state. Though such an innovation is not close at hand, we find that inescapably, our focus on international student security suggests it. We will give this matter more attention in a subsequent book.

In conclusion, by norming cross-border students as the subjects of a universal humanist regime, this provides a heuristic that enables us to examine the extent of, and deficiencies in, the comprehensive economic and social security of those students. It also frees us to explore issues of national and cross-national policy and regulation suggested by the global education market, and more generally by the worldwide growth and ambiguous identities of diasporic populations, in the context of global mobility, convergence and more plural identities. Given there is no good reason to limit the humanist compact to what happens

48 United Nations, 1948.

inside national borders, for example, how might the rights of the globally mobile be governed?

We acknowledge that like all universal humanist norms our human security heuristic creates a prima facie tendency to identify deficiencies (gaps, failings, tensions, contradictions) in the social and economic security of international students. Such deficiencies form the bulk of the evidence in the book. To see this as bias in favour of evidence of a critical kind, neglecting favourable aspects of the student experience, is to misunderstand the study and to miss the point. This is not a holistic survey of student satisfaction or dissatisfaction with international education, or a quality assurance exercise designed as a balanced assessment of strengths and weaknesses. Such surveys and evaluations have their place, but their purpose is different. Still less is this study designed to strengthen Australian exports by building or protecting the reputation of the nation and its institutions. Our sole normative concern is with the international students as people, not with the industry per se. It might be argued that it is in the interests of the Australian industry to strengthen international student security so as to enhance customer satisfaction and secure competitive advantage, but that is also not our object here. Because the book is focused explicitly on this one aspect – deficiencies in international student security – as its object of study, the thrust of *International Student Security* is critical.[49] If it were not primarily critical in nature, this would mean that either international student security was perfect, or our research was deficient.

Part 1 has introduced the global education market, the topic of international student security, the case of Australia, the research study underlying this book and the contents of the book itself. In part 2 we examine student security in the formal welfare domains, beginning in chapter 5 with financial security.

49 We thank the anonymous reviewer for *Higher Education Policy* who required this explanation.

PART 2 SECURITY IN THE FORMAL AND PUBLIC DOMAIN

INTRODUCTION TO PART 2: THE FORMAL AND PUBLIC DOMAIN

The formal and public domain of international student security in Australia is constituted by the ESOS Act, which defines in a particular way the relationship between nation-state, institutional providers and the student consumer. It is also shaped by the conditions governing student visas; and affected by higher education policy and funding, and processes of accreditation and quality assurance (not discussed in detail here).

The branch of government with specific policy responsibility is Australian Education International (AEI), located in the federal Department of Education, Employment and Workplace Relations (DEEWR).[1] AEI promotes the industry, though individual institutions also carry out their own marketing. It administers the ESOS Act and its website is the main official source of information. For the most part AEI relates to students indirectly via educational providers. *The National Code of Practice for Registration Authorities and Providers of Education and Training to Overseas Students* is addressed to providers, not students. Government at a distance means state authority is curiously diffuse. On most matters the students have little recourse to direct demands, confrontation or even questions of government. As much as possible questions of standards and quality are transferred down to their dealings with providers. This is consistent with the principles of subsidiary (devolution to the level closest to the actual service) and academic autonomy, but there is no mechanism of appeal beyond the provider. Nor in most areas are there solid standards by which AEI can be held to account.

1 At the time the interviews were completed it was the Department of Education, Science and Training (DEST).

The main direct dealings between international students and the government that frames the industry are not with DEEWR–AEI but with the Department of Immigration and Citizenship (DIAC) (known as Immigration, Multiculturalism and Indigenous Affairs [DIMIA] at the time of the interviews) in relation to visas.

Issues regulated in the formal domain with implications for student security have a long standing presence in policy and public debate. They include student finances (chapter 5), work (chapter 6), housing (chapter 7), physical and mental health (chapter 8), the safety of the person (chapter 9), and visas and other dealings with government (chapter 10). This introduction will now look at the provisions of the *National Code of Practice for Registration Authorities and Providers of Education and Training to Overseas Students* under the ESOS Act.

THE NATIONAL CODE IN AUSTRALIA

DEEWR 'monitors compliance with the ESOS Act and the standards in the National Code, particularly focussing on student visa integrity and consumer protection'.[2] State and territory governments in Australia register providers for delivery of international student services, and also monitor compliance with the Code. Though both levels of government may enforce the legislation the federal government is 'primarily responsible for investigating and instigating enforcement action for breaches of both the ESOS Act and the National Code'.[3]

The nature of the regime of student security is apparent from the wording of the National Code. The advancement of the industry and the export flows it sustains are paramount, not the security of students. Section A.3.1 states the objectives of the Code are to

1 support the ESOS framework
2 establish and safeguard Australia's international reputation as a provider of high quality education and training by ensuring 'nationally consistent standards and the integrity of providers'
3 protect the interests of overseas students

2 DEEWR, National Code, 2007, section B.4.
3 *ibid*, section B.8.

4 support providers in monitoring student compliance with student visa conditions and in reporting any student breaches to the Australian Government.[4]

Thus the reputation of the industry is placed before the interests of overseas students. These student interests, which appear to be primarily interests in fair dealings in the market and the protection of tuition payments in cases of default, are protected by 'ensuring that appropriate consumer protection mechanisms exist' and that 'student welfare and support services for overseas students meet nationally consistent standards'.[5] For the most part the Act does not specify nationally consistent standards in education and welfare or guarantee possible standards.

The Code repeatedly confirms that the students are seen as subjective consumers of a service, not right-bearing education or welfare subjects. There are no references to political rights.[6] 'The benefits of international education and training depend on the service provided to overseas students, and on public confidence in the integrity and quality of that service.'[7] The concept of 'service' is emphasised and explicitly connected to building the reputation of the Australian industry.[8] The goal is subjective consumer satisfaction. The Code steers away from objective product definition and minimum benchmarks whereby providers could be held to account, except for specified minima. The bedrock assumption is that international students as consumers will regulate standards themselves, by making choices between providers; though, as the Code itself notes, 'overseas students who usually cannot evaluate the quality of a course before purchase'.[9] There is little students can do to pressure the provider to improve services or product. The consumer has real leverage only when the provider breaches its contractual obligation to provide the specified program. The government promotes all providers as world class and in that sense equivalent

4 *ibid*, section A.3.1.

5 *ibid*, section A.3.1.

6 Ninnes, 2005, 150, notes that this approach has been exported into Australian foreign aid ventures in education. In the Virtual Colombo Plan, a World Bank and Australian government sponsored program to provide online education into developing countries, there are no references to political freedoms. The virtues of the Plan are argued in terms of personal career-building and economic enrichment.

7 DEEWR, National Code, 2007, section A.8.2.

8 For example throughout *ibid*, section A.8.

9 *ibid*, section A.6.1

to each other: perhaps this is the meeting of the ambiguous 'nationally consistent standards' in the Code.

The Code specifies the form of the consumer relation but little content. The references to student security are spare and partial. 'The registered provider must enter into a written agreement with the student' that specifies the program of study, monies payable, 'information in relation to refunds of course money'. It is not mandatory to include educational and welfare standards in the agreement.[10]

The agreement must specify circumstances in which the provider may pass information about students to the government, and advise students of their obligation to inform DIAC of any change of circumstances, facilitating the visa regime. Other parts of the Code expand on the obligations of providers to report visa-related matters to the authorities. The National Code contains five pages of detailed standards that spell out the institution's responsibilities in relation to visa requirements concerning student progression, attendance and completion.

> The international education and training industry is closely linked to the Australian Government's student visa programme. Adherence to migration law is essential to ensure public confidence in the student visa programme and to ensure the provision of high quality education and training opportunities to students. Under the ESOS Act, registered providers are required to notify both students and the Australian Government when students have breached their student visa conditions as a result of having failed to maintain satisfactory course progress or attendance.[11]

The immigration provisions of the Code are hard edged. State authority is openly displayed and deployed to make binding and restrictive claims on the students. In the face of it people who lose their student visa status have little redress except a protracted and expensive appeal conducted as a non-citizen from within detention (see chapter 10). The message is clear: in the framing of the mandatory requirements placed on providers, the state's desire to protect the security of its border takes precedence over export revenues and

10 *ibid*, Standard 3, section 3.1.
11 *ibid*, section 10.1.

is much stronger than any concern to protect the human security of temporary immigrants. For many students, especially those working or those in academic difficulties, DIAC punctuates their stay with crucial moments and is an ongoing source of anxiety (chapter 10). Here, in contrast to its handling of issues of educational quality, the government does not rely on market forces as the guarantor of outcomes.

The level of detail on immigration contrasts with the sparse provisions on teaching and learning and the absence of references to language or cultural issues. In this context the Code's reference to the commercial reputation of the industry becomes the primary basis on which the education authorities might stand their ground against heavy-handed actions by the immigration authorities.

In contrast with these direct controls the Code offers some freedoms but they are less potent than the controls it imposes. To facilitate the Australian market and protect student consumers the National Code emphasises that marketing should provide information 'of a high standard, clear and unambiguous, so that intending students and their parents can make informed decisions about their preferred provider and course'. Consumers have 'information about the course, fees, facilities, services and resources offered by the registered provider prior to enrolment', and relevant data on the cost of living and housing options. Recruitment should be 'ethical' and like marketing 'uphold the reputation of Australian international education and training'.[12] Providers must not offer 'false or misleading information or advice' in areas such as 'the employment outcomes associated with a course . . . automatic acceptance into another course', or 'possible migration outcomes'.[13] Predeparture information is not closely monitored, and there is no prohibition of false claims in other respects. Students are to have an internal mechanism for handling complaints and appeals. Providers must also ensure that there is a person or body external to the provider who can handle further complaints or appeals.[14] But there is no mandatory requirement for an external supervisory agent who is genuinely independent, so that ultimately, the provider's commercial interests tend to take priority over student rights.

12 *ibid*, section D, Preamble to Standards 1–4, 10–11; Standard 2, section 2.1.
13 *ibid*, Standard 1, section 1.2.
14 *ibid*, Standard 8, section 8.2.

On welfare, the Code states that providers should ensure 'access to support services and support staff to meet the needs of the students enrolled in their courses'. The definition of 'needs' (by provider? by student? according to regulated standards?) is unspecified.[15] The strongest statement about student security is that 'the registered provider must have sufficient student support personnel to meet the needs of the students enrolled with the registered provider'.[16] Again a definition of 'needs' is absent. The Code states that 'the registered provider must assist students to adjust to study and life in Australia'.[17] There is no obligation for providers to adjust to the background characteristics of students. Curiously, for the most part the Code does not list the mandatory services but lists services that students should be informed about. Information is mandatory but not provision. These services are 'student support services available to students in the transition to life and study in a new environment', 'legal services', 'emergency and health services', 'facilities and resources' and 'complaints and appeals processes'.[18] However, the Code is more directive in relation to welfare services at two points. First, it specifies that 'the registered provider must provide the opportunity for students to participate in services or provide access to services designed to assist students in meeting course requirements and maintaining their attendance'. This assists students' academic progress and supports the visa regime. Second:

> The registered provider must provide the opportunity for students to access welfare-related support services to assist with issues that may arise during their study, including course progress and attendance requirements and accommodation issues. These services must be provided at no additional cost to the student.[19]

This is the only reference to post-enrolment housing services. Counselling is not mentioned. Again, standards and the regulation of standards are unspecified. The Code also regulates emergency services and critical incidents. This is more detailed than other mandatory

15 *ibid*, Preamble to Standard 6.
16 *ibid*, Standard 6, section 6.6.
17 *ibid*, Standard 6, section 6.1.
18 *ibid*, Standard 6, section 6.1.
19 *ibid*, Standard 6, section 6.2.

welfare but contact with students' families is not essential[20] and it is it unclear how far off campus the obligatory provision extends.

In relation to academic services, staffing must be 'adequate and have the capabilities as required by the quality assurance framework applying to the course', which permits variable standards. The statement about learning resources and facilities is similar.[21] The National Code does not mention academic support for students from non-English-speaking backgrounds.[22] The only reference to needs that flow from the global character of international education is the statement that the procedures for complaint and redress have been designed to be accessed by non-citizen students during the period of study as many cannot do so after graduation.[23] This reflects an understanding of the global dimension in terms of trade rights, but like the absence of references to discrimination it is culture blind. Though many dimensions of international student security have a cultural aspect, providers and government have no obligation under the Code to address this.

Beyond provider jurisdiction on campus the ESOS Act and National Code offer no protection or advancement of security, despite the fact that in areas such as housing, personal safety and discrimination (chapters 7, 9 and 15) security is weaker outside the education institutions than inside. Unless the provider moves beyond the terms of its obligations under the Act and offers additional monitoring and/or assistance, gaps in student security are inevitable.

20 *ibid*, Preamble to Standard 6.

21 *ibid*, Standard 14, sections 14.1–14.3.

22 The provisions of the voluntary Universities Australia Code of Practice go a little further, stating that universities should 'take appropriate account of the potential cultural and linguistic difficulties that international students may encounter', as well as meeting students on arrival and providing temporary accommodation. However, it sustains the focus on marketing objectives. 'Australian universities should ensure that academic programs, support services and learning environment offered to all international students encourage them to have a positive attitude about Australian education'; UA, 2008, sections 14 and 17. Successive revisions of this code have tied campus services more specifically to industry promotion and customer satisfaction objectives; AVCC, 1994, 8; AVCC, 2005, 13.

23 DEEWR, National Code 2007, section 6.1

5 FINANCES

It costs money to live here in Australia. Having a budget is very important, and keeping to budget and living within one's means. Living within your means is the safest thing to do here, because if you run out of money I don't know where you can get help. If I ran out of money at home I would go to the village and it's alright. The neighbours would come with a bowl of food for me to eat. I wouldn't be hungry.

~ female, 40, PhD gender studies, Papua New Guinea

INTRODUCTION: 'IF YOU PRICK US, DO WE NOT BLEED?'

In February 2007 the Australian Vice-Chancellor's Committee (AVCC)[1] reported the findings of a national study titled *Australian University Student Finances 2006*. The objective was to clarify the 'financial situation of Australian students'.[2] The reader might assume the report was focused on students enrolled at Australian universities. But this was only partly true. The international students who constituted 25 per cent of students in Australian universities were excluded. The questionnaire used for the study stated that 'This survey is only for domestic students, if you are an international student please do not complete the survey'.[3] Professor Glen Withers of Universities Australia (UA), the rebadged AVCC, defended the exclusion of international students by stating the project was focused on improving

1 Since renamed as Universities Australia.

2 AVCC, 2007, 6.

3 *ibid*, Appendix 1.

income support for domestic students. He also implied that Australian providers had limited responsibility for the financial security of international students. 'The biggest problems are the exchange rate – and universities cannot control that – and expensive housing, and universities cannot control that either.'[4] But while Withers rejected claims that Australian universities treat international students as 'cash cows and don't care about their welfare', there was no parallel survey of international students by AVCC/UA. Their financial needs were ignored.

The AVCC did not explain the exclusion. Why were the financial needs of international students deemed as beneath its notice? International students, like their local student counterparts, also need to find the money required to eat, sleep in shelter, travel to university for classes and finance their computing and communications. Their studies, too, are affected when they do not have enough to eat. In act 3, scene 1 of *The Merchant of Venice* Shakespeare puts a paean against differential treatment and prejudice in the mouth of Shylock. At the climax of his appeal for understanding Shylock turns and says 'If you prick us, do we not bleed?!' We, too, are human. We, too, can suffer. We are the same as you.

The AVCC's failure to investigate or even acknowledge the financial position of international students sat uncomfortably with its own separate *Provision of Education to International Students Code of Practice and Guidelines for Australian Universities*. The Code declared: 'AVCC believes it is essential for all Australian universities offering courses to... adopt consistent and caring procedures in the recruitment, reception, education and welfare of international students'.[5]

This chapter presents data on international student finances from our interviews with the 200 students that indicates that yes, they have financial problems, yes, they can go hungry and yes, it can affect their studies. The fact that international students pay higher tuition charges than local students does not disqualify their problems from attention. It can often exacerbate their difficulties. The chapter begins with a review of the international and Australian literature on international student finances, noting that the situation in Australia appears to be

4 Rout, 2008b.
5 AVCC, 2005.

similar to that confronting international students in other English-speaking countries. It then looks at the regulatory setting in Australia in relation to financial security. Next, the chapter draws on the interview data to cast light on the sources and the adequacy of international student incomes and how the students cope with the financial risks of living and studying in a foreign land. The chapter concludes by arguing that international student financial security ought to be given as much attention as local student finances, in policy, research and pastoral care. 'If you prick us, do we not bleed?' At the same time the distinctive financial issues and problems faced by international students also need to be better understood.

LITERATURE ON STUDENT FINANCES

The research-based literature, both international and Australian, indicates that financial difficulties are experienced by a large minority of international students and that finances are a common source of insecurity and distress.

International studies

In the USA there is a surprising paucity of research data on international student finances despite the size of the international student population there and the extensive literature on some other aspects such as counselling.[6] In recent years governments and university leaders have failed to support research on international student finances, paralleling the situation in Australia. But the international student experience in the USA has been the subject of extensive doctoral research, some of it by international doctoral students. Some of it is by directors or other professionals working in university international offices, who are often encouraged to gain professional doctorates that include studies of the adjustment problems of students in their own university. Certain of these studies include student finances, though unfortunately little of the research has generated publications. This body of work shows that inadequate financial support is one of

6 US studies that do include student finances include those by Church, 1982; Si-Tayeb, 1982; Ogunyieka, 1983; Cadieux and Wehrly, 1986; Barakat, 1988; Al-Shehry, 1989; Feizi, 1990; Lin and Yi, 1997; Cheng, 1999; Mori, 2000; Wang, 2004; Dorough, 2006; Dunn, 2006.

the main issues facing international students. Abu-Ein found, in examining the problems of 416 international students at Texas Southern University, that finances were the issue of greatest concern.[7] Studies by Xia and Cheng agree.[8] Xia found that Asian students not supported by scholarships face greater difficulty than domestic students in the areas of selection and admission, orientation, English language, academic advising, academic record, social–personnel, living–dining, health services and student activities.

In the UK a study of international student problems by Li and Kaye found that financial problems were the problems most frequently mentioned by international students, especially by non-European students. Financial problems occurred more often among students under 25 than older students.[9] But there had been little research by government or the vice-chancellors, though the topic had been taken up in dissertations. Recently, however, UK research has been advanced by the Council for International Education (UKCISA), a charity that serves the interests of international students and those who work with them. In 2003 UKCISA commissioned a review of what is called the 'grey literature' on the international student experience, the large proportion of the British research that is unpublished. This included 'theses and dissertations, unpublished conference papers, internal reports by individual universities and colleges, project reports to ESRC and other funders, and notices of research in progress'.[10] The review revealed that financial security concerned many international students but interested few researchers. In 2004 and 2006 UKCISA produced successive reports on the international student experience in the university and college sector, and further education. Both studies include a section on finance and hardship. Both found that a little over three-quarters of international higher education students stated that they had enough money to live in an acceptable manner, while 23 per cent did not. Those with dependents and research students often reported hardship. Those whose financial support came from a mix of self-funding and other sources were more likely to report hardship than those fully self-funded or fully externally funded. The primary

7 Abu-Ein, 1995.
8 Xia, 1991; Cheng, 1999.
9 Li and Kaye, 1998, 44–5.
10 Leonard et al., 2003.

Table 5.1 Domestic and international students by social class, UK 2006

Social class		Domestic students (weighted) n = 1025 %	International students (weighted) n = 357 %
A	Upper middle class – higher managerial, administrative or professional	8	10
B	Middle class – intermediate managerial, administrative or professional	39	43
C1	Lower middle class – supervisory or clerical; junior managerial, administrative or professional	37	40
C2	Skilled working class – skilled manual workers	9	3
D	Working class – semi and unskilled manual workers	6	2
E	Those at the lowest levels of subsistence; entirely dependent on state for long-term income	2	1

Source: UNITE–UKCISA 2006. 'Unstated' and 'Don't know' have been eliminated. To ensure that the profile of students was representative, quotas were set and data weighted by gender, year of study, subject of study and ethnic minority. For social classifications see National Readership Survey, 2006.

reasons for financial difficulties were deficient pre-arrival knowledge on the cost of living and studying in the UK and exchange rate fluctuations; budgeting was also a significant problem. Few students were protected financially against unexpected difficulties: 35 per cent had medical insurance, 25 percent property insurance.[11]

In 2006 UKCISA cooperated with UNITE, a student housing firm, in the first large scale study to compare perceptions of domestic and international students concerning the university experience.[12] Undertaken across 20 UK universities, the study involved 1025 domestic and 375 international students. One feature of the study is its map of international students' class origins, which it generated using the National Readership Survey instrument. The social origins of UK domestic and international students were heavily skewed towards the affluent, as shown in table 5.1. This is as one would expect, but it is notable that a large minority of international students are classified C1, 'junior management and professional' sector. Students in this category are less likely than most others to be fully supported from home.

11 UKCISA, 2004.
12 UNITE, 2006.

Table 5.2 Problems mentioned most frequently by international students, UK 2006

Q What, if anything, do you consider to be the worst aspect of university life?	**Domestic students n = 1025 %**	**International students n = 357 %**
Having little money/no regular income	50	40
Miss my home/homesick	7	23
Adapting to new way of learning/studying	17	17
The amount of time spent studying	14	13
Needing to work and study at the same time	25	13
Being in debt	44	13
Juggling university work with other commitments	37	13
The academic work is very difficult	10	12
Problems with accommodation	6	11

Source: UNITE–UKCISA, 2006. Respondents were able to select more than one item.

When asked what, if anything, is the worst aspect of university life, 40 per cent of international students selected 'having little money/no regular income'. Smaller but significant percentages cited being in debt (13 per cent) and needing to work and study at the same time (13 per cent). Table 5.2 compares domestic and international student responses to this question. The UNITE–UKCISA researchers also noted that 14 per cent of international students had dropped out or considered dropping out of universities and of these at-risk students nearly three in 10 cited financial reasons as the primary cause for not continuing with their studies.

In New Zealand, Ward and Masgoret find almost 30 per cent of internationals believed they had insufficient funds; for 13 per cent, financial issues constitute the most difficult aspect of living in New Zealand. Consistent with the US and UK literature, Ward and Masgoret reported that 80 per cent of tertiary international students are supported by parents, 15 per cent are self- or partially self-supported, 4 per cent are supported by other family members, 3 per cent are on scholarships and less than 1 per cent have loans or other financial support from home government or employer.[13] Butcher and McGrath found the international students in New Zealand at most financial risk include those poor at budgeting, gamblers and affected associates, those who circumvented immigration requirements, family

13 Ward and Masgoret, 2004.

dependents or those affected by altered family circumstances and those facing unexpected needs, generated by, for example, theft, accidents, fines or tenancy requirements.[14]

STUDIES IN AUSTRALIA

A commercial perspective overhangs Australian government and university research on international students. It has also influenced academic research, as indicated by the relatively high number of doctoral theses and articles that analyse international education and student behaviour from a business perspective.[15]

One exception is the 2006 survey by Rosenthal and colleagues of the health and wellbeing of 979 international students at the University of Melbourne. Students were asked to indicate whether they had adequate financial support and asked to identify their sources of financial support. The majority of students (71.9 per cent) were not worried about their finances, 28.1 percent were concerned and 10.3 per cent said their financial support was 'completely or nearly inadequate'. The Melbourne researchers found that worrying about finances was positively and significantly related to the incidences of depression, anxiety and stress. The association with depression was strongest. They also found that respondents who were significantly more likely to consider their financial support adequate were from Asia, had completed a foundation program, were undergraduates, were progressing as well as or better than expected academically and/or had been enrolled for a relatively long time. International students obtained financial support from a variety of sources. Most drew on more than one type of source. Family was the most common source (84.6 per cent), then dependence on income from paid work (28.0 per cent), and then those drew on their own and/or their partner's savings (20.4 per cent). Only 9 per cent were entirely dependent on their family.[16]

The findings of the Melbourne study were generally consistent with a 2005 survey of first year local and international first year students in nine universities by Krause and colleagues. Compared to domestic

14 Butcher and McGrath, 2004, 547.

15 Mazzarol, 1997; Forde, 2000; Poole, 2000; Mazzarol and Souter, 2001; Chen, 2003; Arambewela, 2003; Sherry et al., 2004; Jiang, 2005; Trestrail, 2005; Thompson, 2006; Jones, 2006.

16 Rosenthal et al., 2006.

students, a larger proportion of the 'international students indicate that their families are their main source of income, fewer report that money worries make it difficult to study and fewer are working part time'.[17] But international students are more likely to feel pressure from financial commitments – 40 per cent, compared to 23 per cent of locals.

Where federal and state government agencies have initiated studies of international student incomes and expenditures, they have failed to ensure that the data are presented in such a way that the state of international student finances and support services is adequately clarified.[18] Presumably, this reflects official concerns about protecting Australia's reputation as a supplier, in that data that show some international students to be struggling are reckoned to be potentially damaging. The recent studies are the least informative. In early studies in 1992 and 1997 the federal government commissioned research enabling total expenditure to be compared with total income. Subsequent studies merely gathered data on where the students spent their money and how much of their income was from Australian sources. Income and expenditure could no longer be compared, the net financial position could no longer be determined and it was impossible to calculate either international student financial wellbeing or the numbers at risk of financial distress.

The 1997 *Survey of International Students Studying in Australia*[19] reported that international students' average discretionary income (income after compulsory fees) was A$368 per week. Average expenditures were $307, which left the average international student with $61 per week for contingencies. There were sharp differences on the basis of region of Australia and country of origin. Table 5.3 presents data on average discretionary income by country and contrasts these data against previously unpublished information on income from work and the 1997 Henderson Poverty Line (HPL), an Australian-based standard for the cost of basic living needs.

Table 5.3 indicates that students from low income countries were likely to have the lowest income and the greatest need to generate an income in Australia. This latter point is highlighted also in studies by

17 Krause et al., 2005, 77.

18 AIEF, 1998; Smith et al., 2000, 2002; Auditor-General, 2002; AEI, 2003; Abbot and Ali, 2005; UQSRC et al., 2005

19 AIEF, 1998.

Table 5.3 Average weekly discretionary income by country of origin, international students, 1997

Country	Discretionary income A$ p.w.	Proportion of students with wages %	Wage Income A$ p.w.	Discretionary income minus wage income A$ p.w.	Discretionary income minus HPL of $237 A$ p.w.
Singapore	475	7.6	5	470	+238
North America	404	16.9	16	388	+167
Hong Kong China	364	8.4	5	359	+127
Japan	359	11.5	16	343	+122
Taiwan	347	9.0	7	340	+110
Indonesia	331	15.3	17	314	+94
India	322	40.9	56	266	+85
Malaysia	294	9.4	11	283	+57
Thailand	223	33.4	33	190	−14
Europe	258	20.8	26	232	+21
China	195	61.8	86	109	−42
Oceania	160	17.6	25	135	−77
South Korea	142	10.1	15	127	−95
Other	207	31.6	31	176	−30

HPL = Henderson Poverty Line. At the advice of the compilers of the HPL we use the HPL figure for 'family head in workforce' without dependants. HPL figures are income after tax, i.e. disposable income.
Source: Adapted from AEIF, 1998, plus unpublished data collected for the 1997 survey.

Mazzarol and colleagues, designed to determine the factors influencing international students when they decide on country of study. The ability to gain employment was particularly important to students from low income countries.[20] Table 5.3 also shows that in the case of students from Thailand, China, the Pacific and South Korea, average net income fell below the Henderson Poverty Line. The calculation of the HPL assumes access to free benefits available to citizens but not available to international students (see table 1.2). It can be inferred that, of the students from poorer countries unable to gain enough work in Australia, many would experience very serious financial difficulties, especially those with children. In the normal course of events some would be forced to discontinue their studies.

The situation may have worsened since 1997. There has been an increase in the proportion of international higher education students from low income nations. Students from China were 3 per cent of

20 Mazzarol, 2002.

international students in 1997, but by 2007 constituted 27 per cent of international students.

REGULATION OF FINANCIAL CAPACITY

The federal government circumvents the problem of student financial security in the same way it circumvents the problem of student capacity in English (chapter 12): by setting visa conditions that formally ensure student competence while making financial support the student's responsibility. This procedure absolves the government of formal responsibility for financial aid to students and safeguards, as far as possible, the economic position of the provider institutions by establishing a minimum benchmark for capacity to pay that covers tuition levels. Which does not solve the problem of student financial security. The level of financial support specified as necessary is not accurate, as discussed below; however, the federal government's regulations specify that education providers 'must not accept an overseas student for enrolment in a course unless the registered provider has given to the student an accurate representation of the local environment in which the registered provider is operating, including location of campuses and indicative costs of living'. The government thereby even avoids direct responsibility for the accuracy of its conditions of financial viability by passing that back to providers.

The process works like this. When applying for a visa, students are compelled to answer the following question and sign the associated declaration:

> Q.41. Do you have access to sufficient funds to support you and your family unit members for the TOTAL period of your stay in Australia (including proposed course fees for you and any school-age family members, living costs and travel costs, regardless of whether your dependants intend to accompany you to Australia)?
>
> Yes – complete declaration below
>
> I declare that I have access to sufficient funds to support myself and my family unit members (regardless of whether they are accompanying me to Australia) for the total period of my stay in Australia.
>
> .... [signature]

Table 5.4 Requirements for student visa applicants intending to enter vocational education and training, higher education and postgraduate research programs, in relation to evidence of income, Australia, 2007

	Amount of living course and school expenses from acceptable source	Travel expenses	Length of time funds need to be held by individual	Evidence of income to accumulate funds	Declaration of access for remainder of course
AL5: No country	Full length of visa	Evidence of funds	5 years	Yes	n/a
AL4: e.g., China, India	First 36 months ($36 000). Postgraduates show 12 months or length of course if less than 12 months	Evidence of funds	6 months, individual defined	Yes	Yes
AL3: e.g., Vietnam in vocational education and training	First 24 months. Postgraduates show 12 months or length of course if less than 12 months	Evidence of funds	3 months, individual not defined, no requirement for postgraduates	Yes	Yes
AL2: e.g., Vietnam in first degree higher education	12 months; cannot include value of item of property	Evidence of funds	0 months	No	Yes
AL1: e.g., Vietnam in postgraduate research; USA, UK in all programs	Full visa length, but access only; funds don't have to be held and evidence of source is not required	Declaration only	0 months	No	Yes

Source: DIMIA, 2007. As these data change from time to time, look for up-to-date information at www.immi.gov.au/students.

The amount of money the student must be able to access depends not only on household size but also on the number of years of planned study and the cost of travelling to and from Australia. For most students the declaration is also supported by documentary evidence. Whether this is required and exactly what documentation is required depends on the country of origin (table 5.4).

In 2008 there were approximately 93 000 students from China, an Assessment Level 4 country. AL4 applicants were required to show evidence of $36 000 in accessible funds, such as the bank account of a parent or sponsor, that would nominally cover them for three years of living expenses and tuition fees. The students were also required to

Table 5.5 Financial requirements for student visas compared to the Henderson Poverty Line (HPL), varying by relation to family size, Australia, 2006

Family size	Henderson Poverty Line (HPL) A$ p.w.	Income required to support visa applications[21] A$ p.w.	Difference between HPL and visa requirement A$ p.w.
Single head of household	330.77	230.76	−100.10
Couple	442.48	311.54	−130.94
Couple +1 child	531.89	357.69	−174.20
Couple +2 children	621.29	392.31	−228.98

Source: MIAESR (2006). HPL figures are income after tax, i.e. disposable income. The cost of children includes that of schooling in Australia.

sign a declaration that they could access funds for tuition and living after the first 36 months. This $36 000 for living expenses equates to $3000 per month or $700 per week if evenly distributed over one year, leaving students with no savings to live on for the next two years. Alternatively it is about $350 a week over two years; or $230 a week over three years. This is ludicrously low.

The starting rate of $12 000 was adopted in 2001 and has remained unchanged despite movements in the cost of living. Thus in March 2008 a domestic independent student living away from home was paid $285 per week, plus a transport subsidy, in government assistance. An international student was expected to live on $230 per week. Clearly, the visa conditions are not set high enough to guarantee financial solvency, especially in inner urban Sydney. Table 5.5 sets down the difference between the Henderson Poverty Line and the income needed to qualify for a student visa, which varies according to household size.

21 Immigration regulations require student visa applicants without an accompanying spouse or dependent children to show they have $12 000 to cover living costs for one year, in either savings or other accessible funds. Those with a spouse are required to show a further 35 per cent over and above the basic rate; for one dependent child a further 20 per cent of the basic rate is required. Further dependent children attract a requirement to show an additional 15 per cent (per child) of the basic rate. The amount that has to be shown also varies according to the country of origin of the applicant. Country categories are determined by economic stability, the risk factor associated with student visa holders from that country based on past patterns and other factors that may affect a students' current and future ability to pay tuition costs and living expenses in Australia. The probability of students breaching visa conditions by overstaying their visa or becoming unlawful and being removed from Australia is also a consideration. These assessment levels are also set for each type of student visa. The assessment levels within a country may, for example, be different for a school student as opposed to a higher education student, or a student intending to enrol in an English Language Intensive Course for Overseas Students (ELICOS). The Department of Immigration and Citizenship (DIAC) has figures that show varying probabilities according to type of institution attended and for nation of origin.

Examination of the websites of universities located in the same city shows that there are varied claims about the cost of living. Clearly, the federal government does not monitor the accuracy of that advice to students. In any case, some providers use the basic rate stipulated in the visa requirements as a guide when determining indicative living costs in their own information provision to students.

An additional difficulty, known to everyone connected with the industry and widely understood by students and their families – and therefore fully known to the government, is that student families can evade the intent of the regulations by producing the necessary on-paper evidence of financial holdings without actually commanding the resources. Parents can borrow temporarily against the value of house or land, and then pay back the money after the visa application succeeds. Home country employers may collude with parents in preparing evidence of regular salary levels and duration of employment. Applicants may certify that they are fully sponsored by a relative who has no intention of paying, and so on.

The visa requirement concerning financial support does not test the financial security of students and their families. It tests their shrewdness in dealing with immigration department systems. It protects not the financial security of the students, but the political security of the government, and the financial security of the industry. This review of the research and the Australian regulations suggest three tentative conclusions. First, that most international students do not experience great financial hardship, though a large minority do have difficulties. It is likely that in Australia the size of these difficulties, and the proportion of students experiencing them, are worsening. Second, students experience financial problems for several reasons, including lack of resources, insufficient knowledge of the challenges of living and studying in a foreign country, currency volatility, inadequate insurance and lack of budgetary skills. But the absence of a safety net to ensure financial security due to inadequate governmental and provider structures and programs is also a key factor. Third, too little research on international student finances has been undertaken. Many international students have had little experience at living away from home and they tend to be highly vulnerable. These three points are now further considered in the light of data from the present study.

The questions on financial security

The present study asked several questions related to student finances:

- Are you experiencing or have you experienced financial difficulties at any stage?
- Who helps you if you ever have problems with money?
- If you were a student in your home country, would you get help with finances? Financial difficulties? Are the authorities more helpful here or less helpful?
- What are your main sources of income?
- Do you receive money from home?
- Do you send money to your family or others back home?
- How do these financial transfers take place? Is the money safe? How long does it take to receive money here? How long does it take for money to arrive back home?

Little was collected on student remittances to home countries. Financial transfers did not seem a difficult issue. The main data on financial security were collected in relation to questions on financial difficulties, sources of income and coping strategies in the event of financial difficulties. In addition, some financial data were supplied in response to questions asked on other topics.

SOURCES OF INCOME

'I don't want my family to support me; I want to be independent'

Consistent with the research literature, the international students had a variety of income sources. Many used multiple sources: family 61.0 per cent, scholarship 34.5 per cent, work 32.5 per cent, other 7.0 per cent. Each basic category took multiple forms. For example, family support was provided not only by parents but also spouses, parents-in-law, grandparents, uncles, aunts and siblings. Family and scholarships was most likely to cover the cost of tuition.

The question was asked: What are your main sources of income?

> In my culture, your parents look after you, and then you look after your parents.
>
> ~ male 19, commerce, Pakistan

> My whole education is funded by my parents. They are providing for the tuition and accommodation. I do work part-time.
>
> ~ female, 22, commerce, India

> Actually, I have two scholarships. One scholarship is from the university; it's $15 000 per year. Another scholarship covers my course fees and my medical insurance for Medibank Private . . . actually if no scholarship I wouldn't come.
>
> ~ female, 26, information technology, Russia

> It's my savings, but you know because I was working for 10 years in Vietnam, it's out of my savings, and this scholarship that I received.
>
> ~ male, 31, PhD, China

Earnings at work were more likely to be used for the less predictable cost of living:

> Now it's my part time job in a chemical company. I do the database maintenance for them . . . Tuition fee is from my parents. Living expenses is from my job.
>
> ~ female, 22, environmental engineering, China

> First my parents fund me for my study and I'm planning to find a part-time job to support my living as well.
>
> ~ male, 25, finance, China

> I work as a telesaler, like for Telstra, and that's basically my job . . . Tuition fee – I'm here on my bank loan. I've got a bank loan from back home.
>
> ~ male, 26, information technology, India

> I'm working as a tutor in the Faculty . . . and I'm also working at the lab, at the help desk. These two jobs and a job in a Sydney café – I am working at a part-time job . . . I basically make coffees. Making some good money there. You work three days and you make two to three hundred bucks. Everything's free, snacks, coffee, everything's free! I work three days there, and two days here [at university].
>
> ~ male, 24, information technology, India

Many students were concerned that their financial situation might place unmanageable burdens on those who cared for them.

> My parents were sending me the course fee but I work part-time casual to earn my expenses . . . I am keeping it to a minimum. Last vacation, the December holiday, I didn't go back home because I was working almost full-time casual and I managed to save about half of my course fee for this final semester.
>
> ~ female, 27 electrical engineering, Singapore

> Initially, my parents supported me, but they could not do it later. I thought of not asking them, because it was . . . I had already taken a lot of money from them. So we both brothers are working and we help each other. When I was studying he was earning and now I'm working and he's studying. So it's like mutual.
>
> ~ male, 23, information technology, India

> So far I still have enough financially, but maybe they are just suffering over there, but they just let me have a comfortable life here.
>
> ~ female, 21, commerce, Malaysia

> I don't want my family to support me, I want to be independent. I try to find part-time jobs to support my living expense.
>
> ~ female, 25 systems engineering, China

> Since I have already done a Masters back at home and I have worked for two years I didn't want to take money from my parents. But I was not in a position to save the entire fees for my course, so I had to take money from them, and some from the bank. I'm working right now part-time. I try to repay it, like every month. I send some money to my parents, whatever I save I try to send some money – at least something to pay back.
>
> ~ female, 25, media and communication, India

For some other students, relations with home were an encumbrance that undermined their financial situation. One student was asked to send money home:

> People at home sometimes think that we are abroad and we've got a lot of money and they sometimes ask us to send money and we do understand that they need also the money. Just recently my brother take a trip to hospital because he was sick and my family asked me to send money and so the money that I saved when I stay here I spend it.
>
> ~ male, 31, community development, Indonesia

Another was told by his parents not to work, but his situation was impossible:

> I'm still really, really struggling . . . my parents don't want me to work, no, because I'm in my final year. And they say you're there as a student, it says so in your visa, it's a student visa, so that's your job . . . I've had long arguments about that, because it's really difficult financially. It's a really tight budget, $16 a day, not including rent . . . it all sort of started happening last year and I had a lot of periods of crying about it, feeling a bit down and really just struggling hard and doing . . . It is still very hard and I still sometimes feel a bit down about it but I've come to accept it a bit better. The way I see it, when I start working, it'll change. The best thing to do for the moment is to have a good attitude about it.
>
> ~ female, 28, communication, Singapore

FINANCIAL DIFFICULTIES

'When my daughter came . . . electricity account, everything was up'

When asked about financial difficulties, one interviewee said that 'Everyone has, it's just big or small'. But this perspective was not shared by the 63 per cent of interviewees who stated they had not experienced such difficulties. They had sufficient funds from home, or were able to manage their budgets or had enough employment in Australia. This finding is consistent with the international literature.

> I'm a lawyer by profession . . . I've been a partner of a jewellery business, which I inherited from my family. I'm not running the business, my brother is running it, but I get a share of it. I'm spending that money for my education.
>
> male, 46, law, Sri Lanka

The existence of a large minority with problems (37 per cent), often acute, is also consistent with the international research findings. The causes of difficulty included the cost of dependents, inadequate information about costs, particularly poor briefing by recruiting agents or institutions prior to departure, inexperience at living and working

Table 5.6 Number of international students experiencing financial difficulty, by age

Age group	20 years or less	21–30 years	31–40 years	40 years and over	All ages
Number in group	17	138	39	6	200
Number in difficulty	3	49	16	6	74
Proportion in difficulty (%)	17.6	35.5	41.0	100.0	37.0

away from home, incapacity or inability to gain employment, currency fluctuations and inadequate support from Australian institutions.

Older students had a relatively high incidence of problems (table 5.6).

Older students are less likely to draw financial support from their parents and relatives, and more likely to have dependant children, as some emphasised

> As an international student it's not always easy. I have two children. They are nine and six and when we came here there was no support so [I used] my savings from the previous jobs . . . and also thanks to my parents. That was the first year how I was funded to stay. But I was pretty precarious because the funds ran out all the time. With the kids, we have to pay fees as international students. We don't have a car. Public transport we try to avoid as much [as possible]. International [students] don't have concession card. My wife found a job . . . for one and half years she has been [the] sole supporter but it means if we are sent back home there are no savings – basically, her earnings go towards either my fees or kids' fees.
>
> ~ male, 40, education, Germany

> When my daughter came my water account, electricity account, everything was up.
>
> ~ female, 33, geography, Bangladesh

> [For] several weeks I had money so that I could give my child five days in childcare but nowadays I'm only giving two. Because if [my child is there] every day I have to spend $17 [per day] . . . If I want to send him to kindergarten I have to spend around $600–900 per month [but] I haven't got that much money.
>
> ~ male, 36, economics, Bangladesh

Table 5.7 Numbers of students with dependent children, by course level and age group

	Number of students in total population		Students with children		
		%	30 years or less	31–40 years	41–49 years
PhD	49	24.5	1	28	5
Masters/graduate diploma	74	37.0	0	9	2
Undergraduate	77	38.5	0	2	0
Total	200	100.0	1	39	7

In the whole study 23.5 per cent of interviewees stated that they had at least one child. Of the 49 doctoral students interviewed, 34 had dependent children.

Some older students did not want to work because they were in the late stages of their course or wanted to finish as soon as possible. Of those who chose to work, or felt they had no choice, a number had experienced financial difficulties because they had not been provided with enough information on the cost of housing and/or the problems of obtaining and maintaining employment.

> At the beginning I only got the scholarship after two weeks . . . I didn't expect that I have to pay bond here and all my money go for [the] house. I have to stay for two weeks with one hundred dollar.
>
> ~ male, 32, engineering, Egypt

> When I was first over here . . . I thought I would get a job immediately, but it took about three months.
>
> ~ male, 27, music therapy, India

Even when adequately informed and in work, the international students were vulnerable to a problem that does not affect locals: currency fluctuations.

> My scholarship is paid in American dollars, so when it comes to Australia it changes with the rates . . . when I came the first time the rate was 0.60. The last time it was 0.74 or 0.75. It's a huge difference. It makes my life more difficult.
>
> ~ male, 37, public health, Mozambique

> My scholarship is paid in US dollars. Three or four years ago when our contract was signed it was okay, but now because of the currency difference between the US dollar and the Australian dollar it covers only 50 per cent of my tuition fee. I'll have to pay the other 50 per cent, so I'm looking for a job.
>
> ~ female, 39, medicine, France

CRISIS MANAGEMENT

'International students should be given some kind of credit'

Most international students have personal strategies designed to ensure that their finances do not become unmanageable. They can identify how they would cope with a potential crises should those strategies fail. For some students this means allowing for contingency within the budget.

> I always keep some money as emergency money, so when you are in a critical situation you still have some money. I put it in a separate account.
>
> ~ male, 22, architecture, Malaysia

For others it means severely limiting what they can spend money on.

> Actually, the stipend which I have is enough for my living here but not for any saving, just enough for my survival here. Just enough for living.
>
> ~ female, 34, PhD in science, Sri Lanka

But even the dutiful can find budgeting difficult. Some make mistakes that render them vulnerable and are periodically in need of temporary support.

> Some things here is very expensive but relatively cheaper in China. But some things here [are] cheap but relatively expensive in China, so it's hard to manage my budget . . . In China we live in the school, we just pay the school. But here you have to find your accommodation by yourself and it's hard to decide how, what kind of one I want and how much it should be – it's just [having] no idea about

> food as well, and for transportation. It's really expensive. I walk so much when I first came here. I thought $1.50 [would] have bought a whole [meal] . . . I feel I couldn't let any dollar go.
>
> ~ female, 25, public health, China

> Yes. I had a very tough time finding a job firstly. First two months I was unemployed. That was affecting my study a lot. Because I didn't want to take money from my parents. Whatever money I've got from India, I get around $3000, it [gets used up] because my rent is very high . . . and other than that you have travelling, eating, everything. So I starved.
>
> ~ female, 36, media communication, India

Both of these students coped with a difficult situation by going without. Another student observed that when he got into difficulties with a telephone company with whom he had signed a contract, his response was to pay the bill, even though he did not understand the cost, and then simply 'avoid contracts'.

Responding to the question 'Who would you turn to if you are in serious financial difficulty?' interviewees provided the following responses: family (61.8 per cent), friends (27.9 per cent), university and scholarship provider (9.7 per cent), other (4.2 per cent) and no one (10.3 per cent). Numerous students indicated they would seek help from more than one source. One had discovered a new method of avoiding financial difficulties that worked better in Australia than at home.

> I found that if you cry here you can make people listen. That's the difference.
>
> ~ female, 36, engineering, South Africa

Even so, most students emphasised the need for self-reliance, even if they also had backup.

> I've managed to keep my head above water and it's been fine, and I know my parents, if I ever need money they'll be happy to help me.
>
> ~ female, 23, organisational and industrial psychology, UK

> We mainly talk to our friends in the community, asking for money to pay back later. The Indonesian community we have here is really helpful to each other.
>
> ~ male, 41, communication, language and cultural studies, Indonesia

> Friends, I think, and I can borrow money from the student council as well. I think they have got 'no interest' borrowing. But it's only for about a couple of hundred dollars. I don't think it will help. Not even to pay for rent.
>
> ~ male, 21, media and communication, Macau

It is disconcerting that only 9.7 per cent of the interviewees felt they could approach their university for help, and that 10.3 per cent indicated they had no one to turn to when in serious need. Few students mentioned crisis resources provided by their university. If safety net bodies and/or programs exist, the overwhelming majority of international students were not aware of them, or how to access them. On the other hand some Australian agencies do provide assistance when international students are in trouble. AusAID stood out in the interviews as an organisation willing to provide financial support to its scholarship holders when in serious need.

> We needed quite a lot of money for the dental operation for my child. And we didn't have enough savings for that, [it costs] more than a thousand [dollars]. AusAID helped ... and I got a loan from university ... the doctor had to extract nine of his teeth ... [AusAID] had an emergency fund. The medical insurance doesn't cover dental.
>
> ~ male, 42, linguistics, Indonesia

> It's difficult to work and study. I do four subjects and there's research work and all that so ... I couldn't basically save money for my fees. I had to get money. I'm looking at possibly getting a loan from ... I tried from the university. It's not possible to get a full loan so I'm looking at the possibility back home. When in trouble I have enquired about many things here. I wanted to take a loan from a bank and I wanted to apply for a credit card, but they said as I am an international student I cannot apply for these things. Even if you are international student with a regular income you can't take loans from banks. I have taken one [university]

> student loan. It is very easy to get a student loan here. So I used that. But it has certain limits so for the rest of things I have to depend on a bank. If I had some problem, if I needed say $5000 [because] accidentally something happened, I know the bank will not help me because I am not a permanent resident. I think this should be changed. International students should be given some kind of credit.
>
> ~ male, 22, commerce, India

CONCLUSIONS

The interviews confirm the three tentative conclusions.

The first of these is that most international students do not experience great financial hardship but a significant minority do and some have severe difficulties. Many students lack ongoing financial security. Students experience financial problems because of lack of resources, insufficient knowledge of the challenges of living and studying in a foreign country, currency volatility and lack of budgetary skills.

Second, in the case of crisis, students do not always have a complete safety net. If a student is in serious financial difficulty the authorities may not know (finances are not monitored) and not all students can rely on friends and family to help.

The third conclusion is that more research is needed.

Given the number of international students, it is extraordinary that we do not have a comprehensive picture of their income and expenditure, including variations by gender, age, field of study, level of course, national origin, location and institution in Australia. This absence of data blocks the potential for development of an effective, economical safety net. While numbers and revenues have grown dramatically, the research has deteriorated. It was clear in the 1990s that a significant number of international students were in financial difficulty. Cynically, instead of probing the problem and finding solutions, it was decided to suppress that knowledge because it might have reduced aggregate student demand for international education or obliged institutions to increase their provision of student financial aid. A 'we just don't want to know' stance lends credence to claims that Australia and its universities see international students primarily as customers who exist to be milked.

Those in the USA and the UK who have taken up the financial security issue note that financial learning is an important part of international student adjustment, and inadequate finances can be a serious source of distress. In both these jurisdictions public bodies have produced documents designed to assist international students in managing their finances. In the UK, UKCISA has initiated studies on the sources of international student income, how and where international students spend their money and how they cope financially. Such studies are needed in Australia.

A review of the infrastructure and programs that support students at risk is also urgently needed. This is made more necessary by the likelihood that provision is uneven across the country. The area is not closely monitored, and universities have unequal resources. We know that such a review is likely to lead to calls for university and government resources to be diverted to constructing a better financial safety net. In our judgment, if the Australian higher education sector wishes to continue its profitable engagement with the global student market it should apportion part of the $2.6 billion it earns in tuition revenues to provide this.

Finally, we suggest that the federal government needs to review the income levels required to obtain a student visa. These levels should provide international students with a clear understanding of the financial burden they will have to bear if they choose to study in Australia. The government must also ensure that universities provide accurate information about finances and work to prospective students. The National Code requires institutions to provide prospective students with 'current and accurate information' on the cost of living, accommodation options and schooling obligations and options for dependant children. But while providing prospective students with accurate information is fundamental, guaranteed income provisions can be avoided and if set too high can act as a barrier to entry by poor students. These are not problems that can be resolved adequately by market forces and by adherence to the buyer beware (*Caveat emptor)* doctrine. Providing accurate knowledge and letting the free market operate does not resolve the situation for students: those who know the reality and take the risk that things will somehow work out, those who think they are secure because of some form of guarantee that fails when put to the test, those who become ill and consequently unable to work, those who are devastated by unforseen shifts in currency rates or in the labour market. Given students can be made extremely vulnerable if such calamities do beset them, governments and universities need to develop policies and practices that provide a viable safety net.

Possibilities worthy of exploration might include compulsory income insurance, a common assurance program to which education suppliers must contribute that provides loans to students in financial trouble, increased efforts to ensure that students do not get into financial trouble by, for example, allocating greater resources to protecting students from exploitative employers, depositing monies advanced as proof of income insurance in a bank with only a limited amount to be taken each month and providing special consideration to students to study part-time and work more hours if they get into financial difficulties. Unless the federal government comprehensively addresses these issues, and unless its efforts (unlike those of AVCC/UA) are supported by research into the financial problems of international students, we are again left with the impression that all the expressions of concern for international student wellbeing are nothing but fine sounding words designed to sustain not student security but the commercial reputation of the Australian industry. And in the longer run, refusing to address this issue might show itself as not just a failure of human rights and pastoral care, but a commercial error as well.

This chapter has reviewed the financial security of international students, the regulatory regime that governs financial security and present gaps in security. The next chapter conducts a parallel review of international students at work.

6 WORK

In my first two years I had to work a lot to support myself, 30–40 hours of work per week, and I was also trying to achieve high marks in my studies.

~ male, 27, India, music therapy

INTRODUCTION: 'ALL THIS FOR $8 AN HOUR'

'Assault, abuse, fare evasion, 12-hour shifts, poor security. All this for $8 an hour.' So ran the quote that was highlighted on the front of the May Day 2008 edition of the *Age*.[1] The main city intersection in front of the clocks at Flinders Street station had been occupied for 22 hours by hundreds of taxi drivers paying respect to a fellow driver who had been stabbed and abandoned by a passenger. The drivers demanded the state government compel taxi owners to fit driver safety shields that would offer some protection from assaults. As was the 23 year old victim, many of the protesters were among the estimated 5000 Indian students working in Melbourne as part-time cabbies to generate the income needed to live and study in Australia. Though it was cold, the young men stripped to the waist and threatened to parade totally naked through the streets to highlight the physical vulnerability of those who labour in a lowly paid occupation in which workers must provide for their own occupational health and safety insurance. According to the Victorian Taxi Directorate this is a dangerous occupation, requiring drivers to 'work alone, work at night, work

1 Schneiders and Lucas with Dobbin, 2008.

long shifts increasing the risk of fatigue, work in isolated and high-crime areas, have cash on hand and always deal with strangers'.

The drivers' occupation of the intersection and their demands were broadcast across India. The *Times of India* observed that driving a taxi in Melbourne can be a nightmare, with limited safety measures to prevent assault. It quoted one of the student drivers who initiated the protest: 'Indians living in India should know about this criminal behaviour of the government here. What is the Indian embassy staff doing here? If an Australian is hurt or killed in India, all hell will break loose. If an Indian is hurt or killed, no one cares. What is our embassy doing in Canberra?'

Though the drivers occupying Flinders Street endured abuse from police and sections of the press, when the community came to understand what the half-naked workers were demanding of government and employers, a wave of sympathy swept across Melbourne. Confronted by the industrial challenge and the economic threat to the largest export market in the state of Victoria – international education – on the second day of the taxi drivers' strike the state Labor government capitulated. It ruled that protective shields must be fitted in all cases when desired by a driver. It could have done so earlier, and it might have headed off a savage attack. The drivers had been calling for protective shields since the murder of an Indian student-driver two years before. It was only when they took action that something was done. But a point missed in the debate was that the young Indian was one of tens of thousands of international students employed in vulnerable occupations across Australia's cities. During their enrolment in Australia foreign students have the right to be employed for 20 hours per week in semester time, an unlimited number of hours at other times and they can remain and work in Australia for up to 18 months on completing their studies if they wish. It is reasonable to assume the conditions governing student work should strengthen the social and financial security of those students. This is far from the case.

Stable, well-paid employment can increase the security of international students. But the need for a job can also render them vulnerable to the physical, social and emotional risks accompanying some forms of employment. On 7 July 2008 the *Age* reported a legal case against security employment contractors at the Australian Open Tennis. An Indian student had been paid the sum of $200 for working over 150 hours as a security guard. Not $8 an hour but $1.33. He was working during summer break to build a cash reserve for income security during semester. When he tried to recover unpaid wages the student had been physically threatened by the security company director. The student's lawyer was quoted as saying, 'Our client is a vulnerable worker – a visitor to Australia trying to scrape together an income while he completes his studies in Australia'. That statement accurately describes the lives of the majority of international students in Australia. Chapter 5 noted that a minority of internationals experience severe financial difficulties. For many their non-wage income is less than half the standard Australian measure of basic living costs, the Henderson Poverty Line. These student-workers are all too easy targets. But they are non-citizen workers. Most of the time no one cares.

A key problem is that many international students need to work more than 20 hours per week in order to survive, but the penalty for working more than 20 hours in a calendar week of study semester is mandatory loss of visa, detention and deportation. Unscrupulous employers who know this can readily impose arbitrary wages and working conditions, in some cases also demanding sexual or other favours, while threatening to report the students to the immigration department if they complain or unionise. At any given time tens of thousands of international students are trapped in exploitative or illegal conditions. Despite this, international student-workers were invisible in the Australian debate on vulnerable employees during 2006–7 in response to the enactment of the anti-labour Work Choices law. Publications that examined the impact of this legislation on vulnerable workers discussed women, migrants, the Indigenous, the disabled and the low-paid but not the then 370 000 international students.[2] International student-workers were not even discussed by contributors who reflected on the impact of Work Choices on youth and local students.[3] Their invisibility is not unique to Australia. In the international literature on vulnerable workers, international student-workers are recognised once, in the 2008 report by the UK Trades Union Congress Commission on Vulnerable Work, which defines these employees as workers who undertake 'precarious work that

2 Pocock and Masterman-Smith, 2005; Cowling et al., 2006; Mathews, 2006; Mitchell et al., 2006; Stewart, 2006; Fenwick, 2006; Burgess et al., 2007; Hodgkinson and Markey, 2007.

3 McDonald et al., 2007.

places people at risk of continuing poverty and injustice resulting from an imbalance of power in the employer-worker relationship'.[4]

The rapid growth of the global education market has generated a new part-time workforce in Australia. This workforce is mostly segmented into a low tier position in the labour market. It is a source of cheap labour. It is vulnerable and its employment experiences are almost unresearched. International student-workers are often compelled to accept a labour bargain unacceptable to local students. At the same time the presence of this severely disadvantaged workforce on a growing scale has the potential to threaten Australian employment standards. If the human rights of these student-workers were recognised, those who profit from education exports, and those responsible for the education and wellbeing of the students, would help them realise their rights in the labour market and workplace.

The chapter begins by reviewing the literature on student workers. It then considers the much smaller coverage of international student-workers, mostly from the USA and the UK, and the official documentation of the area in Australia. It received more attention at the genesis of the education export industry than is now the case. We also contrast the laws regulating student-workers with those covering guest workers. Then, drawing on the 200 international student interviewees, we explore their work experiences, including the proportion who accept employment, the nature of their paid work, remuneration and experiences of discrimination in applying for work and in the workplace itself (see also chapter 14). We conclude with suggestions for further research and for regulation.

INTERNATIONAL STUDENT-WORKERS IN THE LITERATURE

Local student-workers

Research on the paid employment of local students during study time focuses on growth in the number and proportion of student workers, growth in average hours worked, the effect of work on academic results, how universities adapt teaching practices to provide for employed students, student-worker exploitation by employers and

4 TUC, 2008.

whether students displace lower-skilled workers.[5] These studies find that students work primarily because of financial need. Their studies seldom suffer provided they work no more than 15 hours per week, but the students believe they would gain more from their studies if they did not work.[6] Curtis and Williams note that work involves 'acquisition of transferable skills, enhanced employability, increased confidence in the world of work, and the improvement of organisational and time management skills. Sadly, it also involves 'missing lectures and failing to submit coursework on time, low pay... no sick pay or holiday pay, health and safety hazards, and stress and tiredness.'[7]

The literature suggests that continuing growth in the number of students who work is due largely to state policies that compel students and their families to bear a growing proportion of the financial cost of tertiary education.[8] For their part, firms, particularly in service and retail, have redesigned aspects of the labour process to tap a growing body of students who can multitask, make decisions and act in a responsible manner. As Curtis and Lucas observe, many employers 'benefit from an easily recruited workforce of intelligent, articulate young people who are numerically and functionally flexible, conscientious, accepting relatively low pay, and who are easy to control, [can] articulate dislikes about their work and employment conditions, yet... feel unable to challenge their employers'.[9] In companies such as Pizza Hut, up to 60 per cent of employees are students.[10] McDonald notes that student workers tend to be vulnerable to exploitation because of limited work skills, high level of unemployment and underemployment, poor knowledge of their rights and poor capacity to defend these rights.[11] The US Committee on the Health and Safety Implications of Child Labor observes that young student-workers have a high rate of work-related injuries, substance abuse and experience inadequate sleep and inadequate exercise.[12]

5 Long and Hayden, 2001; Neill et al., 2004; Manthei and Gilmore, 2005; Tam and Morrison, 2005; Bexley et al., 2007.
6 Neill and Mulholland et al., 2004.
7 Curtis and Williams, 2002, 5.
8 Dex and McCulloch, 1995; Bexley et al., 2007.
9 Curtis and Lucas, 2001, 38.
10 Curtis, 2000.
11 McDonald et al., 2007.
12 CHSICL, 1998.

Many student-workers occupy jobs that are also suitable for lower-skilled workers. Hoffman and Steijn explored whether their presence in these jobs reflects a substantial displacement of low-skilled workers.[13] They concluded that this is the case and suggest displacement of the low-skilled by students will accelerate when the labour market deteriorates because of employer preferences for students. In noting that students are disproportionately present in low-skilled jobs researchers have also stressed that this is not universal and the group is stratified. Lucas notes that student-workers are segregated by gender – more female than male students are employed – and by skill; a significant minority are in jobs requiring a high level of expertise such as research assistant, librarian, tutor, information technician and/or laboratory technician.[14] Gender and skill segmentation and stratification are highlighted by Christie and colleagues who also show that student workers are stratified by class. The financial position of the student's parents is a primary determinant of the number of hours the student works, and the type of work a student is prepared to accept.[15] The international–domestic student distinction is another source of stratification and segmentation.

International student-workers

The available evidence suggests that international students are concentrated in the lowest strata of student employment, though no major education export country documents this accurately. The factors that so confine internationals include racial discrimination and stereotyping, lack of local kin support, less than optimal language skills, lack of knowledge of the host culture and incapacity to realise rights that accrue to domestic student-workers. In an article discussing the taxi driver protest, Thompson notes that these workers see their occupation as low status and the protest 'can be understood as a rupturing point at the level of respect, where the amount of respect afforded to protesters had dipped too radically low beneath their own levels of self image'.[16] Even so, Indian students are able to monopolise many

13 Hofman and Steijn, 2003.
14 Lucas, 1997.
15 Christie et al., 2002.
16 Skelton, 2008, 11.

service occupations because they tend to have greater English proficiency than east Asian students. 'They [Indians] are comfortable with English – the official and academic language of India for almost a century . . . The thing with Indians is they are highly visible. You can't miss them when they serve you at the supermarket, when you pay for your petrol, or when they drive you home,' notes Sushi Das.[17] The international student workforce is also internally stratified.

But in contrast with the abundant research on domestic student-workers, few studies investigate international student work. Perhaps it is seen as normal for students to work at low status, cash-in-hand jobs. Perhaps the local population, including social researchers, seldom sees international students as workers. Moreover it is likely that education institutions and government agencies fear that if international student work experiences are examined, the resulting tales of exploitation, reported in students' home countries, will damage the industry.

In a US study of discrimination Lee and Rice provide a rare focus on international students at work. While white international students who speak good English rarely experienced discrimination it is different for students of colour and/or relatively poor English. Lee and Rice note that visa stipulations limiting the students to oncampus jobs are seen as discriminatory. The only options left to internationals unable to obtain positions as research assistants, tutors or technicians were low paying oncampus jobs in retail or food services. Lee and Rice also report perceptions of discrimination among those employed as research assistants or technicians. 'You have to know the rules of the game or you'll be killed', said a student from China. An Indian student said that faculty exclude internationals from selected jobs and seek to benefit from their vulnerability because they 'know that as foreign students we have limited recourses' and can be easily exploited. They 'treat you like the scum of the earth', said another.[18]

In the USA and Canada international students were traditionally confined to oncampus work for 20 hours per week, which rendered international student work a marginal issue, though some international students have no doubt been forced by their financial circumstances to work illegally. (There are about 12 million people residing

17 Das, 2008b.
18 Lee and Rice, 2007.

illegally in the USA; many of them also work illegally.) In March 2006 a bill was introduced into the US Senate to permit international students to work offcampus 20 hours per week in term time, 40 hours at other times and to remain and work in the USA for 29 months after graduation. This change would have removed a barrier to less affluent students, eased the passage from student to immigrant and strengthened US education in the global market. The bill was backed by NAFSA, the Association of International Educators, a 9000-member organisation that promotes and researches international education in the USA. In discussion around the bill NAFSA suggested the proposed changes in work rights could also alleviate problems with students acquiring social security numbers. US rules require all workers to provide a social security number to employers. International students have difficulties gaining employment because university human resource departments will not allow students to start work without a social security number, and conversely, social security will not provide a number without evidence of employment, blocking the route to legal employment. However, the bill was withdrawn after 15 months of hearings when the Senate could not agree on how to deal with over 300 amendments, many of which centred on the alleged threat that expanding foreign students' right to work offcampus would pose to Americans' ability to gain employment.

In the UK non-EU internationals may undertake 20 hours of paid work during term time and unlimited hours outside this period, both on and off campus. The representative body for UK universities is concerned about international students' opportunity to work and its impact on potential market share. In 2008 Universities UK released a report on ways of increasing international postgraduate research students that focused on employment, both part-time work while studying and job prospects after graduation. Universities UK noted that 38 per cent of postgraduate research students were enrolled in their courses part-time, about half met living expenses with income from part-time work and in some institutions up to 90 per cent of international research students worked part time, mostly in the university. The report suggested an expansion in part-time work opportunities on campus.

In the UK there has been more research on international student work than in the USA, but it has been limited to studies of level of participation, with nothing of substance on wages, occupations, work conditions or the capacity of students to exercise industrial rights. Baron and colleagues present initial findings of a longitudinal study of international students in Scotland. On the first day of orientation three-quarters of the cohort planned to obtain part-time work while studying.[19] However, a 2004 survey by the UK Council for International Student Affairs (UKCISA) found that only 53 per cent of non-EU international and 46 per cent of EU-international students had worked while studying in Britain. This was little different to the 47 per cent of domestic students who worked while studying full time. There are two possible reasons for the discrepancy between the intention and experience. The first is that international students can face additional difficulties when seeking work. A 2006 UKCISA study that found 58 per cent of international students who wanted paid work found it difficult to obtain: 64 per cent of non-EU internationals compared to 26 per cent of EU internationals. Non-EU students were more likely to report that employers offered lame excuses when refusing them (31 per cent non-EU, 10 per cent EU students), such as false claims that they were ineligible for national insurance. Only 5 per cent of internationals reported open discrimination when applying for jobs, but students from east Asia, southeast Asia, the Middle East and north Africa were most likely to do so,[20] consistent with a Loughborough University survey of employer attitudes to recruiting international students.[21] The second reason is that the international students may have been reluctant to acknowledge work because they had transgressed their visa conditions. When UKCISA asked non-EU foreign students in 2006 about their hours of work, none admitted to more than 20 hours per week. Yet EU-internationals, free of the visa restriction, acknowledged working an average of 22 hours per week. A study by Spencer and colleagues asked a select group of non-EU internationals – those from eastern European countries about to join the EU – about their hours of work and found 75 per cent of students with paying jobs work more than 20 hours per week, with two-thirds working more than 30 hours.[22] These students did not fear they would have their visas revoked.

19 Baron et al., 2007.

20 UKCISA, 2006.

21 Loughborough University Careers Service, 2004.

22 Spencer et al., 2007.

INTERNATIONAL STUDENT-WORKERS IN AUSTRALIA

Australian data on labour market participation and hours of work must be treated with even more caution than the UK data. First, because of the extreme sanctions governing the 20 hour rule. McInnis and Hartley surveyed 1563 local and international students and found that, unlike their local peers, no international student was willing to admit working more than 20 hours per week. They conclude that

> We have some indication that our surveys and interviews did not reveal the full story for some groups of students. Our consultations suggested that there is a strong financial imperative for some full fee-paying overseas students to work their allowed 20 hours and sometimes more. While some can call on substantial financial support from other sources, others are in dire straits financially. Their families can support them through paying fees, however, they are unable to provide living costs and therefore a proportion of overseas students have to work long hours to provide for accommodation and living expenses. Given the limits placed on the number of hours these students can work we suspect that we did not reach many international students in this position or that, despite our reassurances, they did not feel free to divulge the full extent of their paid work.[23]

Second, some Australian studies use a restricted definition of student work. A mid-semester survey of a representative range of Australian universities by Krause and colleagues reports that 23.3 per cent of full-fee paying international students said they worked during semester.[24] Rosenthal and colleagues, likewise researching during semester, found only 27.2 per cent of internationals were employed.[25] These figures have been used to argue that only a small number of internationals work while studying. But neither study asked about work outside semester. When AEI embraced the approach used in the UK and asked international students if they had worked any time in Australia, 59 per cent of those in higher education admitted to

23 McInnis and Hartley, 2002.

24 Krause et al., 2005.

25 Rosenthal et al., 2006.

working, more than the 53 per cent of non-EU internationals in the UK who admitted working.[26]

The AEI found that 56 per cent of international respondents undertook paid work during 2006 compared to 86 per cent of Australians. The discrepancy suggests it might be harder for international students than local students to obtain work, or there is less need for work and/or work is under-reported. Of employed internationals, 80 per cent worked on average five hours a week or more, as did 85 per cent of Australian respondents. Only 33 per cent of internationals stated that the work was related to their field of study. AEI deemed this of particular concern:

> [A] major frustration among international students was the difficulty in finding work related to their field of study. The main reasons stated were that most graduate positions and traineeships required applicants to have permanent residency in Australia. This complicates matters as employers in their home countries expect graduates to have some hands-on experience together with their degree to be eligible for employment. This combination was seen as a major barrier in achieving the necessary credit for their studies overseas.[27]

Of the internationals who did not have a paid job during 2006, the majority had not tried to get one because they did not have Australian work experience, were too busy, did not have a work visa or because there were too few jobs.

In 2006 Melbourne City Council surveyed international students' perceptions of living and studying in Melbourne. It found that 39 per cent of students wanted better part-time work opportunities and 48 per cent believed their ability to connect to the job market needed to improve. Measured against all areas, these two are among the five lowest ranked items on a list of 30 indicators of Melbourne, which is ironic, because many of those interviewed stated that they expected access to part-time job as a reason for choosing Melbourne. When asked what would influence them to remain in Melbourne on graduation, many cited the availability of employment. Respondents also stated that the job market was not an even playing field:

26 AEI, 2007b.
27 AEI, 2007a, 28.

> [A problem is] employers and institutions getting over their ignorance regarding issues related to immigration and cultural diversity. I have spent most of my life overseas and my English is native-like. However, I have experienced more discrimination here than anywhere else in the world; I have lived and studied in the US, UK and Mexico. Most employers will not hire people on a student visa regardless of their qualifications and don't even bother checking you out if the name on the CV and background suggest you are not a native speaker of English.

> Being treated as equals to Australians in terms of salary and opportunities available. I would like to be judged not on my cultural background, but purely based on my actual performance and capability at work.

The Melbourne City Council study also indicates that international students genuinely perceived that they did not have equal rights in the workplace as workers.

> [T]here needs to be more regulations and guidelines for employment. I do observe how underpaid and over-worked most students are. If the government shows a firm stance on this issue, it would relieve countless numbers of students who are currently working for $6 an hour (some of them have proper work visa too!). Also re-enforcing the equal employment policy.

Ong examined the study–work–life balance of international students at Monash University.[28] One in four admitted to working over 15 hours per week part-time. Ong[29] found that half the international students he surveyed were unaware of the mandatory deportation provision but nearly all knew about the 20 hour limit. In a subsequent interview with the authors, Ong confirmed a lack of jobs and argued that this is partly because many internationals are older than domestic students and so cost more for retail companies to employ because they are not paid junior rates. They were often expected to take roles of higher responsibility.[30]

---

28 Ong, 2006.
29 *ibid.*
30 *ibid.*

Ong also argued for a degree of tolerance of subpar working conditions. International students paid below the legal rate of pay do not necessarily complain:

> The word 'exploitation' is a hugely contentious issue as there is a cultural influence in it. In an Australian perspective, it is true that international students are being exploited as they are given lower wages than Australian and not being protected. However, some students may see these 'exploitations' as opportunities for them to learn the harsh realities of life and to train themselves; sounds funny but I actually had this form of thinking before I was involved in international student representation. Technically it is the international students' choice to be exploited (not saying that I support it). At least they must be able to make an informed choice.[31]

> Being paid $5 to $6 for a waitress job is relatively high for many international students. If you compare wages across top source countries (taking purchasing power parity into account), it is two to three times more than what they are paid back home. It is a similar situation in Singapore where well-educated Indonesians, normally with at least a Bachelor degree, are willing to come work as house maids for $400 SGD per month, much more than what they earn as a professional in Indonesia. Another case is that PriceWater-HouseCoopers pay $2000 AUD per month for graduate trainees in Australia and 2000 Ringgit [$637.92 AUD] for the same position in Malaysia.[32]

What may be seen as fair to the individual may not be fair to the group. Living costs are three times higher in Australia than Malaysia, and equal pay is often seen as synonymous with equal respect. Ong also misses the effect on Australian workers, who must compete in the labour market with international students prepared to collude in illegally low wages. A race to the bottom in wages and working conditions undermines the security of both local and foreign workers.

31 *ibid.*
32 *ibid.*

THE REGULATORY REGIME

The implications of international student-workers has been examined in depth once in Australia, as part of the Industry Commission's 1991 report on *Work Rights*. This report, published at a time when there were 60 442 international students in Australia, was little noticed but it provides insights into international student work, the debates about it at the time and its subsequent regulation.

The Industries Commission notes that it is very difficult to accurately survey the number of student workers and their hours of work as workers and institutions have incentives to understate each. Here the Commission cites two submissions received when conducting hearings in preparation of its report. The first was from the ELICOS Foundation, which had interviewed 1483 students and found that

> The section of the survey related to employment, hours worked, payment received and tax paid were not as well answered as they might have been. This could be to poor understanding of the questions and/or a disinclination to answer correctly because it was felt that this was an unnecessary invasion of privacy or because of a sensitivity of the legitimacy of their employment.[33]

On the question of the industrial rights of student-workers, the Commission in its advice to government equates 'work rights' only with the 'right to work'. International students' rights to fair wages and conditions, or how they might realise those rights, are little considered. The main thrust of the report supports the entry of international students into the labour market in deregulated fashion.

> Giving students the right to work while studying increases the attractiveness of Australian education. Many participants thought the current 20 hours a week entitlement was reasonable, allowing an appropriate balance of study and work. At the levels experienced in the past, the evidence indicates that the overall effects on the labour market of overseas students working are likely to be small but positive. No changes are recommended for these students, but

33 Industry Commission, 1991, 98. Similarly, Careers Business College surveyed its students and found that 'It can also be speculated that some students may have failed to respond to the question [on work rights] because they were working in excess of the 20 hour weekly limit, even though the questionnaire was anonymous and confidential; *ibid*, 99.

> dependents of category A visa holders should be permitted to work full-time.[34]

However, the Commission does discuss one topic likely to be increasingly significant in times of high unemployment: whether work participation by international students affects domestic workers. The Commission's analysis of this issue relied on empirical studies by researchers who did not bring to their work the rigor that characterised Hoffman and Steijn's contribution discussed above. It was conceded that there might be downward pressure on wages and a 'crowding out' of Australian residents competing for job opportunities and/or displacement of Australian workers who already hold jobs. The last impact would be greatest in those parts of the labour market in which overseas students are concentrated:

> Students who work potentially displace Australian residents. To the extent that this occurs, the earnings and presumably spending of these residents will be less than otherwise. In addition, resident unemployment may be higher and labour force participation may be lower. The size of these effects depends very much on the groups affected. For example, it is likely that residents working part time (or seeking part-time work), particularly in areas such as service industries, will be more affected than others. If potential resident workers in these jobs are only marginally attached to the labour force, the consequences for measured unemployment and participation will be slight.[35]

The Commission cites econometric evidence from the Centre for International Economics (CIE) and the 1988 *Fitzgerald Report* on immigration. The CIE concluded from its modelling that the 'effect of exports of education on overall economic activity and employment are small, though the contribution is a positive one', while Fitzgerald found that allowing overseas students to work would boost the total number of job opportunities for residents, but there will be winners and losers among the resident workforce. Sectors in which students tend to spend relatively heavily will be advantaged; unemployed

34 *ibid*, 97.
35 *ibid*, 104.

'residents of sectors in which overseas students are likely to search for jobs will be relatively disadvantaged'.[36]

The 1991 Commission understated the likely market impact of international students' work because of its simplifying assumption that international and domestic students had the same reservation wage. This was wrong in 1991. International students lacked access to Austudy student grants, subsidised housing and transport, free medical care, deferred fees and many student loans. Given this situation, a significant proportion of international student-workers would have been willing to undercut the wages of domestics able to access these benefits. Since 1991 the assumption has further weakened. The relative and absolute number of international students from poorer nations of Asia and Africa has increased, and the proportion from more affluent countries, such as Hong Kong China, Singapore and Japan, has decreased.

At the end its discussion, the Commission comments in passing on the suggestion that international students might be subjected to exploitation. The Sydney Committee for Overseas Students (SCOS) had argued to the commission that

> Those (overseas students) that do find employment are often exploited. Their employers, usually from their own ethnic background, pay them well below the legal rate of pay, and in many instances get away with it because it is the only job that the student has been able to find.[37]

However, the SCOS did not provide evidence. The Commission might have been more impressed by the CIE's argument, whose modelling it drew upon and who it possibly also shared a common ideological position with. 'The notion of "exploitation" is a strange idea in that students are willingly making themselves available to employers . . . If there is any exploitation, it occurs when people are denied access to work at wage rates they are willing to accept.'[38] The CIE advocated the right to work as regardless of wages and conditions. The Commission concluded that because of the 'lack of information about the work of students, in part because students and institutions

36 *ibid*, 106.
37 Cited in *ibid*, 107.
38 *ibid*.

are unlikely to disclose practices which may be illegal or at least may be perceived as doubtful, it is not clear to what extent this is occurring'. Despite this lack of clarity it decided not to initiate an empirical investigation of potential exploitation.

By contrast, in 1996 the Bureau of Immigration, Multiculturalism and Population Research sponsored an empirical study of the impact of providing international students with the right to work on the Australian labour market. The methodology underpinning this study was limited to the assembling of secondary sources of data and surveys of higher education international students, employers of these students and higher education providers. These methods led the investigators to conclude the effect of granting international students the right to work was more than offset by the increase in the demand for labour. This conclusion was reached by calculating international student expenditures and contrasting the results against the total number of hours students were legally entitled to labour and the number of hours they reported they did work. The latter figure was deemed particularly important as it suggested international students worked only 2.7 hours per week on average over the course of the year. The low average hours generated by the investigators' survey was accepted at face value and used to dismiss concerns that international students might be displacing domestic workers. It was conceded that there was reason to be concerned at the tendency for these students to crowd into a small number of occupations but this danger was quickly dismissed with the observation that any impact was 'moderated by the relatively small number of overseas students in the labour force'.[39] This calculation reflected not least the fact that proportion of international students studying in Australia at the time was calculated to be equal to only one-half of 1 per cent (0.5 per cent) of the Australian workforce.

The conclusion of the Commission and the Bureau that international student work would have a positive impact overall has informed the policies of all subsequent state, territory and federal administrations. This has been the case even though the number of international student visa holders has risen from 41 500 when the Bureau study was undertaken, to 519 000 in 2008, and consequently the number of international students is now equal to 5 per cent of the labour

39 Baker et al., 1996, 105.

force rather than the half of 1 per cent discussed by the Bureau in 1996.

The employment of international student workers in Australia, like the employment of domestic workers, is currently governed primarily by the Workplace Relations Act. The only difference is that internationals are also subject to the *Migration Act 1958* (Clth), which imposes the limit of 20 hours of work per week during semester and allows those completing at least a two year course to work for eighteen months on graduation in order to gain work experience. The 'light touch' applied to regulation of the work rights of international students and their spouses contrasts markedly with the comprehensive obligations faced by employers of the 70 000 guest workers in Australia on 457 visas for skilled labour. The guest workers have bargaining power. Their employers must provide a return ticket to their home country, pay all medical costs of employees and their family, ensure that the employee is paid at least the minimum salary level that applies when the visa was granted, notify the department within five working days if a sponsored employee becomes unemployed, comply with all laws relating to workplace relations and workplace agreements, and ensure that the employee holds any licence, registration or membership mandatory for the performance of their work. The Migration Act was amended in 2007 to include prosecution of employers whose 457 visa employees breach their visa conditions, with harsher penalties for employers who exploit the workers so as to cause them to breach.

The last change to the Act could also be applied to employers who exploit student visa holders who breach visa conditions. In 2008 DIAC streamlined student work rights by granting these automatically to all visa holders without the need for a separate application. In May 2008 DIAC officials met with an International Student Welfare Reference Group. DIAC noted a dramatic increase in people accessing the Visa Entitlements Verification Online system, which it interpreted as concern by employers that they would be prosecuted for illegally engaging workers. However, the regulatory regime remains indifferent to the exploitation of students. The DEEWR website discusses employment contracts, trade unions and minimum wage rates in abstract but offers no information specific to international student workers. It directs callers with employment concerns to DIAC. Those who call DIAC are offered just two options: 'If you have information about or would like to report people working or living illegally in Australia, press one . . . If you are an employer and would like assistance with understanding work choices and visa labels, press two'. No option is offered students with complaints against an employer. If such a person presses either number, DIAC explains that it does not offer any assistance or keep data on work-related complaints specific to international students.

Thus the government turns a blind eye to the exploitation of its student charges. JobWatch, which monitors industrial exploitation, provides numerous cases of underpaid international students who, when they sought to make a complaint, were told by their employer that the employer would falsely inform DIAC of a visa breach. In 2008 the Australian national workplace ombudsman was compelled by UNITE,[40] a union that seeks to defend fast food and retail workers, to conduct a blitz on 24-hour convenience stores, following international student complaints of pay rates as low as $9 per hour compared to the legal rate of $21.63. UNITE secretary Anthony Main said that 'an investigation by the union had found that franchisees were paying workers considerably less than what was shown on paperwork supplied to the 7-Eleven head office'. Workers were given 'dodgy payslips' showing $22 an hour, with some paid for less than half the hours they worked.[41]

Several journalists have demanded more effective regulation of the international student labour market. In August 2008 the *Australian* reported on international student taxi drivers who not only breached the 20 hours but also worked a dangerous number of hours.[42] Yet governments still refuse to investigate student work for fear of negatively affecting the export industry.

Nor have governments, universities and labour market scholars investigated the extent to which exploitation of international student workers affects the employment conditions of local workers. Since the 1991 Industries Commission report the number of international students has multiplied almost seven times. US research suggests that a significant increase in international student numbers has had a negative impact on the remuneration of local employees.[43] In the years since 1991 this question has become more urgent. In September 2007 the federal government amended the immigration laws to allow

40 The Fighting Union for Fast Food and Retail Workers, not to be confused with the UK accommodation group.

41 Das, 2008c.

42 Kerbaj, 2008.

43 Borjas, 2006.

international student graduates to apply for a temporary visa for 18 months work experience in their chosen occupation. This work experience confers extra immigration points to support applications for permanent residency. It brings onto the labour market a large new cohort of full-time workers, with some prepared to work for low wages or even no wages at all to gain immigration points, as the Victorian Workplace Rights Advocate has noted. In some cases international students are paying employers to provide work experience.

The academic and policy literature on international student workers raises more questions than answers. More research is needed on the number of students working and their hours of work, by industry and category of student. We need a detailed map of exploitative practices at work. Further, we need to understand the impact of what is a largely (though not completely) low status and poorly paid international student workforce on working conditions and wages more generally. The remainder of the chapter reviews evidence arising from our own study based on the 200 student interviews. It throws some light on the first two areas.

The questions on student work

The present study asked several questions related to international student work:

- What are your main sources of income?
- Are you working or have you worked while studying in Australia? (expand, e.g., how many jobs, how did you get these jobs, which areas/industries of work, what hours of work, how much were you paid for this work, etc.).
- How did the bosses and the other employees treat you? What kinds of problems have you experienced at work (including exploitative rates of pay, over-long hours, unfair dismissal, sexual harassment, difficulties with language, etc., other questions as appropriate).
- If you have problems at work, where do you go for help? Who can you talk to?
- If you were a student in your home country, would you get help with work and work problems? Are the authorities more helpful here or less helpful?

Most of the relevant data were provided in response to the first two questions (some data on discrimination are discussed in chapter 15).

A small number of answers to other interview questions also furnished data on work.

WORKFORCE PARTICIPATION

'I had to work a lot'

One-third of interviewees stated that paid employment was their main source of income, and 57 per cent indicated they were employed at the time of interview. A further 13 per cent had worked at an earlier time while studying in Australia; 70 per cent worked at some stage. This level of participation is close to that undertaken by domestic and UK students and much higher than that revealed in survey-based Australian studies. This lends support to our assumption that semi-structured interviews, especially when conducted by a former international student, are more likely to build trust in this difficult area of research than are survey questionnaires.

While not specifically asked 37 per cent of those working provided information about the number of hours they worked. About one in five worked for each of one to five, six to 10 and 11–15 hours per week and one-third worked 16–20 hours; only four admitted breaching their visa conditions by working over 20 hours a week. Given the risk of acknowledging a breach in visa conditions, and the findings of past research in Australia and the Spencer study in the UK (see above), we assume that work in excess of 20 hours has been understated. In the context it is surprising that the four who did acknowledge excessive work were brazen about the details:

> I'm working at two jobs. I work five days in a real estate company as office administrator but I work from 9 a.m. to 1.30 p.m. and in the evening . . . in the Indian restaurant I work only on Thursdays and Fridays. That's from 5.00 to 12 in the night.
>
> ~ female, 25, India, media and communication

Another student, who works as a tutor in his faculty, on the help desk of his IT laboratory and part time in a Sydney café (see quote in chapter 5) was happy about the 'good money' and free food, coffee and other fringe benefits. Others working long hours were under financial and personal strain:

Table 6.1 Number of international students who had worked in Australia, by industry

Industry	number	proportion of total %
Health/medical	2	1.4
University	44	31.0
Other education	9	6.3
Human services	4	2.8
Professional	22	15.5
Labouring	9	6.3
Hospitality	37	26.1
Retail	15	10.6
Total	142	100.0

> I had to work a lot. In my first two years when I was studying I had to work a lot to support myself, 30–40 hours of work, and I was also trying to achieve high marks in my studies.
>
> ~ male, 27, India, music therapy

While this account is not representative of interviews, it may be more representative of the international student community than the data reveals. Given the methods of interviewee selection and the immigration regulations those working long hours were unlikely to be included in the study, and those in the study were scarcely free to complain about the effects of excessive hours.

Though international student-workers are often well qualified they commonly have to work in low skill low paid occupations. Not all specified their type of employment and some named two or three industries or occupations. International students 'do all weird kind of jobs to sort out their financial problems', as one dentistry student from India put it. Table 6.1 presents the range of employment undertaken by the 71 per cent of interviewees who had worked at some time in Australia.

REMUNERATION

'We are paid shift wages'

Table 6.2 indicates that almost one-third of the student interviewees who worked were in universities, reflecting high postgraduate participation in the study. However, many interviewees (43 per cent)

Table 6.2 Students working: hourly pay

$ per hour	**number**	**proportion of total %**
7–10	21	33.9
11–15	15	24.2
16–20	18	29.0
21–25	3	4.8
26–30	0	0.0
31–40	1	1.6
41 +	4	6.5
Total	62	100.0

work in low status occupations where remuneration is low and the rates of pay are often illegal. Almost half of those who have worked, 62 students, provided information on hourly pay (table 6.2).

No student acknowledged working for less than $7 per hour. Of the students who reported their hourly rate, 58 per cent earned between $7 and $15 per hour at a time when the legal minimum was $16.08 an hour for a casual waiter and $17.97 per hour for a casual shop assistant. Of these students, five were under the age of 21 and may have been legally paid a junior wage. Nevertheless, the interviews show many international students were paid well below the legal minimum.

> [I]t's a waitressing job. You're doing everything from cleaning the cutlery . . . we are paid shift wages. I am getting $60 per shift . . . like 5 pm 'til 12 midnight.
>
> ~ female, 25, India, media and communication

This student was working a seven hour shift in a restaurant for less than $8.60 per hour. She worked in another restaurant for an even lower rate of pay:

> It's bad, just $7 an hour. Before they said they gave lunch and then they didn't give me anything after I worked there. She said I gave you probation so I have lunch for a week for free, and then they lied to me. When I started to work properly they didn't give anything.
>
> ~ female, 33, China, education

There were more accounts of this type, many about Chinese restaurants. Students are often exploited by 'friends' from their own national community.

> Chinese restaurant give you very low pay.
>
> ~ male, 19, China, commerce and economics

> [S]urprisingly that's the case with lots of Asian employers. They usually pay you below standard, especially in Chinatown as well. They usually pay you $7 or even $6. I think that is certainly too low.
>
> ~ female, 20, Indonesia, commerce

> I worked for one of my friends to do some paperwork. I worked in Chinese restaurant . . . the pay is very low, like $9 per hour. I don't want to work in the restaurant any more.
>
> ~ female, 27, China, education

Ong comments that some students maintain a strong but sometimes false sense of security with others from the same ethnic background: 'They probably feel threatened if they work in a more Aussie environment'.[44] Same culture networking shows itself also in housing (chapter 7) and friendship patterns (chapter 13). 'Unfortunately, as they develop a working relationship with their respective employers, students find it hard to move away from the jobs – not only because it is more difficult to look for another one, but in most Asian cultures, they must repay the favour to the employer for offering the job to them in the first place.'[45] The interviews indicate that illegal remuneration was widespread across low status occupations in small businesses. For instance:

> I'm doing part-time work . . . cashier in a grocer shop. $8 [per hour].
>
> ~ female, 25, China, business and information technology

Very few interviewees indicated they would become assertive if they had problems in the workplace. Of the exceptions,

44 Ong, 2006.
45 *ibid.*

> If I had a problem I think I would just go straight up to the boss and tell him what's going on, and say I'm not happy with this, not happy with that.
>
> ~ male, 21, Malaysia, commerce

> Nine dollars . . . I wasn't happy with the rate. I went back to the boss, I said I'm not happy with the salary, I think I deserve more and he was happy to increase it by $1.
>
> ~ male, 27, Sri Lanka, technology

These examples confirm Haley-Lock and Shah's contention that often those in greatest need of bargaining support are least able to access the support they need,[46] and Takeda's point, informed by her own experiences as an international student, that internationals work for illegal rates because they are trapped in a small range of occupations. Large numbers of student job seekers are crowded into a limited market. Takeda rejected the notion that her difficulties were a consequence of racism insisting it was simply the operation of the market.[47] Only a minority of interviewees itemised problems triggered by discrimination.

PROBLEMS IN THE WORKPLACE

'She was a nasty piece of job'

Most references to discrimination related to the inability to find decent work, a finding similar to that of the 2006 City of Melbourne survey. A small number of students reported overt discrimination in the workplace itself.

> She was a bit racist (laughs). The boss, she was a particularly nasty old woman . . . Often she'd make remarks sort of leading to the fact like . . . 'You people, you don't know how to clean up, or sweep the floor', 'This is how you sweep the floor', and things like that. Basically, it just meant I'm not doing things her way but she makes generalisations that her way was the right way, culturally.

46 Haley-Lock and Ford Shah, 2007.

47 Takeda, 2005.

> But she's not representative of her culture. She was a nasty piece of job.
>
> ~ female, 26, Malaysia, medicine

> Yeah, plenty of times it's happened. I got the experience from my faculty itself because of one lady working in our department and she's very discriminatory. When you go and talk to her, she really looks at your colour.
>
> ~ male, 24 Indian, information technology

Most interviewees suggested other dimensions to explain unfriendliness.

> In the working place some people are not so friendly. You can't really guarantee that everyone is as friendly as you are so, I don't think its discrimination, just depending on the different personality.
>
> ~ female, 28, China, education

Many students found their workplaces friendly and managers and supervisory staff helpful and approachable. Reports such as 'I can learn English there and the people are nice' were not uncommon (30 year old female from Japan, studying interpreting). But there were many comments on difficulties with language at work, which could lock students into lowly segmented occupations and at times triggered discriminatory responses (see also chapters 12 and 15):

> [T]he problem is because language. One time I work for an Indonesian shop and they all speak Indonesian, I can't understand anything. They just communicate with me in English and sometimes they make a joke of me, so I don't really like it.
>
> ~ female, 21, Vietnam, commerce

> I don't want to name the company. I had gone there and it may be just because of my way of speaking . . . It was a sales job . . . Whatever they asked me I had done very well, but I just didn't get any reply from them. I had a second interview of two hours, but they did not reply to me . . . I have good sales experience back in India but they never took me. I don't know why.
>
> ~ female, 25, Indian, media and communication

Personal appearance could also trigger discriminatory experiences.

> People are not very willing to give me a job because of my appearance . . . they don't want me there, they don't want me to be anywhere where I'm visible.
>
> ~ male, 30, India, dentistry

The student did not directly specify what made him acceptable in a 'visible' occupation but given he was a Sikh his headgear was almost certainly the factor. But unlike many other students he was not prepared to be segmented into a lower status job. This contrasts with another Indian student.

> It's just like the labour kind of work. We Indians we don't get any professional work. I have got another friend in my house, he is 33 years old and he has been working for 12 years I guess in India . . . He is so capable of doing so many things but all he can do now is clean dishes in restaurants or manage the till in 7–Eleven. Things like wash cars or waiter.
>
> ~ male, 23, India, business

Other interviewees attribute their lack of success in obtaining employment primarily to their status as outsiders without Australian residency. Voice and appearance could trigger the perception of themselves as outsiders.

> I feel most of them don't want to give jobs to those from other countries. When they hear our voice and they understand our accent are different, they know that we are from other countries . . . they try to give the excuse that we need people with PR [permanent residency] only, or this is a full-time job, or they say something but they don't give the job to us. I keep trying of course.
>
> ~ female, 34, Sri Lanka, business

The perception that permanent residence (PR) in Australia is a determining element for obtaining employment is not uncommon:

> [T]here is too much discrimination between the international and national students, or the Australian and non-Australian residents, especially in getting work . . . If you apply, maybe they have an interview which you are doing the steps, but finally they decide to . . . give the work to a nominated person that they have from

> previous, and it's very hard to accept, because in this . . . instance, you couldn't do any legal action against them.
>
> ~ male, 40, Iran, physiotherapy

The student may have been unaware that employers are legally required to advertise and interview for some jobs even when the incumbent is reapplying and likely to retain the position. Another interviewee stated that residential discrimination had occurred on the job:

> [S]ometimes they see you're a foreigner so they assign you to some hard job. They separate to different groups and maybe some easy job, good job for the local, but if you're a foreigner they give you a hard job.
>
> ~ male, 25, China, information technology

If those without residential status are given more difficult tasks without additional remuneration, this suggests segmentation within the workplace. Despite this perception, the student wanted to stay because he had a good relationship with the other workers and an 'okay' relationship with the boss. But it was not always easy at work without not only local language but also cultural background.

> [T]he problem out here is the international students are not informed of everything. We are coming from different cultures and the work ethics from the countries we come from are very different.
>
> ~ male, 25, Bangladesh, engineering telecommunication

One student worked in a call centre where she needed sophisticated language skills and a capacity to relate to Australians with culturally specific issues:

> I have many problems. I don't know how to handle the calls and everything . . . When you get a very nasty customer and they've got difficulties.
>
> ~ female, 21, China, commerce

Unable to gain work in what they deem decent jobs, the students occasionally expressed feelings of shame, which sometimes extended to their families:

> I see a lot of Indian students coming. They're working in some situations that they would have never imagined to work back in their country . . . I would have never imagined working as a waitress in India. My parents would have never, never, allowed me in my entire life to work as a waitress . . . [and] they have told me never to tell to other people of my family that I'm working as a waitress.
> ~ female, 25, Indian, media and communication

Some students do not inform their parents about their work experiences, not only because they are ashamed of working in low status occupations, but also because of concerns their parents will worry about the effects of employment on their academic progress. This highlights the need for prospective students to be given a realistic picture of the likely employment circumstances they will encounter.

CONCLUSIONS

The global education market has generated a rapidly growing body of international student workers in Australia. The 200 interviews suggest that the proportion of international students who work is much higher than previously estimated, and some work much more than 20 hours per week. Many students are disadvantaged by lack of English and cultural skills and crowded into a narrower range of jobs than those available to locals. They commonly offset their disadvantages by working for less than the legally defined minimum wage. Relatively few students believe these difficulties are a product of racism, partly because many employers who pay illegally low rates have the same ethnicity as those they exploit.

If the global student market continues to grow, these problems will have increasingly negative impacts unless remedial policies are developed and programs implemented. Governments have eased immigration and labour laws to assist education exports. They have been disinclined to regulate labour markets and practices to close the gap between the factors shaping the bargaining power of local workers and the factors shaping the bargaining power of international student-workers. Reducing this gap is key to reducing the capacity of employers to exploit international students and undermine domestic labour standards. Australia should match its effort at building the export industry, with a program of reform to achieve international student security at work and the security of domestic labour.

In reworking the regulatory framework along these lines, a useful starting point would be to re-examine the issues explored by the 1991 Industry Commission study and the 1996 study of the labour market effects of overseas students. The economic crisis that beset Australia and the rest of the world in 2009 underlines the need to re-examine the assumption that ceding international students the right to work does not displace domestic workers. This is the more so as the earlier studies in Australia assumed any displacement effect would be negligible because of the number of international student-workers was very small relative to the Australian workforce. With the number of international students and their spouses approaching 600 000 in 2009 this assumption needs to be revisited. A detailed and systematic study of international students work rights also needs to examine not only students' right to work, but also their rights within the labour market and workplace. Such an examination should be supported by robust empirical analysis that uses quantitative and qualitative approaches and is able to circumvent the caution that international student-workers apply when questioned about their work experience.

Borrowing from the CHSICL, we propose a comprehensive surveillance system that is able to generate labour market and workplace information on a continuing basis. This system should involve federal, state and territory governments, educational institutions, unions and employers. Information accumulated should enable these agencies to track the number of international student-workers employed, where they work and their conditions of employment, and to investigate injuries and injustices. This system will require agreed definitions and nomenclature, and data must be presented in a form that enables researchers and policy makers to use it. As internationals are often employed under illegal conditions, data collection will include studies designed to document the extent and character of this work.

Health, safety and rights hazards that confront workers in the labour market and workplace, the protections to which they are entitled and the agencies that can assist them to confront these hazards are little understood by international students. Any new strategy must include education and training, using a variety of approaches depending on whether the target audience is the students, teachers, employers, community activists or trade unionists. A simple but necessary step would be to make it compulsory for educational institutions to provide workplace health and safety and rights information during student orientation. The federal government could support pilots designed to essay different educational approaches. It could also formulate and publicise criteria that employers should meet in order to have their enterprises approved as venues to which state funded employment and education agencies can direct students seeking employment.

It is also essential for regulatory agencies to enforce existing laws. It is easy to identify international students who have suffered exploitation in the workplace, yet exploitative employers are seldom prosecuted. Targeted prosecutions could be particularly effective in securing behavioural change. Prosecution should be supplemented by the exposure of repeat violators by such bodies as Victoria's Employment Rights Advocate. These efforts would provide information to international students on their rights as well as the risks they face, which would enable them to make more informed decisions about workplaces and whether they wish to risk their visas; it would also deter employers.

Finally, to make an inspection and exposure regime viable there is a need for interagency cross-training of inspectors and prosecutors. For their part government agencies and educational institutions need staff with a sophisticated understanding of the international education sector, and who are charged with ensuring that the safe environment that education institutions claim for Australia actually does exist in the nation's workplaces.

7 HOUSING

It [was] a one bedroom unit. They lived in the living room, I lived in the bedroom. So inconvenient. He was always there. I cannot get out. I just stayed in my room. That's why I moved. I moved to the other place to the house of my classmate's brother, from Beijing. There were so many people, mum and dad, his wife, him and the baby, and other students. One toilet. So I have to line up, not convenient . . . cooking was always a problem, so many people wanted to cook. I have to line up and wait.

~ female, 33, education, China

INTRODUCTION: 'FALLING WELL SHORT OF OUR DUTY OF CARE'

On 3 January 2008, fire swept through a small house located in busy Ballarat Road in the Melbourne suburb of Footscray, walking distance from the core campus of Victoria University where more than 5500 international students were enrolled. Sleeping in a front bedroom of the house were three students from India: Deepak Kumar Prajapati aged 24, Jigneshkumar Ghanshyandas Sadhu, 32 and Sunil Ramanlal Patel, 24. All three perished. 'We had already heard from callers to 000 [the emergency phone line] that there were people inside and the first crews tried to get in but there was no way they could get to anyone. It was a wall of flame', said Trevor Woodward, a spokesperson for the fire brigade. 'We got the front door open and there was a bloke in the middle of the passage way rolling around, but we couldn't help him', said a neighbour. 'The flames were on both sides of the wall.'[1] Three other people escaped unharmed. The house was gutted.

> The wife of one of the men, dressed in bright pink silk, approached the black wreckage of the house, supported by friends. Firefighters helped her as she combed through what was left of her husband's life. She collected items from inside and put them carefully into a plastic yellow bag. A short time later, friends drove her away.[2]

The fire was later attributed to an electrical fault in a computer monitor in the students' crowded bedroom. The owner of the house told the media that smoke detectors had been fitted. Fire brigade officials could find no evidence of this.

This tragedy triggered widespread media coverage, with follow-up stories about multiple occupancy and crowding in student houses, poor safety in the rental market and risks to the export industry. The fire brigade held a Student Accommodation Fire Safety Forum, which attracted an excellent attendance from educational institutions. Brigade officials commented wryly on the sudden interest. Previously, when university managers had been asked to provide international students with fire safety information, most had been indifferent. Two months later, after two students from Pakistan died in a drowning incident unrelated to housing, a spokesperson for the police harkened back to the much publicised fire in Footscray when she said: 'Victoria takes pride in being a preferred destination for students from overseas. Yet the repeated occurrence of fatal incidents involving international students suggests we are falling well short of our duty of care'.[3]

This chapter focuses on international student housing. It begins by reviewing the academic and policy literature on how institutions finance student housing, the character of student accommodation and how students negotiate private rental markets, combining international and Australian literatures. Then it summarises the crisis in international student housing in Australia, notes the regulatory framework and reports on findings from the interviews with 200 international students. Issues include the nature of the information provided to students before they leave home, assistance on arrival,

1 Perkins, 2008.
2 Medew, 2008.
3 Das, 2008a.

student strategies to gain accommodation, their housing arrangements and conditions and their level of housing security. Conclusions in relation to regulation and to institutional services follow.

LITERATURE ON STUDENT HOUSING

Many universities in Australia and other English-speaking countries that provide international education have turned away from direct provision of student dormitory accommodation in favour of the provision of student housing by non-university agents. This is partly due to space shortages, partly because universities are no longer willing to subsidise oncampus housing despite the pastoral and educational benefits and in some cases also because partnerships with non-university providers of housing provide revenues (see below). There is continuing debate about the role of institutions in providing housing and related services. Student accommodation now embraces oncampus housing, homestay, rooming houses and the private rental market. These options also vary in terms of provision of meals, length of stay, tenure fees or costs and forms of management.[4]

Financing university and affiliated housing

Within education institutions there are two perspectives on student housing issues, shaped respectively by managerial and student welfare goals. Managerialists foster housing policies and programs that further the economic viability of the university. They want to minimise the cost of housing and synchronise housing provision with marketing strategies. Ryan understands the key issues as new sources of finance, minimising the cost of utilities, maximising occupancy and high quality 'facilities and technology' and 'residential life and dining programs'.[5] Some managers fear that if they abandon the direct provision of student housing their capacity to attract students will be undermined. Charging 'reasonable market rents and offering good facilities is seen to constitute a competitive advantage in student recruitment terms'.[6] Managerialists rarely focus on housing for low

4 Harrison Properties, 2009.

5 Ryan, 2003, 68.

6 Blakey, 1994, 3.

income students. In contrast those concerned about student welfare examine the consequences of the turn from direct provision of student housing for retention rates, grades and student integration into academic life. Welfare-oriented scholars argue that efficiency and equity must drive housing finance debates.[7]

The distinction between the two perspectives is reflected in their respective approach to public–private partnerships, arrangements whereby universities outsource the financing and/or building and managing of student housing to private investors.[8] The private partner typically provides finance and the public body contributes inducements that may include land and/or allowing the private partner to use the institution's name for marketing purposes and/or to avoid tax and regulatory obligations.[9] Many Australian universities are enthusiastic about such public–private arrangements while glossing over the fact that private partners are driven by profitability. Most private firms emphasise high cost housing and focus on the needs of students with the capacity to pay high rents. Such projects are presented as responding to student demand as a whole but the definition of demand is selective.[10] In contrast, those for whom disadvantaged students are primary stakeholders insist that universities should provide for all students.

The welfare perspective is exemplified in a study by the UK National Union of Students and Unipol Student Homes. Many British universities are demolishing older residence halls and replacing them with new buildings focused on upmarket housing. NUS/Unipol investigated the effects on affordability of housing, including rent levels, the range of housing options available in terms of cost and amenities and the cost structure of the new provision (for example, are additional amenities charged within an inclusive rent, or add-ons?). Their study found that between 2002 and 2006 the cost of living in university housing increased by 37 per cent, over three times the increase in the UK student loan. Where universities had embraced public–private partnerships university housing was more costly. The letting period was often longer than with traditional arrangements. Landlords were

7 Christie and Dinham, 1991; Thompson et al., 1993; Blakely, 1994; McCluskey-Titus and Oliver, 2001; Zimmerman, 2003; Holdsworth, 2006; Bozick, 2007.

8 Crump and Slee, 2005.

9 Bekurs, 2007.

10 Agron, 1996; 2006.

more likely to charge for 'extras' such as heating and less inclined to cater for students who were disabled, coupled or had dependents. NUS/Unipol state that 'The key message of this report is the need for accommodation managers to stop developing more and more lavish accommodation, and to start concentrating on the needs of poorer students' who might be deterred from entering higher education by housing costs.[11]

A parallel study is yet to occur in Australia despite the widespread use of public–private partnerships in international student housing that provide financial benefits to institutions,[12] and are often structured to evade regulation.

> Affected are students who live in privately owned apartments that have an affiliation with universities or colleges . . . One institute has even taken kickbacks in the form of commissions in return for students staying at a city complex, with bonuses for high occupancy rates . . . The owners of the private apartments avoid scrutiny or prosecution for overcharging the students, mainly from overseas, because they are protected by a loophole in the Residential Tenancies Act. If the accommodation provider has a written affiliation with a tertiary education institute, it is not covered by conditions under the Act.

Some institutions, on top of their tuition revenues, also profit directly from housing.

> One private operator, Taylors College, failed to respond to written questions about commissions and other elements of its agreement with the Contributing to Australian Scholarship and Science (CASS) Foundation, which manages [the student housing precinct] Taylors on A'Beckett [Street]. But . . . it is not illegal. Under the contract signed by two companies linked to 'philanthropic foundation' CASS and to Taylors College, the college is entitled to 5 per cent commission on the rent and fees, including meals, paid by its students in the hostel and 3 per cent of its student rent and fees paid in the apartment section of a city building.[13]

11 NUS/Unipol, 2007, 34.
12 Lebihan, 2007.
13 Gough, 2006.

This suggests that such institutions and their private partners alike should be regulated in the same manner as all other profit-seeking providers of housing.

HOMESTAY AND THE UNAFFILIATED RENTAL MARKET

Because of the shortage of affordable oncampus housing, most students in Australia who live separately from their families, including international students, live in homestays or rental accommodation unaffiliated to the university. Homestay at first glance might appear an attractive option that enables international students to experience the lifestyle of the host nation in a family setting. Where homestay works well it can mark a major contribution to international student security, but many homestay students find themselves in unsuitable environments, and this sector is seldom monitored adequately. Few students prefer the option. Most have to brave the private rental market. This realm is stereotypically characterised by 'bad landlords, noise, damp, run down localities, neighbourhood disputes, cramped conditions, and poor value for money'.[14] In fact there is a broad range of outcomes, from affordable and comfortable properties, to situations that are dire.[15] The distribution of international students across this span is unresearched. But the fact that many live in poor rental housing is well documented. The UK National Union of Students concludes from its research that many international and domestic students live in squalor. According to one study almost one in six student rental properties were vermin-infested, half had no gas safety check certificate, 40 per cent per cent were mouldy and 20 per cent had no smoke detector.[16]

Students live in squalor not through choice but because of the combined effects of two factors. One factor is market forces, not just the patterns of supply and demand for housing of different types, but also their own desires to minimise costs and sometimes to maximise the earnings they can repatriate back home. The other factor is the policies and regulations that shape the housing system. The partly deregulated market sustains a thick layer of low grade housing. Students are forced

14 Kenyon and Heath, 2001; see also Humphrey and McCarthy, 1997.

15 Rugg et al., 2000; Charbonneau et al., 2006.

16 BBC *News*, 2008.

into it by an absolute scarcity of accommodation, or by the desire or necessity to live as cheaply as possible. Governments and educational providers do little to check or monitor housing standards or to provide higher grade alternative on the necessary scale. Because students commonly pool their accommodation resources, often they can rent better quality housing than can individual families,[17] but they are particularly vulnerable to poor quality and exorbitant rents in properties close to universities. Such locations have premium value because of the cost of travelling.

OBSTACLES AND COPING STRATEGIES

The fact that students often pool resources is frequently exploited by landlords to augment revenue, even when the outcome is unsafe or unhealthy conditions. But overcrowding of rental properties is not always instigated by landlords. Students sometimes move in more people than indicated when the lease was signed against the wishes of landlords. Such strategies might be more common among international students because they face special difficulties obtaining housing (racist stereotypes held by landlords and/or their agents is one of the obstacles) and because some may be accustomed to close living. Smith observes that 'International students often rely on help from friends with permanent resident status, who are working full time, to sign lease arrangements, and provide their documentation to landlords or estate agents to secure the housing'.[18] These tactics have negative consequences if they lead to dangerous levels of overcrowding or if landlords and real estate agents become convinced particular groups of students are not to be trusted. In 2007 it was reported that some real estate agents were refusing to rent to students of specified nationalities because of overcrowding.[19]

Another student strategy is to organise accommodation before arrival. This often has good results. But it can be problematic if there is misunderstanding or misrepresentation of the housing market. Because many international students lack adequate knowledge, many

17 Rugg et al., 2000.
18 Smith, 2007, 8.
19 Johnston, 2007.

arrive in the host country without a long-term housing strategy, even though housing security is a primary issue of concern.[20]

There has been no comprehensive research on the accommodation strategies used by international students. In relation to domestic students, Christie and colleagues examine how rents affect budget management by students.[21] For students from affluent families, the effects were modest: parents tended to quarantine rental costs within financial support. In contrast rent was a major problem for limited income students. They tended to reduce rent-stress by working and/or renting low quality housing. Rent strained student budgets severely when work was unavailable, wage rates were particularly low or a housing shortage dramatically increased rent levels. Christie and colleagues also noted that students tended to become more proficient at obtaining affordable housing as they gained experience in negotiating the market.[22] New students are most likely to experience housing 'in poor repair, hard to heat, crowded, and infested with vermin'.[23] Likewise Morgan and McDowell find unscrupulous US landlords commonly target students who have just left home.[24] Similar observations are made by Patiniotis and Holdsworth, and by Bozick, also in the USA.[25] This student learning curve suggests points of intervention for regulation and student assistance. Provider institutions could develop strategies to ease students into the housing market, including transition accommodation, information, advice, and training and skill development to accelerate the pace at which students gain the capacity to negotiate the market.

THE INTERNATIONAL STUDENT HOUSING CRISIS IN AUSTRALIA

In 2006 the mayor of Adelaide, the capital city of South Australia, observed that 'building enough new homes to meet the growing demand from international students is the city's biggest challenge in 2007 and beyond'.[26] In Australia the scarcity of international

20 UKCISA, 2004.
21 Christie et al., 2002.
22 *ibid*, 231.
23 *ibid*, 230.
24 Morgan and McDowell, 1979.
25 Patiniotis and Holdsworth, 2005; Bozick, 2007.
26 Day, 2006.

student housing has increased sharply in the inner urban areas where the largest number of students are enrolled and most student work takes place. The movement of affluent populations into inner city areas, the growth of mass tertiary education and the more rapid growth of the global student market have produced a long-term trend to housing shortage, which is now exacerbated by a scarcity of rental housing in urban areas in most Australian states and territories, and rents rising more rapidly than general inflation in conjunction with limited personal incomes, an increase in the proportion of international students from countries with relatively low per capita incomes (chapter 5), and restrictions on the right to work (chapter 6). At the time this book was being finalised these factors had conspired to generate an international student housing crisis marked by super-rents and overcrowded and unsafe accommodation. In its 2006 survey of international students, AEI asked respondents if their housing arrangements were satisfactory. Only 64 per cent said 'Yes'. This international student housing crisis is the subject of growing discussion in the media, among tenant advocacy groups and in government circles.

Earlier media reporting centred on the investment opportunities generated by the demand for purpose-built student apartments due to the growth in the student market.[27] But as the crisis has mounted, journalists have focused on a new sector, 'average suburban homes converted by landlords to rooming houses',[28] often in a manner that maximises profit and avoids rooming house legislation. Gough states that

> Landlords, particularly near university campuses, are finding they can rent out single rooms to four or more people and can sometimes quadruple the return that they might have otherwise make with a single lease. Up to 12 people can be living in bedrooms and converted lounge, dining and family rooms in an effort to increase profit.
>
> Many have romantic memories of their student share house days – squabbles over dishes, parties – but Sherry Oh's time at a two-storey house near Monash University's Berwick campus has been a slog. Malaysian student Sherry, in her third year of a

27 Houston, 2003; Moynihan, 2004.
28 Gough, 2004.

communication degree, likes being able to walk ten minutes to university. But sharing with ten other students – each with their own room and locks on their doors – made it hard to study, cook and keep clean. The house was designed with three bedrooms, but additional bedrooms have used most of the living space. Visa restrictions, Sherry says, often forced international students to use rooming houses because estate agents require tenants to have a regular income. With ten in the house wanting an evening meal, Sherry sometimes can't use the kitchen until 10.30pm . . . She estimates that the landlord gets $5540 a month in rents alone, compared with a standard three-bedroom house in Berwick, which would attract a rental of $950–$1170.[29]

Marshall[30] notes 'slum-type housing' near La Trobe University in Melbourne's north:

[A] two-year-old and his parents were living in a single room in a house shared by nine people. The unregistered house had no smoke alarms or living room and boarders shared a kitchen, two showers and two toilets. The boy's father, an international student at La Trobe who declined to be named, paid $530 a month. 'It's quite difficult for a student to get a house from an agent. I applied many times and got nothing', he said. The landlord could not be reached for comment.

In Queensland, McCarthy[31] reported the deputy-mayor of the MacGregor–Sunnybank area in Brisbane, on the 'boarding houses' around Griffith University:

[S]ome houses were accommodating up to 15 students and seven cars, with charges as much as $150 to $200 for a shared bedroom or a converted garage . . . They are making a killing and ruining the amenity, but also leaving students with a very sour taste about Australian accommodation.[32]

Later, again in Melbourne, Dun and Sikora[33] report that

29 Gough, 2004.
30 Marshall, 2007.
31 McCarthy, 2007.
32 *ibid.*
33 Dunn and Sikora, 2008.

> A millionaire landlord has been stacking up to 48 Nepalese students in a single house in northern Melbourne and dozens in two other rundown properties, say council investigators... The *Herald Sun* visited the homes following the council raids and found filthy conditions, numbered dormitory-style rooms and mattresses stacked ceiling-high. One room was filled with dismantled bunk beds after government inspectors forced Mr Tamang to reduce tenant numbers in each house to five. Moreland Council became aware of the unregistered rooming houses when locals reported seeing large numbers of foreign students using a nearby park facility as a toilet and to clean themselves.[34]

According to Drill, the mayor of the City of Monash in Melbourne, many properties providing international student housing are a 'disaster waiting to happen.[35] Another Monash councillor observed that 'There are over 16 000 tertiary students attending schools in the City of Monash and over 11 000 rented dwellings and it is of great concern that some student accommodations are found to be in conditions that are substandard and potential death traps'.[36] These stories are supported by one university staff member interviewed by the authors for a separate study, who remarks that international students are so desperate for accommodation close to the campus where she works they have succumbed to landlord demands they pay their rent with sexual favours as well as with money. This claim is confirmed by the university's housing office.[37] Staff of a firm that places international students in Australian educational institutions state that students with low incomes are particularly vulnerable to rogue landlords:

> [W]e find that there are huge disparities between the very wealthy and those who are just really scraping at the edge to be able to fund their son or daughter to go to school... budgets vary dramatically in terms of what they've got left over to be able to spend on accommodation... we've heard horrific stories about students sharing, ten students sharing these two small rooms in doss houses around Victoria – it is happening. We're only hearing a small part

34 *ibid.*
35 Drill, 2006.
36 Miller, 2007.
37 Forbes-Mewett and Nyland, 2008.

> of what's going on out there in the marketplace. The students are really vulnerable, all these accommodation cowboys taking advantage of them . . . It's frightening, but it's occurring.[38]

The Tenants' Union of Victoria produced *International Student Housing. More than just a market* because of a 'sharp rise in the number of queries we receive from international students and the fact that large parts of the housing market catering to these students are either unregulated or non-compliant with tenancy legislation'.[39] The Tenants' Union expresses concern that the emphasis of government strategy 'is on attracting the money that international students bring to the country, without regard to improving the conditions for students once they arrive'. It notes that while most students face difficulties when attempting to access affordable and secure housing, for international students their difficulties are often compounded by limited English skills and a lack of local knowledge. If they rent for a property prior to arrival their choice is often based on inadequate or fraudulent information. Other difficulties are lack of rental history, landlords' insistence on a 12-month lease when the academic year is nine months, and visa uncertainty and consequent lack of time for exploring accommodations options.

POLICY AND REGULATION

In Australia the National Code effectively protects government and providers from being significantly held to account for these problems. As noted in the introduction to part 2, the National Code mentions accommodation twice. First, prior to enrolment, institutions must provide prospective students with 'relevant information on living in Australia', including 'indicative cost of living' and 'accommodation options'.[40] Second, institutions 'must provide the opportunity for students to access welfare-related support services to assist with issues that may arise during their study, including . . . accommodation issues'. These services must be provided 'at no cost to the student'.[41]

---

38 IDP, 2008, interview.

39 Power and McKenna, 2005, 1.

40 National Code, DEEWR, 2008, Standard 2, section 2.1.h.

41 *ibid*, Standard 6, section 6.2.

No standard for the advice on costs and accommodation is specified. Predeparture information, often in the hands of educational agents, who have a vested interest in recruitment, is not always fully passed on to the student. Oncampus services vary but are not closely monitored. The Code does not tie the institutions to the provision of further assistance or make them responsible for the placement services; nor does it make them responsible for either the availability of or student access to safe and/or satisfactory housing. The provider institution is also not obliged to monitor housing quality, which contrasts with the situation in New Zealand where the code of pastoral care specified that the quality of accommodation must be monitored.

Nevertheless, in the face of the gathering housing crisis the laissez-faire approach taken by federal regulation has proven increasingly inadequate . Given this, state and local governments have begun commissioning research to assist the development of a more effective policy response. This has included a 2005 examination by the Queensland Residential Tenancies Authority (QRTA), titled *Research into International Student Accommodation Issues*, and an *International Students Perception Survey* by the City of Melbourne from the same year.[42] The QRTA reported that while international students were generally satisfied with their housing, many had encountered problems unique to international students, such as landlords charging newly-arrived students 30 per cent more rent than domestic students and threatening to have students deported if they dared to protest. In contrast the City of Melbourne study found that accommodation was a major concern for international students. Problems included the level of rents, limited knowledge of Australian housing markets, rights and responsibilities, and lack of knowledge about which parts of the city were dangerous in which to live.

The questions on student housing

The present study asked several questions related to international student accommodation:

- Where are you living at present? How did you obtain this form of housing? Is this arrangement satisfactory for you?

42 McRae, C. 2007; City of Melbourne, 2006.

- How does this compare with your housing back home? If you were a student back home, would you get help with housing? Are the authorities more helpful here or less helpful?
- How closely to campus do you live? Do you have independent means of transport? How much freedom to travel around Melbourne do you have?

Interviewees were also asked questions on friendship and family networks (chapter 12) and on their expectations and preparations before coming to Australia, which elucidated data on living arrangements, including housing.

BEFORE ARRIVING

'They are not very helpful here, to be honest'

Most international students reported that until leaving for Australia they had either lived at home or on campus and had little previous experience with balancing the demands of being a student with the need to pay rent, cook and clean.

For many students, one major difference was the high price of oncampus student housing in Australia; home country experiences were mixed. Students from China and Sri Lanka, and sometimes also Malaysia and Vietnam, reported that cheap oncampus accommodation was available to all. In Indonesia education institutions provided nothing and students either lived at home or, if they were from the country, they had to negotiate the private rental market.

> It is quite different. In China . . . when you are a student the university will offer you accommodation. You don't need to find it yourself. They offer you accommodation, they offer you the food you need to buy so you don't need to pay anything for the accommodation, [although] now they change it and we need to pay something for our accommodation . . . But we don't have many problems in China.
>
> ~ male, 31, computing, China

> The accommodation they [the Australian university] provide us is too expensive, especially the college. It's really different with other

countries where the college is the cheapest place to stay. Here it is the most expensive. Yes, that's really, really weird.

~ female, 21, business, Vietnam

The interviewees were asked if they had particular concerns when preparing for arrival in Australia. For many finding suitable housing was a primary issue.

Worried of course because it's my first time to go abroad. How can I cope with this culture? And then how to apply for suitable place to stay. I am afraid because my English is not good enough.

~ male, 29, arts, Indonesia

Before I came I was worrying, can I really communicate with people from different countries, and can I live with them in the same house and share? . . . Because I never tried to live with other people besides family.

~ female, 24, film and photography, Hong Kong China

Most students did not prebook accommodation. With inadequate information regarding the host country housing market, they were concerned they might be led into commitments that subsequently proved unsatisfactory. Many interviewees, though not all, felt they were not provided with adequate knowledge. Those with good predeparture information had relatively positive initial housing experiences.

Yes, they have sent me a package with the information for housing, and gave me a very good idea about what is happening.

~ male, 37, PhD in medicine, Mozambique

I was lucky. Before I came to Australia I managed to find and secure my accommodation through internet. They had emailed [information about] the student apartments in Brisbane. I asked if they had a place and they give me a place. When I landed in Brisbane I immediately just went to the place and moved in.

~ male, 25, computing, Singapore

University housing officers commonly express exasperation on hearing internationals complain that predeparture housing information was inadequate, inisisting they provide recruitment agents with information and back this up with material on the web. But many students are convinced that those recruiting them provided information that was inadequate, inapproriate and often designed to serve the commercial interests of the university not the wellbeing of the student. Rather than providing students with a full set of accommodation options and costs, website and other data provided by institutions make the housing situation seem better than it is or attempt to funnel the students into university schemes.

> I wrote to the international office asking for some accommodation. They just introduced a dormitory in the uni. It's really expensive and it's not suitable for me.
>
> ~ male, 25, computing, China

> The university doesn't talk a lot about it I think. They should talk more about the fact that there is shared accommodation available for students. It's mostly the colleges which are advertised, and they're $12 000–13 000 a year, which is really expensive.
>
> ~ male, 27, music therapy, India

Interviewees seldom knew about the requirements of landlords and estate agents. They were not given basic information on the nature of bonds, the need to pay rent in advance and the possibility that they might have to purchase furniture.

> If someone is coming from overseas they should contact somebody else with also the same language and the same cultural backgrounds, they can provide good advice. Friends can help much, not the administration. They are different people, different culture . . . We need the guy who is living here; he knows every things he faces, the problem [such as] accommodation.
>
> ~ male, 29, engineering, Bangladesh

Some education suppliers and their agents offer predeparture information on homestay and promote this option as a secure and welcoming choice for first year students. Many interviewees were attracted to this option but found they could learn little of the family with whom they might stay, so rejected it.

> There are so many not very good homestays. All they care about is money. So it'll be a bit hard for them [the students] to live in a homestay family . . . If it's very nice, people will stay there . . . It's really hard to find out.
>
> ~ male, 20, medicine, Japan

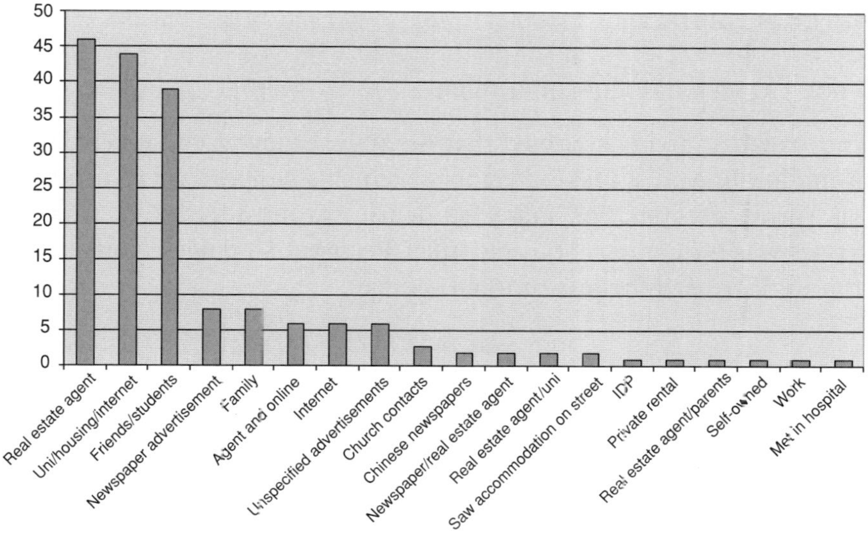

Figure 7.1 How students obtain housing (n = 200)

Many institutions frame the content of predeparture information for students without dependants. Those wanting information on family housing were unhappy with both the predeparture information and the paucity of housing on offer.

> They are not very helpful here [at the university], to be honest . . . I sent them an email from Korea saying I have a family and I need a bigger apartment than you offered me on campus. What can we do? They simply replied back why don't you then rent two apartments? Can you believe it, the rent is $1200 per month!
>
> ~ male, 40, education, Germany

> It would be helpful if specific areas are recommended to students which offer cheaper rates for accommodation for families, as well as those which are closer to university. A little more guidance to help students . . . a little knowledge about all the surrounding suburbs and different rates of accommodation will help them to decide.
>
> ~ female, 37, education, Pakistan

AFTER ARRIVING

'I don't have what you call a room'

The students mostly assumed that on arrival they would receive help in finding housing. The extent to which this support was forthcoming varied greatly. For many students the most effective support service was the campus housing office. Perceptions ranged from laudatory to distressed for institutional service.

> I was really impressed with the support I got when I first arrived here at [university name]. I had nowhere to live and I didn't know what I was doing . . . I didn't know anything and they came and met me at the airport and took us in a bus to the [transitional housing] . . . took me to open a bank account and all this kind of stuff. And they found me a place to live within two days, which was really good. People really went beyond.
>
> ~ female, 23, psychology, UK

> I am very disappointed with the international centre till today. They have not helped me. They are not really giving me any help in term of settling down. You know when I started the course . . . the information given to me [was] that they would take care of everything . . . even they can help me with the accommodation.
>
> ~ female, 29, education, India

A number of students emphasised that new arrivals needed information on how to make choices regarding leases, shared housing and basic services. Many appeared to have depended primarily on friends for advice.

> No one tells you what to do. If you want to share the house, maybe you hear from a friend . . . Electrical connection or phone connection. Which package I should take, and all that? You have to think by your own. If you've luck, you picked the right one. Or wrong one.
>
> ~ male, 28, engineering, Pakistan

SEEKING ACCOMMODATION

Most students obtain housing through real estate agents, via internet-based housing services or through friends. Often students stayed initially in college housing or homestays. These options were expensive and once friendships were established they moved into shared housing.

> At first I lived in homestay because I don't have any relative or friends here. The language school arranged me to a homestay. After living [there] for four weeks found it too expensive . . . I think homestay is very good, especially for newcomer[s] . . . If you're living with local people, you know all the facilities, culture, issues like that, it's really helpful in the beginning.
>
> ~ female, 25, engineering, China

> When I first come I live with my auntie for more than one year, less than two years, because to save money for accommodation and I don't have to worry about eating. After that I move out like for more freedom, move out with my friends, international students so we just all share.
>
> ~ female, 24, management, Malaysia

Figure 7.2 confirms that students have few contacts when they first arrive and over time expand the number of contacts and their understanding of the housing market. Initially, students rely primarily on the educational institution and to a lesser extent family, newspaper advertising and real estate agents. They come to access other opportunities and the pattern becomes more complex and diversified.

Students with children had particular difficulties finding accommodation.

> [I got this flat] through what they call an agent. I saw an announcement and I went to look for houses and applied. I applied to a couple of houses and was fortunate to get this one . . . many people they don't like to rent houses to kids, when you have kids.
>
> ~ male, 37, PhD in medicine, Mozambique

Open cultural discrimination was relatively rare, but some cases were cited.

> Just a few days ago the Malaysian couple that I know, they have to move out of their place . . . they know a house that was vacant,

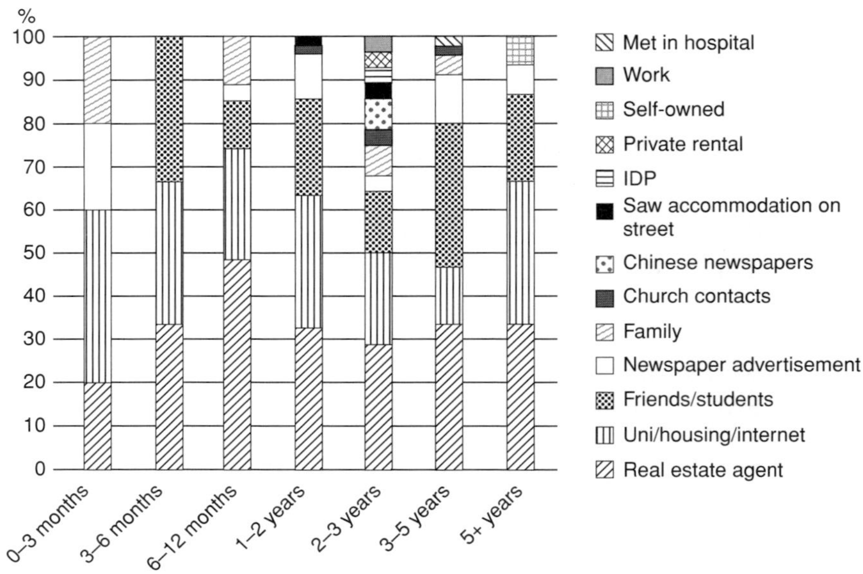

Figure 7.2 Method of obtaining housing and length of time in Australia

and was available, and then they applied for the house. When they went to see the agent, the agent said: 'Oh, I'm sorry, the landlord of that house doesn't want coloured to live in that house. The house is only rented for Australians'. And that I think is a bit too much . . . it's a bit sad. How can people think of us like that?

~ male, 31, community development, Indonesia

LOCATION

As with students everywhere, international students in Australian prefer to live close to campus. Interviewees were asked how long it took to get to university in terms of their most commonly used means of transport. Table 7.1 shows the results.

Some of the international students used a combination of modes of travel to university. Figure 7.3 shows the number using each mode.

Several students reported that when intitially seeking housing they did not know where properties were located in relation to the university. Initial accommodation choices sometimes proved unsuitable.

Table 7.1 International students' travelling distance from university

Distance from university Minutes	Students at this distance n = 200	Proportion of all students %
Less than 10	38	19.0
10–20	61	30.5
20–30	20	10.0
30–60	35	17.5
60–120	4	2.0
Data not available	42	21.0
Total	200	100

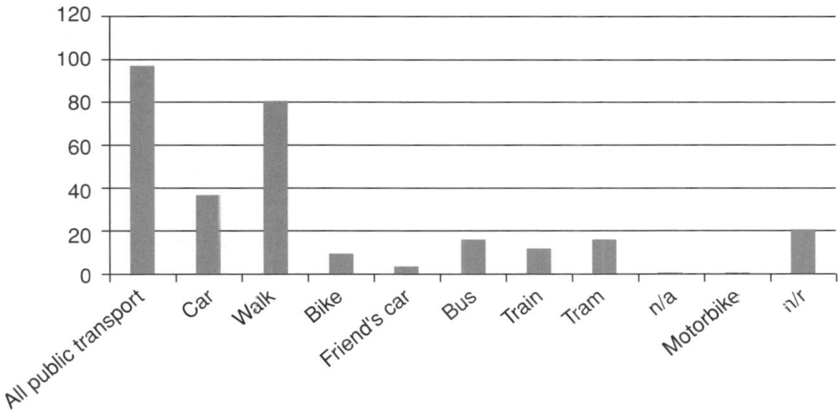

Figure 7.3 Travelling to university (n = 200)

> The first accommodation I found . . . it was very far. I didn't know. I had no idea which one is close to my school . . . They told me to give them deposit for six months and then I had to move out because it's too far to go to school. They didn't want to give me the deposit back.
>
> ~ female, 33, education, China

But living closer to the university could also mean increasing the risk of crime.

> I live there three months and then I changed because my house has been broken [into], my laptop and digital camera stolen. I find it very common thing. Two of my classmates, they also have been broken [into]. Laptop is stole. So I went to move to an apartment,

> but a month ago, it has been broken [into] . . . fortunately when the burglar entered, he entered my bedroom, I was asleep. It's in the morning about 6 o'clock. And I saw him. He opened the door, I heard a noise, I opened my eyes and I saw him. I didn't scream, I just think, he must want to take something and I want to call my friends, but when I move, he saw me and he just ran . . . He didn't take anything, he just break the window. Now, we ask agent to put the lock the window. We have signed one-year contract and if you move frequently it is very tired . . . very tired to find a new house.
>
> ~ female, 22, environmental engineering, China

One student decided the extra travel time was worth the peace of mind.

> I'm staying in an area that is really quiet . . . When I came here I wanted to stay closer to the uni but that suburb is not as safe as here . . . For me maybe it might be different, but raising a teenage girl . . . this is the kind of security that I'm concerned about . . . that's why I ended up finding a place away.
>
> ~ female, 36, engineering, South Africa

DEALING WITH AGENTS

When students utilise real estate agents, unless they the students are clear on rules, obligations and rights they are highly vulnerable. This vulnerability can and is exploited by the unscrupulous. As the literature suggests, this is especially prevelant when international students are learning to negotiate the rental market.

> So many things to think about . . . I learn this from experience: when I move out I have to clean everything perfectly, steam cleaning the floor, otherwise I cannot get my bond back. Yes, this is what I learn.
>
> ~ female, 40, education, Thailand

> When we [aren't] familiar with the rules and regulations we couldn't actually apply for our rights. We don't know which rights do we have, and we don't know how we apply. All interactions actually depend on the other person, not me. [If] the other person doesn't want to do a thing for me I couldn't force him.
>
> ~ male, 40, physiotherapy, Iran

Many international students commented on maintenance of the properties they inhabited and the speed at which agents or landlords responded to problems. As with domestic students, these situations varied dramatically.

> The agents are not as helpful as we expected, because maybe back home whenever there is a problem we just call the agent any time of the day. When I first shifted to this unit, we had a choked toilet and the bath tub was flooding so I called the agent at 5.30 . . . in the evening, because it seemed to be an emergency. Being new here we don't know who to approach. We were told off. 'You should refrain calling this time of the day because the offices are closed.' So I said to her, 'Who am I to approach if the bathtub is choked up? If I'm living alone I don't mind, but the faeces are coming up and I have a kid, and the house is smelling'. So she told me, 'No, we can't send anyone until the morning'. So we ask, 'What happens if it overflows?' And she said, 'No, it definitely will not overflow'. We didn't trust her word so we actually called the emergency number. The plumber came and took a look and said, 'It's good that you called because you were overflowed and you were going to have a problem.'
>
> ~ female, 32, business, Singapore

> The landlord is really good. He trusts me and he doesn't bother me with problems. He says, 'Look, we're a family. If you're not happy, if there's something wrong with the flat just call me and I will fix it'. He's very good in that way.
>
> ~ female, 40, gender studies, Papua New Guinea

> Initially, I had a bit of friction with my landlord. I don't know why, she doesn't want to talk to me . . . but now it's alright. One day when I went there I saw her, I just like chatted with her and I think that eased the whole tension.
>
> ~ female, 27, engineering, Singapore

TYPES OF HOUSING

Interviewees were asked about their housing. The results are listed in table 7.2.

Table 7.2 Types of housing at time of interview

Type of housing	Single students	Married students	Insufficient data	All students
Flat/apartment/unit (sole or shared occupancy)	64	34		98
House (sole or shared occupancy)	53	9		62
University-based accommodation	9	0		9
Hostel	8	0		8
Homestay	5	0		5
Temporary accommodation	1	1		2
Not specified	5	1		16
Data on housing not provided			10	10
Total	145	45	10	200

Most students live in flats or apartments, usually two bedrooms if sharing and one bedroom if alone. Many single students lived in shared houses as did some married students, though three-quarters of married students were in apartments.

> It's a two bedroom flat. Me and my daughter and husband in one bedroom, another couple in one bedroom.
>
> ~ female, 33, environmental management, Bangladesh

Only nine students were in university or college housing. Yet for many interviewees, their in-principle first preference was college accommodation. Living among a large number of peers made adaptation easier and maximised personal safety. Residential colleges provided all the essential facilities and backup.

> I stay in International House . . . it's a residence. It's convenience, because it's on campus. It's nice. No complaints. There are about 200 students, international students.
>
> ~ female, 22, business, India

> You get to meet a lot of people from different backgrounds and you also assimilate very fast into the local culture because there are so many Australians there. You don't just meet them for class. You live with these people, you talk to them every day, you get to see them when you go for supper. I think that helps, in

assimilating me into Australia life in a shorter time . . . Being in a college environment, that is the safest accommodation you can get in the university, because at any one time if you really meet with any danger there are 240 of us to help you. Unless the threat comes from within the 240 people. Thankfully, that has not happened so far and hopefully it will not happen.

I would definitely encourage them [future international students] at least for the first year [to] stay in the college. I think that really helped me in so many aspects. To not worry about food, and therefore time, I have more time to study. It helped me to integrate into Australian society in a very fast way, helped to me socialise, make friends with people . . . It's definitely more costly than if you were to live outside but I think if you want a real overseas study experience, you need to live in a college for an amount of time.

~ male, 24, arts, Malaysia

All other problems like loneliness and study related problems, health problems, travel expenses, all of those are . . . cushioned by the college. We are provided with food, internet connection, book-loan services.

~ male, 20, business, Malaysia

These findings are inconsistent with UK research by Christie and colleagues, who noted that domestic students often moved into private rental housing after a year in college because they did not know other residents and 'encountered a considerable amount of petty theft'.[43] That study did not focus on international students who have special needs for language acquisition and ease of networking. Nevertheless, while it is clear that a great many students in the present study living in shared housing would prefer to reside in college, it was simply beyond their reach. Many cited high prices and low availability, confirming the literature. This study supports the main body of research. Financial capacity shapes housing choices. But having determined they cannot afford college, many internationals find they attain much less in the private rental market than initially envisaged.

It's too expensive in this country. We pay about half of our wages for accommodation and billing only, electrical, gas, water, and

43 Christie et al., 2002, 219.

> telephone billing. First accommodation and servicing for transport, health, clothes, electricity, gas, telephone, water is too expensive.
>
> ~ male, 40, physiotherapy, Iran

Interviewees said prospective students should be better informed about the housing market. One Bangladeshi student said she was giving up, dropping out of her degree, going home. Strenuous efforts to find affordable housing had failed.

Students' descriptions of their living arrangements often suggested they were in rooming house situations, many with more than four flatmates. Some noted that the property might be in breach of restrictions, rules or requirements.

> I don't have what you call a room. Mine is a living room partition. It's not really locked up so I prefer to call it my shack. There is actually a living room and a lounge, the lounge is where the kitchen and TV is. I got the living room.
>
> ~ female, 21, engineering, China

> We have about ten or more people inside a house, that's divided by partition . . . a shared house. The house is specially designed to accommodate students.
>
> ~ female, 25, architecture, Malaysia

> My house is about four rooms, and we are five living . . . Mostly you will find at least two people living in one room. Those real estate agents say you can't sublet and stuff like that, but students have to live like that.
>
> ~ male, 19, business, Pakistan

> There are students from Indonesia, Chinese, Pakistan, Germany and Australia. It's a shared kitchen. We have our own shelves in the kitchen. The owner provides several fridges, two bathrooms and two toilets.
>
> ~ female, 34, education, Indonesia

Interviewees often commented on the negative impact on the social dynamics that results from utilising all the social space in the house or flat as bedrooms.

> Most of the time they just stay in their rooms. It's an apartment of two bedrooms and one living room. We [are] three people. The

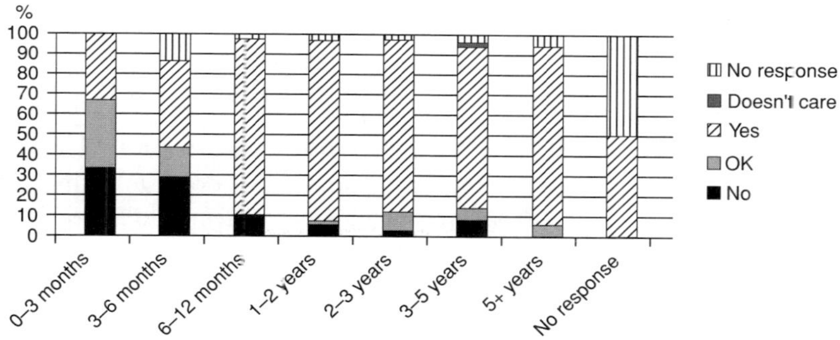

Figure 7.4 Satisfaction with existing housing arrangements

> Chinese boy lives in the living room. There's no common room for the three people.
>
> Yes [I just stay in my room]. Most of the time I like to open my door so that somebody if they have time they can talk with me. But they just close the door.
>
> ~ female, 25, business, China

More life-threatening risks are also entailed, as the tragic January 2008 house fire showed. One outcome of not being informed by education agents, real estate agents or education institutions about relevant housing laws is that students live in arrangements they describe as share houses but which are in fact defined legally as boarding houses under tenancy laws and subject to specific regulations. But frequently, such facilities are not registered with local councils and are often non-compliant with laws enacted to protect health and safety of tenants of boarding houses, such as smoke detector and emergency exit requirements.

SATISFACTION WITH HOUSING ARRANGEMENTS

'It did take me four or five months to find that place'

Interviewees were asked if they were satisfied with their housing arrangements. Given the options available 82 per cent were satisfied. Students who had spent more than six months in Australia were decidedly more content (figure 7.4), which suggests that six months is sufficient time for most internationals to settle, and that during the initial learning period many are in need of assistance. This would seem to support the idea of students living on campus in the first six to 12 months.

> Now I feel very settled, at home, and happy with the people I live with. The first two live-in situations were not quite as good. The first one was a mixture of feeling I was spending too much time commuting, and also not necessarily being comfortable with my room-mates. [With] the second one, the room-mates were fine but I wasn't necessarily happy with the location. Now I'm happy with the people I live with and where I live, but it did take me four or five months to find that place, from July to December. It had an impact overall on my sense of satisfaction with my first few months in Australia.
>
> ~ male, 24, business and law, USA

Of the 45 married students, 33 had brought their families with them. These students usually lived in their own family unit though some families live with one or two other international students or friends. Of the single students, most lived in shared situations with other students; less than one in 20 live alone. Students who lived alone were the least satisfied. Students who did not reveal their living arrangements also showed less satisfaction than other interviewees.

There was an interesting correlation between the nationality of housemates and students' satisfaction. The small number of students living with local students or with a local family unanimously expressed satisfaction with their living arrangements. Students who lived with other international students or in shared arrangements that did not specify nationality showed less satisfaction than students who lived with their family or with students of the same nationality. Chapter 13 provides more detail on the living arrangements and friendship networks. Chapter 15 discusses what was said about cross-cultural relations.

CONCLUSIONS

The housing needs of the three million international students studying outside their home countries is an under-researched topic. In countries where international education has been commodified, as in Australia and the UK, this need is urgent. There university managers have turned away from the subsidised accommodation traditional in university colleges in favour of profit making housing partnerships without regard for the needs of poorer students and/or the transfer of housing responsibilities to the private rental market and to the students themselves.

Our interviewees suggested that oncampus housing offices were a relatively effective service provider, which is an encouraging finding, but housing services are working within a policy framework that is not in students' interests. It is likely that UK and Australian universities will continue to turn their backs on university residences unless they and/or government become convinced that their present housing trajectory is bad for business. But because many students would live in university residences if they could, there is some prospect of change.

The literature on housing, plus the findings in this chapter, suggest six main conclusions. First, an increase in the availability of affordable, good quality international student accommodation is urgently required. Second, students would benefit considerably if universities returned to an emphasis on university-provided housing, subsidised in the case of needy students. In fact almost all international students would gain from a period in university accommodation in at least the first year of study. This is suggested by both the difficulty of working the housing market without adequate knowledge of local conditions, and the larger benefits for international student adaptation and security that university college living offers. Third, the many students in overcrowded accommodation are at risk because of unsafe or unsanitary conditions. Fourth, the regulations governing boarding houses and other forms of accommodation, which are separate from the ESOS Act that governs international education, need to be invoked consistently by state, territory and local governments. Fifth, the mandatory predeparture information is often inadequate, does not always reach the prospective student and needs to be monitored much more closely by government. Finally, the ESOS Act and National Code should be amended so that educational providers assume a mandatory duty of care in relation to international student housing, including inspection of student accommodation, in collaboration with state and local governments as appropriate.

The next chapter examines experiences of health problems and health care.

8 HEALTH

I hate that we should go to hospital and wait... You wait a long time. In hospital you should be very patient to be a patient.

~ male, 31 years, PhD in computing, China

INTRODUCTION: BODY, MIND AND MONEY

Health is essential to life. Physical and mental wellbeing, the prevention and effective treatment of illness and injury, and the stable management of existing chronic conditions are favourable for all activities. For the World Health Organization, health is a 'state of complete physical, mental and social wellbeing and not merely the absence of disease or infirmity'.[1] In encompassing body and mind, wellbeing rests on self-determining agency, and depends on resources and money.[2] Health has objective and subjective dimensions. Health is even more essential to study and living in a foreign country that calls on a high level of energy and resourcefulness. The financing, provision and use of health services are therefore vital to the human security of cross-border students.

International students experience health services differently to local students. As with all aspects of student security, health issues are complicated by mobility itself, by the attenuated flow of information prior to arrival, by language barriers and by cross-cultural relations. Most international students undergo major changes in their personal, social, academic and physical environments. These changes can affect their health. They also enter a new and often unfamiliar health system, sometimes profoundly different in its

1 Danna and Griffin, 1999, 361.

2 *ibid*; see also Diener et al., 1999, and others.

assumptions about diagnosis and treatment and its methods of financing and insurance. International students are also more likely to have incomplete health cover and lack access to particular medical services.

There is much at stake. Research shows that health directly impacts the academic performance of international students and vice versa. Health also affects the student's capacity for relations with authority, informal networks and social life. In turn problems in these mediating areas have further negative effects that are transferred into student learning. The impact of mediating variables in relation to health is an area that is under-researched. Further, the literature on international students and health (especially that from the USA) focuses more on mental health and counselling than on physical health and doctors. From the balance of the literature one would conclude that mental health issues are much more important for international students than are matters of physical health. Yet international students make much more frequent use of medical services than of counselling services, and while serious mental health problems arise from time to time, serious illness or accident are more common. Although more space is given to mental health than physical health in the review of the literature in this chapter, reflecting the composition of the research, in the data from our own interviews the main focuses are on physical health, medical services and health financing.

Perhaps the abundant literature on counselling and mental health reflects the facts that counsellors write more research papers than medical personnel and psychology dominates research on education. Further, while counsellors do fine and essential work and some are notable for intercultural sensitivity, there is a tendency in research and in practice to interpret cultural differences and tensions as pathologies of mental health, and to model counselling as the route to international student wellbeing through cultural normalisation.[3] Some interpret physical health symptoms simply as psychosomatic, though the student may gain more from physical treatments that restore wellbeing and the energy to cope than from psychological counselling, which, at worst, can invoke its own set of stress-creating intercultural tensions, in other words enhancing or even creating the very 'problem' the treatment is then meant to solve. It is a case by case matter, but the point

3 Yang et al., 2006.

is that the cultural assumptions underpinning service delivery are crucially important, and also that the objective of all support and care should be to strengthen not weaken students as independent agents. It is not surprising there is more international student resistance to counselling than to other health services.

This chapter reviews the international and Australian literature on the physical and mental health of international students and on the use of health and counselling services. It discusses the regulatory framework in relation to international student health, health financing and insurance arrangements, and student satisfaction with health services. It then examines findings from the present study. Health-related issues arise also in other chapters, including students' dealings with institutional services (chapter 11) and loneliness problems (chapter 14); issues of mental wellbeing also arise in chapter 15.

LITERATURE ON HEALTH PROBLEMS AND SERVICE USE

Many studies compare international students as a category to domestic students. Some observe relatively high rates of use of health services among international students, others suggest lower than expected use. Some research focuses on variations in use by national or cultural background but variations in student needs receive less attention.[4] Few have attempted to investigate student experiences and satisfaction in depth, especially through qualitative research, and to hear student voices on their own terms. Here the present study might contribute.

International studies

The main source of data about international student health is quantitative research derived from surveys.[5] Much of it positions the students as being in deficit in health status. Pedersen summarises early studies that indicate that internationals are more likely than domestic students to report problems of physical or mental health. One study conducted at Leeds University in 1961 'not only found that foreign students showed more evidence of psychological problems than

4 Harju et al., 1998.

5 For example Cole et al., 1980; Miller, 1987; Faccenda et al., 1994; Norton, 2000; Kramer et al., 2004; Song et al., 2005.

British students, but nearly half these cases were hypochondriacal'. The student experienced high anxiety but doctors were unable to find more than trivial signs of physical illness. Another researcher labelled this 'foreign student syndrome . . . characterised by vague nonspecific symptoms, a passive withdrawn style and dishevelled appearance'. Pedersen comments that 'the theory is that these symptoms of physical illness are the student's way of saving face rather than admitting to psychological symptoms of culture shock'.[6] Furnham and Tresize compare four groups of international students to two British groups on a self-report measure of mental health. The overseas students, as a whole, showed significantly more disturbance than either British control group, while there were no significant differences between the overseas groups on total scale score or subscores.[7] The authors conclude that health status is differentiated by the foreign or local distinction but not cultural specificity. Tendencies to define physical symptoms as absent, pathological or psychosomatic, to ignore or delegitimate cultural difference and to leave unquestioned the modus operandi of health services recur in later studies. Some studies note that views of international students as in health deficit and/or prone to exaggerate health problems are also held by many personnel in student services.

More recent studies question these assumptions.[8] Reeves and Henry, for example, find students from Malaysia in the UK moderated food intake successfully to compensate for the prevalence of higher energy density food and absence of familiar cuisine.[9] They managed themselves effectively, remained weight stable and in energy balance. Some researchers explore difficulties created for students by differences in health care beliefs and practices, and in culture, communication and knowledge and suggest that both the foreign–local distinction and national specificities are salient.[10] Sharif found that many internationals are unaware that campus health services exist.[11] Norton identified students who find it difficult to understand they

6 Pedersen, 1991, 18–19.

7 Furnham and Tresize, 1983.

8 For example Cole et al., 1980; Allen and Cole, 1987; Reeves and Henry, 2000.

9 Reeves and Henry, 2000.

10 Dadfar and Friedlander, 1982; Thomas and Althen, 1989; Norton, 2000; Arthur, 2004; Lee et al., 2004; Rosenthal et al., 2006.

11 Sharif, 1998.

are carriers of tuberculosis without having active tuberculosis.[12] Dadfar and Friedlander concluded that health care beliefs and/or lack of knowledge may affect student safety.[13] Head observes many international students lack adequate knowledge of the association between safe sex and health.[14]

A small study by Harju and colleagues provides insights into institutional health services and insurance policy in the USA.[15] Of the 107 international students involved in the study, 92 per cent used medical services and 83 per cent of women and men were satisfied overall. The most common medical services were treatment of illness or injury (69 per cent), pharmacy (50 per cent), laboratory testing and X-rays; counselling was used by just 14 per cent. Women had a higher rate of medical service use; more than half used the women's clinic. Satisfaction was higher among Asian than European students. The majority of students had concerns about the services. Students from nations with comprehensive health care or low cost insurance were more prone to be critical, especially those with dependents. One in five had no insurance and almost one in four were seriously concerned about the cost of insurance. Many struggled to understand the medical services and wanted to be better informed. There were varied comments about treatment, with the most negative again coming from European students, only half of whom felt understood by the staff. Ten students stated they were not given the opportunity for questions or explanations in relation to treatment because of time pressure on health service staff. Long waits were another concern. Several students complained they could not see a doctor. There were concerns about staff competence, including knowledge about insurance. Students also mentioned lacunae in dental and eye care, and the need for dependent care on campus. They wanted free yearly checkups, immunisations and AIDS testing.

Harju and colleagues argue for a comprehensive and culturally sensitive health program for international students. They note recommendations from the NAFSA and the American College Health Association concerning cross-cultural awareness and training for

12 Norton, 2000, 188.
13 Dadfar and Friedlander, 1982.
14 Head, 2005.
15 Harju, et al., 1998.

staff, international student orientation, respect for differences in beliefs about illness and treatment, sensitivity to language difficulties, understanding the needs of women, facilitation of referral care for dependents and information about health insurance. The NAFSA pamphlet *Health and Wellness*[16] provides advice for international students on health matters. Its *Optimising Health Care in International Education Exchange* is 'intended for reading and discussion by campus administrators working collaboratively to improve health care services for students'.[17] On the other side of the coin, Jong states that strategies of responding to international students should take into consideration the demands placed on healthcare providers. International students can generate language and cultural problems and require prolonged encounter time. Providers fear they will fail to meet patient expectations and their performance will be found inadequate.[18]

Comparing international and domestic students at a German university, Kramer and colleagues noted that the international students[19] 'showed no clear differences in indicators for physical health' but had 'severe disadvantages' in mental health,[20] exhibiting higher rates of stress, less personal resources and lower health awareness. International students were more likely to smoke and to consider suicide, less likely to use bike helmets and car seat belts, and less likely to exercise. Internationals had a healthier diet and less alcohol consumption though this varied depending on gender and duration of residence. Differences between local and international students in risky health behaviour were significant for men but not for women. The researchers advocated programs that support students' original positive health practices and discourage adoption of health-risks, arguing that 'the intercultural competencies of the people leading such interventions will play a central role in their success', and also that augmentation of international students' own intercultural competencies is likely to improve health outcomes.[21]

16 Green, 2002.
17 Rogers and Larsen, 2002.
18 Jong, 2006.
19 In Germany mobile students, not the resident non-citizen students (many children and grandchildren of guest workers from Turkey), are categorised as 'foreign'.
20 Kramer et al., 2004, 131.
21 *ibid*, 131.

On mental health, much research suggests that international students suffer acculturative stress that is correlated to anxiety and depression.[22] Many studies find internationals suffer more frequent psychological distress than local students.[23] Some find higher levels of stress and distress among students from Asia than from Europe. Some US studies suggest that one-quarter to one-half of all international students have diagnosable psychiatric aliments; most of these exhibit symptoms of mental stress and a significant minority are at risk of suicide.[24] The likelihood of such symptoms peaks in the first few months after arrival.[25] Some research finds that experiences of prejudice and discrimination are correlated to the likelihood of depressive symptoms.[26] The probability of distress is increased by loneliness and isolation and reduced by strong social networks and competence in the host country language.[27] Many studies find that student wellbeing is fostered in networks with same-culture family and friends, and also with local contacts.[28]

A large body of research is focused on student use of counselling services. In the study by Selvadurai, 40 per cent of students saw 'personal counselling in health care' as 'unsatisfactory', the highest unsatisfactory rating in 17 areas surveyed.[29] Several US studies found that students from Europe or Latin America are more likely to use counselling than students from Africa or Asia. Dadfar and Friedlander warned that 'ethnic barriers (such as differing language, values in relation to authority) render cross-cultural counselling especially difficult'. They suggested that 'effective cross-cultural counselling requires gaining client trust by acknowledging the conflict over solving problems in a manner that may violate ethnic mores of privacy and independence'.[30] Some cultures stigmatise psychological

22 For example Cox et al., 1981; Furnham and Tresize, 1983; Harju et al., 1998; Leung, 2001; Murphy-Shigematsu, 2002; Lee et al., 2004; Misra and Castillo, 2004; Arthur, 2004; Constantine et al., 2005a; Poyrazli and Grahame, 2007.

23 Summaries by, for example, Bradley, 2000; Mori, 2000; Kilinc and Granello, 2003.

24 Notes on the literature by Schweitzer, 1996.

25 See Poyrazli and Grahame, 2007; see also chapter 14.

26 For example the study of south Asian students in the USA by Rahman and Rollock, 2004; for more discussion see chapter 15.

27 For example Lee et al., 2004, in relation to Korean students living in the Pittsburgh area in the USA.

28 For more discussion on all this see chapters 12–15; see also Leung, 2001, for an Australian study. Tseng and Newton, 2002 focus specifically on wellbeing.

29 Selvadurai, 1991, 277.

30 Dadfar and Friedlander, 1982, 337–8.

disturbance and its public acknowledgement. Kilinc and Granello find this prevalent in Turkey.[31] Carr and colleagues suggested that concerns about physical health 'sometimes act as metaphors for Asian students' emotional or interpersonal problems', echoing an older claim.[32] Fear of losing face particularly affects east and southeast Asian students. Internationals may know little about mental health services or perceive them as designed for locals and culturally inappropriate. Because relations between students and mental health services are culturally specific, for example, for Chinese students in Australia, specific research is needed in each case.

> Cultural values emphasising collectivism and communalism appear to affect both social support seeking and forbearance coping styles among African, Asian and Latin American international students . . . In some investigations, Asians have been found to underreport their levels of psychological distress because of cultural values related to emotional restraint. Although forbearance, minimisation, and even denial of mental health problems may be legitimate and culturally prescribed coping strategies used by some African, Asian, and Latin American international students, these strategies could mask more serious mental health problems.[33]

But research does not always distinguish between a culturally determined reluctance to acknowledge mental health and a culturally determined reluctance to accept the Western counselling regime. Several studies point to the perceived inability of counselling services to manage cultural issues. Baloglu states that international students as a whole 'underutilise' mental health services but there is diversity in coping strategies, expectations of counselling services and patterns of service use. Frequently, counselling staff have not been trained specifically to work with international students.[34] Baloglu studied 170 international students, of whom 29.1 per cent stated that they identified as 'still in their primary culture to the extent that American values had no major effect on their lives'.[35] Students still in their

31 Kilinc and Granello, 2003, 58.
32 Carr et al., 2003, 131.
33 Moore and Constantine, 2005, 343.
34 Baloglu, 2000, 4.
35 *ibid*, 9.

primary culture had a strong preference for support from friends. Likewise Leong and Sedlacek[36] found that in relation to educational problems, international students would rather speak to a parent, older friend or academic staff than a psychiatrist. In relation to emotional–social problems, they would prefer to talk to parents, older friends or other students than to academic or counselling staff. Boyer and Sedlacek note that the tendency of international students to use counselling is correlated to the willingness of services to use 'non-traditional ways of acquiring knowledge', and an 'understanding and ability to deal with racism'.[37] Zhang and Dixon note correlations between students' 'acculturation' and 'stigma tolerance' and their confidence in mental health practitioners.[38] Gender, marital status, age and country of origin independent of acculturation were not correlated to service use.[39] Students at greatest cultural distance from the country of education were least likely to have confidence in and use counselling services. Chang and Chang noted that despite the stigmas that some students attach to face-to-face counselling, online psychological help is not an effective substitute. In their study, international students from Asia and Asian-American citizen students preferred traditional psychological help over online psychological help.[40]

In the UK Bradley's study[41] found that 35 per cent of academic staff reported supervising students with mental health problems. More than half the problems were 'mild mental difficulties', but 28 per cent were 'serious or life-threatening'.[42] The more serious the problems, the more students were unable to communicate them or reluctant to seek help. 'Students may not wish to disclose perceived personal weaknesses to people in authority'. Another problem was 'cross cultural misinterpretation and misunderstanding of communication styles'.[43] Academics noted it could be difficult to detect 'mental health signs' in students from a country or culture other than their own. Some students found it very difficult to discuss complex, half hidden personal

36 Leong and Sedlacek, 1986.
37 Boyer and Sedlacek, 1989, 404.
38 Zhang and Dixon, 2003, 205.
39 *ibid*, 218–19.
40 Chang and Chang, 2004, 146.
41 Bradley, 2000.
42 *ibid*, 420.
43 *ibid*, 421.

problems in a foreign language.[44] Some were reluctant to use university counselling because of its public character and the perceived stigma. Local and international students had similar problems with relationships, isolation, academic pressures, money and accommodation, but international students also emphasised problems in relations with locals, which contributed to the isolation felt by many, and the difficulties in dealing with a local leisure culture centred on pubs and alcohol. International students wanted services that were a safe refuge for those with mental health problems, but were 'suspicious of the counselling service; they were uncertain about the term "counsellor", the nature of the relationship, how the service operates and where the information would go'.[45] 'Students thought strongly that staff needed some form of cultural awareness training since they were likely to misread the signs and get things wrong.'

For international students, there is more at stake in counselling than the use of professional techniques to prevent, diagnose and/or cure problems. Given that some (possibly a disproportionate number of) international students with serious mental health problems are at a long cultural distance from the host country, and such students are the least likely to use services, how could those services, if they were to remained unchanged and steeped in local values, ever help all students in greatest need? Should professional practices, perceived by some international students as culturally invasive, be imposed on those students? Can such practices solve students' mental health problems in a manner consistent with their self-determination? Or should culturally tailored services be provided by culturally specific professionals, at least for the major cultural groups? Some researchers advocate the latter approach. Zhang and Dixon acknowledged that 'almost all counselling theories applied by counsellors are rooted in the values of American culture'. Given the values inherent in counselling services are 'antithetical to the values of international students from Asia'[46] it may be necessary to modify the counselling theories in use or to develop new theories.[47] They emphasise the need for counsellors to acquire a greater knowledge of Asian cultures, especially to

44 *ibid*, 422–3.

45 *ibid*, 427–8.

46 The generic term is used by Zhang and Dixon, 2003.

47 *ibid*, 206.

assist students less acculturated to the local setting.[48] Likewise Mori noted a 'need to modify present counselling practices to be more culturally relevant'.[49] Not only do many internationals not know about counselling services, but it is also probable that 'the most important obstacle to international students' use of services is the shortage of culturally knowledgeable and sensitive counsellors'. Mori suggests the greater use of 'bicultural, bilingual personnel'.[50] In other words, the services need to be acculturated to accommodate the international students, not simply vice versa.

AUSTRALIAN STUDIES

In Australia there have been few studies, and those that exist are mostly limited in compass. Fallon and Barbara[51] focus on pretertiary international students. These researchers sought to clarify how students perceived medical personnel in the original and host countries, the sources of health information and approaches to medication. They found a high rate of medication use, high reliance on family and friends for medical advice and products, some overuse of services and a preference for medical services in the home country. Some, especially Chinese students, were critical of Western health services in general and the available health services in particular. Likewise, in higher education Allen and Cole noted that international students from Asian nations tended to use medical services more when in home countries than in Australia.[52]

Nevertheless, the 2006 Australian government survey of higher education students indicates that 52 per cent of international students used health (medical) services of institutions compared to 26 per cent of local students.[53] Frequency was greatest for students from Korea (64 per cent) and Indonesia (57 per cent) and above average for China and Hong Kong China (54 per cent). Use rates for counselling were much lower and more equal: international students 18 per cent, local

48 *ibid*, 220.
49 Mori, 2000, 139–40.
50 *ibid*, 141.
51 Fallon and Barbara, 2005.
52 Allen and Cole, 1987.
53 AEI, 2007b, 21.

students 15 per cent.[54] For both health and counselling services usefulness ratings exceeded 90 per cent for locals and for internationals but were slightly higher among locals.[55] Usefulness ratings for health services were similar across all national groups though lower for Thais than others.[56] No specific questions were asked about health insurance but the cost of living was a primary concern.[57]

In a single institution study, Bigelow and Kerstjens found that the three reasons most frequently advanced by internationals for being at academic risk were illness of self, psychological problems and illness of family members.[58] Unusually, for these students health created more problems than language. Internationals consulted health professionals at a higher rate than locals. There were many consultations for minor respiratory ailments, which peaked when assignments were due. According to the researchers, this suggested that health services were used to self-manage assessment pressures.

Song and colleagues compared HIV and sexual health among two groups of first year higher education students, again in just one university. The Asia-born had poorer knowledge about HIV and other sexually transmitted infections. Those from China, Hong Kong China, Indonesia and Malaysia, but not those from Thailand, underestimated the prevalence of HIV in their country of birth relative to Australia. However, Asian-born students on average were less sexually active than Australian-born.[59] In a survey of 1155 international students from three Melbourne-based institutions McRae found that 35 per cent of this population had never had access to sexual health education, and that the majority of students from India and Mauritius reported this aspect of education had never been broached at home.[60]

Gonzales[61] compared the help-seeking behaviour of international students by nationality: locally resident students of immigrant origin who use a language other than English at home, and locally born students. Most students did not report health or mental problems.[62]

54 *ibid*, 21.
55 *ibid*, 22.
56 AEI, 2007a, 62.
57 *ibid*, 43.
58 Bigelow and Kerstjens, 2006.
59 Song et al., 2005.
60 McRae, 2007.
61 Gonzalez, 2001.
62 *ibid*, 14.

The level of acculturation was not related to willingness to seek help but was related to help-seeking patterns.[63] The overwhelming majority of students in all groups preferred to seek help from family and friends to any other source. Students from Malaysia, Singapore, Indonesia and Hong Kong China, and local second language students, were more likely than the Australian born to seek help from lecturers. International students were least likely to seek help from university medical and counselling services. Second language students were most likely to approach a doctor. Australian born students displayed more help-seeking behaviour, 'channelled through their use of counselling'.[64] Female students, particularly locals, use counselling more often.[65] Snider compares the attitudes to counselling of internationals from Chinese families out of several Asian countries, internationals from the USA, and 'Australian students'.[66] In total 52 per cent of the American students had previous experience of counselling or other psychological services compared to 33 per cent of Australians and 17 per cent of Chinese students. Some Chinese students felt that if it was known they used counselling services their parents would be shamed; some felt they might be devalued in the eyes of their teachers. There was concern about the confidentiality of counselling. Snider notes that 'the focus of confidentiality is different in the Chinese culture; rather than the individual, it is the family'.[67] No Australian or American students shared these concerns though some feared their friends might think less of them if they were seen to enter counselling.

UNIVERSITY OF MELBOURNE STUDY

In first semester 2005, during data gathering for the present study, the University of Melbourne surveyed one-third of its international students on health and wellbeing.[68] The response rate was 43.9 per cent. The respondents were largely representative of the source population

63 *ibid*, 13–14.
64 Gonzalez, 2001, 4.
65 *ibid*, 14.
66 Snider, 2001.
67 *ibid*, 75.
68 Rosenthal et al., 2006, 2008a, 2008b.

but younger and more female.[69] Compared to the present study the Melbourne respondents were younger, there were fewer PhD students and fewer students from Indonesia. The Melbourne study also differed in that its primary focus was the students' feelings about their health and wellbeing rather than health care experiences and, being framed within psychology, it was more concerned about the psychological health of students than their physical health. In the executive summary physical health data occupy two pages, while data on mental health and self-esteem occupy almost eight pages. This study also utilises an interpretative framework based on student adjustment to host country circumstances. It highlighted the potency of issues of cultural difference to affect wellbeing, noting that 'various measures relating to cultural background, such as country category, coming from an Asian country, speaking a language other than English, act as significant predictors of wellbeing in the different domains'.[70] Students from non-English-speaking homes and backgrounds, especially east and southeast Asian students, are less well connected in the local context, experience a higher incidence of deficit in wellbeing, are more prone to anxiety and depression and are more likely to experience negative effects on their studies due to lacunae in health and wellbeing. But the Melbourne study seems to have pathologised cultural difference as a cause of bad health outcomes. The possibility that cross-cultural pathologies might be generated by the Australian social and institutional setting rather than by international students' emotional responses is little considered. We critique this approach in chapter 15. However, the Melbourne study was rigorously conducted and broadly sympathetic to international students and provides information of value, including, for example, data about health-related behaviours not covered in the present study, including sexual partners, alcohol and smoking, other drug use, gambling, actions of self-harm and suicidal thoughts.[71] The study is discussed in several chapters of this book.

The study found that 64.7 per cent of students had 'very positive perceptions of their general physical health'.[72] While 15.5 per cent

69 Women were 64.0 per cent of survey respondents, 57.3 per cent of the source population.
70 Rosenthal et al., 2006, 5.
71 *ibid*, 52–66.
72 *ibid*, 4, 66.

reported their physical health had improved in Australia, 17.7 per cent noted a deterioration.[73] One in 20 (5.3 per cent) stated that their physical health had interfered with their studies 'very much', 12.8 per cent said it had interfered 'to a considerable degree' and another 27.8 per cent stated 'to some degree'. The study report put a positive spin on the data, summarising 'to some degree' as meaning 'little interference'. In reality just over half the students reported that problems of physical health had not interfered with their studies. In relation to mental health problems the largest incidence was anxiety, with 14.7 per cent reporting extremely severe, 8.9 per cent severe anxiety and 32.3 per cent moderate anxiety. In total 9.0 per cent reported severe or extremely severe stress and 9.6 per cent reported severe or extremely severe depression.[74] There were close correlations between incidences of anxiety, depression and stress, and the last two were associated with lower than expected academic performance.[75] Connections between physical health and mental health were not explored.

On the use of services, 41.2 per cent of respondents had needed university health services during the current year but only 62.2 per cent of these had used them. 'Those with poorer perceived general health', and with depression, used the health service at lower than expected rates.[76] Various explanations are advanced, including judgements by students that their problems do not merit health service attention, lack of information and 'culturally based perceptions', though the last does not figure clearly in the reasons for non-use that respondents were offered.[77] Only 35.9 per cent of students from China who needed help used the university services, but this remains unexplained because the survey gave insufficient weight to non-Western medicine, and offcampus health services. In all 27.6 per cent of students needed counselling service help, but of these only 19.8 per cent used the service. There were no significant differences in relation to service need or service use between Asian and non-Asian students and between different Asian nations. Of the students who needed help, 76.1 per cent wanted academic or educational counselling,

73 *ibid*, 43–4.
74 *ibid*, 45–51.
75 Rosenthal et al., 2008a, 56–7.
76 *ibid*, 4, 66; Rosenthal et al., 2008a, 56; Rosenthal et al., 2006, 110.
77 Rosenthal et al., 2008b, 75; Rosenthal et al., 2006, 68.

60.1 per cent career or vocational counselling and 56.0 per cent wanted personal or emotional or social counselling, a group in which Asian students were under-represented.[78] The most common reasons students gave for not seeking help related to lack of knowledge of the counselling service and how to use it, beliefs that their problem was not important enough or the personnel would not understand them or be able to help.[79]

Of students using the university health service, 70.4 per cent were extremely satisfied or very satisfied. Given that 41.2 per cent of respondents needed health services and less than two-thirds of them used university services, the extremely positive and very positive groups together were 19.8 per cent of the total sample. This was enough for the report to conclude that 'students had very positive perceptions of the health service'. Other data show that 14.7 per cent were extremely uncomfortable about going to the health service, 10.3 per cent were unable, 27.8 per cent somewhat unable to gain an appointment when needed (numbers being higher among Asian students),[80] 7.7 per cent found the health professionals 'not at all sensitive to my needs', and another 21.2 per cent selected 'somewhat insensitive'. In total 13.6 per cent stated it was 'not at all' easy to find information about the health service and another 31.5 per cent said it was 'somewhat easy'.[81]

REGULATION AND INSURANCE

As noted in the introduction to part 2, the National Code does not require institutions to provide health services, only to inform students about what is available. But the conditions governing visas require students to take out initial health insurance. Health insurance was ignored in the University of Melbourne and federal government surveys; in the USA Harju and colleagues found that many internationals criticised the fact that they must pay for health care via insurance or on a fee-for-service basis. Poyrazli and Grahame noted that internationals found insurance costly and insurance policy confusing. Some

78 *ibid*, 66–71.
79 Rosenthal et al., 2003b, 68–9.
80 Rosenthal et al., 2005, 67.
81 *ibid*, 71.

used self-treatment to avoid medical bills.[82] This contrasts with the UK where international students undertaking full-time study of six months or more are entitled to treatment under the National Health Service. Spouse and children are included.

Brown found that internationals are told they must have health insurance prior to entering the USA but know little else.[83] NAFSA's booklet, *Insurance: Not just a good idea*,[84] notes that, like most students, international students are relatively young and healthy. Some, particularly those from poor nations or nations with national health plans, resist paying for insurance or accept cheap but ineffective cover.[85] NAFSA insists health insurance should be compulsory for the full-time the student is in the USA and regrets that the rule that international students must maintain insurance is not adequately enforced. This resembles the Australian situation. While the Australian government requires all international students to be covered by private health insurance concurrently with the terms of a student visa, during the time the present study was conducted this was not effectively enforced.

The Australian approach to health care for international students is not to regulate the quality of health services or monitor their use, but to focus on financial access to those services via insurance arrangements while devolving health care to the students themselves. Students are required to manage their own health insurance by purchasing overseas student health cover (OSHC) from one of the four mandated health insurance providers,[86] whose websites are the primary source of health insurance information. The federal Department of Health and Ageing also offers an informative webpage on OSHC, which provides information for students from countries that have health cover agreements with Australia and who thus do not need to take out OSHC cover. According to the Deed of Agreement between government and insurance providers, the purposes are

82 Poyrazli and Grahame, 2007.

83 Brown, 2006.

84 Green, 2006.

85 Tolbert, 2006.

86 Medibank Private, Teachers Union Health Fund Limited, BUPA OSHC, Australian Health Management Group; see IDP, 2007.

(a) to ensure that the cost of health insurance does not serve as a disincentive to prospective overseas students coming to Australia to study;
(b) to ensure that overseas students and their accompanying dependents have access to affordable medical and hospital treatment while studying in Australia;
(c) to minimise the risk of personal financial crisis for overseas students requiring medical treatment;
(d) to minimise the risk of bad debt to hospitals, doctors and other health professionals;
(e) to ensure the costs of providing health services to government sponsored students are clearly attributable;
(f) to ensure that there is no, or minimal, cost to the Australian taxpayer for the provision of health services to overseas students;
(g) to ensure that a level of service is available enabling overseas students accessibility and a clear understanding of their benefit.

This suggests the primary function is to ensure the flow of fee-paying students is not retarded by health care problems prior to the secondary function of catering for international student needs. But in any case health insurance does not cover all health costs. Dental care and most pharmaceutical costs fall outside basic OSHC. Preexisting medical conditions, aside from pregnancy, are also excluded for the first 12 months. Though students can take out extra health cover for preexisting conditions and some dental costs it is more expensive than standard cover to do so. In addition, while most universities provide free medical services they vary in quality. Not all are staffed by qualified doctors, and the services are often under demand pressure. Cases requiring complex treatment are also normally referred to outside health providers. University services are not accessible 24 hours a day; in cases of emergency students must often utilise hospitals or private doctors.

In 2002 the Australian National University estimated that only 40 per cent of students eligible for OSHC were covered. Strenuous efforts, including penalties for students who failed to renew cover, brought the level up to an estimated 98 per cent in 2006, though no student has been deported for failing to sustain health cover. Some education institutions have introduced compulsory program length cover. At Macquarie University all commencing students were required to pay for OSHC across the full study program rather than annually. But as Paula Dunstan, then president of the International Student Advisors' Network of Australia (ISANA), told a national forum on OSHC in August 2006 in Canberra, 'What happens in relation to OSHC after the visa application process is largely up to the student', and 'not all education providers are able to apply significant resources into renewal services'.[87]

Thus while the regulatory framework opens international student access to the health system it does not guarantee access or ensure full health care. Students are hostage to variations between institutions in the quality and quantity of health services provided, and the extent of and gaps in insurance shape the extent of health security, the sharing of risk and the patterns of service use. The voluntary and partial character of health cover, especially year one, sustains an ambiguity in security. Human needs are met to the extent necessary to fulfil market requirements while minimising costs to insurance companies and the Australian government. Notwithstanding the apparent guarantees of health security at the point of entry, ultimate responsibility for health security lies with the student. Students are provided not with health security per se but with an opportunity to self-invest in partial health security. If they fail to self-invest appropriately and find themselves facing significant medical costs it is 'their fault'. This suggests that some students would not have access to health services when they need them, or would secure access only at significant cost. Further, the students most at risk would be those in the most straitened financial circumstances, who might seek to cut corners by going without health insurance after the first year of their programs, those with specialist medical needs or preexisting conditions not fully covered by insurance and those at the greatest cultural or linguistic distance from the Australian mainstream, who might face significant difficulties in negotiating health services or might prefer another form of health care. These assumptions are confirmed by the findings of the present study, which are now explained.

87 OSHC Forum, 2006.

The interview question on health

The present study asked one principal question directly related to health, as well as further questions as required to illuminate the answers:

> Have you had any health problems while in Australia? What did you do? What medical services did you use, what medical advice did you access?

This line of enquiry was expanded as required, for example, 'Are you prevented from using necessary medical services because of financial restrictions?', and so forth.

Data concerning health problems, services and costs were also provided by students in response to other interview questions, particularly those related to financial problems, discrimination, dealing with authorities (in relation to university health services) and how living in Australia compares with living at home. For a small group of students who had experienced significant difficulties in health matters, the topic often formed a large component of the interview.

HEALTH PROBLEMS ARISING FROM MOBILITY

'It's like my immune system was down'

As a mobile population international students experience problems specific to the transition. Just as many undergo emotional difficulties and stresses when they separate from their families and cultural contexts (see chapters 13 and 14), a smaller number have problems of physical health, triggered by the change of climate, the natural or urban environment or physical and emotional stress. Two students who had moved from humid climates in south Asia to the drier heat of Melbourne underwent treatment for skin problems. In five cases students or their children experienced asthma or hay fever, in four cases for the first time, in the other an existing problem was exacerbated. In one case the consequences were severe:

> The doctor said it's actually the weather problem. It's like my immune system was down.
>
> ~ female, 19, business, Indonesia

> Actually the main health problems are for my kids, due to the change in weather conditions from Iran. For the last one and a half years I think that my kids have been to the doctor more than 50 or 60 times, and four times been admitted to the Children's Hospital. They got asthma or an asthma-like condition after arrival.
>
> Q But they didn't have it before?
>
> A No, no. We didn't have any problem of cold, influenza, asthma-like conditions, or viral infections at all in our country.
>
> ~ male, 40, physiotherapy, Iran

Two students commented that their health had improved in Australia.

PATTERNS OF SERVICE USE

'Nine to five you can be sick, not after that'

Of the 200 students, 41.5 per cent reported no health problems and no use of health services, 46.5 per cent had minor problems and 8.5 per cent experienced serious or life-threatening health problems. The three life-threatening cases all involved appendicitis. Of the 93 students with minor problems, 24 self-treated. Altogether 88 students (44.0 per cent) experienced institutional health care on or off campus (see table 8.1).

East Asian students exhibited higher than average rates of self-care and non-university service use but total group size is too small to break down service use by national or cultural group. Of those undergoing institutional care, 33 students experienced on campus care only, including the three students with serious problems, while 53 experienced outside private or public health care from a doctor, medical clinic, hospital or other health services. Three students had non-campus treatments because they could not gain timely access to campus-based services. Half those with serious health problems were referred to outside specialists by the university service. In some cases oncampus doctors were not available. At least 42 students (20.0 per cent) definitely used oncampus services either solely or en route to another service; the actual total was probably higher as some students provided data only on their final destination of care. The University

Table 8.1 Use of health services by international students

Location of service	Number of students	Proportion of total n = 200 %
No health problems	83	41.5
Self-treatment only	24	12.0
University service only	33	16.5
minor problems	*30*	*15.0*
serious problems	*3*	*1.5*
Used outside health services	53	26.5
minor problems	*37*	*18.5*
serious problems	*13*	*6.5*
life-threatening problems	*3*	*1.5*
Location and problem undefined	2	1.0
No data on health care provided	5	2.5
Total	200	100.0

of Melbourne study found that 25.0 per cent of its sample accessed campus-based services.[88]

Non-Western health

Altogether 11 of the international students interviewed used Chinese medicine, some just self-administrating materials from the herbalist.

> I went to a doctor one time but I don't think the medicine really helps. I would rather use the traditional Chinese medicine from the Indo shop.
>
> ~ female, 25, architecture, Malaysia

> I had a kidney stone problem. I used the university health service and the doctor here referred me to a specialist, a kidney specialist, just to have another person look at it. Instead, I just took some Chinese herbs. I didn't have to pay, I had Medibank Private, but I didn't want to be hospitalised. At the time my family was new here and my wife didn't want to be alone at home with me being hospitalised. Now, I just go to the Chinese herbalist . . . I had two kidney stones but it seems that one is cured now, because of the Chinese herbs. The other one still gives me pain sometimes.
>
> ~ male, 42, PhD in linguistics, Indonesia

88 Rosenthal et al., 2006, 66. As noted, the Melbourne study did not cover outside health services.

Table 8.2 Satisfaction with health services among international students who required care

Service experience	Number of students	Proportion of total n = 112 %
University service was satisfactory	22	19.8
University service was mixed	2	1.8
University service was poor	2	1.8
Other service was satisfactory	32	28.8
Other service was mixed	13	11.6
Other service was poor	2	1.8
Satisfaction unknown	14	12.5
Self-treated	24	21.6
Total	111	100.0

Note: Components of last column do not = 100.0 due to rounding.

Student satisfaction with services

Most of the students undergoing institutional health care stated the extent to which they were satisfied with the services (table 8.2).

There was higher satisfaction with university-based services than outside services. Almost 85 per cent of those using only university services found them excellent, good or satisfactory, similar to the proportion in the Melbourne study. This included the three students whose serious problems were dealt with solely at university. Two students found the service poor; others had lesser complaints. Among those who went outside the university, of those providing data 68 per cent found the services to be excellent, good or satisfactory; 28 per cent had mixed experiences, including the three who had experienced serious problems. Only two students experienced poor services but this included an appendectomy. There was no significant gender difference in satisfaction with either kind of service.

Many students, from a range of cultural backgrounds and both genders, were positive about university services. Typical comments were 'It's really good', 'They're really friendly', 'The health service helps you a lot', 'The GPs are pretty efficient'. A couple of students thought that they had been processed too quickly: 'They never really look through what's going on', and at one university where doctors were not provided, only nursing staff, there was concern about this. The main complaint about university services was difficulties in accessing some of them, including delays for appointments (several days was not uncommon) and the opening hours.

> In Australia they don't even allow you to be sick at night. Nine to five you can be sick, not after that. After 5 [p.m.] people become totally different individuals. This doesn't happen in other countries I know of . . . doctors are good but here doctors have a problem. You can't get hold of them.
>
> ~ male, 19, computing, Pakistan

The main complaint about non-campus services was delays, including several hours spent waiting in hospital emergency, and several months waiting for appointments with specialist services accessed via public hospitals.

> I hate that we should go to hospital and wait . . . You wait a long time. In hospital you should be very patient to be a patient.
>
> ~ male, 41, PhD in computing, China

Students could use private hospitals, cutting delays by paying a higher rate of insurance. Some with chronic conditions had taken this option but others could not afford it. In the three cases where life was at risk there were no delays.

> When I was just 10 days here I got stomach ache and then the doctor diagnosed it as appendicitis so I got the surgery . . . They were very helpful, the doctors here . . . They helped me even though there were many other people waiting in emergency. I came first because my case was more urgent.
>
> ~ male, 27, education, Indonesia

Another student who underwent an appendectomy had a less happy outcome. She developed peritonitis and had to be operated on again; she stayed in hospital for another month and left with a very long scar. She was considering suing the hospital. The small number of students openly critical of general practitioners, specialists or hospitals tended to express themselves strongly.

> I rarely go to the doctor . . . They were very impersonal. They just told me things I could easily have found out from pharmacies. They didn't provide me with enough care. I don't like the doctors here, no!
>
> ~ female, 28, communications, Singapore

There was little discussion of cross-cultural problems. Students uncomfortable about the mode of health care tended to use institutional services less than others. Some delayed treatments until their home country visits (see below). It is difficult to be conclusive about cultural factors on the basis of one interview question.

HEALTH INSURANCE AND THE GAPS IN COVERAGE

'Health insurance really worked that night'

Not all interviewees fully understood the insurance regime. But it was clearly appreciated by some students who did not have parallel coverage at home.

> I got a serious pain in my upper tummy and I asked my friend to take me to hospital in an emergency . . . Compared to home the service here is excellent . . . It was covered by Medibank Private so no need to pay.
>
> ~ male, 31, community development, Indonesia

One student who cut his hand badly and had to use an ambulance and emergency treatment agreed.

> The Medibank Private that students have really worked that night. You don't have to pay anything. It's pretty good. You don't expect international students to have large amounts of money immediately once they need to go to hospital. If they asked me for $2000 to go to hospital, I probably wouldn't have the money at that time.
>
> ~ male, 28, PhD in sociology, Cyprus

For students with Australian government AusAID scholarships, the health insurance costs of themselves and their families were included. They were very positive about their health security. But for some others from developed nations, the transfer from home country to Australia was a downward move in insurance cover, cost and/or accessible services. A large minority criticised the cost or extent of health insurance cover. The main concern was gaps in pharmaceutical costs, and dental and optical expenses. One American student remarked:

> I find the quality of the service very good, but when it comes to paying for prescription drugs, it's not covered. To tell the truth I certainly don't blame the Australian government for not covering foreigner's prescription drugs, but it is a worry. I had a plan in

the US and I was having my parents pay for my plan, and then send over the drugs from there, because the epilepsy drugs I use are very expensive. The insurance company found out that I was away from California for more than six months, and they want to drop me . . . I'd say like that's one of my bigger worries, yes.

~ male, 39, PhD in computing, USA

The student whose children were hospitalised for asthma acquired in Australia had become very precisely aware of what was covered by insurance. He was asked if this created money problems.

Yes, yes. As you know when we go to the doctor sometimes we must pay the difference between the bulk billing and the actual fee that they charge us . . . sometimes in weekends or after the usual time, we must go to our clinic in our street, or another area that works till midnight . . . In the university we don't pay any extra charge. But in the clinic around us we must pay $10 or $15 for each visit. Also we pay the full amount for the drugs. For drugs, during this one and a half years I have paid about $3000, without any rebate.

~ male, 40, PhD in physiotherapy, Iran

One student habitually delayed medical treatment until his annual return to Germany. He was no longer covered by insurance in Germany but the service was still cheaper than in Australia under OSHC, particularly in relation to dental care. Lack of coverage for dental care was noted by seven students.

If I go to Russia for vacation I always go to see the dentist as well. It's very expensive here.

~ female, 26, PhD in computing, Russia

By no means all students had access to affordable dental care on their return home, and some experience dental emergencies requiring immediate treatment.

We needed quite a lot of money for a dental operation for my child. We didn't have enough savings for that, more than $1000. AusAID helped us and I got a loan from university. The second boy got some decay in his teeth, so the doctor had to extract nine of his teeth . . . [AusAID] had an emergency fund.

~ male, 42 years, PhD in linguistics, Indonesia

Another student accessed the emergency help provided by the university health service to obtain a temporary filling. Generously, the university health service turned a blind eye to the dental character of the treatment. She was one of several students who reported treatment from university or public health services outside their insurance entitlement that provided them with essential care.

> The doctor said that if you go to a dentist the least you will have to pay is $1500. She suggested that I go to the health centre in the university. They have emergency help there. They just did a temporary filling, but luckily I can rely on that. I will fix it when I go back home. They are nice people; they understand my financial situation.
>
> ~ female, 40 years, PhD in education, Indonesia

MENTAL HEALTH

'All this group of people helped a lot'

Eight of the 200 students proffered data on problems of mental health and/or the use of university counselling services. The main problem was stress.

> I have assignments due but can't work because I have a pain in my stomach. The doctor said I'm stressed and this is causing my stomach pains . . . They try to help me but I'm too busy. They said that they could give me a course to help me to relax myself, because they said that I don't know how to relax myself. But I don't have time therefore I just ignore it. I still have to hang on doing my work. Then because it continues for around two weeks, the second time I go to see the doctor he tries to transfer me to the hospital to have a check on my stomach or the whole body. But I don't have time.
>
> ~ female, 21, design, Hong Kong China

> When I feel loneliness I always consult with the staff at the international service. They tell me how to [cope]. There are various programs that help to keep me from depression. I walk with another university student, we walk between each other's houses. We do this once a week, maybe for one hour.
>
> ~ male, 25, communications, China

One 27 year old male from India spent two weeks in hospital when stress became 'minor depression'. He was in paid work 30–40 hours a week, trying to achieve high marks at university, had broken up with his girlfriend and had a strained relationship with his mother. Another student, a 25 year old female from China, experienced severe depression for the first five months. The university counsellor advised her to suspend her course for the first semester, saw her regularly during the worst of the depression, helped with rearranging tuition payments and piloted her re-entry. Her professor was also supportive.

> I couldn't help crying all day long like for three or five days. I couldn't stop it and I was very scared when I woke up. I couldn't get out of my bed until afternoon, like then I have to close all my curtains and everything and stay in the dark at home and I wouldn't talk, wouldn't meet people . . . I felt like everyone was so scary. Yes, I couldn't sleep and I couldn't eat until it's getting dark. I felt safer at night but very scared at day time.
>
> Before I saw the counsellor it had [lasted] a month. But it still lasted two or three months. It was hard to decide if I should stay [in Australia] or not.
>
> Q So the counsellor asked you to suspend. So what did you do? Were you under medication?
>
> A No, I just came and talked with [counsellor's name] for two hours once a week. Apart from that I didn't do anything because I didn't know anybody. I just came here for two hours of talk and then went back to my home. I didn't need to go to the uni again. And I tried very hard to do what the counsellor asked me to do.
>
> Q So they helped you?
>
> A Yes, they help a lot with processes in the school . . . they negotiated with my faculty about my tuition fees. The faculty moved all the money from the first semester to the second one. I didn't know it for a long time. I kept worrying for a long time, because in China when a person has such problem nobody cares. We have very little concept of emotional problems. There is some stigma about it, people won't admit that they have mental problems. If other people know you have mental problem they will avoid you. There's no sophisticated services for mental health

in China . . . Even in the modern part of China there's still no such services. If you are physically ill it is seen as very reasonable to take a rest, but not if you are mentally ill, not in China. Nobody will discover your problem until you commit some horrible thing.

Q So you came back the next semester to uni?

A Yes. It takes a long time to really recover. I didn't feel completely okay when I came back the second semester, but I had orientation again, and took part in each step, so it became less scary. The counsellor and I and one of my professors had a meeting to discuss my problem. He said he could help anytime. It really helped to know that when you have some questions you have someone to ask. I felt that Western people really care, and think from your angle . . . All of this group of people helped a lot and after last Christmas I was really well.

~ female, 25, public health, China

CONCLUSIONS

International students in Australia do not have full health security. Insurance is mandatory but at the time of the study inclusion was not 100 per cent, substantial areas of health care fell outside most students' insurance cover and some students lacked knowledge of what health insurance entails.

OSHC is provided on an annual not a program basis. Perhaps annual provision is designed to facilitate transfers between OSHC providers, thereby encouraging competition between them. But a government-regulated oligopoly with fixed prices is not much of a competitive market, not one that should take priority over health security. It is left to institutions to press students into program cover but this is resource-intensive and depends on coercion. It would be better to require program length cover from the start. Portable insurance credits could facilitate movement between providers.

The gaps in OSHC include dental, some optical, most pharmaceutical and some private hospital and specialist charges. Rather than requiring international students to take an extras package to cover some of this, thereby imposing on them the complexities of partial coverage and exemptions used in Australia, it would be better to require them to purchase universal cover at a higher rate, with a ceiling on non-emergency medicine and pharmaceuticals. A simplified universal system would render Australian education more attractive and facilitate synchronisation with home country regimes. Such a system could be extended also to journeys to and from Australia.

There is a need to determine more accurately where and how much the health problems and health needs of international students in Australia differ from those of their domestic counterparts, and to collect comprehensive evidence on international students' experiences of health services on and off campus. This study does not discuss variations between institutions in the quality and accessibility of campus services. But differences in institutional provision viz a viz needs, and differences in offcampus services, which tend to be strongest in inner urban areas, have the potential to closely affect health security. A comprehensive mapping of services is needed. There is also the question of the cultural fit between services and students. A larger scale study would enable this to be more closely investigated.

Chapter 9 considers the personal safety of international students.

9 SAFETY OF THE PERSON

So if the prime motive is education, go to the US. If the motive is immigration, come to Australia. And the quality of life is as good as anywhere else. And it's safer than any other country.

~ male, 23 years, computing, India

INTRODUCTION: THE LOGIC OF DENIAL

In 2006, just after the main body of interviews for this study were conducted, Australian Education International conducted a survey of international students in Australia, including 3585 who were enrolled in the final year of programs in higher education. Respondents were asked to order the importance of factors affecting their decision to study in Australia. Among higher education students the most important reason for coming to Australia was that it was an English-speaking country, which was nominated by 90 per cent. The second most important reason was that Australia was 'safe and secure', or 'a safe place to live', which were nominated by 87 per cent. These two reasons ranked ahead of other considerations, such as the quality of education and the opportunity to experience a new culture and lifestyle. Among students from Indonesia (94 per cent), India (93 per cent) and Singapore and Malaysia (91 per cent), safety and security were the most important reasons for choosing Australia. It ranked highly among students from all other national groupings, including those from China and Hong Kong China (90 per cent).[1]

1 AEI, 2007b, 24–7.

At this time there was no specific emphasis on safety in either the regulatory framework governing the export industry or the policies of federal, state, territory and local governments. Some institutions offered instruction in relation to safety during initial student orientation, and all provided oncampus security. But students were on their own once they left campus and entered the general community. For their part government and industry leaders preferred not to talk about safety issues. Despite accumulating evidence that international students were particularly vulnerable due to inexperience and outsider status, and the fact that most of them lived in inner urban areas where the incidence of crime was concentrated, no further provision was made for their safety. After all, to acknowledge problems of student safety was to undermine the global reputation of Australia as safe and secure, which is what played such a large part in student choice. Australia was not unique in this stance. All export nations have adopted this position at some stage. The first instinct is to treat safety as a word that must not be named for fear its use may negatively impact on consumer confidence. In other words, the refusal to debate international student safety is a tactic designed to protect reputation capital.[2]

But strategies of denial work only so long as the problems they deny – and the act of denial itself – remain hidden from sight. This twin suppression is essential to the success of such strategies. Once the denial is exposed it quickly becomes indefensible. In a market in human services, denial of the real safety problems facing service recipients is not just ethically unacceptable and at odds with corporate social responsibility, but it is also poor business practice. It cedes an advantage to competitors willing to incorporate safety into their reputation management regimes. When the international education industries in the UK and New Zealand began to openly discuss issues of international student safety, the Australian industry did not. But during 2007 and 2008 there were growing reports in the Australian media about safety problems and these reports found their way into the media of nations that supplied international students. Eventually, the tide of evidence became impossible to ignore. Australian authorities began to move from outright and unexplained denial to a strategy

2 Joyce and Thomson, 1999; Gunningham et al., 2004; Rivera, 2008.

of managing perceptions so as to preserve Australia's reputation as a safe location for international education.

Managing perceptions was much preferred to really doing something about safety and so finally naming the problem. But with the cat halfway out of the bag, managing perceptions and nothing else had become more tricky. The logic of denial still held. The more government and industry did to address the perceptions of student safety, the more they were forced to acknowledge it as a problem and the more they opened the possibility of regulation that would install it as an ongoing concern. But still they strived to solve the safety issue once and for all by pushing it back into the bottle so as to regain the old state of innocence in which all was always well in the best of all possible countries. They issued bland media releases that neither confirmed nor denied. They found themselves calling public meetings at which they planned to massage those in attendance into sleepy quiescence. Or so they hoped.

One such effort to manage perceptions was the 1 August 2008 seminar on student security held at the New South Wales parliament for 150 newly arrived Chinese students, journalists from Australia and China and the Chinese consulate. 'Representatives of the NSW Government, the Education and Immigration departments and the police sought to reassure them and journalists from the main Chinese news agencies that the situation was under control', one journalist reported later. The students were told that their safety was a 'high priority', Sydney was 'largely safe' and if they took reasonable precautions safety would not be a problem. The homilies were shattered beyond repair when Zhou Bo, the Sydney-based education consul from the government of China, rose to speak. He provided the students with 'a long list of nasty incidents involving overseas students'. The consulate had surveyed 100 Chinese students and found that more than one in four had been a victim of crime (see chapter 1). Zhou Bo told of a student in Burwood who had been robbed four times and a Western Sydney student killed in her house while she was on the internet. 'By the time he had finished, the initial nervous giggles had turned to gasps of fright.' Zhou Bo called on the Australian authorities to provide better protection for students.[3] China's intervention, which was widely

3 Levett, 2008.

reported in home country media, sent a cold shiver down the spine of the Australian industry. Student safety and protection from crime had been central to China's decision to withdraw support from the New Zealand industry, with catastrophic effects on its share of the global student market. Six weeks after the August 2008 seminar, in a public lecture at the University of Sydney, China's ambassador to Australia, Zhang Junsai, reinforced the message that Australia needed to lift its game. His agenda was exploitation in Australian housing markets and students' frustrations in trying to gain work experience. Chinese students 'deserve better', said the ambassador.[4] But it was student safety and security that, above all, had been the driving issue.

In response Australian education authorities set up an October 2008 meeting in Shanghai with the intent of reassuring the government of China that there was no problem. At the workshop Chinese participants gave priority to student safety in the sessions and the closing plenary. Unfortunately for Australia an eyewitness reported to Chinese readers that Australia's representatives responded poorly.

> *Refreshing approach of the day*: The Chinese candidness about problems they've had with international students and 'bad news stories' such as students being victims of local crime. The Australian side, on the other hand, turned on the spin when it came to international student safety in Australia. My beautiful homeland down under is safer than many other places, no doubt, but it is certainly not a safe haven: many international students are affected by petty and beyond-petty crime, and I have taped assertions to prove it. I hope the denials are only for the sake of maintaining a positive public perception, and not an actual policy position.[5]

Meanwhile, back in Sydney, the Australian government's essay in reputation management was being fatally undermined. As reported in chapter 1, that same day there was a brutal assault on four young international students in Sydney. At the same time newspapers in Melbourne were reporting a continuing series of bashings of south Asian students in the Western suburbs. The students were being savagely assaulted and robbed on trains and as they walked away from the Footscray, Sunshine, St Albans and Werribee stations on their way

4 Armitage, 2008.
5 Suren, 2008.

home from work and study. This targeting of south Asian students by gangs of youths and men of mixed ethnic origins who were citizens or long-term residents of Melbourne, was explicit and unmistakable. Under-resourced police seemed powerless to halt the wave of assaults. It was becoming obvious that a bona fide regime for managing actual student safety (and not just for managing perceptions of student safety) would have to be created. Governments remained reluctant.

The chapter begins by reviewing relevant international and Australian literature on international student safety and discussing the policy and regulatory environment. In part issues of student safety reflect country-specific social, policy and business environments. The USA, New Zealand, the UK, Russia and Australia are briefly reviewed. At the same time there are often similar safety problems and common patterns in the official response: all governments are slow to acknowledge safety issues for fear of harming the national reputation, and in the case of commercial exporters, harming the economic interests of the industry. Nevertheless, once media and student awareness of the safety issue reaches a threshold level, all governments want to be seen to be doing something about international student safety. It is even possible that some in government may try to improve the actual safety of their visitors (as distinct from simply trying to look as if they are doing something).

The chapter then reviews data concerning safety of the person and property from the 200 student interviews, which were conducted when discussion of safety issues was still being avoided by governments and industry leaders who benefited financially from international students. Most international students feel safe in Australia but some believe there are serious dangers to their personal safety. We conclude by examining the steps international students take to remain safe.

THE LITERATURE ON STUDENT SAFETY

The English-speaking countries differ in the incidence of violent crime and in their reputations as safe or unsafe places to live. Reputation and reality do not always coincide. In global perception the USA is a land of high civic menace. Its dangers are the price paid by student sojourners for the stellar life opportunities it provides.

Other nations are seen to offer less opportunity and less danger. This perception is rooted in popular culture. The characteristic

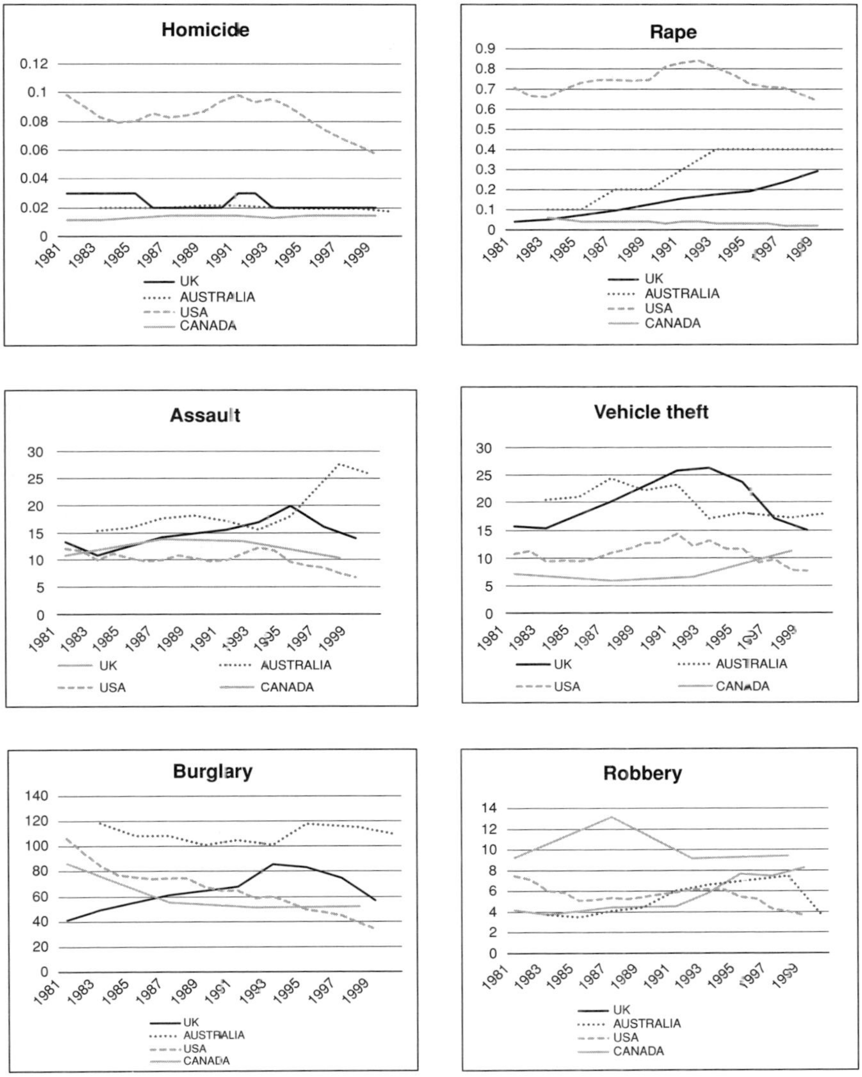

Figure 9.1 Incidence of crime in Australia, Canada, the UK and the USA by type of crime, annual number of crimes per 1000 population (data published in 2004)[6]
Source: Adapted from U.S. Bureau of Justice, Office of Justice Programs, Bureau of Justice Statistics. 2004.

American dyad of death or glory, the narratives of sudden transformation of personal destiny for good or ill, are fostered continuously in the

6 The population compositions vary across type of crime. For example, rape rates were calculated relative to female population 18 years and older; robbery was based on population age 16+; and burglaries were calculated per 1000 households; see US Bureau of Justice statistics for method collection details.

American film and television that drenches the planet. In truth the incidence of urban crime in the USA has declined in the last three decades, much depends on which part of the USA is under scrutiny, US authorities are increasingly conscious of the need for visitor-friendly precincts and intercountry differences are exaggerated. Murder and rape are more prevalent in the USA than Canada, the UK and Australia. These crimes make headlines. But the crimes more likely to affect international students occur more frequently in competitor nations, not only crimes of property, such as house burglary, robbery and vehicle theft, but also assault of people (figure 9.1).[7]

These data suggest that the reputations for superior safety that are held by Australia, the UK and New Zealand relative to the USA are not a forgone conclusion. Perceptions may catch up with the reality of falling crime rates in the USA and the low incidence of crime in some domains and many parts of the nation. If they were so inclined, a concerted effort by US educational authorities to sell the USA as a safe destination for international students might close the gap more quickly (more so if these efforts were joined to a modest gesture by Washington in the direction of gun control).

THE USA

Campus crime is much researched in the USA but the literature seldom distinguishes between domestic and international students. An important early exception is work by Sundeen (1984), which examined fear of street crime among international students at a large US university.[8] The research aimed to determine whether the factors associated with domestic students' fear of crime were identical for international students. Sundeen isolated two variables unique to international students that were correlated with the feeling of being safe from crime. One was frequency of participation in cultural events and activities. Here the direction of the relationship was unanticipated. Sundeen found that the greater the participation in cultural groups and activities, 'the greater the feeling of being very unsafe'. He concluded that while participation in social events may create or strengthen social ties, such activities also entail leaving the safety of

7 Segal, 1994; Madsen, 2006; Kichigina, 2008.
8 Sundeen, 1984.

the home and thus increase potential street crime. He also suggested an alternate explanation: social events enable communication about crime and safety and thereby foster an accumulating sense of mutual danger. The second significant variable was length of time in the USA: the longer international students were there the less they feared becoming a street crime victim. Sundeen suggested that initial awareness of the crime problem in the USA was inflated by warnings in orientation programs and subsequently deflated by daily experience. Two other variables, shared with local students, were also strongly correlated to fear of street crime: the comparative danger of one's neighbourhood and perceived likelihood of total protection.[9]

In part, campus-related crime is an active policy issue in the USA because of high profile court cases in which victims of crime and/or their families have sued the education institution for failing to provide adequate information on the prevailing level of crime on or near campus. Feminist groups have also made campus safety a high profile issue. The USA has developed a legal framework that requires the compilation and public reporting of statistics of crime occurring on campus property and on property that is deemed to be within the campus radius, that is, in the surrounding areas. This regulation, the *Jeanne Clery Disclosure of Campus Security Policy and Campus Crime Statistics Act 1990* (Clth), also mandates the implementation of law enforcement procedures and 'safety from crime' policies. The Clery Act is enforced by the federal Department of Education. Institutions can be fined for non-compliance with its provisions. These penalties are required because many education institutions have been shown to fraudulently hide the extent of crime associated with their institutions in order to sustain or increase their reputation in the marketplace. The extent of under-reporting was revealed when a government audit of 25 education institutions found that 23 had understated the level of crime associated with their institutions. The Act generates a body of public data, which indicates that the types of crime most frequently reported on US campuses are theft of personal belongings, burglary, violence, racial or hate crime and sexual abuse and rape. Most oncampus crime is committed by students.[10] The principal goal of the Clery Act was to increase accountability for higher

9 *ibid*, 12.

10 Fisher, 1995; Brinkley, 2005; Janosik and Gregory, 2002.

education institutions with respect to public disclosure of campus crime statistics. It was assumed that

> Knowledge of the frequency and type of crimes on campus will change the behavior of the students and ultimately make them safer as a result of a heightened awareness of the potential dangers in their environment. In addition, the Clery Act is intended to serve as a resource for potential students and families in making informed decisions about selecting a college based on campus safety information.[11]

Diffusion of this knowledge has been shown to have promoted the adoption of programs that enable students to better protect themselves from crime, raised awareness of the risks to personal safety and heightened student faith in campus-based law enforcement procedures.[12] Janosik and Plummer also found that the Act has generated greater consistency in the gathering and reporting of crime statistics.[13] The influence this information has on decisions by international students and parents is moot; however, it is notable that the higher the proportion of international students on a US campus the lower the crime rate, which might suggest that international students desiring a safe study environment are selecting campuses that have low crime rates and by so doing reinforce the association between international enrolment and relatively low crime rates.[14]

The airborne attacks on the New York Trade Center and the Pentagon on 11 September 2001 (9/11) changed the environment for international student safety. First, following 9/11 there was an observable increase in hate crime and in the discriminatory racial profiling of certain students by police and other authorities. Following the growth of official and unofficial harassment on and off campus, some students left the USA because they feared for their safety. In 2003 Harvard University produced a booklet, *Know your Rights on Campus: A guide to racial profiling and hate crime for international students in the United States*, which, in part, stated that

11 McNeal, 2007, 107.

12 Brinkley, 2005; Janosik and Gregory, 2002; Depken, 1998.

13 Janosik and Plummer, 2005.

14 Volkwein et al., 1995; Larsen, 2008.

> Many immigrants and international students have experienced heightened security and outright discrimination. Racial profiling refers to the reliance by law enforcement officers on a person's ethnicity, national origin, or race rather than behaviour to identify him or her as having been engaged in illegal activity. A hate crime is any criminal act against a person or property in which the perpetrator chooses the victim based on his or her actual or perceived race, national origin, ethnicity, sexual orientation, disability or gender.[15]

The Harvard group confirmed that students from Middle Eastern, Arab and south Asian backgrounds were 'viewed suspiciously because of their appearance or religious and cultural affiliations'. This affected not only individual students, triggering problems ranging from academic difficulties to physical and psychological trauma, but also 'everyone in the targeted group'.[16] The booklet details laws intended to make students safe from hate crime and racial profiling and advises them what they can do if their safety is undermined.

Second, 9/11 triggered what Skinner terms the 'foreign student regulatory dilemma'. Many Americans wish to exclude international students from the USA because they believe these foreigners are a threat to US wellbeing, a longstanding fear that was dramatically boosted by the fact that four of the 9/11 highjackers entered the USA on student visas.[17] Much has been made of this by opponents of the international student program. Borjas states:

> Hani Hasan Hanjour got a visa to study English at ELS Language Centers . . . He did not attend a single class. Instead, he became one of the terrorists in the plane that crashed into the Pentagon on September 11. And two other terrorists were waiting for the official approval of their student visas to attend flight school – an approval that the Immigration and Naturalisation Service dutifully mailed out six months after the attacks.[18]

The message was echoed by Malkin who fomented fear of international students in her provocatively titled *Invasion: How America*

15 Harvard Civil Rights Project, 2003, abstract.
16 *ibid*, 2.
17 Skinner, 2007.
18 Borjas, 2002.

still welcomes terrorists, criminals, and other foreign menaces to our shores.[19] These concerns were echoed officially in the decision of the Department of Homeland Security to subject international students to 'incident reporting technology' that rendered them vulnerable to anonymous denunciation as criminals.[20]

On the other hand educators, business and some state agencies want to sustain the inflow of international students because of their major contribution to American research and were concerned at declines in some country intakes after 9/11, not only Muslim countries in the Middle East and Indonesia but also other parts of southeast and east Asia. Recognising that it was confronting a systemic problem and that international students needed to be partly 'un-Othered' the Association of University Educators (NAFSA) responded by trumpeting the importance of international students to the US economy and national security.[21] It also launched a lobbying effort designed to convince legislators and the public that any dangers to national security posed by foreign students could be contained at a lower level of vigilance than the post 9/11 regime, with less disruption of international students' own security (see chapter 10).[22] NAFSA and US institutions also stepped up efforts to convince prospective students they have nothing to fear in the USA.

US research on international student safety since 9/11 has focused on these issues. Coston confirmed Sundeen where he found that students 'who had heard about the victimisation experiences of other foreign students . . . tended to be more worried about becoming the victim of a crime', and that the longer international students are resident in the USA the less they fear becoming a crime victim. Coston also found that many foreign students believe crime in the USA is no greater than in their home countries, the proportion of international students who become crime victims while in the USA is no greater than the norm in the home countries, the crimes that beset them are similar (primarily theft) and most students minimise the dangers to themselves.[23] Other studies underline that selling the message that the USA is a safe and secure study destination remains a

19 Malkin, 2004.

20 Altbach, 2004; Kichigina, 2008.

21 Bernstein, 2003; Johnson, 2004; Hughes et al., 2008; Urias and Yeakey, 2008.

22 Johnson, 2004, 25, 29; see also NAFSA, 2006, 2008.

23 Coston, 2004, 189.

serious challenge, the more so given the polarisation of world opinion by the Bush administration and widespread disagreement with US foreign policy.[24] In 2008 i-Graduate reported that prospective students viewed the USA as being no safer than China.[25] That same year the Bush administration softened the international student monitoring regime and extended the time students could stay and work after graduation. The November 2008 election of the Obama government provided the opportunity for a circuit breaker. During the presidential campaign Obama promised to reduce the hazards that US visa stipulations posed for international students. After his election, commentators on the global student market surmised an 'Obama effect' in which the USA would become a more attractive destination.[26]

GENDER-BASED VIOLENCE

In the mid 1990s US studies found that 10–20 per cent of all female students experience sexual harassment or assault.[27] Under-reporting is a problem. Sable and colleagues noted that the factors that inhibit reporting of rape and sexual harassment include shame, guilt, embarrassment, concerns about confidentiality, possible retaliation by the perpetrator and fear of not being believed.[28] These factors are likely to compound for international students because of communication barriers, differences between home and host society values, concerns about loss of face, unfamiliarity with support services and legal systems, fear of loss of visa status and greater fears of academic retaliation compared to those experienced by local students. Studies of sexual predation that are specific to international students are lacking.

Another issue needing more research attention is domestic violence.[29] Gendered relations are culturally specific but little is known of how international students and/or their spouses and children cope when their safety is threatened by a family member, how internationals perceive domestic violence practices and sanctuaries, and what help is available to them. Urias found that 40 per cent of the oncampus professionals charged with assisting international

24 Leviyeva, 2005; Madsen, 2006; Pinkerton, 2006, Todd, 2007; Urias and Yeakey, 2008.
25 Archer and Disbury, 2008.
26 *Guardian*, 2008 (quotes from Dominic Scott); Lipsett, 2009.
27 Schweitzer, 1996, 3.
28 Sable et al., 2006.
29 Petersen et al., 2004.

students did not accept any responsibility to act in relation to domestic violence.[30]

> If most U.S. campus international offices are indeed uncertain of the specific number of domestic violence incidents, and many of those offices are opting to defer responsibility to act on behalf of their international population to the campus police or counselling centre, it is clear that those offices are not able to act as advocates on behalf of internationals and their families. While likely reflective of the overwhelming workload placed on international student service offices, which causes those offices to act foremost as enforcers of immigration regulations, there is a disenfranchised campus population that needs help.[31]

Urias urges culturally sensitive strategies that ensure that those under threat make fuller use of legal, economic, cultural and religious resources available to them.

SAFETY FROM SELF-HARM

Self-injury and suicide by students endanger students' lives and threaten the reputational capital of institutions. Whitlock and colleagues found that 17 per cent of students had engaged in such behaviours at least once and three-quarters of these on multiple occasions. International students were more likely to inflict self-injury but less likely to do so on more than one occasion.[32] Gollust and colleagues found the incidence of self-injuring behaviour was similar in both groups.[33]

The situation is different in relation to suicide. Schwartz and Whitaker found that while university students in general are at low risk of suicide international students are not.[34] In 1997 Silverman and colleagues identified the suicide rate among local black and white US tertiary students as 7.5 per 100 000 while the rate for all other students, including internationals, was 21.8 per 100 000.[35] Joffe

30 Urias, 2005.
31 *ibid*, 47.
32 Whitlock et al., 2006, 1939.
33 Gollust et al., 2008.
34 Schwartz and Whitaker 1990, 325.
35 Silverman et al., 1997.

found that at the University of Illinois domestic student suicide is 2.4 per 100 000 but international 10.5 per 100 000.[36] Both Schwartz and Whitaker, and Gordon, argue that international students manifest a relatively high suicide rate in part because they are far from their families.[37] Maris and colleagues accept this point but add that international students commonly come from nations where suicide is higher than the US norm.[38] Stephenson and colleagues remarked that China accounts for 21 per cent of the world's population but 56 per cent of the world's female suicides.[39] Consistent with this, Hayes found suicide ideation is prevalent among Chinese students.[40] There have been no studies of national differences in suicide behaviour among international students.

Hayes suggests that university administrators create networks to identify which students and student groups are at serious risk. Many US university officials find this unappealing because should a student so identified commit suicide, the institution may be vulnerable to litigation. Many US institutions have halted programs designed to identify at risk students. Haas and colleagues concluded that student suicide in the USA is now a 'problem of public relations rather than a matter of student health and welfare' and that international students would be wise to clarify the suicide management practices in the university before they enrol.[41]

NEW ZEALAND

Problems of safety only marginally affect the absolute level of international students enrolments in the USA, but have a larger potential in New Zealand as recent history shows. In 2003 Chinese Embassy officials advised the New Zealand government in Wellington that they were dissatisfied with the level and quality of the attention given to the safety of Chinese students studying in that country.[42] China was concerned about the paucity of resources provided for student safety, the

36 Joffe, personal communication, 2008a; see also Chamberlain, 2003.
37 Schwartz and Whitaker, 1990; Gordon, 2003.
38 Maris et al., 2000; see also Silverman, 2002, iii.
39 Stephenson et al., 2005, 21.
40 Hayes, 2004.
41 Haas et al., 2003,1236.
42 Li, 2007.

licence allowed fraudulent suppliers, the racial vilification of many Asian people in New Zealand and the number of Chinese students who became victims and/or perpetrators of crime while there. Not sufficiently appreciating the significance of the warning by the embassy, the New Zealand government responded merely by referring to the nation's ineffective *Code of Practice for the Pastoral Care of International Students* and making repeated claims that New Zealand was a safe study venue. In short, it responded to a claim of substance with marketing spin. Which turned out to be disastrous. China's Ministry of Education responded in turn by branding New Zealand as unable to protect Chinese students and posted this message on its website:

> In recent years, the number of Chinese full fee-paying students studying in New Zealand is increasing rapidly. The number reached over 30 000 by the end of 2002. New Zealand's limited number of tertiary institutions, its inadequate transport and infrastructure do not have capacity to accommodate such a large number of international students. Most Chinese students are very young and study low-level subjects and courses. They do not have a sense of self-control and self-protection. Therefore, there are many problems with these Chinese students, such as tension with homestay families, traffic offences, violence, prostitution, gambling, crimes, fraudulence, drugs, kidnapping, and murdering.[43]

China's stigmatisation of New Zealand devastated its education export sector. The number of international students fell from 126 919 in 2002 to 90 934 in 2007 (28.4 per cent) due to decline in numbers from China, much the largest source country.[44] The decline triggered studies designed to identify the nature of the risks affecting international students, how to preserve safety and how to restore New Zealand's reputation as a provider of safe conditions.[45] This literature is unique in acknowledging that international students can be perpetrators as well as victims of crime. A small but significant

43 Chinese Ministry of Education, cited by Li, 2007.

44 Education New Zealand, 2007.

45 Ward and Masgoret, 2004; Butcher and McGrath, 2004; Jackson, 2005; Lewis, 2005; Collins, 2006; Xi, 2006; Li, 2007; 2008; Ho et al., 2007; Tan and Simpson, 2008; Yang, 2008.

minority of Chinese students have engaged in extortion, fraud and illegal forms of drug dealing, gambling and prostitution.[46]

Policy makers also responded. Deputy Prime Minister Michael Cullen moved to strengthen the Code of Practice for Pastoral Care and imposed on education institutions, some of which resented the costs,[47] a stronger reputation management strategy underpinned by measures to enhance student safety. Officials from the Ministry of Education International Unit worked with members of ISANA, the body of 'professionals in Australia and New Zealand who work in international student services, advocacy, teaching and policy development in international education', to form a national safety advisory group, which included representatives from the police, immigration, vice-chancellors and insurance firms, and was charged with examining the effectiveness of information for and 'potential safety initiatives' for international students.[48] In New Zealand international student safety has moved from a subject deemed unmentionable in higher education circles to one that requires investigation, debate and promotion.

UNITED KINGDOM

In 1998 the UK Home Office commissioned a report, *Policing the Campus*, which identified higher rates of burglary, theft and violence on campus than in the general population.[49] This led to the creation of a website on student safety and research concerning crimes against students, victim support and associated services, perceptions of safety, fear of victimisation and routine precautions against crime.[50] Research suggests that students are more likely to be victims of crime because of factors of proximity, exposure, guardianship and attractive target.[51] Proximity relates to the housing and residential arrangements: shared housing and multi-unit residences are regarded as high risk for theft and violence. Oncampus violence is more likely to occur in living quarters.[52] The 2004 report of the Home Office,

46 Li, 2007, 2008.
47 Lewis, 2005, 5.
48 Cullen, 2006; McGrath et al., 2008.
49 Home Office, 2007.
50 Barbaret et al., 2004.
51 Fisher and Wilkes, 2003.
52 Smith and Fossey, 1995.

Crimes Against Students: Emerging lessons for reducing student victimisation, includes a section on international students.[53] The report observes that many students are from countries with lower rates of crime than the UK norm and/or countries where problems associated with crime are markedly different. These students are often unaware of the new risks or the safety practices required in Britain, it states. Crime safety messages should reach all international students. The information needs to be region specific and targeted at students and their families. The report regrets an absence of evaluative research on projects on student safety but notes some regions have created a 'package of measures targeted at international students'. One example was a program developed by Sussex police to tackle victimisation of foreign language school students that included the dedication of specially trained police to areas with high concentrations of international students and the profiling of international student communities to render police aware of the safety needs of the communities they had to protect.

In 2005 then UK Prime Minister Tony Blair launched his Second Initiative on International Education (PMI2), a key concern of which was to avoid repetition of the New Zealand experience with China. The message of PMI2 was that the UK provided a sound education as well as rewarding housing, pastoral care, leisure and safety experiences.[54] Research was telling the government that safety was the most important 'hygiene factor' influencing prospective international students when they decided where to study. One study of international students already in Britain found safety to be 'the most important element of the lived experience in the UK'.[55] The UK's reputation as 'one of the safest places in the world to study' was seen as a market advantage to protect.[56] The UK government became increasingly proactive in strengthening and publicising Britain's capacity to provide a safe study environment. A government-funded conference organised in March 2006 by the Office for London and the National Union of Students focused on ways in which parties with an interest in international students in London could work together to improve

53 Home Office (UK), 2004.

54 Merrick, 2007; Humfrey, 2008; CUBO, 2008.

55 CUBO, 2008, 7.

56 i-Graduate, 2008, 4.

student safety and freedom from property crime. That year the British Council distributed, free on the internet, *Safety First, A Personal Safety Guide for International Students*, which advised prospective students that the UK was safer than the USA, while implying that UK degrees were almost as prestigious as American degrees and of higher quality than Australian and New Zealand degrees, pointing to the central position of safety in UK reputational strategy.

The British Council campaign was not confined to the marketing dimension. It enhanced open discussion of student safety issues and there was a spillover to improvements in the actual conditions of safety of international students. Topics discussed in *Safety First* include how to approach the police, property insurance, protection of belongings, protection from identity theft, dangers associated with finding accommodation, racial discrimination and harassment, and physical safety when at home, on the streets or in public transport or taxis. The section on finding accommodation includes the following:

> If possible, take someone with you when viewing accommodation. If you are alone, leave the address you are going to and your expected time of return with a friend or colleague. Find out exactly who might have access to the accommodation apart from yourself. Be businesslike in your dealings with prospective landlords or landladies. If you feel uncomfortable with anyone who is showing you accommodation, mention that friends know where you are and are expecting your return at a certain time.[57]

In 2007 the British Council followed up with *Creating Confidence*, which documents international students' views on safety-related matters, the proportion of students who had been crime victims and steps students could take to ensure safety. Although *Creating Confidence* reports on the results of a survey of international students it is primarily a marketing text, as is apparent in the way survey results unfavourable to the UK are reported. Hate crime, for example, is discussed in a manner intended to reduce fears of racism:

> Some 13 per cent of reported incidents involved personal abuse, ranging from racial comments to having liquids and items thrown but falling short of actual bodily harm. Although disappointing, the

57 British Council, 2006, 10.

> total number of reports amount to just 221 out of 1557 respondents so the incidences are, statistically, very few. Concerns about racial abuse in the UK, which exist in many parts of the world, appear to be largely unfounded.[58]

The Council campaign was underpinned by actions undertaken jointly with other organisations, together with meetings that brought together theorists and practitioners to discuss experiences and develop policy. In 2008 the Council contributed to a conference titled 'Ensuring student safety and security' that aimed to raise safety awareness on campuses and to disseminate information about measures taken to improve international student safety. Meanwhile, the British government created neighbourhood policing teams who had responsibility for campuses and halls of residences. These teams were trialled at Cardiff University. Research showed that student crime victimisation was reduced by 60 per cent. On 1 October 2008 the team strategy was instituted across the whole of Britain.

RUSSIA

In Russia the literature on international student safety focuses primarily on hate crime,[59] which, since the collapse of the Soviet regime, has been visited particularly on African students. The extent of hate crime was long suppressed by the Russian government. However in 2005 the Sova Information-Analytical Centre reported that in 2004 there were 179 attacks on international students across Russia, resulting in 28 deaths and 366 injuries.[60] The following year the *Chronicle of Higher Education* told the story of Simo, a Moroccan ophthalmology student who lived for six years in Voronezh, a university town 400 kilometres from Moscow:

> 'For years we could never go down there; it was like walking into a trap', Simo says of a series of underground walkways at a major intersection. 'That's where Amaru was killed', he says, lifting his chin towards a deep, dark archway across Peace Street. 'Here a student from China was attacked in broad daylight while

58 British Council, 2007, 19.

59 Smolentseva, 2004.

60 See also Smolentseva, 2004; Leviyeva, 2005.

> people stood around and watched, even the cops', he says as he cuts through Eaglet Children's Park . . . '[International students] who fare OK are the ones who smoke, who drink, the ones who involve themselves in the community,' he says. 'The ones who suffer are the weak ones who are afraid, who don't stand up for themselves. They need to be tough because here, in Russia, it's the survival of the fittest. They eat the weak.'[61]

The reporting of safety problems affected recruitment to Russian universities so in 2005 Education and Science Minister Andrei Fursenko declared his ministry would reconsider the list of universities recommended to international students, boost security on all campuses and advise universities to establish councils charged with assessing the security situation and providing advice to students on how to secure their safety. Fursenko observed that while his department bore responsibility for student safety it was imperative that police cease defining the attacks on non-white students as 'hooliganism' and acknowledge that racist violence was a systemic problem in Russia. The problem was not easily eradicated. On 20 April 2007, for example, Russian television reported that international students at the Moscow Sechenov Medical Academy were instructed to stay indoors because racist gangs were attacking 'blacks' as part of their commemoration of Hitler's birthday.[62] Nevertheless, acknowledgement of the problem was a major advance on the strategy of denial prevailing prior to 2005. This acknowledgement reflected an official judgement that Russia's capacity to participate in the global competition for research talent was threatened by violence against international students.[63]

AUSTRALIA

Formal regulation

In Australia oncampus student safety is, in effect, devolved to institutions, without guidelines and to the students themselves. Once they leave campus students must manage their own security. The police

61 MacWilliams, 2006.
62 Finn, 2007; Harding, 2007.
63 Leviyeva, 2005; Todd, 2007; de Witt, 2008.

also have a responsibility to protect the lives and property of international students, as they have in relation to all citizens and non-citizens. But in practice the police have limited resources and cannot be everywhere, as the evidence from the interviews will show. Police cannot cover all threats to safety and security in areas of concentrated public drunkenness or where there is an intensive pattern of assaults. Some international students also feel that as non-citizens or as non-white people they are less likely to be supported and they are reluctant to seek police help.

All institutions provide emergency services of varying effectiveness. Under the National Code of Practice they are obliged to inform students about such services in the mandatory orientation program.[64] There are no further mandatory requirements in the National Code of Practice concerning provision of a safe environment or duty of care of life and property. In that respect the situation is similar to that prevailing in relation to discrimination and racist abuse, areas of behaviour that can impinge on the safety of individuals. Regulation is silent. Among student service personnel the sense of a duty of care[65] often extends well beyond the formal ESOS requirements, but it is not guaranteed. Most institutions offer advice on safety at orientation stage and distribute written information. Some provide dedicated advice services, and a number offer support on safety issues specific to women officially or through student associations. There are no minimum necessary standards for such services. There is no systematic monitoring external to the institutions, of student safety or safety-related services. Students receive little assistance in relation to problems outside the campus except advice.

STUDENTS' CONCERNS

The 2006 AEI survey was not the first or only evidence that safety was a central issue for international students. In 2002 Mazzarol and Souter had noted the level of crime in specific nations and communities was a primary determinant of where students chose to study.[66] In 2006

64 DEEWR, 2008, National Code, Standard 6, section 6.1.c.
65 Ghobrial, 2006.
66 Mazzarol and Souter, 2002.

Table 9.1 International students' feelings of being safe or unsafe, University of Melbourne, 2006

	Proportion of respondents (n = 978) in agreement				
	Not at all %	**To some degree %**	**To a considerable degree %**	**Very much %**	**Total %**
I don't feel safe here in Melbourne	52.7	37.2	8.0	2.1	100.0

Source: Rosenthal, et al., 2006, 28.

Rosenthal and colleagues found one in 10 international students at the University of Melbourne felt unsafe (table 9.1).

The researchers also found that 'female students feel significantly less safe than male students' and that 'Asian students are significantly more likely to feel some concern about their safety in Melbourne than non-Asian students'.[67] In 2007 the Victoria Police identified Chinese international students as a vulnerable group whose safety was at risk because they might become perpetrators or victims of extortion, and noted that Indian students were increasingly victims of robbery and violence, particularly on public transport.[68]

THE SLOW OFFICIAL RESPONSE

In Australia the implementation of the ESOS Act was monitored by AEI from within the Commonwealth department. But AEI was also responsible for marketing the export industry. Perhaps this was why for so long the regulation of international student safety remained loose and safety was downplayed or seen as solely a problem of reputation management, for longer than it was in New Zealand and the UK. Official strategies of denial continued into 2008, despite the increasing number of academic studies, media commentaries and police reports that all pointed to a systemic problem.[69] Only the intervention of foreign embassies in the public debate, especially China, forced the beginnings of a new approach. As discussed above the federal

67 Rosenthal et al., 2006, 29.

68 Tulloch, 2007.

69 *ibid*; Johnston, 2007; Ehrenberg, 2008; Nyland et al., 2008; Forbes-Mewett et al., 2009; Das 2008a; 2008b, 2008c.

government responded by calling a workshop in Shanghai that was designed to put the lid back on the issue. The government of Victoria, where there had been persistent reports of attacks on south Asian students (above), issues of workplace exploitation (chapter 6) and problems with housing and fire safety (chapter 7), created an Overseas Student Experience Task Force to 'review the overseas student experience in Victoria to see what more can be done to improve the experience'.[70] But the executive head of AEI was rebuked by industry representatives when she cautiously suggested Australia should embrace a 'Third Phase of International Education' that would emphasise sustainability and the quality of the student experience as well as growth.[71] Meanwhile, the federal minister continued to insist there was no systemic problem.[72]

Perhaps Australia's protracted semi-denial rested on assumptions that immigration opportunities for international graduates would sustain the flow of students regardless of bad publicity over safety. AEI reported that in 2007, '78 per cent of international survey respondents either had applied (30 per cent) or planned to apply (48 per cent) for permanent resident status in Australia',[73] but on 9 October 2008 the prime minister 'raised the possibility of slashing Australia's record high intake of immigrants should the global financial crisis plunge the economy into a sustained downturn'.[74] Education industry representatives called on the government to maintain immigration,[75] but there were substantial cuts to the skilled labour intake in the May 2009 federal budget.

Signs of a more serious effort to come to grips with the issues began to emerge. Industry and government representatives organised a meeting in Melbourne in December 2008 with consular representatives from China, Indonesia and India. The consular invitees were asked to provide information and advice on issues and problems facing their international students. University and government personnel reported on the steps they had taken yet the 19 December 2008 report from the Victorian Taskforce again papered over the

70 Study Melbourne, 2008.
71 Buffington, 2008.
72 Gooch, 2008.
73 AEI, 2008b, 9.
74 Maley and Edwards, 2008.
75 Bebbington, 2008.

issues: problems of racist targeting and inadequate police responses were not mentioned. Any special problems faced by international students were put down to lack of 'local knowledge that can help them minimise the risks', lack of 'access to support networks if they find themselves in trouble' and the fact that 'many overseas students may also be working and travelling at times that increase their risk'. In other words, the safety problems that international students faced were due to their own deficits. The remedies were for international students to become better informed, improve their support networks and leave public transport to the locals at night. The taskforce recommended a set of steps that would provide better information and increase the length of orientation at educational institutions from one to two weeks. There were no proposals to provide extra resources for safety or change the behaviour of local citizens or law enforcement authorities.[76]

The questions on safety

The present study asked one main question directly related to safety.

> Are you safe and secure in Australia?

Other interview questions covered risks and problems of living in Australia, advice that should be given to prospective students and possible backup systems and protections; some answers to those questions also touched on safety.

ARE YOU SAFE AND SECURE IN AUSTRALIA?

'I feel safe when I don't go out late'

Of the 200 students interviewed 181 (90.5 per cent) answered 'Yes' to the question 'Are you safe and secure in Australia?' Still, some of those who said 'Yes' hesitated, or qualified their answer. Some had been exposed to hate crimes or threats or had heard about thefts and assaults. A frequent response was 'Yes, I feel safe, but I don't go out much at night', though by no means all students felt this and

76 Government of Victoria, 2008, 13–14.

some emphasised that they felt safe at night. The best estimate is that 84 per cent gave an unqualified 'Yes' to the question. The overwhelming majority of interviewees believed they were at least as safe in Australia as at home.

> Yes, I think Australia is quite a safe place. It's not a problem.
>
> ~ male, 41, computing, China

> [Y]ou go home at 2 o'clock, walk alone . . . it's OK.
>
> ~ female, 29, business, Indonesia

> Yes . . . only thing is, I don't really like going out at night.
>
> ~ female, 19, humanities, India

> If you have difficulties around here people will tend not to help because they just don't want to get involved.
>
> ~ female, 39, PhD in engineering, Indonesia

> I just feel people in Australia are different. I mean, people in Australia are not as friendly as I thought. The security here is not as good as I expected. Sometimes when I come home late, you know, late lectures, overtime . . . I just feel little scared to go . . . home by myself. It's a long way and my parents worry about me. They see on TV about killing of overseas students . . . I myself get a little bit scared.
>
> ~ female, 25, business, China

A number of students thought it wise to live in a student environment. This was seen as safer than city locations which were seen as trouble spots.

> [I]t's always better to live in an environment where you have a lot of students and you can relate to them. It's also safer knowing that the students come back at different hours.
>
> ~ female, 32, business, Singapore

> [B]ecause we live in the city, and our street is surrounded by pubs, at night I try not to go out late. Because there are people around, especially on weekends. It's not as safe as I would like it to be.
>
> ~ female, 22, humanities, Singapore

Some interviewees mentioned rumours about major crimes, such as kidnapping and murder.

> To this point I am safe and secure. Although I have heard of a lot of things happening . . . like people get killed, people get mugged and robbed . . . kidnapped. None of these things happened to me or my friends although one of my friends got mugged.
>
> ~ male, 28, science, Indonesia

> A friend told me about robbery and kidnapping, someone taking girls, Asian girls, in a street next to the uni . . .
>
> ~ female, 40, PhD in microbiology, Indonesia

There were differences on the basis of age and gender. All those who said that they felt unsafe were 30 or less. Among women interviewees 12 of the 102 said that they were not safe and secure in Australia, compared to seven of the 98 men. There were larger differences on the basis of place. As Sundeen found,[77] perception of the neighbourhood impacted on the fear of crime. Those who did not feel safe and secure were largely concentrated in Sydney, where 13 students out of 56 in the study (23 per cent) did not feel safe. In Melbourne six out of 133 students (5 per cent) felt unsafe. The interviews were conducted before media reports of regular violence against south Asian students in the west of Melbourne.

> I feel so, I would like to think so, but it's just Sydney . . . compared to Melbourne it gets a little notorious here. Certain places I don't go at night. Near Newtown there's a lot of things happening, there's [nearby] Redfern.
>
> ~ female, 21, computing, Malaysia

There were also differences on the basis of appearance and national or cultural origin. The proportion saying that they did not feel safe and secure was higher than average for students from India (19 per cent) and China (14 per cent). Almost all Indonesian women in Sydney said that they felt unsafe, as did almost all Indian men in Sydney. No Europeans or students from English-speaking nations were affected. Table 9.2 provides a summary.

77 Sundeen, 1984.

Table 9.2 Students' perceptions of safety and security

	Responses to the question: 'Do you feel safe and secure in Australia'?	
	YES	**NO**
	%	**%**
Women	88	12
Men	93	7
India	81	19
China	86	14
Malaysia	94	6
Indonesia	96	4
All students	91	9

> I don't feel very safe, because of my appearance. There might be some person . . . he might not be having a good day and he might just try to do something to me. That is the only thing I'm slightly apprehensive about.
>
> ~ male, 30, dentistry, India

> I feel safe and secure but that's mainly because I'm a big guy. Walking around at night I don't think anyone is going to mess with me. But I have had a lot of friends, especially from countries like Singapore and Malaysia, and girls, who are quite small, they get worried at night. I have a friend who got mugged just around the corner . . . It depends on your physical attributes.
>
> ~ male, 21, medicine, Sri Lanka

HATE CRIME

'Why is there so many fucking Asians here?'

Twenty-three of the students (11.5 per cent) mentioned hate crime, in which they or their friends had been subjected to street abuse, spitting and/or thrown objects.

> Sometimes when I walk down to street, people scream from a car. One time, I went for a walk with my friends, two or three of us, all Asian. Then one of the little kids came up and tried to hit us. She was just a little kid, so we ignored it, but this was quite hostile.
>
> ~ female, 23, nursing, Hong Kong China

> [Sometimes] when I walk around people shout at me. Once people threw an egg at me.
>
> ~ male, 20, architecture, Malaysia

> Once when I passed Chinatown, there was this woman – I don't know whether she was local or not – she was walking behind us. I think she wanted to make her way, but we have no idea because she didn't say 'excuse me', or whatever. She was so rude. She passed us by and then she said 'Why is there so many fucking Asians here?' It was so offensive.
>
> ~ female, 20, business, Indonesia

Hate crime affected both men and women. Female Muslim students who wore headscarves faced difficulties (see also chapter 15). One in a provincial city said:

> I wear my headscarf back in Brunei. When I first came here last year... I stayed at this bed and breakfast and I walk with my headscarf to school and everybody was staring at me. I wore that headscarf for three days and then I started telling myself that it's not safe... so I decided not to wear that. Then when I came here this year I decided I want to wear my headscarf again until... well, we were in the club. Somebody threw stones at the window. And the next week they pointed a red pointer light on to me. I thought it was me but I just kept quiet because I thought probably I'm just imagining things. Then that happened three times. I told my teacher that I didn't feel safe. 'Is it because I'm wearing my scarf?' I asked. My teacher said, 'Yes'. The first time when they threw the stones, my teacher realised that, and he was trying to catch those kids but they ran off... It was some of the students.
>
> ~ female, 35, ceramics, Brunei

An Indian student in a provincial centre said that he and his friends faced continuing difficulties. People there were 'definitely racist', he said. A group of his friends had been bullied at a nightclub. The bullying continued outside the club. Punches were thrown. They had to run, because the locals were a big gang.

> At least in Melbourne you have a big Indian community. You have got the strength, but here it's less so and they can do whatever they want to do.
>
> ~ male, 23, business, India

TRAVELLING AND WALKING

'I was so scared'

There were numerous reports of incidents that occurred when students were in public places. As explained by one student, it was generally safe on campus but this was not necessarily the case in the community, especially late at night.

> Sometimes, especially at night, some people, drunk people, attack people in the street. Sometimes they carry knives . . . in Sydney Road, after we finished praying, it was about 8 p.m., we walked in the street and one guy, drunk guy, attacked people with a knife. There was no policeman in the street. The people [who were attacked] got wounded . . . We can't do anything we have to defend ourselves.
>
> ~ male, 31, PhD in biology, Egypt

Public transport was frequently mentioned as a site of trouble, especially trams in Melbourne and buses in Sydney. Trouble was often triggered by other passengers who were drunk. One student from India was abused by a tram driver. He held back from legal action so as not to jeopardise his application for permanent residency. Women as well as men were attacked, as shown in another case.

> I don't go outside at all. I want to make myself safe. But I did have trouble when I took tram one day. I had a class in the city, I came home late and there was a big man sitting in the back talking to an old woman and I turned around . . . I turned around, and he said 'What's your name?' I was so scared, I didn't want to say anything. He said 'You're so rude, you didn't talk to me'. I didn't know what to do. He grabbed me by my shirt in my neck. The driver said, 'Drop her, otherwise I will call the police'. And he did, after the driver shouted at him. After he got out off the tram, he threw the bottle to me, the Pepsi bottle . . . he wasn't drunk. The driver said to me, 'Why you came home so late?' And I said, 'I had a class, I had to'. And the driver said 'Come home earlier, because the tram is not safe'.
>
> ~ female, 33, education, China

Many international students do not have family or friends to assist them home safely after evening classes. While the tram driver's action was admirable, his advice that the student should exclude herself from public transport is a concern, as was the student's feeling of being unable to protect herself in such a situation, a feeling reported by others.

> Once when I was travelling on the train, I definitely felt that a person probably didn't like me. He started shouting. Things like that happen, not just with me but with a couple of my friends; there were incidents. A friend of mine was walking in Dandenong and somebody threw a beer bottle at him . . . You just keep silent, you can't do anything to them, you can't go and hit them because we don't know what the law of the country is, we don't know whether we can. If it was in my country definitely I would have hit them back if he did that to me . . . [but] this is another land here. I don't want to get thrown out of the country.
>
> ~ male, 24, business, India

ASSAULT

'I gave them everything but they started hitting me'

A small number of students had been victims of assault, robbery and burglary and a larger number had friends who had suffered this.

> I was walking home after work. Eight guys were there. They saw me and started hitting me all over my head . . . I put everything in my hand. I saw them and I was pretty sure I knew what they wanted to do with me. So I said, 'OK, whatever you want, just take it, let me go'. I gave them everything but they start hitting me. They took everything, my wallet, they even took my shirts, I had shirts in my bag . . . digicam, my wallet, my mobile phone, my watch, everything . . . The worse part is they start hitting me on my face and the head, not even on the body. I was just on the ground, try to protect my head . . . I had a really bad headache . . . so I called the police and they took me to hospital. They put me there for the whole night, just to make sure I didn't have any head injury. Actually, the police took my bag, and I called them about the fingerprinting and DNA testing, and they haven't [come back] to me. I called them three times and they haven't even bothered to call me back. I didn't mention anything here [at the university];

> there was no need. They can't do anything. And the police are not cooperating. So what can you expect?
>
> ~ male, 24, computing, India

In this case the police did not provide the level of care that was warranted. Fortunately, there were no other cases of vicious attacks affecting interviewees. There were four cases of burglary, all relating to premises being broken into. Items stolen included computers, cameras, mobile phones and money.

> Before I lived in Coburg. I lived there three months and then I changed because my house was broken, my laptop and digital camera were stolen. I find it a very common thing. Two of my classmates, they also have been broken, laptop stolen . . . fortunately, when the burglar entered, he entered my bedroom. I was asleep. It was in the morning, about 6 o'clock, and I saw him. He opened the door, I heard a noise. I opened my eyes and I saw him. I didn't scream, I just thought, he must want to take something. I wanted to call my friends, I wanted to grab my mobile phone. He saw it, but when I moved, he saw me and he just ran. And he didn't take anything, he just broke the window. Now, we asked the agent to put a lock on the window.
>
> ~ female, 22, environmental studies, China

> When I had been here just three weeks I met a very big problem. At the time I lived with my homestay, and her house was broken into, and I lost my laptop, my cash and mobile. At that time I was very distressed, because I had never met this problem before. I lost my passport. I had to go to the Chinese embassy to apply for a new one.
>
> ~ female, 23, business, China

COMPARISONS

'I feel more safe here'

Seventeen interviewees made direct comparisons between safety in their home country and safety in Australia. Of these 13 deemed Australia to be safer. Students who believed Australia was safer came from Indonesia, India, Pakistan, Papua New Guinea, Malaysia and Zimbabwe.

> Security is better than in my country, very good.
>
> ~ female, 33, environmental studies, Bangladesh

> I do sometimes get news of laptops being stolen, but that happens in any society. Of course, as compared to Pakistan, I feel more safe here.
>
> ~ male, 19, business, Pakistan

> Here is more safe than in our country . . . in Indonesia going around by ourselves is quite dangerous, especially in the evening, but here it's still okay, even though I am living in Footscray where people say it's a very dangerous area. Sometimes I go back home at midnight, but it's still okay.
>
> ~ male, 31, community development, Indonesia

> The biggest difference would be security. Back at home you have to be very mindful of security, where you go. But here you have a very casual time. That's the difference.
>
> ~ male, 36, PhD in engineering, Papua New Guinea

> The safety here is not very bad like in Malaysia. When you walk out in the street at night, you don't have to fear . . . very easy lifestyle, compared to home where it's very tense and you've always got to be watching your back. You've got to lock the door and close the windows.
>
> ~ female, 22, business, Zimbabwe

The four exceptions who saw their home country as safer than Australia were from Japan and Singapore, modernised societies with secure urban precincts.

> In Japan, it's really safe, if you walk from my station to my house . . . My dad would never say, 'Would you like me to pick you up?', because it's not a very big deal, whereas here in Australia, if you were to walk from [university] to a house about five minutes walking, my housemate would always say, 'Would you like me to pick you up?' . . . Security is a big issue.
>
> – male, 20, medicine, Japan

> I felt safe when I don't go out late. In Singapore I walk back home until 12 midnight, late at night, I don't get worried. Over here even when it's half past six I will catch the bus, though it's just a 20 minutes walk, because I think the road here is not safe.
>
> ~ female, 27, engineering, Singapore

A small number of students compared Australia with the USA and the UK and concluded that Australia was the safest option.

> I used to hear about the cases of racism, but compared to UK and America, Australia is OK; I know so many good people. In UK I know there is too much racism.
>
> ~ male, 22, engineering, Botswana

> I feel safe every time I want to go out in the night. I know that nothing is going to happen. Not like America. It's freaky, America.
>
> ~ male, 19, business, Pakistan

COPING STRATEGIES

'They have to learn common sense pretty quickly'

The coping strategies employed by students were mostly simple but effective. Students normally ignored rude or racist remarks to avoid inflaming threatening circumstances. Some Muslim women removed their headscarves to avoid victimisation. Students mostly preferred be in the company of others rather than alone if they could. They learnt the safest modes of public transport, often after unpleasant experiences. However, some found their coping strategies restricted their social activities, especially those who felt they could not go out at night.

Some augmented their personal safety by living in campus residences.

> The thing is, I stay on campus so I'm pretty safe. I am happy with the university's security systems and things like that. For me it's adequate because I don't need to travel in the night and things like that.
>
> ~ female, 22, business, India

> Being in a college environment, that is the safest accommodation you can get in the university . . . if you really meet with any danger there are 240 of us to help you. Unless the threat comes from within the 240 people. Thankfully, that has not happened so far and hopefully it will not happen.
>
> ~ female, 21, business, China

This comment underlines the point that Australian universities seldom provide enough oncampus residential accommodation for students (see chapter 7). Some students saw living near campus as a strategy for remaining safe, though others saw the area surrounding universities as unsafe.[78]

> I usually come home really late at night. So if I live far away from here it might not be good or not safe for me . . . so I decided to move to my friend's, where I live now.
>
> ~ female, 30, food science, Indonesia

Asked what could be done to increase safety, students often made the same point as the mother of the girl who died after falling from a balcony when escaping her attacker (chapter 1). They argued that the Australian authorities did not provide enough information about how to be safe, especially on public transport.

> I think I would tell [prospective students] about the transportation system here I would tell them not [to be] branching out late in the night, just be very discreet about the way you dress and the things you carry when moving in quiet and dark places.
>
> ~ female, 28, engineering, Singapore

Some also stated that universities should provide more transport for students residing near campus.

> I think maybe they [should] provide more transport for the shuttle bus. If you live in this area, the shuttle bus would not have to go . . . very far . . . I have friends, they are Masters students, and their class ends at 9 o'clock. They are girls and they are very scared to walk home alone . . . If they got the shuttle bus, they would just have to go two to three minutes to get [home].
>
> ~ male, 22, food science, Indonesia

One student noted a newly installed university telephone line for reporting victimisation.

> My university just very recently provided special protection for international students, especially in relation to harassment and discrimination . . . it's very good for us international students.
>
> ~ male, 29, humanities, Indonesia

78 Rugg et al., 2000.

But the students also had to be able to survive through their own efforts. They had to form friendship networks and to learn from experience.

> I think almost every student have problems, but the thing is if you want to overcome the problems you should have somebody to help you or somebody to guide you... You should have friends around you. You shouldn't live alone. You should be open to everyone, you should make some friends... so you won't feel lonely and you won't feel unsafe.
>
> ~ male, 25 years, science, Sri Lanka

> I think a lot of people who come down from Asian nations have lived largely sequestered lives, it's true. Their parents have taken care of them. And now they've left the nest properly to go to tertiary education with no in between, with no [period] of branching out and yet coming home at weekends. They don't get that option. When it comes down to being safe and secure they have to learn common sense pretty quickly.
>
> ~ female, 26, medicine, Malaysia

CONCLUSIONS

A reputation for providing a safe environment is a vital and vulnerable asset. Around the world this asset has been devalued. Governments and education suppliers were disinterested, as in Russia, were suspicious of international students, as in the USA or feared that debating the safety issue might undermine the sale of international education, as in New Zealand, the UK and Australia. The logic of denial has been applied even to student suicides, where US welfare programs have been contained lest they reveal information that might undermine an institution's reputation or render it vulnerable to litigation. All five countries are moving away from their former positions of denial and the situation is now in flux. For the most part change was embraced less because of human rights than because of the national interest, specifically, a conviction among industry leaders that a new approach was required to sustain the inflow of international students.

Here an important ally of international students has been public discussion and the generation of knowledge. The media often sensationalises international student safety. Sometimes its coverage (for example in New Zealand) borders on stigmatisation. But the media are indispensable. They ensure a humanist focus on the life and security of the students themselves. Unlike host governments and the industry they have proven hostile to sacrificing student safety to other interests, a vital corrective to official neglect and denial. What this chapter has also shown is that an equally important ally for international students is their home governments. Nation-states have considerable power to affect the flow of international students to host countries merely by letting their citizens know that they believe a specific host does not adequately provide for the students they accept. Governments of nations that supply students are less susceptible to capture by education export industry interests than are the host governments. Further, the discussion of the Clery Act has shown that the market can be an important ally if harnessed in ways that make it mandatory for education institutions to generate public knowledge of the level and form of crime associated with individual education institutions. Recent events also confirm that international students themselves have agency and can be a force for change when they chose to make their concerns public or otherwise known. In New Zealand it was student complaints to the Chinese embassy that led the government of China to intervene in 2003.

Australia long enjoyed – and for the most part still enjoys – a global reputation as a provider of a safe study and living environment. It does not underpin its reputation by mandatory requirements for provision of a safe environment on campus and offers nothing specific to international students outside the campus. Though students' lack of familiarity with the conditions exposes them disproportionately to problems, there is some evidence that they and their property are targeted; police in Victoria have expressed concerns specific to international students. A minority of students have fears for their safety and security, some based on personal or reported experiences, and some do not. Students in some inner city locations and certain provincial centres are especially on guard. Incidents of discrimination and abuse (see also chapter 15) are often linked to perceived threats to personal safety. Australian authorities long preferred to deny there were problems of safety specific to international students and some simply refused to acknowledge the safety issue at all. This slowly began to change in 2008 and 2009. Here Australia followed the pattern of official response common to the export nations but more slowly and less completely than did the UK and New Zealand. The Australian government and industry have yet to fully grasp that just as a reputation for natural safety constitutes a competitive advantage, so can a reputation for the active provision of student safety. Being vigilant and being seen to be vigilant in support of the safety of international students signify a humanist compact that improves the quality of students' experience and reassures their families.

Regulatory protections could be improved by mandating the provision of a safe environment on campus and offering after hours transport to residential zones within a specified minimum distance. Some institutions provide such services, some do not. The larger problems of safety and security lie in the outside community, particularly on and around public transport and in city streets at night. These are beyond the reach of the National Code. Education providers can contribute here by encouraging the collection of comprehensive information about external safety problems and becoming dogged in bringing these data to public and authorities. Night time public transport needs to be cleaned up, which will require higher staffing levels and more comprehensive electronic security systems. Perhaps education providers, international student organisations and support groups could collaborate in a civil organisation dedicated to international student safety that is charged with information collection and advocacy. In this area more than most, recent history shows that knowledge is power, and the dissemination of information can change the policy landscape and achieve results. While government and policing are essential to the solution of safety issues, when the matter is left to government alone all too readily it becomes part of the problem.

Issues of personal safety in the community highlight the informal dimension of students' lives and the role of private and personal resources and networks in student security. Part 3 will expand on this dimension. The final chapter of part 2 will discuss the impact of the government immigration regime on student security.

10 THE IMMIGRATION DEPARTMENT

Dealing with immigration is pretty hard. Extending a visa, it was a big process. It's not easy. You go to the counter there and pick up this ticket number and you have to wait for ages. And people there are not friendly. They never smile, as if we are thieves or have a criminal offence. You go there, you're really tense and nervous. You can't be yourself.

~ male, 27, computing, Sri Lanka

INTRODUCTION: THE ALIENS HAVE LANDED

The relationship between mobile non-citizen[1] students and the nation-state in the country of education is inherently ambiguous and problematic.

We live in a zero sum world in which each nation claims sovereignty over a parcel of territory and each fosters a citizenry, people inherited and chosen, towards whom it exercises jurisdiction and responsibility. Each polices borders that are not just geographic but also imagined boundaries vectored by law, politics and culture. So where do resident non-citizens fit? As discussed in chapter 4 international students have left their nation of citizenship but have not become full members of the nation of education. While the original nation can be reached via communications and the diplomatic mission, those ties have thinned. That nation no longer nurtures and regulates them in a day to day sense. But there is no global state mapped on the growing

1 In this chapter the term 'citizens' includes permanent residents without full citizenship.

population of the globally mobile. In a real sense international students find themselves in limbo, people without a state.

A person without a state is an anathema to clean systems of security in both senses: the security of themselves as people, and the security of nation-states. As chapter 1 showed, international students in Australia have inferior claims to social entitlement and protection. The nation plans to obtain advantages from their temporary presence, and many of them will later become high skill immigrants. But they are not yet citizens. They are still 'aliens' in the legal sense. And aliens are always potential threats to national security and to the privileges of citizenship enclosed within the imagined national boundary. The intentions of international students, as is the case with other visitors, are always seen as questionable. Do they intend to turn temporary immigration into permanent residence without enduring the tortured process that the nation-state imposes on those not born to it who seek to become members? Does their presence jeopardise or undermine the interests of citizens? Are they staying confined within the visa conditions and other restrictions the nation-state imposes on them? Are they the kind of people that we want?

Hence relations between international students and host governments are two-sided. On one hand the relationship is, to a degree, protective and enabling. This is expressed in Australia in the consumer rights and minimum welfare provisions in the National Code and the ill-defined obligations of institutions to provide a quality experience and maintain duty of care. Here students do not deal directly with central government but with the institutions. On the other hand the relationship is harsh and punitive, as can be seen in students' dealings with the Department of Immigration and Citizenship (DIAC, formerly DIMIA[2]). As noted in the introduction to part 2, the National Code defers to DIAC. Institutions are subordinated to visa regulation and must cooperate with DIAC when required. But visas are mostly managed directly by DIAC itself. No one else is trusted. There is no modernist devolution to quasicivil organisations or self-managing individuals here. The national border is protected with a military-like zeal and precision that cuts across the complexity of people's lives. As in the USA, when international students deal directly

2 Interviewees referred to DIMIA, which was the acronym of the department at the time of the interviews. The acronym has been updated here for the sake of clarity.

with the Australian government they deal with a security state. The world is globalising but the security state remains myopic. Its horizon is bound by itself.

The chapter discusses issues in student relations with government in the UK and the USA before discussing DIAC's regulation of international students in Australia, especially the 2006 Senate committee report into the Migration Act. The chapter then reports on what interviewees said about their dealings with government, especially with DIAC. There were no horror stories. None of the 200 interviewees in our study had been placed in detention or deported. But there were many lesser difficulties. It is clear that relations with the immigration authorities, where notions of care and protection are absent, are more fraught than other dealings with government.

RELATIONS WITH GOVERNMENT: THE LITERATURE

The USA

Student surveillance under the American SEVIS system is extensive, intensive and threatening. It is motivated by the security needs of the nation-state rather than international student security. It was framed after the attacks on the World Trade Centre and the Pentagon on 11 September 2001. As Larsen remarks: 'Insecurity, fear and vulnerability are... powerful human motivators',[3] but it is only when a strong state is driven by them that their full power is apparent. Measures of security and control designed to eliminate fear and vulnerability tend to overkill.

In October 2001, one month after 9/11, the Patriot Act authorised US$36 million for student tracking; by August 2003 all international students in the USA were required to have a record in the US surveillance system, SEVIS. Rosser and colleagues report that

> campus-based student and scholar advisers are required to maintain the SEVIS database by reporting events in intervals ranging from daily to monthly. SEVIS has not only dramatically increased the workload and increased the proportion of time spent on

3 Larsen, 2008, 266.

> database management of these advisers, but also changed their relationships with students.[4]

A survey of international student advisers found that 86 per cent said that SEVIS required them to focus more on regulatory compliance than student assistance.[5] NAFSA noted that in August 2008, seven years after 9/11, the system of surveillance of international students still inhibited mobility.

> Despite improvements, the visa process is still unnecessarily onerous. Name checks, especially for students with Arabic names, can hold up visa applications indefinitely because of similarities to names on various watch lists. Students complain of disrespectful treatment at ports of entry. Once in the country, they become subject to a monitoring system – financed with a fee, now being raised to $200, paid by the students – that was thrown up hastily after 9/11 and is easy to run afoul of, which can result in hassle, expense, and even deportation. During their sojourn in the United States, international students are often reluctant to travel internationally for academic conferences, vacations, or family visits, weddings, or funerals, because of uncertainty over being able to return.[6]

As noted in chapter 9 NAFSA and the universities have lobbied to lighten SEVIS, which was modified in the last months of the Bush administration in 2008.

The UK

In *Broadening Our Horizons* (2004), which reports on a survey of 4796 international students, UKCISA reports some negative feedback on the administration of immigration. Many students had faced difficulties when applying for an extension of their study visa, especially in relation to cost. The administration of work rights created problems for 31 per cent. Many were told by officials that they could not work until they had a national insurance number; 26 per cent said employers also believed this, but many students were told by officials they could

4 Rosser et al., 2006, 525.
5 *ibid*, 532.
6 NAFSA, 2008.

not obtain such a number unless they had a job. In actual fact students were free to work without a national insurance number.[7] A 2007 study by UKCISA, *Benchmarking the Provision of Services for International Students*, again draws attention to the ambiguous function of legal regulation in student security. In the UK police are identified protectors of international students as well as being engaged in a level of monitoring that is not always welcome. International students are required to register with the local police station.[8]

In April 2009 the British government introduced a new immigration system that required non-European students and staff to carry identity cards and universities to check students' bona fides and report on unexplained absences. University staff were critical of the system because it turned them into 'immigration agents'. The chief executive of the UK Council for International Student Affairs said that 'it undermines the trust . . . that is an essential part of academic life'.[9]

Australia

The 2006 AEI survey found that significant numbers of international students were dissatisfied or very dissatisfied in relation to the cost of a visa (36 per cent), the length of time before the visa expired after graduation (28 per cent), the time it took to get a visa (27 per cent), the ease of obtaining it (21 per cent), the rules applied to visa holders (18 per cent) and the information available about visas (12 per cent). In each category many students were neither satisfied nor dissatisfied; the remainder were satisfied but this proportion was lower than for other questions in the survey, dropping to just 36 per cent on visa cost.[10] The AEI survey of all education sectors noted that satisfaction ratings in relation to cost were lower than average for northeast Asia;[11] dissatisfaction with the time it took and the ease of obtaining a visa were higher than average for students from China (including Hong Kong China), Japan, Korea and India.[12]

7 UKCISA, 2004, 11–12.
8 UKCISA, 2007, 17.
9 Lipsett, 2009.
10 AEI, 2007a, 16.
11 AEI, 2007b, 49–50.
12 *ibid*, 57–8.

The AEI survey did not enquire further into relations with immigration, where student visas are closely policed. One concern is immigration scams in which agents use the student visa avenue to facilitate people not intending to study but rather to work or do business in Australia, or secure legal or illegal immigration by the backdoor. Such scams may involve organisations posing as educational providers and falsifying records of student attendance and progress, in which case the 'students' themselves are not bona fide and also complicit in falsification. For DIAC it seems that hunting down potential visa breaches takes priority over other objectives, including the commercial market, Australia's reputation and the care of genuine international students. One problem affecting international students, for example, is workplace exploitation. DIAC does not offer help or redress or keep data on work-related complaints (chapter 6), but at the time the research for this study took place the department vigorously investigated those students it believed to be in potential breach of visa conditions in relation to work.[13]

As noted student visas are routinely subject to several conditions, including satisfactory rates of attendance in and progression through the approved program of study, and maximum hours of work. At the time of the interviews for this study students were required to separately obtain an amendment to their visa providing permission to work. The DIAC website specifies that 'You cannot work more than 20 hours a week when your course is in session (other than work which has been registered as a part of the course)'.[14] Longer hours are permitted only during vacation. Any breach of this condition is grounds for mandatory cancellation of a student's visa. In other words, where the grounds for cancellation are established, the visa must be cancelled. Formerly, any breach of the enrolment, attendance and course requirements also triggered mandatory cancellation. There was much criticism on the grounds that DIAC compliance proceedings were invoked too readily and too early, that there was insufficient scope for institutions to exercise educational judgements and there

13 Subsequent to the *Senate Committee Report*, DIMIA/DIAC eased the pressure on students in relation to the work rule but maintained a rigorous approach to overstays and breaches of the academic conditions of student visas. The practice of long-term detention of some ex-students has continued (this note added 8 June 2009).

14 DIAC, 2008.

were too many visa cancellations.[15] On 8 October 2005 the Migration Regulations were amended to allow for 'exceptional circumstances beyond the student's control to be taken into consideration', prior to cancelling a visa for a breach of the conditions concerning attendance and progression. The same flexibility was not created in relation to working hours.[16] If the student works one minute too long, under threat of losing the job or because of extreme financial hardship, the visa is immediately cancelled.

The Senate committee report

In March 2006 the Senate Legal and Constitutional References Committee of the Australian parliament completed its Inquiry into the Administration of the Migration Act 1958, which produced new data concerning the immigration regime for students.

According to the report of the Senate Committee DIAC officers and police routinely search student residences and workplaces to gather evidence that might indicate a breach of visa conditions. Many students so investigated are subsequently detained, many lose their visas and those who appeal against visa cancellation are detained further pending the outcome of the appeal. DIAC's instructions to police state that 'the requirement to detain a person only comes into play' once an officer has formed the 'state of mind' that a person is 'an unlawful non-citizen' or a 'reasonable suspicion that the person is an unlawful non-citizen'. Here 'reasonable suspicion' is 'a reasonable belief or a belief based on the balance of probabilities', or 'probably best described as a degree of satisfaction, not necessarily amounting to belief, but at least extending beyond speculation as to whether an event has occurred or not'. A reasonable suspicion must be a suspicion that 'a reasonable person could hold in the particular circumstances' and 'based on an objective examination of all relevant material'.[17] These provisions are sufficiently enabling so as to catch potentially innocent students in the net.

Chapter 1 told the story of the Alam case discussed in the Senate committee report. Justice Wilcox said in the Federal Court that the

15 *Senate Committee Report*, 2006, 312–13.
16 *ibid*, 310–11.
17 DIMIA, 2005.

Table 10.1 Outcome of student visa cancellations, 2002–3 to 2004–5

	2002–3	2003–4	2004–5
Total number of student visas granted	162 575	171 618	174 786
Number of compliance operations involving student visas	6232	5792	5110
Number of student visa cancellations	8204	8245	8118
Cancellations as a proportion of student visas (%)	5.0	4.8	4.6
Proportion of visa cancellations overturned on appeal (%)	31	40	33

Source: Senate committee, 2006.

case raised 'disturbing questions'. The immigration regulation is 'a drastic, non-discretionary penalty'.[18]

> By what right did the DIAC officers enter and search Mr Alam's home and take away his payslips? They had no search warrant. Nothing in the Migration Act 1958 confers on DIAC officers such extraordinary powers . . . Even if the DIAC officers had power to do what they did, why did they act in such a heavy handed fashion? Mr Alam's request to be allowed to put on a shirt before he was taken to Lee Street was entirely reasonable. Unless it was to humiliate him, what reason could the DIAC officers have had to refuse this request? After his interrogation, Mr Alam was informed he would be detained unless he could put up a $10 000 bond. It was unlikely in the extreme that he was carrying that amount of money on his person, yet he was refused the opportunity of telephoning his sister for assistance. What reason could there have been for that refusal?[19]

Data provided by DIAC showed that in the three years from 2002–3 to 2004–5, as a result of appeals to the Migration Review Tribunal (MRT), the Federal Court and High Court, one-third of visa cancellations were set aside[20] (table 10.1).

> Over one in three cancellation decisions by DIAC which are appealed in the MRT are overturned. The committee considers that this rate is unacceptably high, particularly given the consequences suffered by students whose visas are wrongly cancelled.

18 *Senate Committee Report*, 2006, 316–17.
19 *ibid*, 317.
20 Senate Committee, 2006.

> These consequences include personal and financial hardship for both the student and their family, not to mention the possibility of ending up in immigration detention.[21]

In 2003–4 it took an average of five and a half months to finalise appeals. 'In 2004–05, the averaging processing time for all student visa cancellation cases was 152 calendar days. For applicants in detention it was, according to the department, 91 calendar days'.[22] Some of those in detention have decided to contest their visa cancellation and deportation but cannot afford the bond to release them on a bridging visa pending the outcome of the appeal. The level of the bond is not specified in the Migration Act or regulations. It is at the whim of immigration officials.[23] Those unsuccessful in their appeals are deported and required to pay the costs of detention and removal.

'Students detained for both short and long terms are severely punished for the relatively minor offences which constitute a breach.'[24] Between 2002 and 21 October 2005, 1375 people were detained 'as a direct result of overstaying their student visa or having their student visa cancelled'.[25] Of these 231 were held for one month or more, 31 for more than six months. One former student visa holder was detained for two years and four months and then released on a bridging visa.[26] Michaela Rost, an advocate for people in immigration detention, told the Senate committee that a former student from India was held for two years before giving up the legal battle to have his visa reinstated. On departing for India the Australian government presented him with a bill of $97 000 for the cost of detention.[27]

> The suffering of the relatively few long-term detained students who fight for their right to complete their course is an extreme punishment for failing, perhaps, one subject too many, or working just one hour more than the permitted twenty hours. A speeding driver gets a fine, yet he could have killed someone. However, an overseas student is punished and humiliated through imprisonment for

21 *ibid*, 314.
22 *ibid*, 314.
23 Rost, 2005, 20.
24 *Senate Committee Report*, 2006, 318.
25 *ibid*, 319.
26 *ibid*, 319–20.
27 Rost, 2005, 6.

> a minor offence, even though his parents have made great sacrifices and contributed high fees to the Australian tertiary education system. These parents had entrusted their children into the care of the Australian Government.[28]

Rost further declared that 'Despite students' significant payment for education services and their economic contribution to Australia's sixth largest export industry[29] . . . they seem to receive little understanding, assistance or compassion in exchange'. Instead they are 'subject to harsh, uncompromising and unjust treatment'.[30]

> In particular, the committee is concerned by the levels of student visa cancellations, and the fact that a number of students are finding themselves in immigration detention. The committee considers that this has negative consequences both in terms of the personal impacts on overseas students, as well as the negative impacts on the wider 'education export industry'.[31]

The committee report calls for 'a more flexible and compassionate approach' in relation to visa cancellation. It upholds the principle of limits on working hours but describes mandatory cancellation as 'draconian and heavy handed'. DIAC acknowledged the lack of flexibility in its own statements to the committee. The committee suggests that 'consideration be given to replacing the current provisions requiring mandatory cancellation, with a rebuttable presumption in favour of cancellation'. Problems of 'inappropriate administration and enforcement of the Migration Act and Regulations' should be addressed.[32] These proposals secured no change in policy. DIAC is often obdurate in the face of public debate, its stubbornness and silence apparently part of its claim to be a guardian of national security. Its regulations are complex and less than fully transparent; scope for officer discretion is considerable. The culture of the department, much criticised by the Senate committee, is closer to the military than a civilian bureau.

28 *ibid*, 7.
29 Third largest as of 2008.
30 Rost, 2005, 2.
31 *Senate Committee Report*, 2006, 320.
32 *ibid*, 321.

Other relations with government

Another issue raised by student organisations is international students' lack of access to the public transport concessions available to domestic students in New South Wales and Victoria. In the 2007 Cambridge College survey of 1155 students at two institutions in Victoria, two-thirds of respondents volunteered statements about the need for transport concessions.[33] The AEI survey in higher education also picked up the international student concern about transport concessions.[34]

Questions on relations with government

In the present study interviewees were asked a group of questions concerning relations with government:

- Please describe your experiences in dealing with the Immigration Department and other Australian government departments. Did these departments show understanding of you and your needs? (Follow-up questions were used if required, such as: Did they help you? Did they make things hard for you?)
- What would you do/do you do when the government will not help you with a problem?
- What do you do if the problem is in the government itself?

Other questions went, directly or indirectly, to issues of relations with government, including those on whether 'better or different information' and 'better backup systems and protections' should be provided to prospective students. The data in this chapter include some answers to those questions also.

IMMIGRATION

No other aspect of relations with authority, whether governmental or in education, received as much comment as students' dealings with immigration. Most of this comment was critical. A striking feature of students' remarks about their dealings with DIAC was that when their experiences were not bad this was spoken about as if it were surprising. While students expected university administrative staff to

33 McRae, 2007, 26.
34 AEI, 2007a, 29.

look after them and were critical when they were not well treated, they expected immigration officials to give them a bad time and when it did not happen they were grateful. Having to wait just a few hours at DIAC might be remarked upon favourably, whereas a similar time delay at the university would be criticised.

AT THE UNIVERSITY

'There is nobody who guides students'

Difficulties with immigration began at the university. The universities monitored visa compliance for the government. Often they also provided the student with informal advice in immigration matters, and often but not always they facilitated liaison with the immigration authorities. In some institutions DIAC officials were housed at or near the university international centre. Yet when dealing directly with students, international office personnel often played down their responsibility in immigration matters; some seemed to find it as difficult to deal with immigration as did the students. At this point pastoral care went missing.

> The [marketing] agents of the university, IDP, don't provide information. They said they are education agents not immigration agents. There is nobody who guides students towards these things. And when they [the students] come to Australia, then they realise they have made mistakes. After spending thousands of dollars, they find that they are nowhere.
>
> ~ male, 23, computing, India

Several students noted the failure of the university to generate standardised information about enrolment, progress and change of program that DIAC could comprehend. For one doctoral student the requirements were more complex than for most students and the system could not effectively manage her case. She had changed her program from Masters to PhD and was required to extend her visa for field work and conference attendance. Each time there was no clear-cut procedure. She was sent back and forth between faculty, university international office, the international scholarship office and the graduate school, provided with conflicting advice and sent to DIAC for information that proved to be unavailable there and that the university should have provided DIAC. Academics prepared personal references of no value. DIAC recognised only administrators. 'I received sympathy from them, when at the end of the day what you actually need is support.'

> [All the] information on the immigration website is for undergraduate studies and undergraduate studies are so simple, their curriculum and their status are very straightforward. Every time we have to extend our visa, it seems like the university themselves don't have any clear agreement with immigration. The worse thing is when you ask them at the International Student Office about visa complexities that may arise from our candidature, they simply say, you go to the DIAC website.
>
> ~ female, 29, PhD in architecture, Indonesia

The student argued that there should have been one administrative agency at the university responsible for interpreting and dealing with DIAC's requirements.

The immigration office: 'I hate them'

The questions on relations with immigration triggered lengthy monologues. There were too many stories about bad DIAC days to fully represent them here.

> They are not as friendly as others; they always have this frown on their faces. Yeah, you get a lot of stress, because if they don't renew our visas there is no chance we could continue our studies. You would have to quit halfway through.
>
> ~ male, 27, computing, Sri Lanka

Ordinary politeness regimes, whether local Australian politeness or from another country, did not seem to apply. This student became upset, frustrated, bewildered and resentful just at the memory of his interview.

> I hate the Immigration Department. It really freaks me out, seriously. What I feel is that the people in the Immigration Department, they just want to find some reason to send a student back to their place. That's what I feel. Other international students feel the same. Whenever I have been to Immigration and have had to get the visa extended, their faces are horrible, they've got this look on

their faces . . . like as if they've got some plan in which they would take students directly to the airport and deport them. It's just education. I'm paying my money for getting educated. It is not a big deal. But here they make it a big issue. You have to be like this, that. Australians they do it so . . . they don't have this mental tension like we have. They just pay their money and study. [For us] it's so much of a fight. I really hate it. And the questions they ask, you don't have the answers for them. Why you can do this? Why is it like that? We never even thought about those things. I don't know from where they get those questions.

~ male, 23, business, India

I hate them. I hate them, they're horrible people and they should all be kicked in the asses. Oh, my god, I think generally they are very rude. I dealt with them once and horrible experience it was. I went to extend my visa. First time I called to make an appointment I had a fight . . . because the thing with these immigration people is that one immigration person can state different things from the other. I had this statement from my parents saying they will fund me . . . [one person said] yes, the other person said no. But you never know what is the right thing. When I came there they asked, 'Who actually said that to you?' This person. Well, this person doesn't exist. Stuff like that . . . I probably can't blame them in a way, they have so many [potential] immigrants, but the thing is they are very rude and really non-efficient. I remember they said my visa will be done in one month, it was done in two months. And it expired during that time. It was horrible. I don't like them at all.

~ male, 28, science, Indonesia

Oh, the Immigration Department is the most frustrating thing ever. You go there, which is quite far, and you sit there and lie in wait half a day or something. You go in to beg for an extension of your visa from someone who can't speak English as well as I can, who basically can barely speak English and who is a permanent resident of this country while I'm struggling just to stay here. It's extremely frustrating; I think I'm more Australian than some Australians. It's really difficult to be in this state of limbo not knowing whether you're actually Australian or not, and it's degrading to go there and say, I need to extend my visa and this is why and just hope out of the kindness of their hearts they don't say, 'No you're not, you're going home'... Also I hate the fact that the Immigration hotline is just a bunch of recorded messages, you'll never speak to a person. That is really annoying because everyone is an individual. You have your own problem that has an individual twist to it and you've got your own case to make, it's different. One sweeping tape recorded message cannot possibly solve that problem. The internet site is pretty useless. I would have liked to apply for permanent residency. What I didn't realise until too late, because I didn't know about it, was apparently I could have applied after my third year of Medicine, because I've got a BSc (Med) degree in the first three years. I didn't realise there is a window period of a year between that time and applying. Now it's too late... If you want to know about such things, you have to pay for an immigration lawyer to go through this with you and that's about $150 per half hour session; that's not worth it. They should make these kind of things freely available for people who are educated. It's not like they are a liability for the country. Immigration is one thing that really frustrates me. I hate it. It's based on an archaic white Australian policy.

~ female, 26, medicine, Malaysia

Probably they don't want us to live here.

~ male, 28, business, Bangladesh

The students were made to feel all the insecurities of the stateless. It could all end in a moment, at worst in detention or deportation. DIAC seemed designed to discomfort and intimidate: long waits after applying for a visa, unexpected difficulties switching from a visitor's visa to a student visa, large sums of money needed to establish immigration status, unexpected problems with health checks after arriving in Australia, not knowing whether visas would be renewed or when, finding money for down payments for processing, more like bribes than payments for services because they generated no better service, changes to the immigration rules that affected the transition from student status to permanent residence when students were halfway through what were non-optimal enrolments (several interviewees complained of this), which bridging visa to apply for and what was needed to secure it, how long the student's money would have to last while waiting for an application, what to do about accommodation while waiting, and so on.

The most common criticism of DIAC proceedings was about processing time – the weeks and months waiting for visas, the hours spent in offices. Students with appointments often had to wait well beyond the scheduled time.

> It's just irritating. It irritates you a lot.
>
> ~ female, 21, business, Bahrain

> I advise immigration in this country to change all persons of the Australian embassy in Tehran, because they make so [much] trouble, so [many] problems for all people . . . I have a scholarship but they made too many problems for me. It took about three months to get only a student visa. It's not fair and it's not logical.
>
> ~ male, 40, PhD in physiotherapy, Iran

> I went there to apply for my working visa and it was really disappointing. It took me more than three hours, just waiting, and when I told them that I had been waiting three hours outside, the officer was surprised, because she said she has nothing to do inside.
>
> ~ female, 28, education, China

> When I applied to renew my visa it took half a year. I know there are a lot of applications there but I don't know why it takes that long.
>
> ~ female, 21, business, China

The treatment of student applicants, like all applications for entry to Australia, was discriminatory without being fully transparent. Prospective students from countries considered more likely to generate visa overstays experienced longer delays, more security checks and tougher conditions. It was better to enter from the UK than Asia, and from within Asia better to come from Singapore than China or the Middle East. International students sponsored by Australia under schemes such as AusAID received preferential treatment in immigration processing.

Feelings of anxiety and helplessness about having few or no rights were compounded by contrary or incomplete advice. Apparently identical student cases, even students from the same cities, could receive divergent treatment. Many officials assumed that applicants had a higher level of knowledge than they possessed.

> I tried to extend my visa. I rang them up for information and all the information they gave me was, like, very negative. They didn't

> tell me that if I put in the application to extend my visa I would have a good chance. Some of the staff that worked there probably didn't know much about what they were doing, maybe because they were just recruited. They gave me different answers to my questions [among themselves] and it got me worried. I was under a lot of pressure because I was thinking that if I reapply they might cancel my visa. It would have been better if they had known what they were talking about.
>
> ~ male, 27, computing, Papua New Guinea

One 22 year old female student from Malaysia wanted to pay the costs of visa processing but was told that cash would not be accepted. She would have to pay by credit card. She had not been in Australia long enough to establish a bank account and credit card so she offered to pay using her brother's credit card. The DIAC official told her that she could not use someone else's credit facilities and scolded her. She broke down and cried. Two days later the payment was accepted by another DIAC official. There was no apology. 'If I need further study at Masters level, I will go to another country', she said. Other students told stories about how changing their course necessitated a longer stay and extension on their student visa, but were told this meant applying for a new visa, undergoing another medical check and paying $600 in processing fees for no good reason.

Immigration difficulties are not unique to Australia. Some students said that initial processing was slower in the USA, but Australian visas were more expensive.

LEARNING TO COPE

'These are the rules'

A minority of interviewees were more positive than negative. Dealing with immigration was less strenuous and traumatic than they expected.

> Just recently I had to deal with them about extending my visa, and that was really quick and helpful. I had no troubles there.
>
> ~ female, 22, business, Zimbabwe

> They are cool guys. I never got any problems from them.
>
> ~ male, 24, computing, India

'It went very well', said one business student from Indonesia. 'Any business I have with them is solved.' A German doctoral student in engineering said that his visa renewal 'ran very smoothly' although he had friends who experienced long delays. 'Extremely positive. No difficulty', stated a humanities student from Sri Lanka who had just obtained her work visa. A business student from Sri Lanka said that he always received a 'very good service' except for one time when he sought a work permit and had to queue for three hours. But, he said, 'I think that was beyond their control'. On the other hand a doctoral student in pharmacology from China complained strongly about waiting two hours for a work visa. Perhaps students' expectations of DIAC were variable because of differing bureaucratic regimes at home. One student from India, who experienced much to-ing and fro-ing in relation to the initial DIAC health check, nevertheless stated that

> The main difference [between here and home] is when you're dealing with the government departments everything is done very professionally. Back home in India it's a very big hassle to get anything done . . . Since there are Indians in the Australian High Commission the culture becomes like an Indian culture, they keep on making excuses and things like that. When I came out here, when I applied for my visa, the problem was sorted out and I got it very fast.
>
> ~ male, 30, dentistry, India

A number of interviewees said that officials were helpful although overworked and for that reason slow. It was better to go when they were less busy.

During the period of the interviews DIAC shifted to an online mechanism for work permits. This was welcomed by several interviewees. 'I got my visa very fast', said one from Indonesia. Not all were so fortunate. The biggest plus was avoiding direct encounters with officials. The department also modified its earlier practice of sending student appointees to far away locations to spread the workload between different DIAC offices. One student from Germany appreciated the changes.

> The first time they provided me with the wrong information, and it was a disaster . . . [The official] said I can only apply outside Australia for permanent residency, which is clearly wrong. The second

time was even worse. They suddenly developed this system of an 'express' lane and another lane. I went to the counter . . . and said I need some information about student visas and permanent residency. 'You are express lane.' I waited for a long time, even though it was express lane, and when I got to the counter all they said you can't ask any questions. Why is it that you are in express lane? I can only sell you a brochure. I said 'This is ridiculous' . . . Now the system works much better and they are much nicer. I think they have improved heaps. I used to dread to go to DIAC but now I don't mind. Even though you wait a very long time they are helpful and patient. They used to be really bad, in particular one person; I always ended up with this person. It is much better now.

~ male, 40, PhD in education, Germany

Experience in dealing with immigration bred in students the skills necessary to tolerate it, survive and work their way past the obstacle to their goal, whether in education or migration. They became more practical, patient and hard-bitten.

My experiences have been good. I've never had any problems because I stick to the basics and I stick to the rules. I don't think there is any way I'm going to win an argument if I'm having the argument with Immigration. It's not going to happen. If I have to fill in a form, if I have to do the medical and if I have to do it at a certain time, if I have to maintain the state of my visa, these are the rules. I'm in a foreign country, I have to do as the rules say.

~ male, 26, business, Botswana

They are there to stop me going through so what do you expect? They are there to make the international student's life miserable. They do accomplish their task indeed. Also they are there to make the immigrants or the alien residents of Australia miserable and they accomplish that task too. They do a good job, they do the job they are given. Those people are there for that purpose, what do you expect them to be? I don't like them much, but . . . they do [that job] very well indeed.

~ male, 33, PhD in medicine, Spain

OTHER DEALINGS WITH GOVERNMENT

A small number of other relations with government were discussed. Some interviewees mentioned officials who had been unexpectedly sympathetic. One praised the tax office for its professionalism and cheerfulness in its dealings with him. Another newly arrived student received extensive assistance from a Centrelink officer, though she had no entitlement to the service.

> When I came I didn't know about childcare facilities and I didn't know where to get information. So I called Centrelink. The officer was so kind. He made an appointment knowing that I'm not entitled for any entitlements. He sat down and he told me where to look for childcare, what the fees were like and stuff. He spent like one hour with us, knowing that we are foreigners. So we are very thankful.
>
> ~ female, 32, business, Singapore

Students from Indonesia and Vietnam with federal government AusAID scholarships spoke highly of the aid program. AusAID officers provided help with immigration, medical insurance, an emergency fund, and social and sporting activities. They backed up the students on matters in the university, including sensitive areas such as problems with doctoral supervisors. Students spoke well of their AusAID officers. 'When I talk to her she is really helpful, she is really kind and close to students', said a 21 year old female business student from Vietnam.

Unless they are covered by scholarship international students in Australia must pay school fees for their children (see chapter 4). AusAID scholarships include children's school fees but many foreign country scholarships and Australian university scholarships do not, as several interviewees noted. This contrasts with some other nations where international scholarship holders receive free schooling for their children in the country of education.[35] A French student in postgraduate medicine faced difficulties. Her scholarship was funded by the company that employed her and did not cover school fees for her sons. She had expected that education in Australia would be free.

> My oldest boy is six years old and going to primary school. My younger one is [still] in child care. I must admit that was a major

35 In 2006 the Victorian government announced that government school fees would be abolished for the families of all international students holding research degree scholarships.

> disappointment in Australia and we are struggling to stay on here. We have experienced a 50 per cent increase in the fees for primary school this year, which was not at all expected and put us in big financial difficulties, but we've not given up yet.
>
> ~ female, 39, medicine, France

A 40 year old male student from Laos, enrolled in a PhD in medicine and supported by a World Health Organization scholarship, was forced to leave two of his three children at home because he could only afford to educate one in Australia.

CONCLUSIONS

International students in Australia are governed by two state apparatuses: consumer protection-oriented governance led by AEI and managed by provider institutions, and the immigration regime policed by DIAC. Integration is less than perfect. In itself the university–AEI relationship is a stable system of authority but DIAC is something else. The concern of DIAC is not just to sustain global people mobility but also to secure the nation against it. The overall regime is coherent only because AEI and the universities defer to DIAC. At times the demands of immigration regulation, such as sudden arbitrary changes in visa requirements or costs, threaten to destabilise the industry. The universities can provide little check to DIAC, which has power over visas and reputations and the universities need its goodwill. Forms must be filled in accurately and breaches reported up the line. Mostly, though, AEI generates enough negative feedback to ensure corrections: after all the nation needs exports. Students' relations with government are pulled back and forth within the ebb and flow of the cold war between departments.

But international students experience government and institutions as one block of bureaus that know each other better than they know students. Those in institutions and government are all too aware of the gaps and tensions between and within each, but these are rarely accessible to student strategies. Here again we see the success of Australia's governance model, at least in its own terms. Responsibilisation, the chain of devolution downwards from nation-state, to educational provider, to informal networks and the private domain, does not subtract from authority or control. Institutions exercise a mix of hard and soft power. DIAC carries the big stick. The losers are the students.

They are frightened by immigration, which weakens their capacity to develop place-based identity in Australia, which in turn diminishes not only their learning experience but also their potential agency. At best DIAC is burdensome and fosters insecurity. At worst it is deeply menacing. The statistics on inappropriate visa cancellations and detentions are truly shocking and if the full nature of immigration policing was understood by prospective students and parents then demand for Australian exports would fall.

Immigration is an older form of state power that displays awesome force in that it diminishes the potential of self-managing subjects rather than empowering them to do its work. Aliens are less suitable vehicles for empowerment, less bound into the web of benefits and obligations than are citizens, who are thereby rendered safe. Global mobility poses a difficult challenge for regulation. Draconian immigration regimes are a means not of meeting the challenge but of avoiding it. What is needed is a more complex system of regulation encompassing more than one nation. Instead the security state stands athwart globally mobile and multiple identities like some latter day Colossus of Rhodes and imposes itself as a singular identity with categorical power. The world of DIAC is a crude world in which obsolete barriers are resurrected, loyalties are interrogated and binary distinctions forcibly policed. You are a citizen or you are an alien. You behave like a supine alien or you are out. Government stands at the gateway of Eden like an angel with a flaming sword and woe betide those who do not fill in all the forms or who work a minute longer in one calendar week than they are permitted because they will not remain therein.

Here the old Weberian authority of the nation-state makes its final stand. Standing warlike at the border, towering over the tiny human figures scurrying ant-like below, it casts a long traditional shadow over the economic, educational and cultural purposes of cross-border education. Spectre of Westphalia. Grizzled resistor of universal human rights. Sui generis hugger of its own territory in a global world. This is its grandeur and its gravitas. Not that of Augustus, but that of Don Corleone. Arbitrary and cruel. Insular and self-referential within a wider space, with no other principle or larger purpose. Strangely unworkable and anachronistic.

PART 3 SECURITY IN THE INFORMAL AND PRIVATE DOMAIN

INTRODUCTION TO PART 3: THE INFORMAL AND PRIVATE DOMAIN

In the security of international students, the formal domain of policy and regulation is ordered by the legal compacts between government and education institution, and education institution and student. As discussed in part 2 it is in the formal domain that recognised policy issues of student security such as housing and health care are played out. But as noted in part 1, beyond the formal domain of international education lies another domain, equally important to student security. That is the informal domain, larger and more complex than the formal domain, more shadowy in a public sense but more familiar in students' own lives. The informal domain begins with the semi-formal relations between education institution and student, inside and outside the classroom, that contour student life. Beyond the institutions is the world of intimate family and student households and networks of friends, religious observance, sport and arts and clubs and advocacy groups. While the formal domain is largely invariant and standardised, the informal domain is different for each person. It is always changing, shaped by students' successive encounters with authority and each other, with local people and life on the street. It is also the domain of the private self, of thoughts and sensibilities, feelings and imaginings. Though most of the informal domain is visible to provider institutions, this solely private space is normally invisible.

The informal domain is not recognised by policy or regulation except as personal details on file, but it is essential to students and to the care of students. Student security is advanced in the informal domain. It can also be lost. And, as we have seen, the informal domain has an essential role within the student security regime. Under ESOS the responsibility for student security is devolved down from government to institutions, and down again through the institutions to students themselves and thus to their families, networks and organisations. From day one institutions work hard on this second devolution. They encourage newly arrived students to band together in shared accommodation and student clubs that provide social support. The relationship between the formal and informal domains is symbiotic. Yet it is also in tension. There are overlaps and gaps. For a small number of students the informal domain scarcely exists. Some others have many problems in the informal domain, and often formal student security fails to identify or fix those problems. And while the economic health of the export industry partly depends on the willingness of individual university staff, motivated by vocation, to assist students in the informal domain as required, this does not always happen. Institutions are also striving for financial surplus in a commercial export market. Some enrol over 10 000 international students. They have to limit their capacity to monitor, supplement and protect students unless formally obliged to do so. Fuller student security is a privilege available to some students in some institutions some of the time. It seems that it is easy to draw a line around the accountability of the institution and to shift anything outside that line onto the students themselves.

The role of the non-formal dimension in student security is desirable and inevitable. The right of individuals and groups to make their own life is a central human value. We have argued that any regime of human security ought to protect and advance this. But there are limits to the degree to which security can be engineered from above by nation-states. When governments play too large and direct a role in people's lives they are more likely to undermine security than provide for it. When security functions are devolved into the less formal realm, security becomes more changeable, less transparent and more ambiguous. It is not always clear where lie the respective responsibilities of home and the Australian government, educational institution, academic unit, other university authority, non-government organisation (NGO), student society, informal social group and family. Which 'personal' matters are legitimate matters for external intervention? Lines of accountability are readily blurred. The limits of states are unclear. So are the rights of individuals, not only to privacy but also to protection and help. An Anglo-American-Australian system of security is too quick to hand the ultimate responsibility to the individual. It is an irony of self-freedom, highly problematic for international students alone in a strange country with varying personal resources. Some are significantly at risk. Here it is too easy to blame the victim, which is where Anglo-American humanism shows its limit, unless it is corrected.

When things go wrong with informal security they can go badly wrong. This is clear in relation to pathologies such as child abuse and domestic violence that routinely attend the family, the most important informal institution. But in most (though not all) cases the private problems of households are known to others because people's lives are connected between households. It appears that for international students this is less likely to be the case. Chapter 1 noted the case of Hong Jie Zhang, who was murdered in her flat in Canberra, and then left undiscovered for six months. The university vice-chancellor blamed the failure of discovery on Hong's 'peer group' because they did not notice she was missing. He expected that, as a matter of unsupervised routine, Hong would have social networks based on common-culture friends and that these networks should have not only provided for any lacuna (life threatening or otherwise) in Hong's life, but they should also have supplemented, and where necessary replaced, the responsibility of the university in pastoral care and the administration of enrolment. Invalid assumptions. Yet according to the regime of international student security the vice-chancellor was on solid ground. The university might have noticed Hong's failure to re-enrol in her program of study, if only to sustain the economic relationship. But Hong, being dead, had failed to signal her continuing importance to the university by renewing her fee payments, and even if she had, there was nothing in the legal or educational framework of student security that spelt out an obligation to provide Hong with pastoral care. The ultimate responsibility lay with uncodified social networks because it lay with Hong herself. She died and her body was neglected for half a year because she had failed to make friends. She had chosen the wrong boyfriend who harmed her instead of nurturing her. She had failed in the care of the self. Responsibility for care of the self has been deeply embedded in the Western tradition since the Stoics and Marcus Aurelius,[1] but some people fall through the cracks. The Western tradition also provides formal and informal safety nets,

1 Foucault, 1986.

even in Anglo-American polities such as Australia. But non-citizens such as Hong do not enjoy the citizen's access to common safety nets.

Australia's diffuse, voluntaristic and low cost student security regime, embodied in the spare provisions made in the ESOS Act, which was a child of the high deregulation era in 1990s public policy, works most of the time but not all the time. The firmness of contractual relations conceals a more diffuse reality. The one moment of clarity in relations between student and nation or university is when tuition fees are paid. This seems to settle matters, whatever they are, but then matters begin to blur. It is not a question of reading the fine print so much as reading what is not there at all. It would have been difficult to recruit Hong to her Australian university if it had been explained to her family prior to fee payment that once they left the university grounds students had to look after themselves against dangers without and within, and that this was the Australian way. But the elegant cynicism of the framework lies in the manner in which even the periodic failure of protection is represented as a form of freedom. It would have been wrong for the university to tell Hong and her networks how to manage their lives – at least until legal and moral claims against the university had to be evaded, blame had to be assigned, and her peers (but not her university) reminded of the common obligations of humanity. Thus the function of upholding the common good, devolved from state to civil institution, is finally dissolved into that pure private life that is the terminal point of the neoliberal imagination. Through the expedient of responsibilisation – devolution without certainty – the individual gains the freedom to act in exchange for the risk of arbitrary danger and violence. This freedom as danger is explained away as the most natural outcome of a naturalised market, as the price of the right to mobile consumption, as if the student cannot have both economic freedom and human security together. But this reduces international education. The devolution of human security on the basis of uncertainty, on the basis of insecurity, renders security impossible. By definition, security requires certainty.

Thus education is re-imagined as a market game in which risk is inevitable and there are losers as well as winners: Hong was one of the losers. Nation and university are remodelled from paternalistic bureaucracies to enterprising exporters and spare, economical and minimalist service providers. The opportunities bought by investing in mobility are held to justify the risks. And foreign students, or buyers, are 'liberated' to find their own unimagined pathway through this 'natural' world of riches and terrors.

Unlike Hong most international students experience their stay as largely happy, successful and free from danger. But Hong's life should not be explained away in terms of the inexplicable arbitrariness of violent crime, which from time to time destroys people even in the best kept communities. Still less should it be understood in terms of the pathology of the victim or flaws in the networks she kept. She was not protected. Many smaller problems also go unattended because of the sparse character of the security regime. And the security of all international students is affected for better or worse by the informal zone. We now need to look at that zone in detail.

The interviews with the 200 participants in this study suggest that for mobile students these informal relationships are configured in certain distinctive ways. First, the oncampus relations with teachers, service staff and administrators (see chapter 11) are very important. Not only do these relations mediate the formal domain of security (see part 2), but they also affect the potential of the informal and private domain and help shape the student ability to act. The effects are ambiguous. The data show that university staff often help individual students to survive and to manage their lives effectively. Often also, dealings with authority, mixing good and bad experiences in the manner of such encounters the world over, reinforce students' all too easily acquired sense of being powerless. Others in a foreign country. International students find themselves too dependent on educational and administrative systems that are unable to be nuanced for each individual case. Those systems lack the resources and skills needed for customisation.

Second, for the majority of international students, who come from English as a foreign language (EFL) countries, mastery of English is crucial to their security. Language is so central to everything, from academic success to dealing with landlords and surviving on the streets. Yet as chapter 12 notes, though Australia is officially a monoculture, language is largely treated as a matter of informal rather than formal regulation. Once they have satisfied the mandated English test at the point of entry, students' competence in language is primarily a matter for them to determine, not the responsibility of the institution, though some provide extra help. Still less does the Australian government assist with English language skills.

Third, there are family and same culture or similar culture friends. Chapter 13 maps out the field of students' personal and social networks. Bonding ties with the parental family have a continuing importance for many students. The sentimental power of these ties is evident. Nevertheless, for single students they are mostly conducted at a distance and their capacity to fulfil emotional needs is partly voided and partly displaced. The diasporic character of relations with parents facilitates the splitting of identities. This is the source of both ease of movement between contrasting roles and values, and tensions within the student's sense of self. Close bonding friendships with one or more people are often pivotal to students' lives. A consistent finding of the research, confirmed in our data, is that such friendships are almost always with a person or people from the same cultural and linguistic background. Interviews with many students suggest that these friendships operate as partial substitutes for the home family. Beyond close friendships is the larger set of less intimate friends and acquaintances. After a review of different ways of understanding networks, including social capital and actor network theories, the chapter uses a social network analysis to investigate network dynamics.

Chapter 14 looks at the other side of that coin, which is international students' experiences of loneliness and isolation while studying and living in Australia. The majority of students in our study experienced these feelings at some point during their stay, often associated with a sense of displacement of the self as self-determining agent, even students who had strong same-culture networks with fellow students. Chapter 14 develops the notion of cultural loneliness to help to explain this.

Finally, there are relationships with people in the country of education, also crucial in shaping the experience. These can be good, less than fully satisfactory, pathologically bad or non-existent. Data reported in chapter 15 on intercultural relations suggest that while cross-cultural problems such as discrimination and abuse that were reported by some non-white students in our study are mostly experienced outside the campus, in the general Australian community a primary difficulty is that most international students fail to form bridging friendships that they want with local students, and this weakens their external integration and sense of belonging. Here the study confirms a long string of research in Australia and the other English-speaking countries. What are perceived by students as cross-cultural barriers tend to force them back on same-culture networks as their primary or sole associations, thereby slowing the acquisition of English, weakening the capacity to manage multiple identity and value conflict. In this setting students' unfulfilled needs for home culture, language and emotional attachments are not just addressed but also reinforced. Some overcome these difficulties, some do not.

Here mobility and the cross-cultural setting combine and reinforce each other. Perhaps it is above all in this reciprocal interaction between mobility and cultural difference, in which individual students are partly open, partly adventurous, partly vulnerable and with variable resources for protecting, advancing and changing themselves, that the international student experience in Australia is shaped. Personal change is rarely easy to manage, but it is easier to manage in accustomed settings. We are in awe of what these students achieve in surviving and remaking themselves. Our point here is that the students' vulnerability, and their variable resources, are conditioned by gaps in the informal and private domain of security. This again places in question Australia's reliance on a narrow student-as-consumer conception of rights and the thin level of formal support provided.

11 THE UNIVERSITIES

When you first come here, you have no idea what to do. You end up like finding out about the whole university because they throw you from one place to the other.

– male, 28, science, Indonesia

INTRODUCTION: THE CONSUMER AS SUPPLICANT

'Do but despise understanding and science, which are the highest of all human gifts, and you have surrendered yourself to the devil and must surely perish.'

So says Goethe in *Mephistopheles*.[1] And, as websites of universities around the world tell us, those who desire 'understanding and science' must enrol at a university.

Those same university websites also describe their institutions as the path to individual enrichment and prosperity. That message might be more potent. After all it is Accounting and not Aristotle that puts bread on the table. But universities are very large and only intermittently friendly. It is not very easy to access scientific knowledge and professional careers in a foreign university in a strange country.

International students have three sets of relations with the university: with administrative processes, with academic staff and with student services. As the evidence below will show the harder moments are mostly with administration. Relations with services are more positive than negative. Academic experiences are mixed, but fraught because much is at stake. Often internal university

1 Hegel, 2008 (1820), 9.

dealings are mediated by an international student office, especially in the crucial early weeks. Normally international students are provided with meet and greet and orientation assistance. After that practices vary, depending on whether the institution has specialised international servicing or integrates services and administration across the local–international student divide.[2] Most teaching and learning are integrated. At one time or another all international students are treated as having distinct issues, and all are treated like other students. In both modes the tone of relations is often as important as the outcome. Thus each individual student's experiences are shaped semi-formally and informally, in day-to-day relations with the personnel of a large institution. It is a chancy business.

No one likes being treated as just a number with no right to negotiate. Even one ally on staff who treats students with respect can make a great difference. Too often though, as Lee and Rice note in their study of student services in the USA,[3] the system provides little opportunity to learn its processes, fails to create trust, translates cultural differences into deficits, responds to appeals for help in ways that make things worse, and tends to drive students away. A persistent pattern in the research on student encounters with services and university administration is that internationals have more problems than do locals (chapter 15). For international students, emotionally vulnerable and with less backup than locals, and for whom the hurdles are high and the bureaucracy strange, there is often too much at stake in their prosaic day-to-day encounters with the university.

This is because international students need more help from their universities than they have a strict legal right to expect. Under ESOS universities are meant to link with students but as part 2 described, the Act sketches this function in scant terms. The obligations of provider institutions are restricted by the primacy of commercial objectives, the thinness of the legal clauses concerning student welfare and educational matters, the lack of references to cultural difference, language needs and antidiscrimination. There are also the other agendas of universities, especially their need to minimise costs. The gaps in mandated

2 In the UK, UKCISA notes that in 2007, specialist support and advice for international students was provided by international offices in 51 per cent of institutions, general student services in 65 per cent of respondent institutions and by the student union in 48 per cent; UKCISA, 2007, 13.

3 Lee and Rice, 2007.

student security ensure that for the most part institutions can do it well or badly without violating the formal requirements. Either way, there is little students can do. At the same time, universities are not as difficult as the Department of Immigration. Regardless of the talk of students as consumers, as does DIAC, universities position the student as dependent on and subordinate to authority. But university decisions are rarely as mandatory and final as those of immigration. At university there is usually more than one way through the maze. University staff help students when they can. At best, unlike DIAC, they build not reduce the capabilities of international students; many individual students testify to this. The problem is that universities are not always at their best.

From the point of view of student security there is an inescapable ambiguity about relations with university authority. These relations augment student security and subtract from it. From the university side, there are thousands of international students. How could the institution provide a personalised service for every one? For students, the information asymmetry intrinsic to education markets is a permanent handicap: the provider always knows more about the product. The asymmetry is elongated in the global market. Initial buyer decisions are made from another country far from the action. It is difficult to penetrate marketing claims. Language and cultural difference retard information flow and the capacity to ask questions. Once the student arrives, a second asymmetry comes into play. The official language and procedures are novel. The student may be uncomfortable with how authorities behave, might feel the lack of old politeness regimes and the customary right to be related to in certain ways. Such feelings have to be put on hold. It is essential to make it work because changing university is a sanction of last resort. Fee paying students can attract other sellers, but transfers must be approved by DIAC, and wherever the student is enrolled, academic success rests on the goodwill of teaching staff and university officers. Complainants are told there are no repercussions, but this is not always true. Many-headed university authority has a thousand open and hidden ways to make its wishes known. Being an international student is a complex mixture of suppliance and sovereignty.

The chapter begins with research on relations between international students and educational institutions. In a comprehensive review of the literature on international education Harman notes that international students and their experiences constitute the largest part. But there are few studies on relations with universities (even less on relations with immigration).[4] A little can be gleaned from the literature on service utilisation, on teacher–student and supervisor–student relations, and surveys of student satisfaction. The rest of the chapter presents findings from the interviews with the students that focus on dealings with university staff and processes.

RESEARCH ON STUDENT–UNIVERSITY RELATIONS

International literature

Research data from the USA and the UK concerning relations between international students and universities mostly go to relations with faculty (academic staff), research supervisors and student services. Few studies focus on student experiences in dealing with administrative processes. A significant limitation is that most studies are generated in university service units and start from the prima facie position that international students should become integrated into the host community without any necessary change in the latter. As Lee and Rice remark it is assumed that 'host institutions are impartial and without fault'. Few studies focus on how universities purposefully or inadvertently marginalise international students.[5]

Relations between international students and university personnel are affected by the fact the students are non-local, which renders those relations more important to students and more difficult to conduct, and by language and cultural difference. Some US studies have found that students from non-Anglo-European cultural backgrounds and countries where English is learnt as a foreign language have relatively high needs for services, including culturally tailored services, but this does not always translate into higher rates of usage.[6] Factors related to language and cultural difference are associated with the highest levels of student dissatisfaction,[7] as noted in chapter 8 in

4 Harman, 2005.

5 Lee and Rice, 2007.

6 Hanassah and Tidwell, 2002, 305; Zhang and Dixon, 2003, 218; Yang et al., 2002, 204, 211–12; Chang and Chang, 2004, 140.

7 For example Selvadurai, 1991, 277; McGrath and Hooker, 2006, 11; Lee and Rice, 2007; Baloglu, 2000, 3; Mori, 2000, 140. For a fuller discussion of cross-cultural issues see chapter 15.

relation to health and counselling services. The literature also contains positive stories about student–institution relationships that build capacity. Yang and colleagues, for example, discussed the careers service at the University of Missouri, which was tailored for cultural differences, and which provided targeted information and superior generic skills.[8]

Some studies have found that 'faculty often misinterpret the behaviour of international students and need greater understanding of their academic, social, emotional and psychological challenge', as Andrade put it.[9] East Asian students[10] and Turkish students[11] may have expectations of teacher–student or supervisor (adviser)–student relations different to those of faculty, which can create potential for misunderstanding, disappointed expectation and conflict. Because intensive engagement is required the relationship with advisers brings these issues to a head. Kim investigated the student–adviser experiences of eight Korean students in the USA. Interviews were conducted in Korean. He found 'discrepancies' between advisers and students 'generated serious problems' and 'significant conflicts'.[12] 'It is not unusual to find advisors who are insensitive' to students 'from societies and values far distanced from the host country'.[13] All eight students had language difficulties but some faculty 'interpret poor communication as a sign of intellectual incapacity, underestimating the student's academic potential, rather than seeing communication problems as a transactional issue'.[14] Often students did not understand their advisers and found it especially difficult to make themselves understood, especially with non-verbal signals. 'The Korean students tended to form expectations about their relationships with American advisors based on their experiences with teachers in their home country', where they 'experienced the deep, almost parental involvement in their schooling of Korean teachers'. They 'expected the American advisors to play a similar role[15] ... The traditional parental image held by Korean

8 Yang et al., 2002, 206
9 Andrade, 2006, 149.
10 For example Wan, 2001, 39–42.
11 Tatar, 2005; see also Andrade, 2006, 137.
12 Kim, 2007, 179.
13 *ibid*, 174.
14 *ibid*, 174.
15 *ibid*, 183.

students of their teachers was of a strict and demanding individual who was also capable of being generous, attentive, supportive, protecting, and caring'.[16] Kim described it as 'warm authoritarianism', a Confucian combination of king, master and father. 'Contrary to their expectations, Korean students did not see American advisors playing the multiple roles similar to their Korean counterparts.' The students expected their advisers to closely supervise them but 'their advisors seemed to expect students to be independent and make decisions on their own'.[17] One student said, 'I didn't know why my advisor didn't give me work. Later, I realised I had to create work myself and do it. I felt overwhelmed'.[18]

Unable to solve these difficulties, students became passive, unwilling to take a lead. Kim noted that 'while intercultural awareness would help international students and their advisors understand each other better, it does not guarantee they will immediately alter their cultural traits and approaches to the advising relationship'. Respect, tolerance, concern and empathy for the other are also essential.[19]

Gender is also at play. In their survey of 640 international students at UCLA Hanassah and Tidwell found women exhibit higher levels of need for campus services.[20] Nasrin noted that research on graduate students shows women receive less support from academic departments, but most literature on international student 'adjustment experiences' is gender blind and does not tell us whether female problems are the same as male problems.[21]

Academic faculty are more likely than student services workers to neglect cultural factors, though there are exceptions. Whereas faculty may see creation of productive student–institution relations as voluntary for them and a function of student effort, services personnel are more likely to see such relations as instrumental to student survival. In Finland, Hoffman cites student service personnel at an oncampus international conference on racism, who when discussing faculty attitudes made comments such as 'We tell the faculty about this every

16 *ibid*, 183.
17 *ibid*, 185.
18 *ibid*, 184.
19 *ibid*, 189.
20 Hanassah and Tidwell, 2002, 305.
21 Nasrin, 2001, 15, 24–5.

year – it never sinks in', 'The international advisers see this as a pattern, while professors view these things as one-off incidents' and 'This is a faculty problem thrown back in our laps because the faculties don't understand it'.[22] In the UK Bradley found that 'some academics may actively seek to keep students at "arm's length" personally and emotionally in order for them to pursue other priorities',[23] while noting also that students found it difficult to express themselves emotionally in a second language.[24] The 2004 UKCOSA survey found that 'East Asian students showed lower satisfaction with teaching and academic support': 87 per cent of all students were satisfied with the course but 81 per cent of east Asians.[25]

Australia

In Australian-based research, the lesser focus on relations with teachers and research supervisors reflects the priority given to service delivery aspects and Australia's lesser role in global competition for doctoral students. A strength of the work is the insight into student–institution relations, including administration.

Volet and Tan-Quigley conducted interviews at two Western Australian universities. They spoke to 36 students from Singapore and Malaysia in Australia for one year or more, and 28 Australian administrative staff members who interacted with international students on a daily basis, including discipline-unit administrators, library staff, staff in residential colleges and general administrative staff.[26] They examined 'how some "awkward" cross-cultural incidents between southeast Asian students and Australian staff at university in Australia may be interpreted in terms of the cultural, subcultural and individual differences in the social rules governing this category of interactions'.[27] The researchers noted that 'People's personal views of what are socially unacceptable behaviours are mediated by their culturally bound values, belief structures and identities'.[28] When, for

22 Hoffman, 2003, 82–3.
23 Bradley, 2000, 421.
24 *ibid*, 422–3.
25 UKCISA, 2004, 10, 27.
26 Volet and Tan-Quigley, 1999, 97–8.
27 *ibid*, 95.
28 *ibid*, 96.

example, a southeast Asian student refers a complaint to the staff member's superior this may have a different cultural meaning to the student than it does to the staff member.

> [C]ulturally bound cognitions, values and expectations can contribute to misunderstandings in the interpretation of everyday behaviours and in turn to breakdown in cross-cultural communication between staff and students . . . misunderstandings, ethnocentric and egocentric attributions of meanings can lead to communication breakdowns and reciprocal negative stereotyping. Thus the importance of fostering the development of intercultural communication competence, knowledge of other cultures, and ability for social decentring.[29]

'Different cultural perspectives on administration and administrative matters have the potential to undermine many of the daily individual interactions between staff and international SEA students.' Volet and Tan-Quigley do not essentialise cultural factors, noting that relations between students and administrative authority are also affected by 'distinct agendas',[30] differences in purpose and intentions.

> According to Haas,[31] both the structural and cultural aspects of work situation determine people's roles on both the personal and professional levels. The structural features, which represent the stable, historically realised aspects of a work environment, are assumed to dictate the social and political structure, and, in particular, the power distribution within a given hierarchy. The cultural features, which refer to 'the norms and expectations which govern the actions of people in their work situation', have their roots in the social psyche of a cultural community and are instinctively understood and, to a larger extent, accepted by those functioning within its confines. In the case of cross-cultural encounters, however, the different norms and expectations of the two interacting parties may create misunderstanding and social friction.[32]

29 *ibid*, 95–6.
30 *ibid*, 96.
31 Haas, 1979.
32 Volet and Tan-Quigley, 1999, 96–7.

A theme common to several reported conflicts is that students do not take no for an answer.[33] In interview, administrative staff referred to 'socially inappropriate "persistent behaviours" '.[34] Staff were more inclined than students to explain this in terms of cultural differences in styles of negotiation. Students were more inclined than staff to say that 'the behaviour reflected different views of the importance of the administrative issue'.[35] The students saw themselves as having rights as fee-paying internationals to an education of high standard in Australia. While some misunderstandings could be put down to 'differences in overall cultural beliefs and values' between Australia and southeast Asia, 'others reflected differences in the subcultures of Australian administrative staff and southeast Asian international students'. They add that 'The range of interpretations within each group highlighted the magnitude of individual differences and should serve as a warning not to overgeneralise or to stereotype group behaviours, reactions or perceptions'.[36] The authors conclude that cross-cultural understanding requires more than an understanding of the cultural foundations of social relations. It requires the capacity to reflect on own and others' cultural assumptions in order to select 'a socially ethical course of action most suited to the occasioning situational and environmental variables'. They argue for a 'shared, collective responsibility in intercultural interactions' including a commitment to 'reciprocal understanding'.[37]

Another enquiry focuses on students' sense of belonging at university. Comparing international Muslim and local Muslim students, Asmar notes that both groups exhibit a much stronger sense of belonging in relation to teaching and learning than the university as a whole (table 11.1). Comparison with another study of local non-Muslim students suggests that while Muslims and non-Muslims have a similar level of belonging in relation to teaching and learning, non-Muslim students are much more at ease with their place in the university as a whole.[38]

33 *ibid*, 99–100.
34 *ibid*, 98.
35 *ibid*, 100.
36 *ibid*, 113–14.
37 *ibid*, 114.
38 Asmar, 2005, 130–1.

Table 11.1 Belonging, international and local Muslim students, 13 universities

	Yes %	To some extent %	No %	Total %
International students (n = 62)				
I feel part of a group of students and staff committed to learning	75	20	5	100
I feel I belong to the university community	34	57	10	100
Local students (n = 112)				
I feel part of a group of students and staff committed to learning	53	38	9	100
I feel I belong to the university community	30	61	10	100

Source: Asmar, 2005, 300.

Asmar's findings highlight the cultural determinants of students' relationship with the university not the local–international student distinction. It would be useful to investigate parallels between, say, Chinese-background Australian citizen students compared to international students from China. Perhaps in some matters cultural distinctions are more determining, in some the local–international distinction is more determining, in some structural relations between institution and student are more determining, that is, relations between social variables are not constant. In their survey at the University of Melbourne, Rosenthal and colleagues also asked about student–university relations. More than half the students agreed that 'I don't feel I really belong here at the university' (table 11.2). There was 'a statistically significant difference between the responses of students from Asian countries and other students; students from Asian countries feel significantly less at home in the university (mean = 1.6) than other internationals (mean = 1.2)'.[39]

Studies that touch on relations between academic faculty and international students in Australia find that as in the USA students perceive some staff to be indifferent to cultural factors, insufficiently communicative and/or unable to adjust teaching to the specific needs of international students who each have 'her or his own different and particular transnational educational history', as Singh put it.[40] Descriptors such as 'aloof', 'unfriendly' and 'speaks too fast' recur.

39 Rosenthal et al., 2006, 28; see also 93. Note that the study contained some students who were at the university for only two to three months, which probably reduced overall levels of connectedness.

40 Singh, 2005, 10.

Table 11.2 Sense of belonging among international students at the University of Melbourne, 2006

	0 Not at all %	1 Some agreement %	2 Considerable agreement %	3 Much agreement %	Total %
I don't feel I really belong here at the university *(n = 973)*	11.2	35.7	42.0	11.1	100.0

Source: Rosenthal, et al., 2006, 28.

Robertson and colleagues noted 'An overwhelming desire by students to be accepted by their fellow class students and staff' but 'a shortfall in many of the staff responses'.[41] Faculty involved in transnational teaching are often more adaptive to the cultural context of students than faculty onshore in Australia.[42] In transnational settings teachers deal with one group of international students in the home context, not a miscellany of less confident international students far from home. The teachers have to do more adjusting than the students. This can make for richer learning.

Australian studies confirm cultural difference and language barriers as factors affecting student service use. Gonzales noted that 'Trust also appeared to be an important factor in help-seeking behaviour and greater cultural distrust was associated with a more negative attitude towards seeking help'.[43] Snider discussed underuse of counselling services by Chinese students, which he attributes to conflicting views of confidentiality (chapter 8)[44] and other cultural factors:

> With few exceptions, ethnic Chinese students in the focus groups voiced negative sentiments about the staff and the settings. The most common theme was the ethnicity of counsellors. The Chinese students questioned the counsellors' abilities to be effective because 'only Chinese can understand another Chinese'. When questioned

41 For example Robertson et al., 2000, 94, 100–1; Ramsay et al., 1999, 137; see also Naidoo and Jamieson, 2005. In some studies, for example Ramsay et al., 1999, 136, the critical findings are balanced by instances of positive feedback.

42 For example in the discussions of teaching by staff at the University of Ballarat and the University of South Australia, in Marginson and Eijkman, 2007.

43 Gonzales, 2001, 6.

44 Snider, 2001, 75.

if the comment referred to language or ethnicity, both were identified as concerns. One student said, 'We don't trust strangers; only family and friends. Not a non-Chinese'.[45]

Student satisfaction survey, 2006

In its 2006 survey Australian Education International found international students had lower levels of positive response than domestic students on questions of studying in Australia, the course of study, the university and the quality of education. The largest gap was on satisfaction with the university. When asked if they would recommend to family and friends the university they attended, 75 per cent of international students said 'Yes' compared to 88 per cent of locals.[46] Satisfaction with the quality of education overall (where the survey respondents had a personal stake in the reputation of the degree) was greater than was satisfaction on all particulars related to the delivery of education.

Of the items on relations with university personnel, international students (71 per cent satisfaction) rated the commitment of staff lower than did local students (78 per cent), 64 per cent among students from China, including Hong Kong China. On opportunities for one-to-one contact with staff, satisfaction was 58 per cent for students from China, including Hong Kong China.[47] On course content, assessment and study workload, international satisfaction was 5–10 per cent lower but internationals were more positive than locals on quality of small classes, range of subjects and group projects.[48] The AEI noted that 'Satisfaction with the dimensions of educational delivery was lower for respondents from countries with greater cultural incongruence with Australia, notably Japan, Korea, China, North Asia'.[49]

When asked if they were treated with respect and courtesy by administrative and support staff, 85 per cent of international students

45 *ibid*, 76.

46 AEI, 2007a, 19–20, 24. There were much larger differences in the level of perceived respect and courtesy in relation to other categories, such as people in the Australian community, and in relation to international and local students; see chapter 15.

47 AEI, 2007b, 75, 80.

48 AEI, 2007a, 20.

49 *ibid*, 7.

Table 11.3 Satisfaction with study in Australia, course, university and aspects of the experience: international and local students, 2006

	Proportion of students 'satisfied'/'very satisfied'					
	Local n = 7064 %	**International n = 3608 %**	**China and Hong Kong China %**	**India %**	**Indonesia %**	**Malaysia and Singapore**
Study experience in Australia	91	85	81	82	86	88
Course	88	83	78	85	83	86
Living in Australia	–	84	77	87	86	83
University	88	75	Not available	Not available	Not available	Not available
Quality of education	81	77	73	76	83	82
Commitment of staff	78	71	64	79	74	71
One-to-one academic contact	72	69	58	76	79	72
Methods of teaching	74	69	66	77	71	70

Source: AEI, 2007, Higher education survey, 20; AEI, 2007, *All Sectors Survey Report*, 10–17, 72–84.

said 'Yes', not far below the 88 per cent of local students. In relation to whether they were so treated by teaching staff, 89 per cent of internationals said 'Yes' as did 92 per cent of locals.[50]

International students were twice as likely to have used university health services than locals (52 compared to 26 per cent) and accommodation services (41 compared to 20) and more likely to have used employment services (32 compared to 18), careers advice (25 compared to 20) and study support services (28 compared to 18). Ratings for the usefulness of the services were similar for both groups, though international students were less positive than locals about accommodation services (88 compared to 96) and employment services (83 compared to 93).[51]

50 *ibid*, 30.
51 *ibid*, 21.

Questions on relations with the university

Interviewees were asked a number of different questions concerning relations with the university.

- Please describe your dealings with your university – not your course and your teachers, the other parts of the university – from the time you first arrived.
- Are you aware of the student services that are provided to assist you at university – for example, student counselling, student health services, financial advice?
- What would you do/do you do when the university will not help you with a problem?
- What do you do if the problem is in the university itself?
- Please describe your experiences in dealing with your teachers and other people involved in your course(s) from when you first arrived. Are the people understanding of you and your needs?
- What would you do/do you do when your teachers will not help you with a problem?
- What do you do if the problem is in the course, the teaching, itself?

Most of the material in this chapter is drawn from those answers. Other questions in the study also raised questions concerning relations with the university, directly or indirectly, for example:

- If you were a student back home, would you get help if you were lonely or isolated, e.g., help from your education institution? Are the authorities more helpful here or less helpful?

Similar questions were asked in relation to help with finances, help with work and work problems. Questions about backup systems and protections also elucidated some comment on the universities.

SERVICES AND ADMINISTRATION

Students did not speak much of the university as a whole. In their first impressions and early experiences some saw it as a single alien entity. As their dealings with personnel and processes multiplied it became a miscellany of different academic, servicing and administrative systems and authorities. For many if not most students the international office was where it all came together, more so than the academic unit or classroom, the other important site.

Services and the international office: 'Very warm hearted'

Early experiences of staff and services on arrival and at orientation were mostly positive or very positive, though in a handful of cases meet and greet or other promised new arrival services were not provided.

> Yes, when I first entered the university I was not very familiar with the rules. I just ask the staff, whoever I find. They are just very warm hearted in regard to me.
>
> ~ female, 25, business, China

Individual experiences could vary. At one institution that provided initial help with accommodation, for example, one student was happy with the service, another cited broken promises, a third queried the expectation of six months rent in advance and a fourth was told by the student housing office that she would have to continue paying rent for university accommodation after moving out. This latter problem was later straightened out by the international office. Overall, though, students were mostly positive about student services personnel, especially health services (chapter 8). Clearly, in several cases professional staff members had been crucial to student survival.

Relations with the campus international office were the most positive, both in universities where administration and services for international students were channelled through that office, and those where it had a less comprehensive role. International office personnel understood international student needs better than did other parts of the university, especially in relation to cultural matters.

> What is good here is that the international office employs people from overseas. They are Australian residents but they come from overseas.
>
> ~ male, 28, PhD in social sciences, Cyprus

> In semester one I talked to one of the international student people, [saying that] I want to change course. They were really helpful . . . Because I'm an international student so they really care about me.
>
> ~ female, 19, business, Indonesia

'I have a good relationship with the staff at the international office', stated several. 'When I feel loneliness I always consult with the staff at the international office', said a male communications student from China. 'They are very friendly and helpful', declared a male business student from Indonesia. 'The office is like a second home for international students', said a female business student from Singapore, though she had a different story about her previous institution:

> The lady in charge, she's a local . . . I remember that when I first came my grandma was very sick. It was a life and death thing and [my grandma] was already bedridden and the doctor said to get ready . . . I tried to get visa to go home and she [in the international office] thought I was pulling a fast one. She refused to give me any leave and she accused me of lying. I was willing to take my exam early and then go back, but she insisted that I was lying. I felt so terrible I broke down.
>
> ~ female, 32, business, Singapore

Commercial services

'It's becoming profit first'

Where services involved monetary exchange, especially commercial services, there was more resentment about quantity or quality. One business student from India was concerned that the university charged for items that he thought should be free. Another student criticised the orientation of commercial services such as catering as well as the minimalist approach of free services such as security:

> The main issue that I have is with subsidiary services, for example, food providers as well as with the security services . . . It's [the university's] becoming a bit too much of a money grabber, it's becoming profit first and providing education second . . . A recent example [was] international union week . . . They offered cheap food prices during that week, but the week after that they eased the prices up. It's a well-known fact that the prices that you find [on] campus are about the same as commercial providers that you find outside campus, and the service that you are getting is not really as good as what you get from commercial providers. We expect to get subsidised services here on campus because we are after all paying a very high amount of tuition fees as well as our union fees to the university. It is reasonable to expect that we get a certain amount

> of value for money services back, but a lot of international students are not getting that. As for security, just recently when I asked them to come up and lock this office here, they were actually a bit reluctant to do that because they say that they're not really in charge of security, they are actually only in charge of maintaining security.
>
> ~ male, 23, business, Singapore

Administration

'It's just the way the uni works'

Students' relations with university administration spanned the good, the bad and the ugly. Behaviours of administrative staff were sometime recalled warmly. When asked whether he had experienced any particular problems in his dealings with university personnel, one student replied:

> Not at all actually. It's really, really smooth, so much better than in Germany. People are really nice, they get stuff done and no, I have absolutely no problems I would say. It was always good.
>
> ~ male, 28, PhD in engineering, Germany

A few students told of administrative staff, mostly from the international office, student services or in academic units, who had gone out of their way to help. More often encounters with administration in central university agencies were recalled with a shudder. There were also some criticisms of faculty level administration. Perhaps criticism of administrative staff is a reflex in most populations, with bad experiences almost fondly remembered and positive ones taken for granted. There were many complaints about the speed of administration, with comments such as 'It's very slow', 'Sometimes it takes ages, we have to wait', and 'They are very lazy!'; there were also complaints about contradictory advice. There were common stories of repeated phone calls, of messages not being passed on to staff, staff not calling back, being sent back and forth between staff and other symptoms of administrative overload. In a few institutions staff still used manual recording processes. In some places online systems functioned poorly. One female business student said there were no problems with administration because 'We do most of the admin stuff over the internet', but delayed replies to email was an issue.

> Although I'm happy with the university it's quite slow and quite messy at times.
>
> ~ male, 22, architecture, Malaysia

> They tell you what they have been told. They're not creative, that's the thing.
>
> ~ male, 24, social science, Vietnam

> Once I was asking about course requirements. They weren't very helpful. They were, like, very abrupt and cut you short. 'Read this.' They are like that to everybody.
>
> ~ female, 22, business, Malaysia

> When I first arrived . . . the degree programs officer she was very rude, very rude. She just did not connect with me, didn't understand my problems.
>
> ~ male, 27, music, India

> Teachers are really good, but the administration is so bad . . . if you want to get something from them, in computer science, it's the worst. It takes a lot of time and every second person is telling us a different story.
>
> ~ male, 24, computing, India

> This university . . . oh, God . . . the university personnel here is horrible. I thought the bureaucracy here would be pretty good but you get thrown from one place to another and the people here don't know exactly what you have to do if you have a problem . . . You have to get student coverage . . . go there! You have to pay student fees, go somewhere else! Transfer? Go somewhere else! If they had just one centre for it, then everything would be done right.
>
> ~ male, 28, science, Indonesia

One students who was a leader in the postgraduate student association had learnt that in order to get things done, he worked around administration rather than through it. He saw the university bureaucracy as disabling, not enabling.

> The administration in this university tends to be what stops everything. If you have a plan, a good idea or whatever and you have to go to administration, chances are that . . . you're going nowhere. I tend to go around administration. Basically, I do things by

> myself and when it doesn't work I get my supervisor involved, because he calls the boss of the person I'm talking to or the boss's boss, and then something gets done. But [if I go] to the research office . . . That's useless . . . as soon as they see I'm a student they tell me 'No, it cannot be done'. It is a 'We'll call you back' and the call never comes back.
>
> ~ male, 33, PhD in medicine, Spain

Some students alleged instances of discrimination (see also chapter 15). In response to a question about whether she had experienced any particular problems in her dealings with the university, one student replied:

> Not me in particular but my friend . . . she was trying to get help from one of the ladies at her school. The woman [was] just so really really mean to her. Before she went up, there was an Aussie person and she was helpful to the guy. Then when [my friend] came up she was just really different. My friend was asking more or less the same thing [as the guy]. We wanted to send a complaint, but I don't think she ended up sending the complaint. Another girl from Kenya told her that after she sent a complaint she started to get into more trouble from everyone else, she got problems.
>
> ~ female, 22, business, Botswana

Several students had run into difficulties with the university's handling of course credits at commencement or when moving between institutions or between programs in the same institution. One student from India who had attended a prestigious national university was told by student services in his Australian university that his degree was not good enough. The matter was later sorted out at faculty level. Such problems compounded when the university did not use a single system of standardised credits, when the student received different information from different parts of the university or when the student experienced an unanticipated rise in fees when moving to another program level. One student complained that administration routinely sent official mail to his parents' address in the USA, though his residential address was close to the campus, causing a two week delay. The university had then fined him for late payment of fees. Clearly, for many students dealing with university administration, like dealing with immigration, was a survival skill that was slowly and sometimes painfully acquired.

> I wouldn't say I have had any real problems, but maybe sometimes just the sense that you have to go to too many different points to get the answer to a question. When I arrived I just had no idea of where I was supposed to go.
>
> ~ male, 24, business, USA

> At first I felt that the university didn't really care personally about us, not like [the staff in] the foundation program. But I came to realise that it's just the way the uni works. They help a lot of people. You need to read the things and follow the system. As I get used to it I feel that really they are very helpful.
>
> ~ male, 18, engineering, Indonesia

Teachers

'Some are very nice and some just don't care'

Interviewees were less critical about academic teachers than about university administration. Positive and negative statements split 50:50. Many interviewees had mixed experiences. It was not just that some teachers were more friendly – though students often couched it that way – but across the academic staff there were also inconsistent approaches to culturally mixed classes: whether and to what extent to differentiate between students with different needs, how to deal with students from non-English-speaking backgrounds with partly formed skills in academic English, whether to make extra efforts for them. Some students had happy stories about the support they received, especially in the early stages of steep learning curves. 'Patience' was often mentioned. Approachability was also important.

> There are some brilliant professors. Some of them are very helpful, some of them are very nice and they would take the time out to deal with you personally and then some just don't care.
>
> ~ female, 22, business, India

> I am deeply touched by their patience and kindness. They are mostly Australian but the cultural diversity in the class is very huge. If you take 10 students, you get 10 different accents. But still the lecturers listen to them with patience and they try to help.
>
> ~ female, 34, business, Sri Lanka

Some academic teachers were criticised because they gave more attention to local students than internationals. Others were criticised because they failed to discriminate by taking account of the distinctive problems of international students:

> There's just one [teacher] . . . She seems to think that Asian people are not as smart as local people. We just feel that she puts more attention to local students. Not many teachers, just one.
>
> ~ female, 27, business, Indonesia

> They just see us the same as local people.
>
> ~ female, 24, communications, Hong Kong China

Research degree supervision required more complex and engaged support. Doctoral students in the study mostly had a good rapport with their supervisors, especially when the student worked on staff as a teaching or research assistant.

> My teachers accept me as a colleague . . . I have a very good rapport with my supervisor. She's asked me to take a lecture every semester. I respect her and I look up to her and I ask for help when I need it.
>
> ~ female, 40, gender studies, Papua New Guinea

CONCLUSIONS

The size and the wholly commercial character of the industry make it impossible for universities to fully service all international students individually. As noted the industry is also partly carried by the willingness of some staff to go the extra mile for students when it is needed. Given the scale of the industry this no longer suffices, if it ever could. One staff member, who had worked in an international office for a decade, told the research team that every year a small proportion of international students constituted serious mental health cases. When there were only a few cases each year they were referred to state mental health services and treated without charge. This was needs-based provision outside commercial frameworks and the abbreviated student entitlements of the National Code. But growth meant the university now had 100 or more such cases each year and the state mental health authority could no longer carry the cost. Nor did the international office have staff to manage the cases. In this situation, the ESOS framework is attractive to institutions. It enables them to hold students at a distance. The loser is the mentally ill student, suddenly made responsible for her or his own fate.

The industry in Australia has been built more by augmentation of services than of academic capacity. But given the imperative to minimise unit costs, service provision wherever possible is rendered generic to locals and internationals alike. When they can, the universities avoid tailored services, such as the careers service exclusively for internationals proposed by Yang and colleagues,[52] or high cost targeted welfare with no commercial payoffs as in the case of mental health.

> The irony is that marketisation, ostensibly in the customer's favour . . . may even produce a worse experience for the student where a business calculation does not make it worth the institution (or educator's) while to produce service of a high standard.[53]

Students experience relations with the university as uncertain. It fails to provide sure backup in a crisis. It also fails to meet many routine non-crisis needs in the areas discussed in this book, such as finances, work, health, housing, immigration problems, English language assistance, loneliness and lack of social networks. Here the problem is more than one of a spare commercially driven cost structure joined to system and service overload. It is also communication failure and organisational pathology. The university does not always synchronise with students. First, students experience the university as fragmented and episodic. It fails to constitute an integrated system. Often information banks are poorly integrated, especially between academic and non-academic units. Universities with strong, well-connected international offices come closest to providing a coherent interface with students. Second, language barriers often prevent students from raising problems and establishing ongoing service relationships with university personnel. This is convenient for universities. It protects them from more extensive and intensive servicing responsibilities. It also conceals serious problems, and throws students back onto the less reliable protections and capacities of family and informal same-culture networks. There is something deft in the way universities do this. But it is also a form of work shedding. And it is the transfer of

52 Yang et al., 2002.
53 Scott, 1999, 200.

expectations, which are uncodified but real, that universities normally provide their students with full pastoral care. 'Consuming' families and students do not necessarily accept the limited ESOS Act view of their entitlements.

And what happens when university personnel who are nominally there to help are themselves the source of the student's problem, or protect the source (and universities defend their own)? This is the heart of the ambiguity in student–university relations. Often the university is the only place where students can go for help with a formal matter. Yet such formal difficulties are often generated by the operations of universities themselves. The solution is the problem. The problem is the solution. This dilemma again forces students back onto the support structures of the informal sector. But informal mechanisms are better for coping than solving.

Institutions expect and encourage students to sustain same-culture networks. No doubt these have a growing potential as international education expands, but given the crucial role of those informal networks as supplementary to universities in student security – as backup in a crisis, as fillers for holes in university servicing, and as point of reference when the university itself is the problem – then the universities should monitor the informal domain more effectively than they do. Universities should, for example, identify instances of students who lack private social networks. But the Act does not require this, and as the universities see it, informal networks are there to relieve them of responsibility, not to create more work.

The next chapter looks at international students' experiences in using English, a threshold condition of most relationships and all student security.

12 LANGUAGE

There's a tutor, she was about to fail my first assignment which I thought I had done perfectly. She was so awful. When I walked into her office, the very first thing she said, 'You are an international student, right? So does this happen to you often, has it happen to you before?' She assumed that English is my problem and it had been happening since I started university... Yes, I'm an international student, but I don't deserve the description of someone who is more likely to fail.

~ female, 23, social work, Taiwan

INTRODUCTION: LANGUAGE AND STUDENT SECURITY

Language shapes our mentalities and makes communication and association possible. For international students, cross-border mobility is mobility from one zone of social communication to another. Language fluency not only affects ease of mobility, but in some respects it also determines whether mobility takes place. Students' capacity in the language of the country of education governs academic success, as well as with whom students talk and the nature of their day-to-day life. Language capacity also determines whether students can deal with problems and emergencies on their own behalf. Communication is essential to survival and security in almost all situations.

If there is one theme that stands out in the research literature on international education in English-speaking nations, it is that of international students' language-related difficulties, which can be particularly severe for students from countries where English is learnt as a foreign language, being at best a medium of instruction in the classroom and sometimes merely a subject of study, rather than a language of daily interaction. These countries include China, the world's largest source of international students and the largest single provider of students in Australia, Japan, Korea, Taiwan, Vietnam, Thailand and Indonesia.

As this chapter will show, students see language as key to the experience. Improving English proficiency is almost as important as the degree itself. The rapid growth of international education corresponds to the spread of the global role of English[1] and of demand for English-medium skills. Further, communicative competence and confidence in English mediates the informal domain as much as the academic experience to define the student's networks and spheres of activity. Yet research in Australia, as in other English-speaking nations, has found that the language difficulties experienced by international students are not necessarily overcome during the period of study, even among students who successfully complete their degrees. One study even suggests that some students graduate with skills in English that have deteriorated since their arrival.[2] If this is true, then not only is their day-to-day security in jeopardy but much of the point of investing in a foreign education has also been lost. Here the role of language in learning and student security intersects with continuing and often heated debates about language testing and standards at entry, the level and type of English inherent in degree programs and the support (or lack of support) for language formation during the period of study.

The chapter begins with a discussion about research on international students and language, and then presents findings from the interviews on language-related issues pertaining to student security. These include students' language difficulties, the resulting social challenges and their views on language support services. Issues of teaching and learning, to the extent they relate to student security, are touched on briefly. (Study data in this area will be largely published elsewhere.)[3] Relations between language and discrimination are further explored in chapter 15.

1 Crystal, 2003.

2 Birrell, 2006.

3 Marginson and Sawir, forthcoming; Sawir et al., forthcoming.

RESEARCH ON LANGUAGE FACTORS

For reasons of space a full survey of the international literature on international students and language, potentially a book in itself, is not attempted here.[4] The discussion focuses on relations between language competence and confidence, self-determining agency and interaction with host country nationals.

International studies

The role of language in the adjustment of non-native speakers of English is the subject of much research in the USA.[5] Yang and colleagues state that 'Because communication skills are essential for satisfying everyday needs, many scholars argue that competence in intercultural communication and in the language of the host society is crucial for fulfilling those needs'.[6] Church, in a study of mobile business personnel, noted the positive relationship between language proficiency and social interaction with host nationals.[7] Hayes and Lin remark that 'English proficiency has been found to be an important factor in social interaction and adjustment',[8] that 'the inability to speak the host language fluently is a primary inhibiter to becoming socially involved in the host society'[9] and 'to fill the void' some international students 'form strong in-group oriented ethnic communities', which enables them to 'establish new primary relations' in place of the lost family and friends back home.[10] Redmond surveyed 644 international students at one university, finding the effects of 'intercultural communication competence' on the level of student stress are 'fairly constant' regardless of students' cultural values.[11] Nasrin conducted focus group interviews with four students from Bangladesh, Cameroon, Taiwan and Venezuela concerning adjustment experiences and coping techniques.[12] The students were concerned about oral

4 There is further discussion in Marginson and Sawir, forthcoming.
5 For discussion of the notion of adjustment, see chapter 15.
6 Yang et al., 2006, 490.
7 Church, 1982, 546.
8 Hayes and Lin, 1994, 8.
9 *ibid*, 11.
10 *ibid*, 8–9.
11 Redmond, 2000, 156.
12 Nasrin, 2001.

communication, particularly understanding the American accent, and class presentations. The students knew their university subjects but could not effectively communicate their understanding.

One line of enquiry points to an interdependency between communication in the host language and the self-determining agency of international students. Communicative competence mediates and interacts with the level of contact with host country nationals. Both factors augment self-confidence, which facilitates more local encounters and furthers language development and academic success. MacIntyre and colleagues found that self-confidence is a more important predictor of language use and 'acculturation' than is language competence.[13] In a study of 81 international students from non-Western backgrounds in Canada, Yang and colleagues hypothesised that frequent intercultural contact contributes to student adaptation and the link is mediated by English language self-confidence. They confirm this hypothesis, and also find that a sense of self-determining agency or 'independent self-construals' predicts 'greater English self-confidence'.[14] Conversely, 'communicative competence in the host language directly promotes better wellbeing, perhaps because the language provides a vehicle of self-expression and identity negotiation'; and 'given that comfort using the language of the host society facilitates the fulfillment of everyday needs, self-confidence was associated with better ability to carry out everyday tasks'.[15]

> The findings reveal that some people with particular self-ways are more likely to experience better cross-cultural adaptation during international student sojourns. That said, personality characteristics are not the only determinants of adaptation, as communicative competence and comfort in the host language play a pivotal role in this process. Not only do language and communication processes (indexed by self-confidence) mediate the relations between host cultural contact and psychological and sociocultural difficulty, but they also mediate the influence of self-construals on adaptation. These findings suggest that although some people might be better suited to international sojourns because of their personality

13 MacIntyre et al., 1998; Yang et al., 2006, 491.
14 *ibid*, 501–2.
15 *ibid*, 502.

characteristics, by developing linguistic and communication skill and comfort in the host language, many people can have a positive experience with international education.[16]

Strong agency helps students to acquire communicative skills and to attempt and execute communications. Communicative capacity helps sustain and augment effective agency and self-worth amid the downward pressures on status and self-questioning of one's day-to-day competence. Communicative capacity by itself does not ensure agency, but it helps. Other studies in cross-cultural psychology focus on reciprocity between communicative activity and agency, using various notions of agency: Li and Gasser on 'cross-cultural self-efficacy',[17] Hullett and Witte on 'uncertainty control',[18] Matsumoto and colleagues on social interaction.[19] Ward and colleagues combine communicability and agency as 'extraversion'.[20] Studying graduate students at one university Perrucci and Hu find that 'academic satisfaction is most strongly related to contact with US students, language skills, and perceived discrimination', while 'social satisfaction is linked with marital status, language skills, perceived discrimination and contact with US students'.[21] Communicative capacity is associated with self-worth and linked in a virtuous circle with interaction with host nationals, bringing a sense of belonging.

> [The social] satisfaction of international graduate students with their experiences in the host environment is largely shaped by their language skills, self-esteem, and a feeling of positive involvement with their social environment. Contact with U.S. graduate students is probably facilitated by language proficiency and strong feelings of self-worth and competence on the part of international students. When these individual and social resources of students are combined with a perception of the host environment as accepting and positive toward them and their country, the basis for satisfaction is established.[22]

16 *ibid*, 503.
17 Li and Gasser, 2005.
18 Hullett and Witte, 2001.
19 Matsumoto et al., 2001.
20 Ward et al., 2004.
21 Perrucci and Hu, 1995, 491.
22 *ibid*, 506.

Likewise research focused on stereotyping, segregation and discrimination in intercultural relations identifies the centrality of language factors. In research on the stereotyping of foreign students by local students, Spencer-Rodgers noted that

> Aside from the occasional, extremely negative response such as 'they should study in their own country' and 'creepy', the most derogatory descriptors elicited in the study were related to language barriers. For instance, foreign students 'can't speak', 'can't communicate', and 'shouldn't be TAs [teaching assistants]'. Internationals were evidently perceived as deficient in English language ability (23 per cent).[23]

In Fatima's study of female graduate students from non-European countries in a US university in the deep south, the term 'discrimination' was introduced by the study participants not the researcher 'while the participants were discussing about the language problem'.[24] Lee and Rice noted the centrality of language factors in studies of international students and discrimination.[25] Perceived differences in speech can trigger communication barriers, including stereotyping of international students, prejudicial attitudes[26] and abuse. Prior stereotyping and assumptions of local superiority may create expectations of communication problems even when there are none (see chapter 15). Again we find reciprocity between relations of power and communicative relations. While most non-native speakers want their identities to be acknowledged, they do not want cultural differences to disable them. But it is difficult for them to seize the verbal initiative and shape the terrain of conversation so as to optimise communicative understanding and mutual cultural respect.

In a study of international students at one UK university Li and Kaye likewise found that language difficulties, and separation or segregation, are circularly linked.

> Students who have English language problems tend to have difficulties in mixing with UK students; on the other hand, the students who do not mix with UK students have less opportunities to

23 Spencer-Rodgers, 2001, 652.
24 Fatima, 2001, 43.
25 Lee and Rice, 2007, 389–90.
26 Spencer-Rodgers and McGovern, 2002.

communicate in English and are likely to continue to have English language problems.[27]

Butcher and McGrath investigated international students in New Zealand.[28] Their academic needs included proficiency in English so they would be able to understand textbooks and lecturers in class, grasp questions, assignments and the use of research skills, to communicate verbally and have an understanding of non-verbal aspects of communication, including humour and knowledge of New Zealand history. Li and colleagues focus on language difficulties specific to international students in New Zealand.[29] They gathered data from 23 students from China, India, Sri Lanka and Myanmar by means of group and individual interviews. Language difficulties constituted significant barriers to learning in unfamiliar settings, student interaction in the classroom and cultural adaptation. These difficulties varied by discipline. More conceptually based degree programs, for example, such as management, required greater accuracy in written English than did computing or accounting.

Australia

Australian-based studies are largely focused on teaching and learning. Pantelides[30] and Robertson and colleagues studied learning difficulties as perceived by students and academic staff.[31] Research by Feast and Carroll investigated the relationship between English language proficiency and academic performance.[32] Prescott and Hellstén considered factors affecting the academic transition into Australian classrooms.[33] Sawir considered the effects of prior learning experience on the conversational English of international students.[34] There are data on language factors in broader studies by Singh, Daroesman and colleagues, and Rosenthal and colleagues.[35] Proficiency in

27 Li and Kaye, 1998, 48.
28 Butcher and McGrath, 2004.
29 Li et al., 2002.
30 Pantelides, 1999.
31 Robertson et. al., 2000.
32 Feast, 2002; Carroll, 2005.
33 Prescott and Hellstén, 2005.
34 Sawir, 2005.
35 Singh, 2005; Daroesman et al., 2005; Rosenthal et al., 2006.

academic English helps students to survive and succeed as students, which contributes to their wellbeing. But the more important effect for international student security is that it augments broader communicative capacity. This larger dimension of communicative competence is little researched.

Pantelides interviewed 12 non-English-speaking background (NESB) international students in engineering and four members of academic staff. The staff noted that although the students had achieved the minimum standard of English required for entry, their academic skills were inadequate. Staff were sympathetic but had little knowledge of language learning per se and did not always recognise student unease. Staff also noted that extra efforts in support of NESB students were not recognised or rewarded. When asked whether they adapted lectures for the students they said 'No'. The students agreed that language difficulties hampered academic progress, and were frustrated at the failure of staff to take their learning needs into account. When seeking language assistance, they mostly turned first to friends or relatives, and then to dictionaries, grammar books or computer software. The last resort was to consult the lecturers.[36]

> Many teachers have little understanding that NESB students may be working in their second or third language and from very different cultural understandings. Similarly, many do not appreciate the effects of students' English language difficulties on their ability to comprehend and articulate their understanding of content in what is primarily a very traditional, behaviourist-type assessment context.[37]

Pantelides goes on to argue that even when lecturers are sympathetic to the students' problems they may not recognise symptoms of student unease; when they do recognise the symptoms they may not know how to deal with them. But she adds that language proficiency is not the only predictor of academic success, and research indicates that international students with low English competency are able to survive and succeed at university if the environment is conducive enough.[38] This suggests that the primary solution is not to

36 Pantelides, 1999.

37 *ibid*, 66.

38 Asmar, 1999; Stoynoff, 1997.

raise standards at the point of entry. It is to transform preparation and make language-related assistance integral to the whole curriculum, not just to provide partial and exceptional support services that carry with them the stigma of deficit and remediation. 'If we accept that language is the key to learning, all educators have a clear and pressing responsibility to support students' language development.'[39] Robertson and colleagues[40] also gathered data from students and staff. Both groups emphasised learning problems associated with language. The students said that lack of confidence with English further inhibited learning by, for example, hindering classroom speech. The study concluded that the main problems of international students are language-related. Similarly, Gatfield and collaborators find the students are more concerned about the difficulties of academic learning in English than any other factor.[41] Other researchers note that while acquiring foundational language in the first months of study, students deal with other learning challenges that interact with language proficiency: discipline-based critical thinking and problem solving, lecturers' expectations, workloads and time management,[42] familiarity with the Australian academic context, autonomy, motivation and maturity,[43] and integration into the broader university environment.[44]

Research highlights problems of speech and writing. Writing presents challenging difficulties because it is nested in culturally specific conventions and styles. People from varied linguistic and cultural backgrounds organise discourse differently.[45] Wilkinson and Kavan suggest that in Western academic writing style meaning is developed in a linear way whereas in much Asian academic writing, especially southeast Asian, meaning is negotiated by using circling inferences.[46] This goes beyond vocabulary and grammar to embrace politeness regimes and what is persuasive in argument. There are also differences between the academic disciplines in how a piece of work is written. This is confirmed repeatedly in the literature, for example

39 Pantelides, 1999, 64.
40 Robertson et al., 2000.
41 Gatfield et al., 1999; see also Malcolm and McGregor, 1995.
42 Hill et al., 1999.
43 Borland and Pearce, 2002.
44 Grayson, 2005.
45 Gonzalez et al., 2001, 20.
46 Wilkinson and Kavan, 2003; in McLean and Ransom, 2005.

Zhu on writing tasks.[47] Spack argues that the general language and study skills taught in most preparatory courses are not always transferable to discipline-specific tasks, academic skills are 'not fixed' and 'all academic work is socially situated'.[48] Not only do skills and conventions vary between disciplines but the disciplinary variations are also culturally variant. Business education in Thailand is two removes from its equivalent in Australia.

Hellstén and Prescott used interviews with 48 international students to investigate relations between cultural practices and pedagogy.[49] Asian students felt inadequate in spoken English, which hinders their classroom participation, but these students were wary of suggestions that lecturers should adjust their style downwards to meet students' communicative competence, which they saw as a 'gesture that further marginalises them from the mainstream students'.[50] Another paper by Prescott and Hellstén used the interview data to examine social and cultural experiences on arrival, friendship and peer relationships, and students' beliefs about how they were coping.[51] The difficulties facing international students in making the transition from prior learning environments were exacerbated by language factors and the absence of customary social and/or cultural zones. Language-related factors also enhanced time pressures. Study and assignment preparation took longer. Lectures were recorded and listened to again. Cross-cultural conversation was slowed by mental translation. 'If you are a native speaker you can response very quickly, you can think in English very quickly, but . . . in my case, when I think in English it takes more time than in Japanese', stated one student.[52] Students in difficulty often failed to approach staff, especially when the problem was lecturer behaviour, for example, speaking too fast. The students often preferred to avoid confrontation, again a culturally specific response.

Singh conducted interviews with students from China in the final year of first degrees in Australia. Learning American or British textbook English had not fully prepared the students for Australian

47 Zhu, 2004.
48 Spack, 1997, 50.
49 Hellstén and Prescott, 2004.
50 *ibid*, 347.
51 Prescott and Hellstén, 2005.
52 *ibid*, 86.

speech.[53] The students identified ways to improve linguistic and cultural competence such as making friendships with students from other countries, and obtaining part-time jobs that would generate English-language conversations, thereby enhancing confidence and independence. But it was difficult to make friends with local students, partly because of language barriers.

Using a questionnaire administered to 2555 international students at the University of Melbourne, facets explored by Daroesman and colleagues included student expectations about learning programs and their extra curricular activities.[54] Students had problems with writing, aural understanding and class talk. Language difficulties also affected them outside the classroom and were a constant issue. Rosenthal and colleagues found that international students who had spoken some English when growing up had a stronger sense of connectedness (chapter 13), lower cultural stress, more satisfaction in living arrangements, higher involvement in paid work and a more satisfactory balance between study and social life. Students who had not spoken English before had higher levels of stress and a lower connectedness, and often restricted themselves socially to same-culture friends (chapter 13). Language-related variables were more strongly correlated than was country of origin with a sense of connectedness.[55]

Devos focused on the public media positioning of international students and their difficulties with English as drivers of an alleged decline in academic standards.[56] Though the theme was not addressed by interviewees in the present study, this public positioning constitutes a potential threat to student security.

Language testing

Most students entering Australia are required to undertake an International English Language Testing System (IELTS) test, which assesses students in speaking, listening, reading and writing. The same test is used to determine permanent residence visas after students graduate.

53 Singh, 2005.
54 Daroesman et al., 2005.
55 Rosenthal et al., 2006, 89.
56 Devos, 2003.

Most universities set a minimum average IELTS level of 6.0 or 6.5 at entry, though institutions have discretion. Some students enter from secondary school or vocational courses in Australia, others from a foundation English course offshore, without sitting an IELTS test.

The IELTS score is widely accepted as an indicator of language proficiency and endorsed without question by the Australian government.[57] In public debate it is often assumed that testing standards could be raised to ensure that all students are adequately prepared for the academic and social environment. This would only be true if students achieving IELTS standards were prepared in all the required academic and communicative skills and that language was the only barrier to transition from home country to host country education system. But Pantelides found that some students with the IELTS standard are inadequately prepared for academic programs.[58] Carroll discussed the language difficulties of international students who meet the IELTS score but encounter problems later.[59] Of the four skills assessed in IELTS the writing tasks are much shorter than university writing tasks in many disciplines. 'The test can give some indication of students' overall language skills but offer little guidance as to abilities suitable for an academic environment',[60] suggesting that students should be prepared for a more advanced level of academic writing. In addition, the composite IELTS result may conceal a marked variation in the scores for the four skills. A student with an IELTS average of 6.0 may have a much lower score in writing or speaking.

Some studies indicate a positive relationship between students' English language proficiency as measured by the IELTS score and their performance as measured by their grade point average (GPA).[61] Poyrazli and colleagues investigated the relationship between the reading and writing subtest, academic achievement and student adjustment.[62] Students with better writing and reading proficiency as measured by IELTS had better academic adjustment. Those with poor writing and reading skills were more likely to have difficulty in class,

57 Feast, 2002.
58 Pantelides, 1999; see also Coley, 1999.
59 Carroll, 2005.
60 *ibid*, 37.
61 For example Elder, 1993; Hill et al., 1999; Poyrazli et al., 2001; Feast, 2002.
62 Poyrazli et al., 2001.

stress and adjustment problems. Other studies indicate the reading section test is a significant predictor of academic performance.[63] Feast suggested the required IELTS score should be increased, while noting that this could trigger a fall in international student numbers.[64] Other studies found no statistically significant relationship between IELTS and academic performance. Dooey found that students with higher IELTS scores tend to have higher not lower failure rates at university, and those who do not fully meet the language requirement for admission may still succeed academically.[65] The contrasting findings raise questions about the role of IELTS in selection. Is testing, including testing offshore, adequate? Is preparation for study in Australia adequate? Is this adequately measured by IELTS? Can preparation designed to help students across the selection hurdle that is the IELTS test, ensure that students have adequate foundations for academic English in Australia? Does IELTS capture the required broader competences in social language?

Birrell examines the outcomes of IELTS tests conducted at the point of application for permanent residence for the 2005–6 graduate cohort.[66] More than one-third of graduates had IELTS scores below the normal operating competence required for professionals in Australia. Many had IELTS scores below the level normally required for entry into higher education, which suggests that English proficiency may have declined during education. Birrell's conclusion must be qualified, however. The IELTS is not an exhaustive measure of language proficiency. The contexts of each phase of testing are not strictly comparable. Pre-entry IELTS score might be inflated by teaching to the test, but the study again underlines the point that not all academic programs inculcate adequate English, thereby worsening student problems inside and outside the classroom. Birrell's findings are also consistent with the concerns of some academic staff[67] that the drive to maximise export volume is associated with a weakened commitment to academic standards, especially where standards include English expression.[68]

63 For example by Kerstjens and Nery, 2000; Bayliss and Raymond, 2004.
64 Feast, 2002.
65 Dooey, 1999.
66 Birrell, 2006.
67 Alexander, 2007.
68 For example Ewart, 2007.

Questions on language

The present study included the following questions about the use of English.

- Before coming to Australia, how good were your English language skills for listening? Speaking? Reading? Writing?
- Now, how good are your English language skills for listening? Speaking? Reading? Writing?
- If you completed a bridging course, preparatory course or other course to assist you in the use of English before you commenced your main course in Australia, was this preparation in English sufficient to meet your academic needs?
- Talking about the situation now, does English create difficulties for you in your academic work? In making a verbal presentation? In following technical descriptions? In writing an essay? What kind of difficulties?
- Do you need someone to assist you in your use of English in your written work? If so, do you have all the assistance that you need? (expand, e.g. who provides this assistance? Is it the University, the Faculty, is it funded by yourself or your family? etc.).

The bulk of the data in this chapter are derived from direct answers to the last two questions. Interviewees also commented on language issues and problems when answering other parts of the interview schedule.

ENGLISH LANGUAGE SKILLS OF INTERVIEWEES

According to Ryan and Carroll international students experience three shocks: culture shock, language shock and academic shock.[69] The 200 students in the present study were more competent in English than the average international student; the study excluded students in first semester and was weighted in favour of older students, postgraduates and especially PhD students. The methods used to compose the group, selection by staff in international offices and self-selection favoured those with communication skills. A countervailing factor is the

69 Ryan and Carroll, 2005.

under-representation of students from Singapore and Hong Kong China, who have relatively good skills in English. Taken together these factors suggest that the difficulties faced by these students are likely to be worse among internationals as a whole.

The study confirmed other findings that language and related cross-cultural issues pose challenges for international students in academic, social and work settings. When asked the question 'When you first decided to study in Australia, at the time, was there anything that worried you about this?' the majority of interviewees said they had worried about language proficiency. Comments such as 'You have to speak English all the time and it's very challenging' were common.

> Of course, it's quite different country. I have grown up in a non-English country so language was the first thing I was worried about.
>
> ~ male, 25, computer science, Korea

Various interviewees referred to language problems when discussing their studies, finding suitable housing, resolving problems, making friends and social networks. The domains where language was associated with difficulty varied.

PROBLEMS IN TEACHING AND LEARNING

Does English create difficulties for you in your academic work?

Almost one-third of students (*n* = *60*) said that they had language-related academic problems, though this varied according to national origin (table 12.1).

No students from India or Bangladesh reported difficulties.

> No, not at all because in India our education was in English, I was brought up in an English environment, and my work was in English. English is a first language in India as well. I have no problem with English.
>
> male, 27, business, India

But language difficulties were a serious problem for the majority of students from China and other parts of east Asia, and for some from southeast Asia. Nineteen out of 28 students from China reported

Table 12.1 Self-reported language difficulties in academic work, by country of origin

Region or nation	Students interviewed	Interviewees with problems	Proportion of all interviewees who had problems %
East Asia			
China	28	17	61
Hong Kong China	5	3	60
Other east Asia*	9	6	67
Southeast Asia			
Indonesia	49	19	39
Malaysia	18	3	17
Singapore	11	0	0
Laos, Cambodia and Vietnam	6	2	33
Other southeast Asia and Pacific**	6	4	67
South Asia			
India	21	0	0
Other south Asia***	19	4	21
Other			
Middle East, North Africa	7	1	14
All sub-Saharan Africa	7	1	14
Europe	6	0	0
Canada, US, UK	5	0	0
Latin America	3	0	0
Total	200	60	30

* Korea, Japan, Taiwan, Macau
** Brunei, Thailand, PNG
*** Sri Lanka, Bangladesh, Pakistan, Nepal

problems. Some students from other nationalities expressed sympathy for the difficulties they faced.

> No. In fact language is one of my best points because I'm good at English and I'm good at my Urdu as well . . . But [there are] some students who are not good at it, they have a lot of problems in first year . . . especially [students] from Chinese backgrounds . . . They don't know that much English even if they have done courses. They have to work so hard. The same thing which I come to know in one hour, it takes them 10 hours. I really feel bad for them . . . Now the teachers can't teach in Chinese or Malay. They have to teach them in English.
>
> ~ male, 19, commerce, Pakistan

Table 12.2 Areas of language difficulties experienced by international students

Proportion of students reporting each aspects of language as being difficult n = 200; total number of students reporting academic language difficulties = 60 (30.0%)							
Following lectures	**Oral presentation**	**Writing**	**Reading**	**Technical terms, vocabulary**	**Speaking too fast**	**Slang and colloquialism**	**Accent**
8.5%	13.5%	26.0%	3.0%	2.0%	3.5%	5.5%	12.0%

Some students cited more than one aspect of language difficulty. Difficulty in writing was the most cited problem, followed by oral presentation or classroom participation and understanding the Australian accent (table 12.2).

'I was just tongue-tied'

Perceptions that writing was the most challenging issue confirms Pantelides[70] and other studies. Differences in academic practice in the home country contributed to the problems of writing. As one student from Malaysia put it, 'You have to reference academic writing, different from home'. Some students had difficulty in writing full sentences and linking them together. Others had difficulty with grammatical aspects and expressing ideas and structuring arguments. Many needed to translate English language material in and out of the native tongue.

> My difficulty is in writing, because, you know, academic writing is very different from, like, informal English writing . . . If I want to make a sentence in English I just make it in Indonesian, and then translate it into English. But then somebody who is a native speaker, when that person reads my writing they say, 'Oh, it's not English, it's another kind of language.'
>
> ~ female, 30, food science, Indonesia

The demands of academic writing were discipline specific.

> So far we don't have to do any writing . . . It's more about programming.
>
> ~ female, 27, engineering, Indonesia

> Like, doing assignment . . . sometimes in order to write one sentence I have to think three hours or something. It's so difficult, so tiring.
>
> ~ female, 33, education, China

Students with prior training in writing had much less difficulty. One Indonesian student said that he liked writing in English: back home he had worked as a freelance journalist. Another student, from France, had a good command of English because she had been working in

70 Pantelides, 1999.

an international company. The prior learning experience of students needs to be taken into account.

Various factors contributed to difficulties with oral presentation, such as lack of prior experience in English classes at home and feeling intimidated by native English speakers who dominated in class. Lack of confidence and being shy and nervous also contributed. Some found it impossible to ask questions of teachers.

> [I]n Brunei we don't give presentations . . . I was just tongue-tied when I got up. I didn't know what to say. I was intimidated by these people staring at me You're just out of place.
>
> ~ female, 35, ceramics, Brunei

Other concerns were the accents of lecturers and classmates, speed of speech, pronunciation, local idiom and cultural references. It was not the English that students had learnt at home, British or American English, or English as taught by an Indonesian or Sri Lankan, not Australian English.

> Because all my schooling right from my kindergarten to my post-graduation was completed in English I was comfortable with English even before coming here. It's [difficulty] only with the accent, which is different from that of UK.
>
> ~ female, 27, primary education, China

> Sometimes they are speaking fast and they regard us maybe [as if] we are native English speakers.
>
> ~ male, 31, community development, Indonesia

Many students felt that they should have received more help. But being recognised as having language difficulties was not always advantageous.

> English is not my first language, so you just got try hard . . . but I don't like people to say to me that 'Well it's okay, your English is not good' . . . I just don't like people to point it out. I don't know – it's a kind of dilemma, I know.
>
> ~ female, 23, social work, Taiwan

SOCIAL BARRIERS AND DISCRIMINATION

Are there significant barriers in making friends across cultures?

A clear majority (61 per cent) said there were barriers in making friends across cultures. Most of them mentioned language differences, sustained and compounded by cultural differences and lack of mixing outside class (chapter 15).

> When you use English to communicate, somehow it's hard to have very deep communication.
>
> ~ male, 41, information and technology, China

Language difficulties, lack of local and topical knowledge and other cultural dimensions hindered interaction with locals and other nationalities. Even students with a good command of English found some nuances beyond their reach. People from different cultures had different topics of conversation and often different senses of humour as well.

> You don't know their jokes. You don't know why they are laughing. Their humour is different and you don't know their culture, what they are talking about. Although you know every word, you don't really understand the true meaning of the sentence.
>
> ~ female, 24, industrial relations, China

> Sometimes, if I want to talk to them, I don't know what the topic of conversation should be. So we always talk about school stuff.
>
> ~ female, 22, commerce, Malaysia

> Yah, when it comes to actually owning the language, I find it difficult. Because there are certain nuances that cultures bring in and it's difficult to read those things, though I am quite good. I have to pause to understand what they mean.
>
> ~ female, 29, education, India

> Behind each culture, I think, there are different underlying assumptions. There are certain rules in each society which do not exist in another . . . I don't really think it's the language issue. I speak really good English compared to Australians but the problem is our underlying cultures are different. When I sit in the dining hall with a group of Australians and just talk, sometimes I fail

> to strike conversation. That never happens when I'm in a group of Asians . . . I don't think it's because they are particularly racist, we're just different.
>
> ~ male, 24, arts, Singapore

A total of 64 per cent of interviewees had worked in Australia at some stage; 21 per cent of them had problems at work (chapter 6). Several mentioned issues of oral communicative competence, especially barriers created by accents.

> The real estate person . . . he just says I need to change my accent, because I have a strong Indian accent. Since I'm in a real estate job and I'll be handling their clients, I need to improve – listen to a lot of news, read a lot of newspapers, and it will be okay.
>
> ~ female, 25, media and communication, India

Have you experienced hostility or prejudice while in Australia?

When asked whether they had experienced hostility or prejudice while in Australia, 50 per cent of interviewees said 'Yes' (see chapter 15 for fuller discussion). Frequently, those who said 'Yes' joined discussion of racism, discrimination or stereotyping to issues of communication. Students experienced discriminatory actions ranging from subtle to explicit. They paid a sometimes severe price for their limited English, which could trigger discourtesy, a refusal to speak or aggressive hostility. In some cases they paid a price for the perception that their English was limited, even when it was not. Their appearance alone could trigger that perception. Some reported 'unwelcoming' looks when people heard a non-English accent. Native speakers made a quick judgement that their communicative competence was inadequate and after that made little effort to understand.

> [It's] not explicitly stated that we don't like you because you speak English different. That's not explicitly stated but it's implied . . . Some people don't make an effort to understand what you are saying when you speak with a different accent. It can be in a shop or it can even be in the university. Especially when your English is basic, they don't make an effort to understand. It is like a prejudice; they are probably not aware but it is a racist prejudice that this person is not able to communicate with me . . . that

> is the assumption behind it. It sounds trivial but it's actually very important when it happens systematically . . . it kind of puts you off.
>
> ~ male, 28, sociology, Cyprus

Often international students became frustrated when others did not make any effort to try to understand them, did not show any interest in them and lacked the patience to deal with them. More than a failure of politeness, it was a failure of mutuality that blocked the possibility of symmetrical exchange. Because the international students were trying hard to communicate in English they felt native speakers should respect their efforts to reach out and make a reciprocal effort to understand them. But native speakers did not share their motivation.

LANGUAGE PREPARATION AND LANGUAGE SUPPORT SERVICES

IELTS: 'It is only focused on the test'

Some interviewees questioned whether preparation for the IELTS test was adequate to Australian academic requirements.

> I don't think IELTS is sufficient. For your daily life it's enough that you can communicate and understand someone. But for academic purposes it's far from enough [for] how to organise your sentences, how to express your point of view very accurately.
>
> ~ male, 26, IT, China

> It's harder to improve the very general aspect of your language because it [the preparation] is only focused on the test.
>
> ~ female, 25, business and IT, China

> For long term you have to learn the environment; it's very important.
>
> ~ female, 25, accounting, China

Some students were highly critical of the minimalist IELTS standards regime, which seemed to serve the industry better than it prepared the students.

> I deal with two students in the beginning of this semester whose IELTS test results are good but they cannot understand what people are talking about.
>
> ~ male, 30, IT and business, Taiwan

> I think it's something to do with IELTS . . . lots and lots of people in my faculty of business have really, really bad English. They don't even understand what the professors are saying at all. I think the university is just ripping them off. They're just making money out of them. Why give them admission if they don't even understand English? In the end they're getting like 50 per cent, 55 per cent. They're much more intelligent [than that suggests], they're better off doing it in Chinese or something. They'd probably get 80 per cent. They come here and they don't understand the language at all and get 50 per cent..
>
> ~ female, 22, commerce, India

Other interviewees stated that IELTS preparation had been positive in helping them to improve their writing skills, though it was less effective for oral communication.

> When I take the IELTS test, writing is good but I always fail in the oral English test when chatting with some local students . . . I need time to think about it, and to organise my sentence structure. So sometimes maybe it just feels very boring. They don't want to talk with me.
>
> ~ female, 23, international business, China

Prior preparation in English

Interviewees were asked 'If you completed a bridging course, preparatory course or other course to assist you in the use of English before you commenced your main course in Australia, was this preparation in English sufficient to meet your academic needs?' In response, many of the students provided data about preparation in English prior to commencement of their courses. Most home country schools and universities emphasised academic reading and writing more than oral communicative competence,[71] hindering the fit with academic and social life in Australia:

> The English course when I studied in the university is not suitable, because... you have no opportunity to speak... The teacher always speaks Chinese while telling you how to learn English.
>
> ~ male, 25, telecommunications, China

Some students had completed a bridging program in their home country and another in Australia before commencement. Mostly, the former was more useful.

> Yes, I did complete a bridging course before coming here... We AusAID awardees from Indonesia must take the English preparation in Jakarta or Denpasar, Bali. I did my English preparation in Jakarta. It was very good and very helpful for me and I think also for my friends as well, but the English preparation here seems to repeat so it is not very helpful.
>
> ~ male, 36, Indonesian studies, Indonesia

The Australian-based bridging program would have been more effective if it had been integrated with the student's field of study:

> The [bridging] course is not sufficient. It's true that we are taught academic writing skills, but sometimes it depends on the academic fields of the students. For example the way to argue in a certain field is different from other fields. According to me, the bridging course here in Australia should be specific to [the] student's field.
>
> ~ female, 40, education, Indonesia

LANGUAGE SUPPORT SERVICES: 'IT IS NOT ENOUGH'

The students provided many comments on the need for better language support. Existing services were mostly seen as insufficient to meet extensive and complex needs. Time restrictions often prevented students from using support services effectively. The services were often under-resourced relative to needs and overly generic, given that each student has a specific learning background, trajectory and problems. One student had to cheat to gain extra time for consultation.

71 Sawir, 2005.

> The learning skill teachers tell you that you have to make an appointment. But the time is very short. So, like, you study two sentences, and then finish. So it is not enough. I don't have any place to go. It is hard, very hard. I had a problem with the learning skill teacher; she is so bad. One day I needed to finish my Masters thesis. I had to get that done. So I wanted to see them [in the learning skills unit]. But I had finished my time there. Each student is allowed to see the learning skills people two times, and I had finished already the two times, a long time ago. So I used my classmate's name, Lyn [pseudonym]. But Lyn didn't go, I went. So she [in the learning skills unit] said 'Your name is Lyn?' I said yes; I pretended. [Later] she said 'What's you name?' I forgot, I said my real name. She said, 'It's supposed to be Lyn. How come you're here?' I said I was sorry and that Lyn said that she wanted to give it to me. Lyn wrote a letter. She said 'I don't care, it doesn't mean anything. You need to go now because you are cheating'. I went back to my course coordinator. The course coordinator was angry and wanted to complain about her, but nothing happened.
>
> ~ female, 33, education, China

Balancing this, others told stories about how they had received extra help with language from lecturers or supervisors, or had been provided with extra classes to prepare them early in the course or extra classes on an ongoing basis.

Some students suggested an introductory course in interpreting the Australian accent. Others suggested orientation briefings in how the university worked, for example how to deal with problems and how to deal with university staff.

What would you advise other students?

Interviewees were also asked 'What would you advise other individual students coming to Australia, about the risks and problems of studying and living here? Several emphasised the need for prospective students to be prepared in English and to mix with English speakers after arrival.

> Be aware of the language problem before coming here.
>
> ~ male, 40, medicine, Laos

> I think if you're studying here, you should at least have basic foundations of English, of English communication skill.
>
> ~ female, 21, commerce, Indonesia

> It's better not to stay together with students from the same countries . . . try the homestay.
>
> ~ female, 30, chemistry, Thailand

Confirming the literature, interviewees saw language competence as the key to active agency in the English-speaking environment, thereby moving beyond the passivity often associated with international students. The assumption that Asian students are inherently passive is deeply problematic but was not endorsed by any interviewee in the study. The point is rather that as the foregoing suggests, in many east and southeast Asian classrooms there is less emphasis on discussion. This factor combined with lack of fluency and confidence in English generates the behaviours attributed to the stereotypical Asian learner in Australian educational institutions. One interviewee focused on the importance of active learning.

> Most importantly they should try to be more outspoken, to be more active, because I notice that most of the time they're usually silent and more passive. So I want them to be more active, to be more involved in what they are doing in class, and also to prepare their English as good as possible, like say by reading novels, or attending the conversation class.
>
> ~ female, 20, commerce, Indonesia

Language brought with it the capacity to mix and integrate on a broader basis. In turn broader social mixing fed back into language learning and confidence:

> Mainly I would advise them to really actively learn English when here. If they don't, then they are better to stay back in their home country. If you study in Australia the language is English. Many of my friends they just hang out with their own country-people so they hardly learn English at all. You need to actively join other clubs maybe, and societies so you can make the most of your studies here, not just academic but also social life with the Australian people while you have a chance.
>
> ~ male, 23, arts, Macau

> First suggestion is, don't mix with people from your own country. It's not good for you [if you want] to improve your English. I'm lucky, when I came here there were no Chinese in my house. My only friend went back China the first day I reached here. So in the first few months, I had no chance to practise my Chinese. It's really good for me to improve quite quickly. And secondly, talk as much as you can. Go outside, look with your own eyes, don't always stay inside.
>
> ~ female, 26, pharmacology, China

One student took this argument further.

> I would suggest avoiding having too much contact with home, because students must not feel homeless . . . like, you feel sad and you call your mum, or you call your friends, and then you're, Awww . . . what am I doing here? The best thing to do is just step away a little bit from home. Forget your language a little bit, don't speak in your language, otherwise you'll never learn English. Your brain still works in your language, far away from family and friends. That's what I did. I called my friends and I called my mum and said, 'I know you want to talk to me, but this is causing me a lot of problems. I know maybe this is selfish but I need the space. Don't talk to me; I'll talk to you later' . . . I started to feel more interactive here. I'm used to the culture, the food and the language, and now the brain starts to work in English.
>
> ~ male, 27, science, Mexico

The advice to break home ties would not have been supported by most other students. It must be said though that the cultural distance from Mexico and Spanish to Anglo-Australia and English is not as far as the journey from, say, China to Australia.

CONCLUSIONS

Competence in English is primary in the social and economic security of non-citizen students studying in an English-language country. Not only is English the medium of learning, but language also enables students to understand, cooperate and exchange with lecturers and each other, to navigate the regulatory and administrative requirements of governments and universities, to deal with financial institutions, the health sector, the housing market and the retail sector, to manage the tasks of paid work, especially when these involve direct dealings with the public, to establish a broad network of friends and contacts, to navigate through problems and crises and to exercise their rights as students and humans. Competence in language brings with it connectedness and confidence. It allows international students to respond at need and to be proactive and self-determining agents.

The data from the interviews are consistent with most literature on issues in the use of English in the country of study: for example the inadequacy of the IELTS testing regime as preparation, the time pressures created by the foreign language environment, especially early, difficulties with academic writing, underpreparedness in oral communication and lack of classroom confidence and the need to mix with locals. The policing of standards varies in intensity: some teachers compound students' problems by using rapid speech or colloquial language, and only some take the trouble to understand the prior backgrounds of students. We see the centrality of language as the students struggle to progress their degree programs and deal with problems of daily life. The study draws attention to the role of cultural factors in conditioning language acquisition and use. It strongly confirms the link between language competence and active student agency. It also links oral communication to problems of interaction with locals and discrimination.

The interview data suggest that the contribution of Australian institutions to language formation is insufficient and uneven in time and place. The commercial mass international education industry applies a minimalist and generic approach to preparation and support services that are only sometimes varied upwards to meet needs. Typically, economic minimalism is joined to the conservative, monocultural approach to university education that is still the norm in Anglo-American nations. Many if not most tertiary programs still proceed on the assumptions that students have completed local secondary school and achieved the necessary standard in English, the one compulsory subject, that students are familiar with local academic conventions, that students enrolled in particular university disciplines are familiar with the prior school subjects at the foundation of those disciplines and that students know Australian society, culture, norms, idioms, slang and jokes. They also assume that if students are deficient in any of these attributes it is their responsibility to acquire them. It cannot be the responsibility of the university. But while many students absorb the local culture and language at near miraculous pace in the early months, these assumptions do not hold. To treat international students as if they are local students is pedagogical negligence. To shift the responsibility back onto the students themselves is the educational and social equivalent of throwing them into the deep end of a swimming pool without teaching them how to swim. To neglect their formation in academic English is to retard the communicative competence that is foundational to their human security beyond the classroom.

In teaching and learning, the solution lies in comprehensive diagnostic testing prior to the degree together with mandatory provision of bridging programs tailored to the student's prior learning environment and the intended discipline in Australia. For many students from English as a foreign language countries the bridging program would need to be six to 12 months long. During the period of preparation a learning audit, which could be prepared for each individual, would identify areas where particular assistance was needed, inform teaching and learning strategies and inform the monitoring of later progress. The bridging program could be split between the home country and country of education. This immediately raises the problem of financing in an industry in which institutions and students have an interest in minimising unit costs. One possible approach would be for the Australian government to identify full preparation in academic English and the production of graduates certified as strong in English skills as primary to the Australian brand. This could be supported by a formal compact on language services underpinned by joint financing by institution, student and government. Government guaranteed English language standards that were more than spin and be officially subsidised, would send an attractive signal to the global market and move Australia ahead of competitor English language nations. It would constitute a change in global positioning strategy. Instead of competing on the basis of marketing, non-academic services and high volume or standard cost–quality production,[72] Australia would compete on the basis of higher educational quality.

---

72 Marginson, 2007.

Extended transition strategies, such as foundation or bridging programs, make a large difference. Transparent pathways from the different Asian education systems, all distinctive and all nested in language and culture, to education in the English-speaking nation would facilitate the intercultural dimension of local programs, encourage mutual pedagogical learning and creative hybridity and enable the issue of multiple Englishes – variations in global English – to be tackled. But further development of these themes is beyond the compass of this study.[73]

Another essential component is comprehensive ongoing academic support, particularly focused on language competence and tailored to the needs of individual students. The goal is to foster not ongoing dependence and client relationships but independent learners with communicative competence. In turn augmented language skills and confident student agency would facilitate interaction with locals as well as day-to-day safety and security. The ESOS Act could be amended to install ongoing language support as a mandatory student entitlement. The other area where public authorities can assist is the regulation of academic standards. In its five-year audit cycle the Tertiary Education Quality and Standards Authority, TEQSA (successor to the Australian Universities Quality Agency, or AUQA)[74] could require universities to provide the infrastructure of diagnostic testing, bridging programs and language help in degree program, and emphasise benchmarking and continuous improvement in each of these areas.

The next chapter looks at student networks, primarily family and same-culture friends. The theme of language and intercultural relations returns in chapter 15.

---

73 But see Marginson and Sawir, forthcoming.

74 AUQA, 2007; Government of Australia, 2009.

13 FAMILY AND FRIENDS

Family, that's your comfort zone. You have to build a whole new comfort zone, and you try to find where you are going to fit. You can't really keep on holding on to . . . I'm in Australia but I'm still very Malay, I do things the Malaysian way. Yes, you have to find that balance.

– female, 21, computing, Malaysia

INTRODUCTION: NETWORKS, RELATIONSHIPS AND STUDENT SECURITY

The literature on social capital distinguishes bonding and bridging networks. 'Bonding' means ties of family, kin, locality, friends like oneself and ethnic or fraternal organisations. It tends to exclude outsiders. 'Bridging' ties are more open and inclusive. They bring people together with others different from themselves.[1] Educational institutions can facilitate horizontal bridging between people of different classes, localities, cultural backgrounds and nations.[2]

Both forms of association contribute to international student security. Weiss argues that 'different types of relationship make different provisions'. People have varying needs and multiple linkages and networks. He nominates six kinds of provision: 'attachment, social integration, reliable alliance, guidance, reassurance of worth and opportunity for nurturance'. No relationship fulfils

1 Putnam, 2000.

2 Woolcock, 2000. Woolcock noted a third form of association, 'linking' social capital, which consists of vertical relations with people in power, for example employer–employee, interest group–government minister.

all needs, though intimate relations with a partner may fulfil several of them.[3] Weiss distinguishes 'social loneliness' triggered by desires for social integration, attachment and alliance, from 'emotional loneliness'.[4] In a study of university students DiTommaso and Spinner confirm the categories of social and emotional loneliness and, within emotional loneliness, distinguish between family loneliness and romantic loneliness.[5] The desire for family is not just for attachment per se. 'For people in their early university years, the defining feature of their family relationships is having family members to whom they can turn for guidance and advice.' Family also offers reassurance of worth.[6] The separations between social networks, close friends, family and partner are not absolute. 'All the social provisions were found to relate to the three forms of loneliness, suggesting that intimate relationships and those afforded by one's social network each may provide many or all of the social provisions.' Nevertheless, DiTommaso and Spinner, like Weiss, find 'attachment and guidance' are the best unique predictors of romantic and family loneliness or unloneliness. Social loneliness is most strongly affected by social integration.[7]

> In addition to the social integration that both friends and acquaintances provide, having closer friends who provide feelings of attachment, and can be turned to for advice are associated with less social loneliness . . . a network made up only of casual acquaintances may not be as effective in preventing social loneliness as would a network that also contains close friends.[8]

Relations are also culturally nested. Immersion in collectivity, and meanings of the terms 'family', 'friends' and 'closeness', vary by culture as well as personality.[9]

At the same time bonding relations are not confined to kin or culture. They can, for example, be formed in a common profession. In universities bridging relations can become bonding relations, which is the cosmopolitan potential of the experience, its capacity to transform

3 Weiss, 1974
4 Weiss, 1973
5 DiTommaso and Spinner, 1997, 419.
6 *ibid*, 424.
7 *ibid*, 425.
8 *ibid*, 424.
9 Church, 1982; Triandis et al., 1988; Misra, 1999.

both self and friendship. But this study confirms the literature (below) in finding that most student friendships are same-culture or similar-culture friendships, more bonding than bridging. Friendship is mostly less deep than family but closer at hand. Some friends come to Australia together, especially from nations sending large numbers, such as China, India, Malaysia, Singapore and Indonesia. Most friends are found after arrival. There are varied opportunities to make friends and some find it easier than others. Fluency in local language and customs affects the capacity to initiate (chapter 12). Overall students from EFL nations are less confident in bridging and more dependent on same-culture networks. There are pros and cons in this. As with all networks, same-culture networks include and exclude. The tighter the protection they provide, the greater the opportunity cost for other associations and activities, especially immersion in local networks. This trade-off is only avoided by students adept in multiple roles. More find bonding–bridging potentials in relations with same-culture locals and other-culture internationals.

But the pathologies of same-culture networks can be overstated. Prospects of real local friendships are limited. For many the alternative to same-culture networks may be no network at all. Social isolation threatens student welfare and academic progress. Others have inner family bonds fraught with problems. Both groups should concern universities and governments. Those in greatest difficulty are the most invisible, a serious weakness in international student security.

The informal and private domain of student security is more than just a matter to be left to the students themselves, to globally elongated family ties stretched near to breaking, to the uncertain resources and social imaginings of student clubs or religious communities, to the volatile market in personal encounters and to the fluctuations of private emotion and volition. Inevitably, these are part of the picture, but informal student security is also affected by policy, people management and the resources each student has. Student welfare and rights are better secured when the pastoral responsibilities of authorities are clarified and opportunities to network are available and flexible in the range of possibilities they provide. The fluctuations and gaps in informal student security cannot be abolished by the actions of universities or governments. Nor can this be attempted without violating student freedoms and the scope for personal growth. But the gaps can be monitored, compensated and supplemented with a light but effective touch.

The chapter begins with theorisations of networking and the research on same-culture international student networking (for cross-cultural relations see chapter 14). It then moves to the interview data. Students reflect on the displacement effects of the transition to Australia, the early weeks and efforts in new relationships, continuing ties with parents, kin and communities at home and, in some cases, intimate family relations in Australia and varied forms of friendship.

The interviews also provided information on international student loneliness and how students respond to it, matters that are addressed in chapter 14.

NETWORKED RELATIONS

Social capital theory

Social capital can be defined as the networks of affiliation to which people belong (families, friendship groups, professional and business contacts, formal or informal organisations and groups) plus those qualities of agents that facilitate networking.[10] Political economists focus on the contribution of social capital to productivity and wealth. Sociologists, such as Bourdieu,[11] focus on power, hierarchy, division and order. He notes that people move beyond contingent relations in family, locality or work to create 'social relationships that are directly usable in the short or long term'.[12]

> Social capital is the aggregate of the actual or potential resources which are linked to possession of a durable network of more or less institutionalised relationships of mutual acquaintance and recognition – or in other words, to membership in a group – which provides each of its members with the backing of the collectively-owned capital . . . The volume of the social capital possessed by a given agent thus depends on the size of the network of connections he/she can effectively mobilise and on the volume of the capital

10 OECD, 2001, 4; Bexley et al., 2007.
11 Bourdieu, 1984, 1986.
12 *ibid*, 249.

> (economic, cultural or symbolic) possessed in his/her own right by each of those to whom he/she is connected.[13]

The group augments the social and material advantages of each member. Continuing the economic metaphor, Bourdieu finds 'the profits which accrue from membership in groups are the basis of the solidarity which makes them possible',[14] and each member is a custodian of 'the limits of the group'.[15] Unlike family ties, voluntary social networks are produced by 'endless effort'. Bourdieu is interested in groups in the upper echelons of society that use networks to sustain privilege and exclude others. His social capital is a relational form of power in a zero sum social market. Some gain social capital at the expense of others. An Australian Productivity Commission study made the related but not identical point that some gain social capital at the expense of the common good: 'strong group bonds can reduce tolerance of outsiders and create an undue focus on the group's needs to the detriment of the broader society'.[16] In part contrast Coleman[17] found that social capital can strengthen the social position of groups of people otherwise marginalised, that in some social networks people engage in altruistic sharing inconsistent with economics and there can be win–win outcomes in which everyone advances. Coleman and Bourdieu both emphasise the potential of education in forming networks that constitute social capital, though for Coleman closed networks such as family and church are the primary sites of social capital.[18] Arguably, Bourdieu describes, say, elite law students in exclusive universities, whereas Coleman's description is closer to the bonding behaviours of international students.

In a study of networking that draws on theorisations of social capital Thune states that 'networks of relationships between people and organisations can be seen as resources available for an agent to utilise in the course of action'.[19] Such ties can be either strong or weak. Strong ties, typically, for international students with parents and immediate family, are characterised by close and frequent

13 *ibid*, 248–9.
14 *ibid*, 249.
15 *ibid*, 250.
16 Productivity Commission, 2003, xi.
17 Coleman, 1988.
18 Bexley et al., 2007, 16.
19 Thune, 2007, 159.

interactions. They have benefits in coordination and resource sharing. Weaker ties, typically, between acquaintances where contact is less frequent or there is less emotional investment, can 'give access to new opportunities, carry novel information and increase variance'. Networks of acquaintances exchange knowledge. 'Access to common cognitive resources increases the exchange capabilities of partners', bridging between groups and different sites of activity, reaching across borders and spreading the influence of groups and ideas.[20] The cross-cultural relationships of international students often take this form. Weak or loose ties are also typical of internet-mediated relationships. But networks are more than containers for atomised individuals. The ideas of Bourdieu and Coleman suggest that as well as strong or weak (loose) networks determined by the intensity of relations, the aggregated social capital of a network may be strong or weak, depending on the relations of the network to other powers.

Social network analysis

Social network analysis imagines 'a reciprocal relationship between individual and society'.[21] It defines a social network as 'the amalgamation of ties among actors'. 'Social structure' is the pattern those ties assume.[22] Each actor is separable but also a 'node' within the network, interdependent rather than wholly independent. 'Actors are related through links that channel information, affection and other resources.' The structure of social relations 'both constrains and facilitates action'.[23]

> The capacities of an individual to act in society, and the implications of that action, depend not only on his/her attributes but also on the pattern of relations within which he/she is located (but both attributes and patterns of relations are dynamic and can influence one another).[24]

---

20 *ibid*, 160; Vera and Schupp, 2006, 413.

21 *ibid*, 408.

22 In actor network theory the entities seen to be linked in a common network, whether people or machines, have no intrinsic qualities and acquire their attributes only through relations with other entities; see Latour, 1999. But cross-border students have an existence prior to their networks in the country of education.

23 Vera and Schupp, 2006, 408.

24 *ibid*, 408.

Social network analysis also provides terminology for analysing networks. 'Nodes' are individual agents or actors in the network. 'Lines' or 'ties' are links or relations between agents. The number of connections of each actor is the 'degree' of the node. 'Density' is the proportion of all possible connections within the network that actually exist. 'Closeness', the distance between two nodes, is the number of 'steps' needed to move from one to the other. 'Betweenness' is the extent to which a node connects different elements of the network. 'Connectivity' is the minimum number of nodes or ties that need to be removed to disconnect part of a network. 'Transitivity' and the 'clustering coefficient' refer to the extent to which neighbouring nodes are linked, measuring the local density of connections. Together closeness, betweenness and clustering coefficient indicate 'centrality'. These indicators can be calculated for nodes in the network ('egocentric' analysis), and for the network as a whole.[25] 'Hubs' are nodes with a larger than average number of connections. Hubs 'shorten the distance between any pair of nodes' (agents). By concentrating connections they reduce the number of steps between nodes. Hubs 'centralise the diffusion of information, thereby increasing the closeness value of the whole network'. The fluidity of communication does not depend primarily on the density of a network, but on the existence of hubs.[26]

Social network analysis alerts us to the dynamism of networks, in which innovations, bridges, node dissolutions or concentrations can lead to marked and sudden change across the system as a whole.[27] Networks are also overlapping and multiple. Mische and White focus on the 'switching' process by which people move from one network to another'.[28] These insights are consistent with the openness, volatility and multiplicity of cross-border student life. Network analysis is often applied to cultural domains and in intercultural and comparative studies, including global studies.[29] On the whole it is better to imagine social relations in terms of open connectivity than to identify barriers, separations and enclosures. It might be better in mapping the lines, nodes and intensity of networked connections than the dark spaces

25 *ibid*, 408–9.
26 *ibid*, 418.
27 *ibid*, 424.
28 Mische and White, 1998.
29 *ibid*; Knox et al., 2006.

between networks and the characteristics of the unconnected. Nodes with few or no connections are by definition peripheral to networks. But in international education these nodes are real people, such as Hong 'Steffi' Zhang.

Factors shaping networks

Research on cross-border networking draws on psychology and sociology. Much of it focuses on factors that define, condition or generate networks. Definitional factors include size, density, strong or loose ties, frequency of contact, closure or openness to outsiders, multiplicity of networks and interconnectedness between networks. Additional factors that condition or generate networks include the capabilities of individuals, for example language and communication, religious, ethnic, national or socioeconomic affiliations, shared patterns of living, such as worksites or accommodation, and personality. All else being equal, people with higher self-esteem are more popular with peers and more facile in networking.[30]

For Stokes one variable is the extent to which network members are attached as relatives or confidants, that is, how social and emotional ties are configured in relation to each other. Denser networks, and networks where some attachments are emotional, enhance a sense of belonging and are 'associated with lower levels of loneliness'.[31] The quantity of people to which an individual is connected is less important. Lonely students are not necessarily isolated (chapter 14).[32] Close bonds are better at alleviating loneliness than having a large number of friends.[33]

Much research emphasises the benefits of friendships. Student peer networks can enhance self-esteem and concentrate and universalise the motivation to achieve.[34] Students with 'strong support networks exhibit better psychological and physiological wellbeing particularly during periods of high stress', according to Sarason and colleagues.[35] Co-nationals are 'an extremely important resource for success, with international students far more willing to disclose a "personal

30 Nurmi et al., 1997.
31 Stokes, 1985, 983.
32 *ibid*, 987.
33 *ibid*, 982–3.
34 Eggens et al., 2008.
35 Sarason et al., 1997.

problem" to a co-national' than counselling personnel, Pedersen noted.[36] Networks help international students to feel supported and more in control; they cope better with emotional, social and educational problems. The character of ties varies by age. Green and her colleagues found that for young adults size of network is more significant than for older adults, for whom closeness of relations and life partners become increasingly significant. However, for young people one close friend may play a key attachment role,[37] especially if their parental family is remote. Carstensen confirms that the needs provided for by social interaction vary with age. For older people, for whom the future is seen as limited, there is less motivation to engage in functional but emotionally meaningless linkages; emotionally important bonds dominate social contact.[38] For younger people, such as university students without children, for whom 'the future is perceived as largely open-ended',[39] social contact is often driven by information and opportunity seeking. Such young people typically sustain a range of weak friendships that shade into acquaintanceship. These may not provide emotional attachment but are functional in other ways.

> When information seeking is the goal, novel, unfamiliar people are often the best sources. Thus, when a person is exploring the world, trying to understand how it works, what the culture is like, how he or she compares with other people, and what other people are like, interactions with novel social partners have greater potential to fulfil this goal than would interactions with familiar social partners. The period from adolescence to young adulthood likely represents the peak emphasis on . . . information seeking and, consistent with the theory, is a time when people are establishing their independence from long-time family and friends and seeking out new social contacts.[40]

This describes the networking behaviour of many international students. But sources of information can be restricted. The literatures on mobile personnel and international students discuss the differences

36 Pedersen, 1991, 21.
37 Green et al., 2001, 281–7; see also DiTomasso and Spinner, *op cit*, 424.
38 Carstensen, 1995, 152–3.
39 *ibid*, 153.
40 *ibid*, 152.

between same-culture and other-culture relations. Researchers see cross-cultural relations as positive but are ambivalent about same-culture relations that protect and exclude. Weak integration with locals is associated with lower 'adjustment' and 'adaptation',[41] and with higher stress.[42] Church's business travellers form 'enclave groups' that insulate sojourners from potential for conflict between host and sojourner cultures and minimise feelings of powerlessness and the need for adjustment. 'Such enclaves also serve as reference groups with whom the new environment can be discussed, compared and interpreted.'[43] They 'largely determine the living arrangements, friendship patterns, and organisational affiliations of the sojourners'. Often members are intolerant of those who become attached to the host culture.[44] For Church 'restricting social interaction with host nationals to superficial encounters can be self-defeating in the long run because it inhibits learning the language, values and customs of the new culture and can reinforce a sense of alienation'. But while 'hosts often view sojourners as not seeking host friendships, many sojourners report wishing to have more interaction with host nationals'.[45] Some sojourners experience awkwardness when switching between local and sojourner networks and have 'difficulty in defining the optimal balance between identification with home and host culture values ("overlapping membership conflict")'. The optimum position, states Church, is a 'genuine cosmopolitan orientation'.[46]

These issues recur in the literature on international students, though the latter exhibit stronger desires for interaction with host nationals than did Church's business travellers. Some researchers assume students from 'collectivist' Asian cultures are more likely to form same-culture enclaves.[47] But local students from individualist English-speaking cultures also form enclaves. While nominally one's choice of associates are one's own affair, international students do not have full control over their choices. Those from non-English-speaking countries are limited by language (chapter 12) and intercultural relations

41 For a critical discussion of these concepts see chapter 15.
42 Rosenthal et al., 2006, 13.
43 Church, 1982, 551–2.
44 *ibid*, 551.
45 *ibid*, 552.
46 *ibid*, 553.
47 Triandis, 1989, 1994; see also Hofstede, 1980, 1998.

(chapter 15). Experiences of barriers and occasional abuse propel networking down some paths and not others.

Australian study of connectedness

Rosenthal and colleagues use an index of connectedness, comprised by international students' responses to questions about whether they had people 'I can ask for help', 'who care about me' and 'I can talk to about my problems'. 'About 70 per cent of students in the sample have a considerable to strong sense of connectedness',[48] and 'over 90 per cent of students indicate that they have someone or some people in Melbourne who can provide help, caring and support'.[49] Less than 6 per cent felt substantially isolated. More students had access to people who could help them than people they were close to and people with whom they could discuss their problems. (The study did not distinguish relations with family and kin from those with friends.) Higher connectedness was positively associated with student satisfaction with academic progress, living arrangements, financial position, self-esteem and health,[50] and with a lesser incidence of cultural stress, as defined in the study. Connectedness was correlated to all of same-culture networking, networking with locals, the 'capacity to contact a caring family' and belonging to organisations.[51] Rosenthal and colleagues found that 'the critical issue is to achieve an optimum balance between interaction and identification with the home and host cultures'.[52] But only one-fifth of survey respondents had 'a reasonable degree of contact with Australians' on campus or outside it.[53] (The Melbourne survey did not distinguish local Australians with Asian backgrounds, some of whom shared international students' languages, from other Australians. These students appeared as 'Australian' in some questions and 'people with . . . a cultural background similar to my own' in others. The study also used a generic 'Asia' that combined ESL and EFL nations and inadvertently conflated problems specific to Muslims with problems specific to east Asians.)

48 Rosenthal et al., 2006, 3.
49 *ibid*, 22.
50 *ibid*, 6.
51 *ibid*, 3.
52 *ibid*, 13.
53 *ibid*, 23.

Students who tended to lower connectedness scores included those early in the period of study, separated from children left behind at home, not doing well academically, who spoke no English while growing up, who spoke a language other than English outside the university and were from China.[54] These results confirm the importance of language and culture as factors that affect not only networking patterns but also a sense of belonging and support. The fact that language-related variables were more strongly associated than was country of origin with variations in connectedness[55] reflects the fact that the category of national origin may cover more than one language group and cultural background.

The researchers find that 'the pattern of students' responses shows that they tend to see mixing with people of similar cultural background as an alternative to mixing socially with Australians'.[56] Yet the data suggest this is true only for some students. For those from Asian countries, mixing with co-culturals and mixing with Australians were each positively associated with connectedness. For other internationals only mixing with Australians was associated with connectedness. Asians were more likely to form dominant networks with same-culture students, and less likely to do so with Australians, than were other international students. The same was true of students who spoke a language other than English at home (95.1 per cent of whom were from Asia). The countries of origin with the strongest pattern of same-culture networking had the largest groups of students at the university: Singapore, Indonesia, Malaysia, Hong Kong China and China. The exception was south Asian students, who formed strong networks with Australians more often, perhaps due to lower language barriers.[57]

More controversially, the study also found that 'students from Asian countries see a negative relationship between mixing with co-culturals and Australians, while students from non-Asian countries see no relationship between them'.[58] It is likely that this finding is partly an artefact of the methodology. As table 13.1 indicated, respondents

54 *ibid*, 22.
55 *ibid*, 89.
56 *ibid*, 23–4.
57 *ibid*, 88.
58 *ibid*, 24.

Table 13.1 Dominant international student networks, University of Melbourne study, 2005

	To a considerable degree %	**Very much** %	**Total (considerable + very much)** %
At the university, I mix socially with other international students	32.0	27.9	59.9
At the university, the people I mix with socially have a cultural background similar to my own	40.1	27.3	67.4
Outside the university, the people I mix with socially have a cultural background similar to my own	32.7	44.0	76.7
At the university, the people I mix with socially are Australian	17.2	4.2	21.2
Outside the university, the people I mix with socially are Australian	15.0	5.8	20.8

Source: Rosenthal, et al., 2006, 23.

were required to name dominant patterns of networking ('The people I mix with socially are . . . '). International students with strong networks within and across cultural lines could not nominate both sets of links as strong and were forced to choose one, or, alternatively, found themselves recording contrary responses, for example choosing 'very much' or 'to a considerable degree' across all categories. Students with active links with many local students who spent more time with same-culture fellows might seem to rank their local networks low. Framed thus the analysis suggests a larger gap in local connectivity than might be warranted. As Thune points out, bridging ties between different social groups are typically more loose, weaker and less dense than bonding ties. Clustering coefficients are lower. But these bridging ties might still be vital in connecting students to the local setting with all its potentials. Rosenthal and colleagues may have overstated same-culture ghettoisation. Contrariwise, the method of selection in the present study attracted students relatively competent in English and cross-cultural communication and might lead us to understate ghettoisation.

The Melbourne survey also found that older students and postgraduate researchers were more likely than younger students to form dominant networks with Australians and less likely to do so in same-culture manner. Students from Asian countries who completed a preparatory foundation program were more likely to take the same-culture path. This may have been a selection category effect, rather than a program effect: on average students participating in such programs probably had less English languages skills than those who did not.[59] The study also found that on campus, female international students were less likely to form dominant networks with locals than were male international students.[60]

Questions on bonding and networks

Interviewees were asked a group of questions concerning family and personal ties and other relationships, associations and networks.

- Do you maintain contact with your family at home? Which family members? How frequently do you speak to them? How frequently do you travel home?
- If you have a partner in Australia, does your partner fully support your activities and needs as a student?
- Who are the people you see most often while here in Australia? Describe your closer friends. Have you made many new friends while here?
- Do you practice a religious faith? Do you worship regularly?
- Are you involved in regular group or club activities? What organisations are you involved in?

Students often proffered information beyond the immediate confines of the questions. The study did not gather comprehensive statistics on the number, range and intensity of student networks comparable to the research by Stokes[61] and others, but did enable mapping of networks (below). The study did not look closely at partnering

59 *ibid*, 5.
60 *ibid*, 24.
61 Stokes, 1985.

Table 13.2 Composition of students' networks within Australia

Networks and associations include	Number	%
Intimate bonding		
Immediate family/relatives located in Australia	61	31.5
Close friends, including boy/girl friends	113	56.5
Other bonding		
Casual friends: other international students	183	91.5
Casual friends: local students	113	56.5
Activity in social organisations such as clubs	96	48.0
Q Are their significant barriers in making friends across cultures?		
A Yes	110	55.0
No	90	45.0

Note: Some students mentioned more than one association; total does not sum to 100 per cent.

activity. The findings are strongest on family and friends, the history of such relations in Australia and on the role of cultural factors.

MAP OF NETWORKS

Table 13.2 summarises the within Australia networks of the 200 students. It includes family in Australia but excludes parents, relatives and friends in the country of origin. The table covers the above questions as well as those on cross-cultural relations (chapter 15) that followed. Altogether 91.5 per cent of students had at least casual friends among other international students. More than half had casual friendships with locals, some of which were same-culture friendships.

Almost one-third of students had family with them. This was highest among doctoral students, for many of whom the travel and educational costs of families were covered by scholarship. Boyfriends and girlfriends fell between close friend and family member and could take the characteristics of one or both. The suggestive data on barriers to making friends across cultures are discussed in chapter 15.

The educational institution can be an important influence in fostering student friendships. Other networks have their genesis more wholly in the informal private domain, through civil and religious organisations outside the institution or, more often, family and friends. Each of these areas is now considered in turn.

UNIVERSITY-STRUCTURED NETWORKS

Arrival: 'They become sort of your protection, your family'

Care of international students peaks at arrival. Universities often meet their clients at the airport, take them to temporary accommodation and provide them with comprehensive attention. Students are in most need of help at this point. Most arrive on their own having partly disconnected from all ties. Excitement is mingled with apprehension and a sense of loss. Many are fragile, especially younger students. As Weiss noted, a sudden loss of relationships, particularly intimate relationships, is felt more strongly than a long term lacuna.[62]

Some students in the present study said that structured university programs, including peer support schemes and new arrivals pairings, had kick started friendships. Programs varied by institution. Pre-class orientation activities could be important, which placed latecomers at a disadvantage. Some peer support teamed new arrivals with international students of similar backgrounds, some with partners from a different country or with local students. These programs were maximised when students had sufficient agency, social confidence and language fluency.

> I get involved in a lot of things that involve all foreign international students like the Peer Support Program . . . I've been on that twice. Being far from home . . . the more people you know, the less homesick you're going to be. And the more friends you have, the more they become sort of your protection, your family.
>
> ~ male, 26, business, Botswana

Accommodation: 'I was lucky to be in the college environment'

University-based colleges or residences provide the optimum framework for making friends across a range of cultures. De facto segregation could still occur but there were broad social opportunities and it was a secure environment for experiment. One student shared college with 240 others from many nations.

62 Weiss, 1973; see also Hayes and Lin, *op cit*, 7.

> That's the great thing about living [in college], you get to meet a lot of people from different backgrounds. You also assimilate very fast into the local culture because there are so many Australians there. You don't just meet them for class, you live with these people, you talk to them every day, you get to see them when you go for supper . . . There is a relatively big Asian community in my college. A little bit segregated from the Australian community. But within ourselves we are quite united and close. I see most of them, they are my close buddies. I go to them when I have problems. We are like brothers and sisters.
>
> Of course [I have experienced periods of loneliness or isolation]. I was lucky to be in a college environment because there I'm not the only one who is new and lonely. When you are faced with that there are two things you can do. You can hide in your room and cry alone, or you go out and try to meet people and talk to them, and say 'Hey, hello. How are you?' And then you say 'I'm sad and lonely', and they say 'Hey, I'm sad and lonely too. Let's talk, okay?' That is how I developed one of my closest friendships here. A Pakistani friend, totally from the other side of the world. I'd never really heard of Pakistan. He's Muslim, but we became really good friends and within a year we were the best of friends.
>
> ~ male, 24, arts, Singapore

In residential colleges information was readily diffused and the close proximity of others provided opportunities to participate in dense networks in which many or most potential connections were realised. Residences were hubs with many connections and short distances between the students or nodes. More accurately, they functioned as two or more loosely linked hubs in close proximity to each other, like neighbouring castles with drawbridges between them. Providing there is active traffic between the castles or hubs, international students benefit from same-culture and other-culture networking without the pathologies created by too exclusive a dependence on either ghettoisation or fraught identity.

Campus-based organisations: 'Almost every month we have a major event'

In their study Rosenthal and colleagues noted that 49.9 per cent of respondents had no involvement in university-based student clubs and only 21.4 per cent were involved to a 'considerable degree' or 'very much'. Male students, younger students, undergraduates and students without partners had higher than average levels of involvement. Students with club involvement reported higher than average levels of connectedness.[63] These results are consistent with the present study. The minority involved in clubs, more often in religious or cultural or national organisations than in clubs based on sport or specialised interests, often reported heavy involvement and emphasised the value of the club as network.

At their best student clubs were powerful hubs with high levels of betweenness and centrality, with close connections (short distances) between students and high clustering coefficients. One student was president of the campus Buddhist Society.

> We've got weekly English and Chinese dharma talks. Dharma talks are like Buddha's teachings. We invite either monks or nuns or Buddhist teachers to give these talks. We have a sports section also. Almost every month we have a major event. In the last week, we had a Buddhist exhibition which went for one week. At the end of May we're having a Vesak day celebration. During winter break we're having winter retreat. In August we're having a performance by our members at [name] auditorium. Then we have AGM and at the end of the year we have the cook of the year, whereby all the members come together in groups and prepare dishes in a competition. Yeah, it's around 200 odd people. It's a very good experience for me.
>
> ~ female, 26, arts, Singapore

These hub organisations could be highly sustaining. A 21 year old female from Malaysia in the same religious society said, 'My Buddhist friends' especially helped in difficulties with university work. 'I very much appreciate having these friends.' Likewise for some students, particularly but not only Muslims, regular worship and associated activities together were an important part of the week.

> Indonesian Muslim students have weekly meetings. Saturday night. We recite the Qur'an and we pray together, and after that we have

63 Rosenthal et al., 2006, 25–6.

> our dinner and we discuss what we're going to do back home after finishing out study.
>
> ~ male, 27, community development, Indonesia

Several interviewees were office bearers in same-culture student clubs. Some joined more than one club, for example Singapore and Hong Kong China associations. Several interviewees discussed an active network of AusAID scholarship students. There was common approval of the mix of 'Aussie' and cross-cultural functions: barbeques, dances, food mixes, cultural nights. At some universities general international student clubs were important.

> In the last two years, I've been working with the International Student Services Unit with a club called Unimates, which is designed for international students. I'm the president of it currently. We design activities for international students to give them an opportunity to meet other people if they're having problems. I've got quite a few friends through that, but they tend to be the transient ones who are going off after six months somewhere else.
>
> ~ female, 24, law, UK

Another student, a 24 year old male from Vietnam studying social science, was president of the university international student association, which had been broadened from same-culture to cross-cultural mixing. The association had 500 members. The president's work included planning, fundraising, advertising and membership drives. Annual activities included camping, BBQs, dancing clubs and balls, as well as football, tennis, a music club and so on. Another interviewee had been president of the university postgraduate students' association. A third, from Egypt, had helped to found a cross-cultural postgraduate student society.

Only a handful of students reported doing voluntary work outside club frameworks.

> I am in the Student Ambassador Leadership program. We do volunteer work. I chose to do conservation. We go to the park and clean up and do weeding. I wanted to try something different and this is something different.
>
> ~ female, 22, business, Malaysia

There was less international student involvement in field of study-based clubs, though a few interviewees had held leadership positions. The main activity was in economics and business where international student numbers were very high. The weak capacity of such organisations to draw student involvement brings into question the suggestion by Rosenthal and colleagues that the disciplines should be primary sites for building connectedness;[64] however, changes in the level of interaction with local students at discipline level might be fruitful (see chapter 15).

PARENTS AND FAMILIES

The attachment of international students to their families is often compelling. As chapter 14 will show the main commentary of students on loneliness is about missing families, especially in the early stages. Almost all students had active relations with the immediate family, and many with the extended family. Most students maintained family ties only via communications and travel. Some had partners and/or children with them. A small group lived with siblings, parents or other family members in Australia. Another small group maintained no family ties.

Again these results confirm Rosenthal and colleagues, who noted that 'students generally have strong links to home'. More than 90 per cent testified to support from family, 95.2 per cent stated that their families were concerned about their welfare and 92.9 per cent could contact home at need, though only 45.8 per cent could return home at need. Cost was the barrier. 'Young single female undergraduate students from Asian countries (especially Singapore) find it easiest to return home' at need.[65] Rosenthal and colleagues also found that 46.1 per cent felt 'stressed by the need to do well for the sake of my family'.[66] In the present study there was no specific question on this theme. It was little mentioned by students.

64 *ibid*, 8.

65 *ibid*, 26; these data combine the responses recorded as 'to a considerable degree' and 'very much'.

66 *ibid*, 30; data interpretation as for the previous note.

FAMILIES AT A DISTANCE

'I call them every tonight'

For nearly all with families abroad it was a short step to connect by phone, text or internet and almost all students did so, most often by voice phone (video calls were not in wide use at this time). But there were varied attitudes to the family ties. For a few students the emotional bond had been fractured. For more it had been partly displaced, strained, attenuated or otherwise changed. For many it continued under changed circumstances alongside new networks. Many found it a crucial form of continuing support. Others felt unable to open up to their parents about what was happening to them. Many developed substitutes for family, not always satisfactory and with varying levels of closeness: intimate friends, larger friendship networks and sometimes (perhaps to substitute for parental authority) teacher–student relationships. Some students attempted to immerse themselves locally.

For most students communications to home peaked in the early weeks and then settled into a rhythm. This could range from daily communication to once a fortnight or a month. A typical pattern was a phone call two to four times a week and trip home once a year. Some students, in Australia for several years, said that the gap between calls had lengthened. For those who talked daily it was central in their lives and met a strong need for close bonding. Several students sustained dense family networks in an active manner through multiple communications.

> I call them every tonight.
>
> ~ female, 23, business, Malaysia

> Three or four times a week. Mostly my mum. I want to listen to her voice.
>
> ~ female, 33, education, China

> Every day. My mum, dad, sister, my friends. Actually, my phone expenses are too much, I spend a lot of money on that.
>
> ~ male, 24, computing, India

Though in many cases there was no clear connection between relationships back home and the patterns in Australia, some students suggested there was substitution between them, in that when close friends or partnerships began in Australia the need for home diminished. On the whole students living with people who spoke their own language seemed to have a less burning need for contact with home. Those with partners or children left behind had a strong need.

> I talk to my parents once a week usually. I talk to my girlfriend, my fiance, three times a week.
>
> ~ male, 27, business, Indonesia

> I speak to my wife and son every day.
>
> ~ male, 35, law, Indonesia

In some cases calls to home were determined by the students and their own emotional (or financial) needs. When busy with their studies they rang less often. In response to questions as to which family members students spoke to, and how often, one student replied:

> My parents, my brother, my auntie, my grandma and grandpa. When I got depression, like every other day, because I felt if I didn't talk to them I felt I was invisible. But now, once every two or three months.
>
> ~ female, 25, public health, China

Another said:

> My Mum mostly. I talk to my Dad strictly if I need something [money], and my Dad says okay, bye. So if I call him just to talk to him, he says, like 'Yes, what do you need?' Once I said 'No, I don't need anything I just want to talk to you'. With my mum it's like, 'What are you doing? What are you eating?' and things like that.
>
> ~ female, 21, computing, Malaysia

In other cases the parents set the pattern. Effective phone costs varied with the student's budget, the destination, the phone company and the deal. Calls to Singapore were cheap, Indochina expensive. Phone cards helped. Mobile and internet use increased sharply during the period of the interviews.

> My mum she calls me. They got like a special offer in Macau, so if she calls me at a certain time on weekends it is cheaper. It's so expensive for me to call from here to Macau.
>
> ~ male, 23, arts, Macau

> Now all of my friends and relatives have got mobiles . . . It's not so expensive, $10 for hundreds of minutes.
>
> ~ male, 29, PhD in engineering, Bangladesh

> My mum and my dad, sister. Once a week, regularly. If I just call them but through SMS, every day.
>
> ~ female, 24, business, Indonesia

> I call them sometimes and email them very often.
>
> ~ female, 32, PhD in education, Vietnam

Not all parents were comfortable with text and email or chat and some lacked access. In a few cases even phone communication was impossible.

> Letters maybe come once a term. My parents are in the village where there's no access to a telephone . . . I talk to my boyfriend every day. He's the only one.
>
> ~ female, 40, PhD in gender studies, Papua New Guinea

Whereas many found in talking with their parents an essential renewal of intimacy, for a few calls the home were distancing and disturbing. Some wanted to evade continuous surveillance and emotional control. Others found it difficult to switch persona between sites, essential because their parents did not understand what they were going through. Sometimes it was better to talk to a sibling, another relative or family friend, than re-enter the parent–child relationship.

> Usually I don't call my parents. I don't want to make them worry. I usually call my friends.
>
> ~ male, 25, computing, Korea

> I seldom call back actually. You know, the parents . . . even if you complain about a little thing they think it's quite serious. I don't want to make them worried. I just tell them I am very happy here.
>
> ~ male, 41, education, Indonesia

A number of interviewees celebrated the sense of self-determination that independence from their parents had provided.

> In China I live with my parents. I have to go back home every night, before 11 o'clock. If I don't I have to call them and tell them. But now here I have a lot of freedom . . . It's [a different] attitude to life. Before, everything was done for me because I am the only child in my family: I don't need to do any housework, my father arranged work for me, that kind of thing. Now I have to do everything for me. It's good. I have learnt a lot being independent.
>
> ~ female, 27, education, China

Many students travelled home regularly, at least once a year and sometimes more often. A small number of students were visited in Australia regularly by parents. One student from Japan effectively lived in both countries.

> When I was in high school, I went home three times a year. But since I came to uni, once a year, for three months at a time.
>
> ~ male, 20, medicine, Japan

Most families could not afford that much travelling though. Some students had not travelled home during the period of study. 'It's so expensive', said an Indonesian female, 39, doing a PhD in engineering. For students with children in Australia the need to travel home was less strong and multiple fares were expensive.

FAMILIES IN AUSTRALIA

'Don't come alone'

For those with siblings, partners and/or children living with them, the experience was very different to that of solitary others without intimate ties in Australia. There was less of the feeling of emptiness many of the latter reported. Asked what would they advise to other individual students coming to Australia about the risks and problems of studying and living here, one student said:

> It would be good if they have a family members here for support . . . don't come alone, it's really difficult.
>
> ~ female, 28, PhD in environmental studies, Singapore

And in response to a question as to whether they had experienced periods of loneliness or isolation, one student replied:

> Not really because I have family here.
>
> ~ male, 40, Laos, medicine

One Indonesian student in engineering, who lived in an apartment with his brother and sister, was financed by parents. His aunt and uncle were in the same city and could be reached easily if there were problems. The same student had completed the last four years of secondary school in Australia, had fluent English and no difficulties in cross-cultural relations. It was almost the perfect basis for the international student experience, although the investment cost was high.

Others in Australia for a shorter time still benefited from sharing the experience with family.

> When you're back in your home country if you have any problem you can talk to your parents, ask for their suggestions. Here we have to face it. This makes me and my brother's relationship closer because we support each other.
>
> ~ female, 22, science, Malaysia

Several commented on the essential support provided by their spouse. When asked if the work in the home was shared with the partner and family and if, in their opinion, the sharing was balanced, one student from China replied, 'She does it all'. In response to the interviewer's remark that that wasn't fair, the student replied:

> Because I need to work on my studies. She wants me to teach [following graduation with the doctorate] as soon as possible.
>
> ~ male, 41, PhD in computing, China

> Yes, yes, we share. He helps with cooking, cleaning, yes now he helps a lot. My subject, environmental management, it is quite something. Every day I have a class. Every night I work. So it's a little bit difficult. If he was not here . . . when I'm in the class he's looking after my daughter, feeding her, send her to bed.
>
> ~ female, 33, environmental studies, Bangladesh

Not all could bring their children with them. One PhD student had his wife with him but the three children had remained behind. He had an Indonesian provincial government scholarship that did not cover children's school fees.

> [I maintain contact] with my children, every day.
>
> ~ male, 45, PhD in education, Indonesia

But having family present in Australia could multiply the problems.

> I always missed them and it was not good, because it broke up my concentration . . . and now they are here, I cannot concentrate also. [laughs] I think my problem is not the wife, it's my autistic boy. He takes a lot of my time . . . very overactive boy. Yes, she spends most of her time with him.
>
> ~ male, 42, PhD in linguistics, Indonesia

Moreover, having the family was not always enough to overcome loneliness. There was still cultural loneliness (chapter 14) and the loss of parental bonds. Students were asked if they had experienced periods of loneliness or isolation.

> Oh yes, even though I came with my family. I think the first year here was terrible. It took me very long to adapt. Maybe it's a new environment plus new faces, everything new, so even though my family are with me I still feel lonely. I miss my [parental] family.
>
> When I first came I went to Holmesglen so I used talked to the lecturer there. They have this thing about student welfare. If you have any problems, even personal, you just talk to them. Yes, they have counsellors there. I used to tell them I'm feeling homesick. I don't understand why even though I'm here with my family, but maybe it's a long space of separation . . . I think after talking to someone you feel relief and yet you feel like you've got it off your chest, someone actually understands what you're going through. I thought I was the only one feeling like this until when I met more new friends they told me 'Oh yes, I feel it for the first year, in fact we are still going through the same thing'.
>
> ~ female, 32, business, Singapore

Some student families were nested in larger groups of same-culture friends, providing spouses with shared childcare and families with a slice of home cultural context. Some mixed successfully with other-culture families. Others were less fortunate, especially those spouses isolated at home with small children.

NEW PARTNERS IN AUSTRALIA

'They come and go'

Many students had acquired boyfriends or girlfriends in Australia. For some it was the beginning of family formation. For others it was less engaging but helped to fill the gaps in closeness, transitivity and connectivity. Deniz noted on Turkish students that 'The loneliness levels of university students who have a romantic relationship were found to be significantly lower than the loneliness levels of other students'.[67]

67 Deniz, 2005.

Away from parents students had a greater freedom to form romantic ties on their own terms. Same-culture couplings were most common but some formed partnerships with locals or with international students from other backgrounds. One student from Taiwan, with a broad range of friends from Indonesia, Malaysia and Thailand, married a Thai fellow student he had met in Australia. A student from Colombia was 'very close' to her local boyfriend's family in Melbourne. Another student, from Malaysia, maintained a little distance from her local partner: In response to the question whether a student's partner fully supported their activities and needs as a student, one replied:

> Oh yeah, all the time. He is offering moral support. He's a doctor now, but he's saving and working hard for his future. I won't need him once I'm working, but it's nice to have him around. But of course he's white so he doesn't quite understand sometimes.
>
> ~ female, 26, medicine, Malaysia

For others, romantic involvements were inappropriate, or did not run deep.

> I don't have girlfriends because that's not in my religion.
>
> ~ male, 19, business, Pakistan

> Mmm, yes . . . they [girlfriends] come and go.
>
> ~ male, 23, business, India

None of those with active romantic partnerships in Australia reported being severely unhappy. In their study Rosenthal and colleagues noted that one-third of students had one or more sexual partner, and 'having a sexual partner in Australia is associated with a stronger sense of connectedness'.[68] They also report 'a small but significant positive relationship between number of partners and sense of connectedness'.[69] The present study did not go to that level of detail.

---

68 Rosenthal et al., 2006, 101.
69 *ibid*, 52–4.

FRIENDS

The size and internal diversity of friendship networks varied greatly. The triggers of friendship also varied, from accommodation, to the study program, to work, to common interests, activities or identification. Same culture associations were more important than cross-cultural ones. Housing was more important in creating or sustaining friendships than sharing a course of study or workplace.

MAKING FRIENDS

'I'm so picky'

Some interviewees were noticeably cosmopolitan. They had active friendships with international students from different nations and with locals, and were confident in switching between them all. One student from Singapore had close friends from Malaysia, Palestine and Australia. A student from India had good friendships among other Indian students, local Anglo-Australians and Italian-Australian. 'I consider myself a very social person and I make friends easily'. At the other end of the spectrum were those who found it difficult to make friends.

> I am single, I find that in Australia I don't meet any body, even a woman . . . The classmate is always busy. They don't want to talk to you.
>
> ~ female, 33, education, China

> No, [I have] not [made] many friends. I'm so picky about friends . . . I may have only two friends.
>
> ~ female, 21, business, Bahrain

Another used the internet to achieve more limited relationships.

> I use the internet to chat with whoever is on line. I don't care who they are as long as they don't know who I am, they don't know where I am and they don't know my background . . . I got someone to talk to, and I can express myself. I also get my confidence . . . and I can practise my English as well.
>
> ~ female, 23, social work, Taiwan

Forming friends was a matter of motivation, opportunity and commonality. The compatibility requirements included age and interests.

> The international students around here tend to be very young. It's not that I have anything against them, it's simply that they have another set of interests, so it's difficult to meet such friends. I'm 33, I'm married, I'm not going to go partying wildly with guys. I am done with that.
>
> ~ male, 33, PhD in medicine, Spain

As Green and colleagues note,[70] while younger people often have many acquaintances, older people tend to value a few closer friends.

For students not living with family or host family or in university residences, the core friendship group was often shaped by the shared house or apartment. Many had made good new friends when thrown together in this way. Often shared houses were minihubs in which each member bonded with the others and became more loosely connected to their networks of family and friends. The closer the extent of sharing in the house – common finances, meals, studies, leisure activities, friends – the more intensive the centralising hub effects.

Interviewees were asked who they saw most often. Most reported spending the largest amount of time with housemates. Some said their housemates were their only friends, the people they would turn to for advice, help and support when in trouble.

> Here, well, my family, I mean, sorry, my room members. Housemates.
>
> ~ male, 28, business, Bangladesh

> I think we are good friends. Just some limits. We are good for each other but we don't interfere in each other. But if you have some trouble or you know if you're homesick and you want somebody to talk [to], yes, they are there for you.
>
> ~ male, 25, computing, China

But not all housemates, same-culture or other-culture, were this compatible. For some students friends and networks developed less through housing than through study. 'Most of my good friends are my classmates', said one student in education from Indonesia. Work, for example in data programming, retail or hospitality and fast foods, was another source of new friendships.

70 Green et al., 2001.

> Most of my good friends are from the restaurant where I waitress. They are all uni students there. I made lots of friends through there.
>
> ~ female, 23, psychology/social sciences, UK

SAME-CULTURE NETWORKING: 'GOING BACK TOWARDS MY FRIENDS FROM MALAYSIA'

Most interviewees confirmed the research literature by saying that same-culture networks, usually involving common language, were especially important. There was a strong tendency to group in same-culture households. Students were asked who were the people they see most often while in Australia and if they had made many new friends while here.

> In the house, my friends, they're from India.
>
> ~ male, 26, business, India

> I don't want to share with any other nationalities because I don't know them, but Chinese is familiar.
>
> ~ female, 33, education, China

> I found a housemate. She's Singaporean Malay as well so it's a good thing for religion and things like that.
>
> ~ female, 21, computer science, Malaysia

Even so, in some same-culture households the students had little in common. They had their meals at separate times and sometimes fractious conflicts arose over shared bills for water or power. In certain houses that were composed by subletting, the agent, who had the same cultural background as the students, discouraged the formation of close bonds among members of the house.

References to same-culture association were ubiquitous in the interviews. Sharing a common language was crucial.

> Yes, I have close friends. My classmates. We are very close. All of them, they are from Japan.
>
> ~ female, 30, interpreting, Japan

> I try to have a circle of friends from different countries . . . most of the time I find myself going back towards my friends from Malaysia.
>
> ~ male, 20, architecture, Malaysia

> There is a French family living not very far from our house so that I would say would be the most frequent people I see . . . We haven't really met much people.
>
> ~ female, 39, medicine, France

> Several of my close friends are all from China. We speak the same language. We have the same topic in the lecture notes, that sort of things. It's very hard to make friends with the outside community. It's very hard to enter the Australia group.
>
> ~ female, 24, business, China

Same-culture networking occurred not only with people from the same country but also extended to neighbouring and related countries with language, religion or values in common. One PhD student in medicine from Laos noted that Laotians found it easier to become good friends with people who shared an Indochinese background, for example Thai students and those from Vietnam and Cambodia, though Indonesians were further away. 'We feel some barrier between us.' [39] At the same time, Indonesians and Muslim Malays spoke of a common heritage with each other, as did Europeans about each other. 'My best friend is from Colombia', noted one student from Mexico. Notwithstanding the plurality of Chinese languages, Chinese background provided many opportunities for friendship.

> I've got two very close friends from Singapore. Most of my friends are from Singapore and Malaysia.
>
> ~ female, 22, business, Malaysia

In same-culture networking on campus religious worship appeared as important as national clubs. Outside campus, religion was more important than any other binding factor apart from common language. Religious practice actively shaped the lives of a large minority of students in the study. For regular worshippers it provided a dense supportive network, involving not just friendship or quasi-family but also housing, sport and/or shared community service.

When asked the question, 'How did you get this house?', one student responded:

> Actually, I had a friend, she lived here and so I used to visit her. She's from my church. After she went back to Malaysia I moved into her room.
>
> ~ male, 25, science, Sri Lanka

Some Muslim students attended local mosques and were in contact with local Muslim families. Some helped to organise Islamic students' societies on campus.

> I am one of the committee that set up a prayer room on campus and I like to follow the progress of the society.
>
> ~ male, 45, PhD in education, Indonesia

DOWNSIDES OF SAME-CULTURE NETWORKS

'I really feel for them'

But a number of students were uneasy about same-culture networks, in which all connections led back to the same hubs and where the density of connections multiplied. These students preferred the extensivity of connections with its larger learning potential.

> Actually, the biggest issue that is affecting me now is that to live together with friends from the same country is not good for your English.
>
> ~ female, 27, business, China

> It's better not to stay together with students from the same countries. If you have more money try the homestay. My friend came here at the same time as me but her English is very good because she stays with the local people.
>
> ~ female, 30, science, Thailand

> Most of my friends are actually like not Singaporeans here . . . It's a bad experience just mingling with same [culture] friends.
>
> ~ female, 22, arts, Singapore

One student from Malaysia stated that many students from China were not adequately prepared in English prior to their arrival and this encouraged inwardly focused networks. They became overly dependent on same-culture enclosures and their skills in English remained underdeveloped, which reproduced the problem.

> A lot of people from the Republic of China (we all say PRC) have a lot of problems with spoken English. I really feel for them because they get despised so much by Australians. Their English is so poor that even a primary two or three is better than them. They can't even communicate well. Their written English has all

grammatical mistakes. They can't differentiate between 'is' and 'are'. Australians, the university in Australia, want to make money, they are profit-making . . . but it's not [the] way to make money, out of students that can't even speak English . . . It just drags the whole educational level down, the standard down. They can't even understand. They have no interest, they always stay in their own, the Chinese community . . . They just survive with their Chinese newspapers, Chinese magazines, Chinese food, Chinese people all around. That's all they do.

I have a lot of Chinese friends. But they have major, severe difficulties in terms of language and, especially during presentations . . . I think VCE [Victorian Certificate of Education] English for ESL is too easy. As long as you pass, you can go to university. A lot of them have borderline marks, 25, 26, 27. They can't even speak English . . . They say the language school is useless. Definitely useless . . . They say all I do is meet other people from China.

~ female, 21, architecture, Malaysia

Same-culture enclosures were not confined to students from China. There was a more limited potential among students from Malaysia or Indonesia. Same-culture enclosure effects could be modified by relationships with siblings or cousins already established in Australia, and with locals from the same cultural background, as well as with other international students (see below).

Some students tried to avoid or modify same-culture approaches. They lived with local students or international students from other countries, or used English when communicating with same-culture housemates.

Sometimes my roommate wants to practise English, so much English . . . I said no, so I speak Chinese and she speaks English. She wants to practise. I don't want to speak English; it's too much!

~ female, 33, education, China

I don't generally like clubs, especially the nationality clubs. In my first year, I was a member of the MSL, the Malaysian Students' Association, and I found that it just sets you aside from other people. Everybody else is interracial . . . If you join a student organisation that is about a particular race or particular nationality, you've just labelled yourself. You've just put yourself in that group of people.

~ female, 26, medicine, Malaysia

She was then asked, 'What would you advise to other individual students coming to Australia, about the risks and problems of studying and living here?', to which she replied:

Keep an open mind, and don't sequester yourself to friends of your own nationality . . . If you want to get to know Australia, live as an Australian. Yeah.

BONDING/BRIDGING

'Not many local students, more likely ABCs'

Many internationals from Chinese backgrounds networked with local Australians from Chinese families, fluent in both Chinese and English, which provided them with functional entry into the local culture. In Sydney and Melbourne, each with large Chinese background populations, such bonding/bridging networks were potentially large. Too central to be tagged enclaves, they potentially constituted strong social capital in the collective sense. Those in rural regional institutions lacked points of entry into the dominant Anglo-Australian communities, which made them more dependent on same-culture networks but with fewer people to build them with.

All of my close friends are from the youth group, church, and most of them are Chinese speaking. They may be from Malaysia, or Singapore, but they all speak Chinese.

~ female, 25, public health, China

Most of [my friends] are from China. I mean their original mother is China, but some of them are residents.

~ female, 21, business, China

Friends? Yes, lots, mainly from China. Few international students. Not many local students, more likely ABCs, Australian born Chinese.

~ female, 25, engineering, China

In response to the question, 'Have you made many new friends while here?', one student said:

> My communities, my supervisor who is also Chinese, office friends, and every Sunday I go to Chinese Christian church. I have many Chinese friends. I tried to make friends with students from different cultures but I/we don't have that many activities together.
>
> ~ female, 40, PhD in engineering, China

Such networks reproduced some of the limitations of same-culture enclosures without the students becoming cut off from the local environment.

NETWORKING WITH OTHER INTERNATIONALS

'Usually still Asian'

The shared experience of being an international student within an Anglo-Australian environment, where all international (especially non-white) students felt Othered, encouraged bridging friendships with students from other countries with different languages and/or religions. This was another strong theme in the findings.

Students were asked if they had made many new friends while they have been here.

> A lot – most of them are from Pakistan, China.
>
> male, 26, computing, India

> Yes, I've got a very good friend from Japan, another one from Korea and one from Malaysia.
>
> ~ female, 32, business, Singapore

They were also asked if they had been able to make friends with people from other cultures while in Australia.

> Yeah, a lot. They are all Asian but born here. I didn't meet many Thais.
>
> ~ female, 18, architecture, Thailand

Some students emphasised the value of living with students from other nationalities and sharing with locals to improve one's English.

> The best way to study here is to share houses with as much internationals as possible . . . share a house, try to talk to people, try to socialise.
>
> ~ male, 28, engineering, Germany

Mixed-culture households offered a broader set of networked connections than same-culture households, functioning like mixed student residences on a miniature scale and at a higher level of transitivity and coherence.

> Two students are from Australia, one is from China and one from India. Well I'm very happy actually, because I speak in English with my friends, especially my two Australian fellows.
>
> ~ male, 27, community development, Indonesia

LOCAL STUDENTS

'I don't think they are really friends'

Many interviewees mixed some local friends with their same-culture and other international student friends. A repeated pattern across the study was that interviewees nominated degrees of friendship and relegated the locals to the outer circles (chapter 15). Some younger students who had many acquaintances freely labelled the local students as 'friends', although some of these ties were no doubt loose. Others, especially older students, used the term 'friend' more carefully.

> Indonesia, Malaysia, Singapore . . . I do [have local friends] but not like very close, because they have a different lifestyle. Our thinking is different as well. But they are very nice to talk with. Mostly they are friends from my course. Yeah, sometimes, we meet in school, we talk together, but we never hang out together outside.
>
> ~ female, 21, business, Indonesia

> With local students I don't know . . . I've got friends from China, from Japan . . . I think it's a little bit hard to get friends from Australia. I don't know, until now I don't have a friend from Australia . . . I think language [is the barrier].
>
> ~ male, 35, law, Indonesia

CONCLUSIONS

In forming and sustaining personal and social relationships, all university students, including internationals, have certain advantages. A large majority do not carry major career responsibilities and most (though not all) have no children of their own. The world they inhabit is open, fluid, flexible and relatively cosmopolitan, with freedoms that are both alarming and attractive. Students have, in Weiss' terminology, the liberty to 'install' new attachment relationships. The loss of older ties provides opportunities (and pressures) to enter new associations. If network density is one key to reducing loneliness, especially among younger people, internationals can multiply their associations quickly. They are in regular seeing distance of dozens of others and have many avenues of extracurricular activity. Against this, relationships take time and effort. Internationals are already hard pressed to manage course loads and cope with communications; many also work. As well, the density of networks is not enough to satisfy needs for quality of association, through cultural fit underpinning a deeper social integration and/or through intimacy, sufficient to overcome family loneliness or romantic loneliness.

International students typically exhibit a combination of strong and weak ties, in the sense of intensity. Analysis is complicated by the fact that some families at home remain close and others are distanced, contact with friends may be more frequent and intensive than with families and some friends are substitutes for family bonds. Certain ties reinforce the student's sense of self, others have more prosaic benefits. Thune's notion of networked relationships 'as resources available for an agent to utilise in the course of action' applies more to friends than family. The strength of networked social capital is also a function of the network as a whole. If most same-culture friendship networks constitute weak social capital, marginalised in relation to government and university, when students band together in student organisations they can constitute stronger social capital.

International students need emotional and cultural continuity and they need to engage with the new. Individual students vary, but all want to learn and change. Despite the binary way the choices are framed by some researchers, students do not make absolute choices between the old and the new, though they are aware of potential tensions between them. In continuing their links with home and parental family or in nuclear relations with partner and children in Australia, they remain immersed in home culture and language, thereby sustaining continuity of self. They also draw from intimate relationships some of the emotional, intellectual and material resources with which they deal with challenges and remake themselves. Yet parents, kin and partners are not necessarily changing in the same way at the same time. This can generate misunderstandings, especially with parents and kin, compounding the uncertainties and vulnerabilities of mobility. Distance rarely means that close bonds are severed in an absolute sense. Nevertheless, no longer sharing the same living space with parents and communicating largely by electronic means can exacerbate the feelings of loneliness and cultural displacement and trigger a sense of disjuncture when switching between family and friendship networks. Most students feel the need for compensating relations with people close by. This heightens the role of friendships with other students, especially close friends. For some students, having their own space away from family is welcome because it facilitates personal exploration and change. Some feel more free, but some of the lonely ones feel more powerless (chapter 14).

Personal and social relationships and the boundaries between them can be unstable and volatile, especially in the early days. Relationships and networks develop and alter quickly. Acquaintances become close friends in a few days. Friends and sexual partners become surrogate family. Groups in same-culture networks suddenly function like extended families. The drivers of new patterns are the hole in the heart, the need for intimacy, the need for accommodation and the drives to cope educationally and survive and prosper in settings in which English is spoken. Accommodation often determines personal associations. Some houses and student residences constitute hubs within a larger setting of many partly joined networks. Shared same-culture households at best provide a quasifamily setting in which cultural continuity is leavened with the shared opportunity to learn day-to-day English and link to the host society. These dual elements are best provided for in mixed-culture houses and student residences with a well-developed degree of transitivity across boundaries. This evidence strongly confirms chapter 6 on the potentials of university-based residences. Nevertheless, simply bringing students of different backgrounds into one place does not guarantee optimum connectivity.

For the most part this study is consistent with the literature. Ties to parents and family at home were central, especially for younger students. Close friends, mostly from the same culture, were part substitutes. A broad range of same- or similar-culture friendships and friendships with other internationals was open to most but not all. Interviewees worried about obstacles to cross-cultural networking, though some had good local friends. Many worried that they spent too much time with people like themselves, and some tried to reduce self-imposed obstacles such as always using home languages. The study confirms the ambiguity of same-culture networks. These are necessary but not sufficient to the international student experience. Same-culture networks facilitate agency and action. They provide emotional sustenance, living support and help with learning; they can also constrain action inside enclosures. Insularity reduces the achievement of groups as well as individuals. At worst same-culture norms stifle individual freedoms or block the formation of bridging behaviours with outsiders, which are seen to breach solidarity and trust. Where they exclude others, same-culture networks lessen the educational experiences of locals as well as internationals. But even self-ghettoising student groups can advance academic performance and student security, and thereby contribute to the social good as well as the good of the group.

The study suggests potential for Bourdieu-ian tradeoffs in which some gain social capital at the expense of others. It can be argued, for example, that in Australia insular local student groups secure cultural advantages. Perhaps there is equal potential for win–win and lose–lose effects. Arguably, when same-culture groups become too separated from each other everyone loses the potential offered by the cosmopolitan experience. Moreover, because international students are less powerful than elite lawyers or public servants in Bourdieu's France, exclusive networks have as many downsides as upsides for those enclosed inside.

The study also extends the literature. First, it demonstrates that it is essential to disaggregate the large international student populations in English-language countries not only by nationality but also by cultural background, language and religion. Students from different groupings exhibit varying needs for sociability and bonding, a point recognised by some researchers but not always by educational providers. Students have differing capacities to network cross-culturally (language is one key to this). Students are differentially placed to form same-culture networks because of varying group size. Students from Bahrain, Laos and sub-Saharan Africa had fewer compatriots in Australia than do those from China or Singapore. Students are also differentially placed to penetrate locally based groups and associations.

Second, the study points to the bonding/bridging potentials, in immigration heavy countries, of networks with same-culture locals. These potentials again vary by student grouping. This also raises questions about the sharp distinction drawn in the research literature between same-culture and other-culture associations, or sojourners and locals. These conceptions entail a monocultural notion of locals. Local societies can be culturally heterogeneous, especially in a globalising environment in which immigrants, whether temporary (as are many international students) or more permanent, maintain contact with their place of origin, return home from time to time, and sustain much of the old in the new setting.[71] It is a peculiar omission in the research, indicating that the migration-heavy English-language countries are not always immigrant sensitive.

For policy makers, educational providers and student parents the most important finding concerns the volatility and variability of networks. To repeat the point, some students have no personal networks in the country of education. They are poorly placed to handle not just crises but also daily life. Too often institutions assume that 'because international students are resourceful and resilient, they do not require additional assistance'.[72] This comforting notion that personal networks are always there must be exploded. On the other side of the coin it is sometimes argued[73] that universities should do more to establish personal care themselves, which is not very different from the view of some international students that lecturers should extend beyond teaching to become personal mentors and guides. This is equally impractical. Australian educational institutions cannot compensate in quasi-affective fashion for social and emotional lacuna in the private sphere. What they can do is monitor, back up and strengthen the informal forms of security.

It is essential to respect the distinctions between the formal sphere of government, the semiformal university and the informal and private sphere. There is boundary ambiguity but this does not obviate the need for the division of labour. The issue is not whether and how institutional provision and private security can or should substitute for each other, it is how they can most usefully complement and supplement each other within the overall framework of security.

Educational providers can facilitate students' relationships with family and friends in practical ways. First, as first noted in

71 Appadurai, 1996.
72 Lee, 2005, 5.
73 Rosenthal et al., 2006a, 91.

chapter 11, they can monitor the situation of each student to identify those lacking friends or other ties and place a safety net under them (see chapter 14). These students need extra care. Second, institutions can facilitate the role of the original home in student security by establishing direct lines of communication and accountability from institution to parents, informing families of major problems of welfare or academic progress and funding communications in emergencies. This would assist the security of family and student. Third, not all institutions provide a full program of structured mixing and buddy systems on arrival. Universities could provide two kinds of pairing: one with another international student from a same-culture or similar-culture background, the other with a local student. Fourth, we again make the point (chapter 6) that more university-subsidised student residences would considerably advance the potential for successful relationships of all kinds. Fifth, institutions can do much to facilitate student activities in the form of clubs, religion, sport and culture by providing subsidies, venues and facilities.

There are two other domains in which a larger change in the security of international students can be achieved by changing patterns of networking and relationships. Each of these domains contributes directly to the formation of students as active agents. The first move is to improve foundation language skills (see chapter 12). The second and related move is to integrate international students more effectively into the local context. That thorny problem is addressed in chapter 15. Prior to that chapter 14 looks more closely at international student loneliness.

14 LONELINESS

I think the biggest problems most international students face is that of loneliness, and I mean it really gets to the point of depression. Some of the people I know that I've met, it's really . . . they don't know what to do, they don't know who to go to, because they have come from countries where it is not acceptable to go and ask for help. You have to do it yourself.

– male, 29, business, India

INTRODUCTION: THE LONELINESS OF THE LONG-DISTANCE STUDENT

Not all international students are secured all the time by bonding relations. Often networks with family and friends are attenuated by distance or by cultural displacement just when they are most needed. For others traditional bonds do not meet all their needs for sociability. Many experience loneliness during their stay. For some loneliness becomes a permanent condition that constrains their agency.

A person is lonely when the need to belong is unsatisfied. As with feelings of hunger, joy and sorrow, loneliness is a human condition that almost everyone has known. Feelings of loneliness cannot be wholly eliminated but they can be modified through the actions of the agent and/or others.[1] Loneliness is more likely to occur under circumstances such as prolonged foreign travel or the loss of significant others. It is one of the defining features of the international student experience.

1 Rokach and Brock, 1998.

For many students it is acute, especially in the first few months, and often longer in the case of those students who have few co-culturals to talk to. For students who are isolated, whose emotional and/or social bonds are weak or distant or non-existent, loneliness is hard to escape. But it also affects actively networked students who nevertheless find themselves displaced, whether in geographical, social, educational, linguistic or cultural terms. Loneliness affects not only wellbeing and confidence but also the capacity to learn and grow in the country of education. Loneliness and coping with loneliness are among the primary factors that shape student security.

Some studies suggest that loneliness stems from deficits in emotional bonds and social networks, while others highlight personality as a predisposing factor. A middle group of studies takes in both these explanations. A small number of studies, including a previous paper from the present study,[2] focus specifically on the loneliness of mobile people in cross-cultural situations.

The present study is the first interview-based investigation of international student loneliness in Australia conducted at scale. It may constitute the largest qualitative investigation of international student loneliness yet published. The chapter begins with the literatures on loneliness, factors affecting it, coping with loneliness, and cross-border students and loneliness. It then moves to student responses to the interview questions about loneliness and other responses touching on loneliness-related issues. It concludes with implications for universities and policy makers.

LITERATURE ON LONELINESS

The need to belong can be understood as the need to form and maintain a minimum quantity of interpersonal relationships. If this need is not sufficiently satisfied, negative feelings are generated, including feelings of loneliness.[3] According to Russell and colleagues, loneliness reflects 'an individual's subjective perception of deficiencies in his or her social relationships'.[4] Most literature on loneliness explains it as a singular and universal quality. We should specify at the outset of

2 Sawir et al., 2008.
3 Baumeister and Leary, 1995.
4 Russell, et al., 1984, 1313.

this chapter that while loneliness is a common human condition we do not consider that all people experience the same loneliness: perceptions and expressions of loneliness can vary among individuals and between groups. Social relations and communications differ between cultural groups and are affected by gender, age and other factors. People's expectations and needs also vary on the basis of personal disposition and values, physical health and energy, and will and imagination. For two people in much the same circumstances, the incidence and intensity of loneliness may differ. Remedies and coping strategies also vary across individuals and groups and are socially, economically and culturally nested.

Weiss[5] distinction between emotional loneliness and social loneliness, based on the difference between intimate personal ties and more distanced social ties, is foundational in much of the literature on loneliness. We use the terms 'personal loneliness' and 'social loneliness' here, noting that personal loneliness can be either romantic or non-romantic (chapter 13). As noted, between the different forms of loneliness lie ambiguities, overlaps and some scope for substitution.

According to Weiss emotional or personal loneliness results from the loss or absence of an intimate tie with spouse, lover, parent or child. It is characterised by anxiety and apprehension. It can be partly or wholly remedied by installing a satisfactory attachment relationship, though there are limits to substitutability. Social loneliness is triggered by a lack of an engaged social network with peers, those who share one's concerns or view of the world. As with personal relations, a sudden loss of social relations is felt more intensely than is the longer-term lack. Social loneliness brings with it boredom and a sense of exclusion.[6] Osterman noted that 'Being accepted, included or welcomed leads to positive emotions such as happiness, elation, commitment and calm', while 'Being rejected, excluded or ignored leads to often intense negative feelings of anxiety, depression, grief, jealousy and loneliness'.[7] The obvious remedy for social loneliness is integration into an existing or newly-formed social network. Weiss states:

5 Weiss, 1973; 1974.
6 Weiss, 1973.
7 Osterman, 2001, 327.

> Social networks provide a base for social activities, for outings and parties and get-togethers with people with whom one has much in common; they provide a pool of others among whom one can find companions for an evening's conversation or for some portion of the daily round. Social isolation removes these gratifications; it very directly impoverishes life.[8]

While Weiss appears to conflate loneliness and isolation, the two are not identical. Isolation is one trigger of loneliness, but not all isolated people are lonely, nor are all lonely people necessarily isolated (see below). As Misra puts it 'One may be alone without being lonely, and feel lonely in a crowd'.[9] Some socially networked people are lonely for personal ties. Some long for social ties different to those they have. Isolation is a measurable human condition. Loneliness is a subjective feeling often – but not always – associated with the objective condition.

Causes of loneliness

Many studies investigate causes of loneliness.[10] Some focus on external events such as the fracturing of social and personal relationships. Rokach[11] refers to 'traumatic events' such as the death of a spouse, divorce or loss of a friend. Separation from loved ones may also occur on relocation, which severs contact with social networks and support systems. Rokach[12] refers to 'relational deficits'.

Another group of studies uses network analysis. Stokes[13] explored the statistical relationship between social network variables and undergraduate loneliness. As noted in chapter 13 the most significant correlate of loneliness is network density. All else being equal denser networks enhance the sense of belonging. Green and colleagues[14] examined the effects of network size, closeness ratings of members of the network, presence of partner, presence of intimate other, and

8 Weiss, 1973, 150.

9 Misra, *op cit*, 1.

10 For earlier examples in the literature see Peplau and Perlman, 1982; Rokach, 1988, 1989; Stuewe-Portnoff, 1988; Lunt, 1991.

11 Rokach, 1988.

12 Rokach, 1989.

13 Stokes, 1985.

14 Green et al., 2001.

network density. They found that social loneliness is related to the closeness of people in the network and to the number of people in it. Carstensen[15] confirms these conclusions. DiTommaso and Spinner[16] found that integration into a social network is the best predictor of lesser social loneliness. The crucial element is close friends who are able to provide meaningful personal advice rather than just casual acquaintances. Here the line between personal and social relationships is blurred.

Loneliness and individual characteristics

A third set of studies considers the relations between loneliness and the qualities of human agents, including personality, age, gender and cultural identity.

One body of work focuses on personality traits and learnt attributes that may exacerbate the potential for loneliness, for example characteristics that reduce the desire for social relationships, or result in countersocial behaviours in social situations or lead a person to change their actual social relations.[17] These characteristics can include lack of social skills, physical disability, feelings of being unimportant or fear of being rejected. Peplau and Perlman suggest that people unusually prone to loneliness are often shy, introverted and less willing to take social risks. Some are more than usually anxious, depressed and neurotic.[18] Typically, extroverts are surrounded by large networks to which they feel close.[19] Paradoxically, those who appear more self-sufficient and less in need of others find it easier to attract others and maintain successful relationships. Research identifies a link between low self-esteem and severe loneliness.[20] Conversely, loneliness may trigger reduced self-concept. Rosenberg and colleagues note that loss of 'specific self-esteem' is correlated to reduced school performance.[21] Poor language or communications capacity is another factor. Being

15 Carstensen, *op cit.*
16 DiTommaso and Spinner, 1997.
17 Peplau and Perlman, 1982.
18 *ibid*, 9; Hojat, 1982; Stokes, 1985.
19 *ibid.*
20 For early examples see Peplau and Perlman, 1982; Hojat, 1982.
21 Rosenberg et al., 1995, 167–8.

anxious about communication correlates with loneliness.[22] Among many internationals, problems of language competence inhibit potential relationships and augment loneliness.

As noted in chapter 13 bonding ties can vary with age. Green and colleagues find the negative correlation between loneliness and closeness to members of the network is more significant for older adults. The negative correlation between loneliness and the number of contacts is more important for young college students.[23] Stokes reports similar findings. Often the loneliness of college students is reduced simply by increasing the size of their networks.[24] We note that these studies are culturally specific in that their subjects were mostly people from the USA; they may or may not apply to international students from all nations.

There are contradictory findings on gender and loneliness. Weiss found that women are more apt to be lonely than men. Hojat argues that women have lower self-esteem than men, which, given the association between low self-esteem and loneliness, suggests women are more prone to loneliness.[25] Borys and Perlman suggest that reported gender differences in loneliness do not result from differences in the incidence of loneliness. Rather, the finding that men are less lonely derives from men's greater reluctance to disclose such feelings. Some men might even refuse to admit to themselves when they are lonely.[26] We suggest also that women may place higher importance than men on interpersonal relations and deficiencies in such relations. Further, research suggests that women rate themselves as better at emotional expression than men,[27] while men are more likely to report expressing emotion only in intimate relationships.[28] These gender differences might also be subject to other variations, such as age or cultural background. Constantine and colleagues noted in relation to the 'cultural adjustment experiences' of Asian college women that one Vietnamese student missed both mother and grandmother, and talked of a lack

22 See among others Solano and Koester, 1989.
23 Green et al., 2001.
24 Stokes, 1985.
25 Weiss, 1973, *op cit*; Hojat, 1982.
26 Borys and Perlman, 1985, 69.
27 Brody, 1996.
28 Brody and Hall, 2000.

of 'female role models' while living in the USA.[29] But Russell and colleagues found no gender differences in relation to loneliness,[30] and Deniz, confirming Ari and Hamarta, found that loneliness levels among male students are higher than among females.[31] It is suggested that loneliness may be greater among males because emotional expressivity, emotional sensitivity and social control are higher in females. Male students are more inclined to suppress and conceal loneliness (an interpretation that receives some empirical support in the present study; see below). Female students display better attachment skill, which leads to greater success in making relationships, thereby reducing loneliness. Stokes and Levin agree that men have higher levels of loneliness,[32] partly because the quality of close relations determines loneliness among women, and women in the study tended to develop close and dyadic social ties, while men were more group oriented in friendship and often conscious of deficiencies in group relations.[33]

There are few studies of cultural and cross-cultural aspects of loneliness. As noted the dominant approach is culture blind. Loneliness is treated as a universal experience. Some studies do argue that loneliness is caused or exacerbated by specific cultural norms related to coupling, relations with parents and peers and/or social relations in general.[34] To the extent that loneliness (and not just isolation) are constituted by lacuna in personal bonds and/or social networks, it follows that loneliness and responses to loneliness must be variable to the extent that personal relations and social networks are variable. But no study has examined loneliness across several cultures. Most studies focus on just one or two cultures.[35]

COPING WITH LONELINESS

Strategies and resources people use in coping with loneliness vary among people and groups. Research[36] suggests there are three

29 Constantine et al., 2005b, *op cit*, 167.

30 Russell et al., 1984.

31 Deniz, 2005; Ari and Hamarta, 2000.

32 Stokes and Levin, 1986.

33 Likewise male adolescents are more willing to make new friends than are female adolescents: Savin-William and Berndt, 1990; findings confirmed by Nurmi et al., 1997.

34 See also Rokach, 1989.

35 Misra, 1999.

36 This includes Rubensten and Shaver, 1982; Paloutzian and Ellison, 1982; Cutrona, 1982; Rokach, 1990; Rokach and Brock, 1998.

overlapping coping strategies. First, strategies in which lonely subjects work directly on themself to manage feelings of loneliness. Andre refers to self-acceptance of being alone as 'positive solitude'.[37] Rokach and Brock discuss the promotion of 'individuality, creativity, and self-awareness by allowing the opportunity for contemplation, self-exploration, and insight', which can enhance self-esteem and alleviate the pain of loneliness.[38] The lonely person can also contemplate the causes of loneliness and develop self-knowledge in order to solve the problem. Some other lonely people further distance themselves from others, retreating into an isolated and closed inner self (this use of isolation to cope with loneliness again indicates that loneliness and isolation are not identical). But this strategy may sublimate loneliness rather than abolish it and become associated with pathological behaviour.[39] Another strategy is to focus on religion, which can bring strength and inner peace.[40] In the study by Kirkpatrick and Shaver participants who described their relationship with God as a secure attachment were less lonely and depressed than those with insecure attachment to God.[41] Pergament and colleagues suggest that 'God can be viewed as another member of social network who like other network members can at times offer help in the coping process'.[42] Other strategies include new activities that provide adventure or other challenges or pampering oneself via consumption.

Second, there are strategies to augment social relations or the potential to engage in them. The lonely person can systematically become prepared by learning new thoughts, behaviours, communications and social skills. Third, there are strategies of seeking help – professional, institutional or personal – to achieve either emotional self-management or augmented sociability. Note that the choice of coping strategies can be affected by cultural background.[43]

---

37 Andre, 1991.

38 Rokach and Brock, 1998, 112.

39 See for example the case of Huan Xiang at Monash University in 2002; Wikipedia, 2005a.

40 Rokach and Brock, 1998.

41 Kirkpatrick and Shaver, 1992. This has interesting theoretical implications. It might suggest that the interlocking network of formal and informal and private agencies that comprise student security might be extended to include the student's imagination.

42 Pergament et al. 1990, 815.

43 Rokach, 1999, finds the use of religion and faith to cope with loneliness is most prevalent among people from south Asia and the West Indies.

INTERNATIONAL STUDENTS AND LONELINESS

What does research say about cross-border international students and loneliness? Brislin and Yoshida found that many students report a strong sense of loss and isolation, persistent anxiety and confusion, and disappointed expectations about the host country.[44] Studies report early feelings of intense loneliness even for students in regular contact with people from their own city or culture. In most cases, this intense loneliness diminishes in time. Expectations change. Agency becomes more grounded and proactive. Students learn to cope, extend their social circles and make new kinds of friends. Without such transformations the intense initial loneliness may persist and become entrenched as longer-term social alienation that stunts the capacity for self-determining action.[45] Brennan noted that loneliness together with problems in crucial relationships can be 'extremely debilitating' and contribute to loss of motivation and student failure.[46] In Turkey Demir and Tarhan found that 'as the level of loneliness increased, academic achievement decreased'.[47] These problems are exacerbated for students with a 'social skills deficit', such as difficulties with language and/or networking. 'Lonely adolescents may experience difficulties in forming and maintaining satisfactory relationships' and miss strategic opportunities for 'mutual learning' such as academic skill building.[48]

Networked relationships play a key role in sustaining confidence and agency and helping students to deal with emotional, social and educational problems (see chapter 13). The literature also reveals patterns in student support. Leong and Sedlacek found that when seeking help with emotional–social problems, students opt for parents, older friends or other students. When seeking help with educational–vocational problems, they prefer faculty advisers, parents or older friends.[49] Baloglu found that friends are the most preferred source of help, followed by parents and teachers, and that friendship networks provide the most important support when away from home.[50]

44 Brislin and Yoshida, 1994.
45 Moroi, 1986.
46 Brennan, 1982, 271.
47 Demir and Tarhan, 2001, 113.
48 *ibid*, 120.
49 Leong and Sedlacek, 1986.
50 Baloglu, 2000.

Table 14.1 Aspects of international student loneliness, University of Melbourne, 2006

	To a considerable degree %	Very much %	Total (to a considerable degree plus very much) %
It is lonely for me here in Melbourne	21.0	11.3	32.3
It's hard being away from the people I love	27.9	22.8	50.7
I miss the familiar way of life in my own country	26.6	23.8	50.4
I feel less important here than at home	26.5	14.4	40.9
I feel uncomfortable in the Australian culture	13.1	2.6	15.7

Note: n = 973–8, depending on question.
Source: Rosenthal, et al., 28.

Student counselling services are often underutilised due to cultural factors (see chapters 8 and 11).[51]

In Australia a relatively high incidence of international student loneliness was noted by Leder and Forgasz,[52] who interviewed 13 students, including five internationals. They concluded that 'university counselling services may need to address the issue of loneliness proactively'.[53] The only large scale Australian study of international student loneliness, lacuna in networks and related issues is by Rosenthal and colleagues[54] (table 14.1). Unlike the present study, the Melbourne study did not ask whether students have been lonely in Australia at any stage, but whether they were lonely on the day the survey was completed.[55]

The study found that about 70 per cent of international students have a strong sense of connectedness, which is 'fundamental to students' wellbeing'. Only 6 per cent or less of students 'feel quite isolated'; a larger proportion were homesick. The most positive finding was that 42.4 per cent ticked 'Not at all' against the statement 'I feel uncomfortable in the Australian culture'.[56]

51 Schweitzer, 1996; Baloglu, 2000; Mori, 2000; Jacob and Greggo, 2001; Snider, 2001; Rosenthal, 2006, *op cit*.

52 Leder and Forgasz, 2004, 194.

53 *ibid*, 196.

54 Rosenthal et al., 2006.

55 Thus the Melbourne study does not distinguish between initial experiences of loneliness and longer-term patterns as discussed here. However, it noted that the initial period constitutes a distinct set of difficulties; Rosenthal, 2006, 13.

56 *ibid*, 28. This finding is not included in table 14.1; see source for full findings.

Questions on loneliness

Interviewees were asked, 'Have you experienced periods of loneliness or isolation?' If the answer was 'Yes', they were asked 'Who do you turn to?'

These questions were among the most fruitful in the study. Altogether 131 students (65 per cent–66 per cent of women and 63 per cent of men) answered 'Yes' to the first. Some answers distinguished between loneliness and isolation. Many students proffered further data and narratives in relation to one or another question. Some who answered 'No' also provided more data. Because this detail was unsought we can surmise that, as with the questions on dealing with immigration (chapter 10), the loneliness questions touched a chord in many students, who felt strongly about their experiences of loneliness and wanted to tell. In addition, some other questions produced data related to loneliness, including those on family and networks (see chapter 13) and cross-cultural relations (see chapter 15).

The proportion answering 'Yes' to having experienced loneliness or isolation was double that in the University of Melbourne study, as noted primarily because the Melbourne study asked about loneliness only on the day of the survey. All research suggests that the incidence of loneliness peaks in the first few months.

The interview data enable us to compare the networks of those reporting loneliness and isolation to the networks of those who did not. Strikingly, those reporting loneliness had a greater incidence of networked relations (table 14.2).

The comparison in table 14.3 illustrates that same-culture networks are not a universal cure all for social needs. It might suggest a minority category of students who are both isolated and contain their loneliness within. It also highlights the question of integration with the local setting. Of the lonely, 65 per cent identified barriers to cross-cultural friendship, compared to just 37 per cent of the non-lonely.

ONLY THE LONELY

In response to the question, 'Have you experienced a period of loneliness or isolation?', many students replied that they had.

Rates of loneliness were above average for students from Malaysia (72 per cent) and Singapore (92 per cent). China (61 per cent),

Table 14.2 Comparison of lonely and non-lonely student networks

	Lonely (n = 129)		Not lonely (n = 71)	
Networks and associations include	***Number***	***%***	***Number***	***%***
Immediate family or relatives	36	28	25	35
Close friends, including partner boyfriends or girlfriends	77	60	36	51
Casual friends: other international students	129	100	54	76
Casual friends: local students	77	60	36	51
Social organisations	72	56	24	34
Q Are their significant barriers in making friends across cultures?				
Yes	84	65	26	37
No	45	35	45	63

Note: Some students mentioned more than one association so the total does not sum to 100 per cent.

Table 14.3 Self-reported problems with loneliness, by national origin and gender

	Female students		Male students		All students	
	Total	**Loneliness**	**Total**	**Loneliness**	**Total**	**Loneliness**
Southeast Asia and Pacific						
Indonesia	22	12	27	18	49	30
Malaysia	13	11	5	2	18	13
Singapore	7	6	4	4	11	10
Laos, Cambodia, Vietnam	3	1	3	2	6	3
Other southeast Asia and Pacific*	5	4	1	1	6	5
Northeast Asia						
China	22	13	6	4	28	17
Hong Kong China	5	3	0	0	5	3
Other east Asia**	3	3	6	4	9	7
South Asia						
India	4	2	17	10	21	12
Other south Asia	5	3	14	7	19	10
Other						
Middle East and North Africa	2	2	5	3	7	5
Other Africa	3	3	4	3	7	6
Europe	2	2	4	1	6	3
Canada/USA/UK	3	0	2	2	5	2
Latin America	2	2	1	1	3	3
Total	101	67	99	62	200	119

* Brunei, Thailand, PNG

** Korea, Japan, Taiwan, Macau

Table 14.4 Triggers of loneliness

Total students interviewed = 200
Number of students answering 'Yes' to the question 'Have you experienced a period of loneliness or isolation in Australia? n = 129 (64.5%)

Self-perceived triggers of loneliness	**Number of lonely students mentioning trigger**	**% of lonely students interviewed**
Not specified	60	47
Personal (emotional) loneliness	46	36
Shock of the new culture	30	23
Obstacles to social networking	6	5
Difficulties in handling problems*	6	5
Personal characteristics of interviewee	3	2
Total students answering 'Yes'	129	100

Note: Some students mentioned more than one cause of loneliness, so percentages do not sum to 100.
* All but one of the specified problems were academic in nature.

India (57 per cent) and other South Asian nations were below average. Loneliness was almost universal among students from Africa (table 13.3). While half the students did not specify causes of loneliness or isolation, the cause mentioned most often was a lacuna in close relationships, normally with families (see table 13.4). Another large group of students referred to the shock when they encountered an unfamiliar cultural setting in Australia. A small group had difficulties in securing adequate social networks.

Personal loneliness: 'I'll cry and cry on the phone'

Those who had lost the warmth of personal relations with parents, spouse, children, siblings, relatives and close friends often reported a profound sense of loneliness. For some the experience was very painful and challenging.

> Yes, yes, oh, especially right at the beginning when I first got here. I didn't have anyone to talk to, that was the thing. It was really hard because I couldn't have contact with anybody. Initially, I came all by myself... Exactly who to approach, who to talk to, I had no clue. I used to be on the phone every day with my dad, 'I wanna go home'. Every single day, I'll call my dad and cry and cry on the phone.
>
> ~ female, 22, business, Zimbabwe

Yes, it does affect you when you come in. Like pulling out your comfort zone and putting it in a different place. Definitely it affects you.

~ male, 28, business, Sri Lanka

The experience was more daunting for students who left the nest for the first time. Some, especially those with extra problems or burdens, lacked confidence about living on their own and faced serious difficulties.

When I first came here it's very lonely because it's my first experience of going into abroad and staying alone. It's very hard . . . and, you know, I got a little, small baby and . . . Just 10 months. This is very hard for me.

~ male, 35, law, Indonesia

The sense of isolation increased when the student became sick and was without parental care or, alternatively, when a family member back home needed care. The familial bond was there but frustrated, which could trigger an intense feeling of loneliness.

It [loneliness] happens when you're sick. It happens a lot. You remember your mum and family when you are sick, but that's natural.

~ male, 19, business, Pakistan

Last weekend I got a call from my brother saying my mother was sick and in hospital, and I just completely lost my . . .

~ female, 40, PhD in gender studies, Papua New Guinea

Christmas and other religious or national festivals had special meaning. Those separated from home at such times could feel distressed. Weiss noted that Christmas is 'a time of reaffirmation by kin of their fundamental commitment to another'.[57]

However, having family members in Australia did not always solve all loneliness.

Not isolation, it's just lonely. Even though my sister has come, I still feel that. When I talk to her she doesn't always understand

57 Weiss, 1973, 18.

> what I'm talking about because she's too young. Although she's around 18, we still have a generation gap.
>
> ~ female, 21, design, Hong Kong China

Shock of the new: 'We are in the very strange place'

In the early months the old hubs were inaccessible and the new still undiscovered. When separation from family was raw, and even same-culture friends were few, loneliness was raw too. Often loneliness began with initial feelings of profound unfamiliarity, extending from culture, language and people to the urban ambience; things looked and smelt different, some said; and unfamiliar bureaucratic systems. It was less a sense of node without connections, more like lost in a strange jungle. The sense of everything new confused and unbalanced the students, leaving them permanently uncertain about what to do, where to seek help, and the resources available. This magnified the sense of isolation and retarded the processes of learning and changing. Some also experienced financial problems or loss of status, which compounded that feeling of helplessness or lack of agency that often seems to accompany feelings of loneliness and might be integral to it.

> The first year here was terrible. It took me very long to adapt. Maybe it's a new environment plus new faces, everything new, so even though my family is with me I still feel lonely.
>
> ~ female, 32, commerce, Singapore

> Apart from the family, we are in a very strange place, different culture; it was difficult to find help. All things make you very, very, strange at the time.
>
> ~ male, 31, community development, Indonesia

> After arriving we had much problems with settlement of my children – sickness, the change in their weather conditions, the change in their environment, new kids, new child care, new neighbourhood house . . . For the first couple of months we had too many problems.
>
> ~ male, 40, physiotherapy, Iran

> The first three months were really hard. I'd walk around and say, awww . . . God, I feel so lonely. I can't hang around . . . I want to go

> home. I would usually call my friends or my parents back home. I spent a lot of money calling my friends . . .
>
> ~ male, 28, biochemistry, Indonesia

> Yes. Yes, like . . . probably something close to depression. I've never feel like this before. This is the first time I've been alone for this length of time . . . I was used to working in Mexico, I was used to have my own money . . . But, you don't have money again, you're a student again.
>
> ~ male, 27, science, Mexico

At this stage many felt the cultural difference very sharply. To compound the personal deficit and the social deficit, they also experienced culture deficit. For some their identities were continually being bombarded. It was not always easy to make friends or share their feelings of loneliness with other students from a different culture.

> It's hard because you come from different countries. If you have a lot of friends, so much less you have loneliness in this country. [If I feel lonely I] play some music, talk to someone and try to overcome. You must face it because it is a challenge.
>
> ~ male, 31, computing, China

Obstacles to networking: 'Everybody here lives in their own world'

Friends could not always solve all problems of loneliness. But when friends were lacking and transitivity was low, that became the problem in itself. This also confirms Weiss' point that paucity of social networks can lead to boredom.

> I talk to myself only. When there's nobody in the house I just watch the TV but sometimes I have been so bored here, because here everybody lives in their own world so it's very . . . In India we used to go out with our friends.
>
> ~ male, 23, business, India

Obstacles to social networking included incompatibilities of age, nationality or patterns of socialising, communication difficulties and money limitations.

> When I came most students in campus were a little bit younger . . . After one year two other students came in under the

> same supervisor and they were my age, so it became a little bit easier. During the first year I was really alone.
>
> ~ female, 26, computing, Russia

> For the first one or two years I was very seriously homesick. Firstly, because my English level is not that good and secondly, because I didn't have a friend, like I have now.
>
> ~ male, 23, business, Taiwan

Loneliness in the institution: 'If I knew I would be so isolated . . . '

After initial settlement some students felt new loneliness in the academic setting. Relationships with teachers or administrators often triggered it. Students expected those relationships to be socially or personally supportive, found they were not, and then had nowhere else to take their educational or administrative difficulties.

> Sometimes . . . not at home, yes in university. Sometimes people are very busy. I feel it's not the right environment, not the right conditions. Sometimes I can't concentrate well.
>
> ~ female, 40, microbiology, Indonesia

One PhD student thought she would be able to develop her knowledge and research skills in an active research culture, but it did not happen.

> If I knew that I would be so isolated doing my PhD here, maybe I would not have come here . . . I thought I would have more chance to attend conferences, express my ideas, take part in discussion groups.
>
> ~ male, 31, PhD in community development, Indonesia

Without classes to attend research students lacked a surrogate social network with its opportunities for genuine friendship. Doctoral students spend most of their time on their own. It was not always easy to discuss one's research with others.

> It's a different type of loneliness, let's say topic-related loneliness. I can't talk to anybody, not even to my supervisor, because it's a field no one really has worked in.
>
> ~ male, 40, education, Germany

Table 14.5 Coping strategies of lonely international students

Responses to the follow-up question 'Who did you turn to?' (n = 129)		**Total**	**%**
Relationships in Australia			
Family and relatives	Spouse, siblings, other relatives	13	10
	Partner, boyfriend or girlfriend	2	2
	Subtotal	15	11
Friends	Subtotal	71	54
University staff	Supervisor or lecturer	5	4
	International office	2	2
	University counselling	4	3
	Subtotal	11	8
Landlord	Subtotal	1	1
Total		98	75
Relationships in home country			
Family and relatives	Subtotal	45	34
Friends	Subtotal	12	9
Total		57	44

Note: Some students used more than one strategy so the total does not sum to 100 per cent.

Personal characteristics: 'I'm an insecure person anyway'

A few students discussed loneliness in terms of their own attributes. For some a 'relational deficit' was 'positive solitude': they liked being alone or accepted it. For others, a sense of personal inadequacy compounded their misery.

> I am not an extroverted person. I don't mind being by myself. It doesn't bother me.
>
> ~ female, 34, education, Indonesia

Coping strategies

Nearly all 129 students felt lonely or isolated; of these, 113 students (88 per cent), turned to personal and social networks or more formal relationships in the educational institution (table 14.5). A small group of 13 students (10 per cent) became immersed in activities; 20 students (15 per cent) found resources for coping inside themselves. Several mentioned more than one strategy.

The most frequent categories of support were friends in Australia (54 per cent of the lonely students) and family and relatives at home

(34 per cent). Three-quarters of the lonely students turned to people in Australia. Almost half contacted people back home, mostly phoning parents or other relatives. Institutional relationships were less important in coping strategies (8 per cent).

Personal support: 'You just call home'

Even for those who gained emotional support from friends there was often more comfort and familiarity turning towards home.

> Everybody's busy with their own life so you feel very, very lonely. You just call home.
>
> ~ male, 24, computing, India

> I talked to my family. I called them. Or read Qur'an.
>
> ~ male, 37, accounting, Egypt

> I mean there are some things that I would confide to friends here, but . . . I often call home, not only to my parents but often to close friends from home. It is cheap to call back to the US.
>
> ~ male, 24, business, USA

But some students tried to avoid their parents when they were lonely or have problems. It was easier to make the call than to achieve mutual understanding.

> I don't want them to worry so much about me. I just stay in my room . . . sometimes I cry [out] and when I cry out, I feel better.
>
> ~ male, 21, business, Malaysia

Some students had access to parents, partners, siblings or other relatives in Australia.

> It was very depressing. I just felt very, very lonely. I think because it was my first time that I had left home.
>
> When asked who she turned to, she replied:
>
> Nobody. Just my brother and my family . . . it's good [to have my brother here] . . . together we came.
>
> ~ female, 21, business, Bahrain

Social networks: 'I felt better speaking the same language'

Many students turned to friends of the same nationality, though the capacity of friends or boyfriends or girlfriends to provide support was not unlimited.

> I talked to other Indonesian community [members] here, some friends. I felt better speaking the same language.
>
> ~ male, 41, education, Indonesia

> Yes, yes. I was with my boyfriend at that time, but he couldn't help. I guess we both had the same problem and we kind of lost the ability to help each other. But you don't find him as someone you can talk to and help you like he – I guess maybe he was the wrong person . . . He showed very clearly his selfishness in this very difficult situation.
>
> ~ female, 25, health sciences, China

University staff: 'I went to the counselling service'

A less common source of support was university staff. Students were not always aware of the support systems available at university, especially early in the stay.

> I think there was a time where I would call my parents. But if I was really sad, if I had problems and didn't get the support I was used to, then I would call my good friends, I mean those who had known me for quite a long time in Indonesia. Actually, I have been to a counselling service as well . . . At that time I didn't really have someone who was really close to me, and I don't like talking about my personal problems. So I went to the counselling service.
>
> ~ female, 27, engineering, Indonesia

Sometimes the university service made a crucial difference.

> Being the first child in my family, I was never one to talk about my problems and a lot of things had been building. I was getting really depressed and lonely. I felt I was just alone and fighting this whole battle. So I talked to this friend of mine, and then after that, I went to the . . . counselling service and I talked to them. And then I thought, I need a change. So I changed my course and I changed towns and I've been happy ever since.
>
> ~ male, 26, business, Botswana

Positive solitude: 'I can manage this'

A number of students stated that they did not talk to anyone when they felt lonely. They preferred to manage their loneliness by themselves.

> I think I'm older, I can manage this.
>
> ~ male, 25, computing, China

> I'm a very introverted kind of person. When I have something I keep it to myself.
>
> ~ female, 25, media and communication, India

Another tackled isolation and loneliness by going to crowded places.

> Sometimes I felt isolated or far away from the people I love... I didn't talk to a particular person but I just go to the crowded place, such as library and laboratory.
>
> ~ male, 27, community development, Indonesia

Several male students saw coping in solitude as intrinsic to their gendered identity. No female interviewee voiced such sentiments.

> Because I am a man, I usually keep [my loneliness] to myself. If it gets bad, I usually talk with my friends, my close friends.
>
> ~ male, 28, business, Indonesia

> A lot of times, but... I'm an insecure person anyway. I think most females are, and I think everyone can say they've experienced periods of loneliness.
>
> ~ female, 26, medicine, Malaysia

ONLY THE NOT LONELY

A common characteristic of many students who had not experienced loneliness was that they started off very well. Students in university residences found ready-made social networks were at hand, including same-culture and other international student groupings as well as local students (chapter 13). Others were used to travelling or being alone, or quickly took to the greater personal freedom in Australia. When asked if they had experienced loneliness when they arrived in Australia, many said that they had not.

> No. Because I've stayed away from family for a long time before. When I was working, I stayed in a different city. I kind of got used to that. My parents were in Delhi, I was working in Hyderabad. Whether it's 200 kilometres or 2000 kilometres, away from home is away from home.
>
> ~ male, 29, business, Indonesia

> When I first came here, I was so eager to explore the new world, yeah.
>
> ~ male, 22, science, Vietnam

In many positive stories cultural tensions were minimised, or cultural difference was positive:

> No loneliness, never. I love it here. I'm comfortable. You see the thing is, I fit in over here. I don't fit in in India. I'm a feminist, OK, I'm a strong minded woman and in the India subcontinent, it is very difficult. Here I have the freedom to lead my own life and I am not expected to come home and . . . I don't have all the social pressures to deal with. I have my life.
>
> ~ female, 19, arts, India

Well networked: 'You can easily find friends'

Others simply said they avoided personal loneliness because family was with them, or overcame social loneliness through same-culture networks.

> There are a lot of Chinese students here. You can easily find friends.
>
> ~ female, 24, industrial relations, China

Personal characteristics: 'Not much time for getting sad'

Some said they avoided loneliness through personal characteristics or behaviour. They were extroverted, or used to being independent or too busy to think about it.

> I'm used to living in different places all over India, so I suppose I'm not finding it difficult to adjust [to Australia] . . . My father is in an industry that means we keep moving from one place to another.
>
> ~ male, 21, business, India

> I was quite independent when I was in China. I live independently, I did everything for myself.
>
> ~ female, 25, business, China

Others set their feelings aside by concentrating on studies or activities.

> I've always been busy, so I haven't noticed to tell you the truth. The first year I came here I spent my first semester just doing my Masters. I just worked hard, so it kept me busy. Then the next six months I engaged in being president [of the postgraduate student association]. And that was that, my agenda filled up automatically.
>
> ~ male, 33, medicine, Spain

As did some lonely students, non-lonely students, too, found solutions within.

CONCLUSIONS

As Grinberg and Grinberg put it, in immigration 'one ceases to belong to the world one left behind, and does not yet belong to the world in which one has nearly arrived'.[58] As with all immigrants, temporary or permanent, international students experience personal and social loneliness. They geographically separate from family members, mostly while retaining contact, and exile themselves from face-to-face friends. They are in relational deficit if not social isolation. Yet these students need personal and social support more than before, just when their accustomed networks are in disarray. In the midst of a dramatic and often traumatic relocation, their physical and cultural environment has changed sharply and they face daily problems of language, study, finances and accommodation. They must negotiate new institutional rules. Many also experience a unprecedented personal autonomy and begin to recreate their identity in the new setting.[59] They absorb new social customs while defining themselves as foreigners who are staying, neither in nor out of the country. Without much support they must handle unpredictable encounters, idiosyncratic messages and instances

58 Grinberg and Grinberg, 1989, 23.
59 Baker and Siryk, 1986.

of discrimination. Anxiety is a normal response in such situations.[60] Emotional correlates of loneliness range from wistfulness and quiet longing, to boredom and annoyance, to extreme pain.

The present study confirms other research at many points: the impact of loss of family support, the positive role of social networks, how problems of loneliness are compounded by language difficulties. The interviews confirm that students who are isolated and/or feel lonely are less confident as agents. Likewise, positive self-concept modifies loneliness. There is some evidence that male students are more likely to deal with loneliness by containment or denial – 'Because I am a man, I usually keep [my loneliness] to myself' – but this study does not tell us whether women or men are more liable to loneliness. The study also confirms other findings on the positive potential of educational institutions, especially in the vital early months, in grounding the agency of students and assisting with same-culture and cross-cultural networking: new arrival services, help in communicating with parents, buddy programs, university residences, help with shared accommodation, clubs and other associations – all can help to modify isolation and mitigate feelings of loneliness. The study also confirms findings on the positive potential of same-culture activities and networks outside the universities. One interviewee suggested that universities encourage same-culture residents in the city to meet with the students when they arrive. The locals could play a nurturing and mentoring role.

The study also makes its own contributions. First, it highlights the fact that formal and semiformal sites can generate alienating experiences contributing to loneliness. These arise in encounters with university administration, classrooms and services, and with government immigration (chapters 10 and 11).

Second, PhD students need special attention. Isolated projects carry potential costs, which suggests the need for research groups in which students engaged in related areas of enquiry can discuss their topics and work together at need. If an institution cannot constitute such a group because it lacks critical mass in the relevant field(s), then it should help student to connect with researchers outside.

60 Pedersen, 1991.

Third, the study highlights the vulnerability of the Steffi Zhangs, students who are isolated or severely lonely. To the extent that severe loneliness robs them of agency these students cannot help themselves. Because of the extent to which they are isolated, no one can see their difficulties. There are several implications for regulators and institutions. We suggest institutions should conduct regular network audits that review the communicative competence and social supports accessed by each individual international student. Universities should also benchmark their services against the loneliness issue. How does each service contribute to modifying and solving loneliness problems? Where are the gaps? What kind of students are not helped? Why? Are academic and service staff fully sensitive to loneliness issues? Does the institution have a collective radar capable of spotting emerging individual problems? How close to failsafe is it? What kind of students is it likely to miss?

Perhaps the most vital and delicate institutional task is provision of a safety net for students who may be at personal risk. These students do not make themselves obvious, so the institution must know the life circumstances of each and every student. As suggested earlier, this requires institutions to provide a comprehensive safety net and undertake individual monitoring. This can only work if intervention is culturally sensitive, informed, is spare and targeted to need. But, inescapably, this takes us beyond Australia's present framework of an exclusively commercial industry that provides a minimalist generic service at below US and UK prices.

Fourth, the study adds to our knowledge of loneliness and cultural difference.

Most international students in Australia are from cultural backgrounds where large family networks and locality bonds are the norm. The values and norms they bring with them shape their encounter with the predominantly Anglo-Australian values the find, which emphasise competition and individual achievement and pay less regard to extended family, tradition and place. For some international students, the direct pressure on them as unsupported individuals, and the human bonds that appear loose and detachable, signal personal exposure, instability and even danger. Sometimes cross-cultural encounters directly trigger loneliness. Often they colour loneliness, as was repeatedly evident during the interviews.

To Weiss' categories of emotional (personal) loneliness and social loneliness we can add another: cultural loneliness. Cultural loneliness is conditioned by the absence of the preferred cultural and linguistic environment. It interacts with and reinforces personal and social loneliness. The propensity to cultural loneliness explains why certain students in this study, who had fine social networks, some with intimate family on hand, still reported acute loneliness. Many find access to their own cultural and language community is crucial, regardless of other factors.

But should not international students engage with the new cultural setting? Does that not offer a clear solution for isolation and a potential lateral solution for cultural loneliness? It is true that integration into local networks, particularly with local students, can powerfully alleviate international student loneliness. Here better relations between international and local students mean more than just better networking. Theorisations of networking and loneliness suggest what is important is the quality of the network, including the personal bonds within it. Such bonds could reduce the tendency of cultural loneliness to amplify personal and social loneliness. They could be central to satisfying the need to belong and could help international students find a middle zone where they engage with local culture without abandoning their sense of self. The students know this is a vital issue. As noted, two-thirds (65 per cent) of those who experienced loneliness or isolation had faced barriers in making friends across cultures compared to 37 per cent of non-lonely.

> They just interact with the same people. Hang on, I've come to Australia, I want to meet somebody else. If I wanted to meet my own countrymen I would stay back in my country. So it's a question of how do you break down the barriers, how do you get people to interact?
>
> ~ male, 29, business, India

It would be easy to conclude that internationals should adjust to local norms quicker and better, and that universities should facilitate this. That would be nothing new. It has often been said or implied, in theory and in practice. The prevalence of the term 'adjustment' in the research is one sign (chapter 15) of this frequency. But the standard notion of adjustment is one way. It begs the question of where the obligation to adjust should fall. It assumes local Anglo cultural and educational environments are unchanging and perhaps unchangeable. It begs the question of whether local educational and social settings are conducive to engagement with internationals and whether engagement is based on cultural reciprocity or domination. It implies that the core problem is international resistance to adjustment. Yet all the evidence shows that internationals want to integrate better and are frustrated when they cannot.

If we expect international students to simply set aside core elements of their identity to integrate locally and thereby banish loneliness, we must recognise this approach to international education carries severe individual costs. Should students have to reduce their love for the extended family to cope in Australia, the USA or the UK? Must they acquire not just English but also an ideology of possessive individualism to be happy? Should they have to drink alcohol, regardless of preference and belief, to be accepted by local male students? Often this is what international students are asked to do (more in some places than others). But even if it were feasible and desirable to secure such adjustments, this is not a practical formula for international education. International students are often very flexible in the face of their many challenges, but few adopt local values holus bolus, just to minimise loneliness or for any other reason. International students should be able to combine old and new. They should not have to jettison one to gain the other. Why should they? It is not necessary for academic success or personal survival. It implies that for every cultural gain there is a cultural loss, as if identity were a zero sum game without potential for hybridity and multiplicity. The solution to loneliness is not one-way adjustment and an assimilation that worsens personal displacement. It is integration on the basis of self-determining agency and cross-cultural relations in which both parties change. Chapter 15 looks at these issues.

15 INTERCULTURAL RELATIONS

There was one incident that I'll never forget. It happened to me when I was up in Melbourne, in my first six months here. I was at the South Yarra train station. I was standing next to this woman, and she turned round to me and started abusing me. 'Why don't you just go back where you came from? We don't want you here!' It really took me aback. It was the last thing I expected... I was blind. I was walking into town... I just carried on walking. It was so embarrassing. Ever since that, I've been more conscious about being different, about my colour, my nationality.

– female, 22, business, Zimbabwe

INTRODUCTION: INTERCULTURAL RELATIONS AND STUDENT SECURITY

People want synchrony and harmony with their conditions of life.[1] 'Harmony' means inclusion, membership and acceptance. 'Synchrony' refers to mimetic coordination with the world around, social and institutional relations that speak of timing and easy grace. People want to coincide with each other. Though this is often seen as a conforming impulse it also powers innovation and creativity. Much of the energy in globalisation lies in the drive to synchronise across geographical and cultural distance, to reach out for new friends and do things together.[2] In this more global era there are millions of cases. Many involve international students.

1 They also hanker after new sights and feelings. But even the novelties are mostly semi-familiar, ritualised and aligned to others, thus the compelling power of consumer culture that satisfies the need for controlled change in a safe and sanitised manner. But that is another story.

2 Marginson, 2009.

Synchrony and harmony are also at the heart of student security. People feel secure when they can instinctively go with the flow by recognising social signals, responding as required and fitting in without much thought. They understand and respond to necessity, doing what they have to do. They know the potentials, limits and expectations of voluntary behaviour. Student security has both a protective aspect and a proactive aspect. Harmony is protective because it is inclusive. The achievement of synchrony further legitimates inclusion. It also establishes the basis for proactive, self-determining autonomy in the country of education, and synchronous relations with locals are vital in both defence and advance.

Yet the kinetic life, the mobile existence of the traveller, is a continuous challenge to the sense of harmony and synchrony. Synchrony and harmony are impossible when people first arrive in a new country. They take time to emerge. They rest on ease in language and exchange, and politeness, customs and social symbols, on accumulating experience of the day to day cycles of life, the larger calendar and rhythms of events, and modes of communication and organisation. For international students the process of adjustment or acculturation, much discussed in the literature, is a journey towards synchrony and harmony. It is not, as some researchers and university personnel believe, a journey from difference to sameness. It is not a metamorphosis into local identity, whether in part or whole. It is the process of learning to survive, to cope and be effective in the new setting.

But the self, even a synchronous and harmonious self, can be many different people. Even as internationals change to absorb the new requirements, even as they grapple with elements beyond their control such as language and university bureaucracy and local resistance, they are also choosing what they will be.

Self-formation in international education is culturally reciprocal and culturally separated. It is reciprocal when it entails interaction between internationals and locals. At best this leads to mutual learning and change. International education becomes an intercultural process. Often relations between internationals and locals are merely cross-cultural, with no necessary implication of deep engagement and mutual transformation. Frequently, the visitors change out of choice and necessity while locals remain stubbornly unmoved by the desire or need to engage. The transformation of internationals occurs separately from the locals.

As this suggests international education calls on international students to synchronise in two domains. First, the domain of same-culture peers where a familiar harmony is found. Second, the local domain – the university, classes, staff and students, and the community beyond. This is difficult terrain but it must be traversed. As chapter 13 described, in the interstices between these domains, closer to the first, many cultivate relations with internationals from other countries. Often but not always students feel tension between the domains. One finding of this study and much of the literature is that some students are more comfortable than others with ambiguity and plural identity. Some want to synthesise the different strands of their lives. Others synchronise in different ways in plural domains. Many students are remarkably and reflexively inventive. They are flexible in their self-formation.

Yet to borrow again Marx's dictum, international students make their own lives but under conditions they do not control. Our interviewees reflected critically on the proportion of time they spent in same-culture versus local domains. They wanted to engage more with English and with Australian virtues and idiosyncrasies. Yet the balance between domains, indeed, the very opportunity to achieve synchrony and harmony, were not always theirs to choose. The separation between same-culture and locals is sustained by more than communication barriers, and more than the laziness of Anglo-Australian students who gain nothing (as they see it) by adjusting to the newcomers in their midst. The separation is also propelled by the entrenched dynamics of cultural segregation. It is locked down by stereotyping and by cultural closure and discrimination, which enforce binary categories, block the route to local relations and consign international students to an outsider status from which harmonisation is impossible. It is hammered into the heart of one non-white international student after another by pathologies of racism and occasional moments of brutal abuse. Nothing in the topic of international student security seems more important than this. It is with these vital and terrible matters, which touch human rights at the deepest level, that of the right to exist and find a secure path through a turbulent world of hopes and fears, that much of the chapter is concerned.

In sum the cross-cultural and intercultural aspects of international education discussed in this chapter are synchronisation with local requirements, including a critical examination of the adjustment hypothesis in cross-cultural psychology, friendships and barriers to friendship with local students, and discrimination and abuse inside and outside the universities. The 200 interviewees provided much evidence. There is also a large literature that we do not fully explore here. The original literature review now constitutes the main part of a separate book on intercultural education and self-formation;[3] issues of teaching and learning are addressed separately in that book. For language and intercultural relations see chapter 12; language and discrimination are addressed here.

RESEARCH ON ADJUSTMENT

Psychology focuses on adjustment by sojourners in host countries. Bochner sees this as cultural learning.[4] The task for international students is not to absorb the new culture but to 'learn its salient characteristics' so as to operate effectively.[5] The problems of sojourners are not symptoms of individual deficit, rather they indicate a lack of learnt skills.[6] According to Berry, 'acculturation occurs when two independent cultural groups come into continuous first-hand contact over an extended period of time, resulting in changes to either or both'.[7] It includes adaptation by groups or individuals 'in response to environmental demands'.[8] There are two dimensions of acculturation: maintenance of the original cultural group and formation of relations with other groups.[9] Various combinations are possible. Berry favours 'integration', a 'bi-cultural' process whereby the group becomes 'an integral part of a larger societal framework' while its cultural identity is maintained.[10] 'Integration can only be "freely" chosen and successfully pursued by non-dominant groups when the dominant society is open and inclusive in its orientation to cultural diversity.'[11] Both Bochner and Berry imply that students can augment their original

3 Marginson and Sawir, forthcoming.
4 Bochner, 1972; Furnham and Bochner, 1986.
5 Pedersen, 1991, 26.
6 *ibid*, 26.
7 Berry et al., 1989, 186.
8 Berry, 1997, 13.
9 Berry, 1974; 1984, 1997; etc.
10 Berry et al., 1989, 188; Berry, 1997, 11.
11 *ibid*, 10.

'identity and customs'[12] and shape new intercultural relations at the same time.

In major research reviews Church[13] and Pedersen[14] noted that international student experiences vary according to the cultural background of students, and are accessible to varying interpretations according to cultural standpoint. These insights open the way for researchers to model international education in terms of plural cultures without always privileging one culture over others. This has been our approach in this study. Issues and data need to be considered on merit, not explained using essentialist cultural categories. Much of the work in cross-cultural psychology on adjustment fails this test. Here internationals are seen as journeying from original identity to host identity, as if one cannot have both, as if the relation is zero sum. It is assumed that the closer students' cultural fit with the host country, the better will be their adaptation, adjustment, happiness, social engagement and academic success in the country of education.[15] Often same-culture groups become seen as inherently problematic. They are seen to block the potential for relations with local students, as if internationals must choose between the two kinds of network. At bottom, the notion of cultural fit, like Hofstede's theory of the differences between individualist and collectivist cultures,[16] rests on cultural essentialism. It models cultures as fixed and external to human agents, attributes too much explanatory power to them and enables the privileging of one culture over others, which is ethnocentrism.[17] Leong and Ward state that 'Individuals who make cross-cultural transitions are *generally expected to conform* to the normative values, attitudes and behaviours of their host countries'.[18] Social science as ideology.

But the ethnocentric argument is vulnerable. Cultures are made by human agents. Internationals select freely from cultural practices old and new. Cultures are dynamic and continually evolving as humans

12 Berry et al., 1989, 186.
13 For example Church, 1982, 563.
14 Pedersen, 1991.
15 For example Ward and Kennedy, 1994; Ward and Chang, 1997; Ward et al., 1998; Leong and Ward, 2000; Ward et al., 2004; Ward and Masgoret, 2004; Ward, 2005; Ward, 2008. Berry gives some comfort to this approach in, for example, his discussion of Ward and Kennedy, 1994; Berry, 1997, 18, where he advocates the use of the term 'adjustment'.
16 Hofstede, 1980; 1998; see also the critique by Stephens, 1997.
17 Volet and Ang, 1998, 7.
18 Leong and Ward, 2000, 765; emphasis added.

struggle to survive and adapt, and they are no more pure than they are fixed. They are always stained by each other.[19] Cultural identity is not always primary. It interacts with other factors such the local–outsider distinction, power, economics and personality. The notion of cultural fit fails to separate adaptation and acculturation from a one-way 'assimilation',[20] which suppresses the agency of the students and denies the observed reality of their lives. Advocates of the cultural fit thesis have failed to ground it empirically, despite persistent attempts.[21]

The ethnocentric approach has proven resilient. The reason is less intellectual than institutional. Much of the literature is in counselling psychology and ethnocentrism speaks to counselling strategies in many American universities in which local worldviews are unquestioned and the object is to shape international students as quasi-locals. Cultural fit allows local staff and students to remain comfortably unchallenged by the different students in their midst. In Australia and the UK, where cost minimisation is integral to the industry, an ethnocentric kind of adjustment confines claims based on cultural difference, justifies normalisation of diverse international populations to fit standard services and helps shift the onus for student survival and success from the institution to the students themselves.

BEYOND ETHNOCENTRISM

Some counselling-based studies are sympathetic to the cultural backgrounds of internationals,[22] and recent papers in psychology move further from ethnocentrism. These studies normalise plural cultural domains and set aside cultural fit as a universal explanatory device. This work does not model cultures as holistic or superior or in deficit. As noted in chapter 12 it highlights two factors central to student success, happiness and intercultural engagement. These are communicative competence and self-determining agency, including the

19 Rizvi, 2005, 334–335; see also Rizvi, 2008; see also Casrnir, 1999, for one attempt to capture the dynamic character of intercultural communication.

20 Zhang and Dixon, 2003, 208.

21 For fuller discussion, the distinction between psychological and sociocultural adjustment and the critique of the cultural fit hypothesis, see Marginson, 2009; Marginson and Sawir, forthcoming; see also Anderson, 2006.

22 See Constantine et al., 2005a, 2005b. But this work seems to treat identity as fixed and may underestimate the self-formative powers of students.

centred will and capacity to manage uncertainty.[23] We will examine one further paper. Kashima and Loh studied 200 international students in Melbourne,[24] 61 per cent of them from Singapore and Malaysia.[25] These researchers focused on networks, communication and agency. They investigated the need for cognitive closure as a factor in acculturation and cross-cultural relations. 'An individual difference [in the extent of the need for] cognitive closure . . . reflects the degrees to which one desires a clear and firm solution over uncertainty, confusion, and ambiguity.'[26] Students with low need for cognitive closure tolerate some ambiguity in identity. They are not prone to either/or binary thinking. Though Kashima and Loh do not use these terms, ambiguity in identity can take the form of multiplicity or hybridity. 'Multiplicity' refers to people living in more than one cultural zone, operating somewhat differently in each. 'Hybridity' refers to the combining of different cultural elements in a newly formed self. Kashima and Loh mapped variations in the need for cognitive closure against three kinds of interpersonal network: same-culture internationals, other internationals and local students. They looked at these factors in conjunction with acquisition of host cultural knowledge and Australian university identity, and home culture (heritage) identity. They expected to find that patterns of personal ties and differences in the need for cognitive closure would effect acculturation.

The findings are consistent with our argument. Kashima and Loh first built an open picture of self-determined agents. 'International students' social identities may change dynamically during their acculturation'[27] (as in the interviews for the present study). It is often assumed that heritage cultural identity is maintained, not 'transformed dynamically in the host society'. But heritage identity can be 'more salient once in the foreign cultural environment'. Ties with other internationals and locals may 'enhance newcomers' heritage cultural identity' by encouraging them to compare the heritage culture with other cultures and 'thereby recognise their own distinctiveness'.[28]

23 See for example Perrucci and Hu, 1995; Hullett and Witte, 2001; Leung, 2001; Matsumoto et al., 2004; Savicki et al., 2004; Li and Gasser, 2005; Yang et al., 2006; Chirkov et al., 2007.

24 The usable response pool was 100.

25 Kashima and Loh, 2006, 475.

26 *ibid*, 473.

27 *ibid*, 471.

28 *ibid*, 473.

A cross-cultural environment, with its multiple perspectives, enhances the scope for cultural relativism and reflexivity in agents.

High cognitive closure is linked with lower 'psychological adjustment', that is, stable happiness, and with 'sociocultural adjustment', meaning competences that enable cultural learning. Conversely, all else being equal a capacity for ambiguity is associated with happier students with stronger relational competences. Given that psychological and sociocultural adjustment correlate to academic success, this has added importance. Further, ties with locals and other internationals predict greater psychological adjustment, same-culture ties do not, except among students requiring high cognitive closure.[29] Notably, among students requiring high cognitive closure, same-culture ties did not diminish sociocultural adjustment.[30]

Next, the study highlights networks with internationals from other cultural backgrounds,[31] 'a neglected topic in the acculturation literature which tends to focus more on effects of conational and host cultural contacts'.[32] Kashima and Loh found that 'Students with greater international ties also tended to identify more strongly' with heritage culture and Australian university and, as a result, 'the better adjusted they were'.[33] Australian university identity was also enhanced by ties with co-nationals and locals.[34] Heritage cultural identity was marginally strengthened by co-national ties, though not among those with high need for cognitive closure and unaffected by local ties.

Time in Australia made no difference to the strength of heritage identity.[35] When internationals develop more complex identity configurations, including ties with locals and other internationals, they do not have to discard heritage culture. There is no trade-off necessary between heritage identity and local ties, or same-culture ties and local ties, which again stymies the idea of a binary either/or adjustment journey from home country identity to host country identity. It also undermines the assumption lurking beneath such research that

29 *ibid*, 478–9.
30 *ibid*, 480.
31 Some of whom might nevertheless share heritage, for example Chinese background students from other parts of Asia.
32 Kashima and Loh, 2006, 472.
33 *ibid*, 481–2.
34 *ibid*, 481.
35 *ibid*, 480–1.

something is intrinsically wrong with same-culture networks. These networks do not necessarily block cross-cultural relations or retard student learning. The keys are language competence, effective agency, and tolerance of ambiguity and plural cultures. The optimum is strong networks in all three domains. The ideal student is cosmopolitan and embraces cultural diversity within the common humanity.

This is not a new idea. Much research finds that cosmopolitans make the best sojourners[36] though there is debate on exactly what 'cosmopolitan' means.[37] But if internationals are cosmopolitan while local students are not, there are limits to intercultural relations. Nasrin reports interviews with female graduate students from non-European countries studying in the USA. The students said Americans lacked knowledge about other countries and cultures. They volunteered the word 'ignorance' and provided examples.[38] Singh notes that local students 'have yet to think of themselves as Others'. They are yet to relativise their own identity in the larger global setting,[39] to commit to intercultural exchange and adopt the modest willingness to alter themselves typical of internationals. Volet and Ang note that much literature focuses on the tendency of international students to form same-culture groupings but is silent on the same habit among local students. The unspoken assumption of normal practice is that the local enclosure is a natural grouping and it is inappropriate to problematise it. This hides 'the extent to which both groups share responsibility for the lack of intercultural contact'.[40] Lee and Rice found that

> Not all of the issues international students face can be problematised as matters of adjustment, as much research does . . . Some of the more serious challenges are due to inadequacies within the host society . . . the responsibility is often left to the student to 'adjust' or 'adapt' to the host culture rather than for institutions to understand and try to accommodate their unique needs.[41]

36 Gardner, 1962, and the 'universal communicator'; Adler, 1977; Bochner, 1977; Church, 1982, 554; Hannerz, 1990; Pedersen, 1991, 18; Bennett, 1993; Hall, 2002; Allan, 2003; Gunesch, 2004; Anderson et al., 2006; Deardorff, 2006; Stone, 2006; Rizvi, 2005, 2008.

37 For example do cosmopolitans retain a place-based identity?

38 Nasrin, 2001, 45.

39 Singh, 2005, 16; see also Ninnes, 2005; Doherty and Singh, 2005.

40 Volet and Ang 1998, 7–8.

41 Lee and Rice, 2007, 381, 385.

This is a particular problem for non-white students, who deal with heightened obstacles.

> White European students face fewer integration issues . . . issues that go beyond language difficulties to involve prejudice tend to emanate from the host society rather than from the students. We find that most of the literature concerning international student experiences describes their difficulties as issues of adapting or coping, which embodies the assumption that international students bear the responsibility to persist, overcome their discomfort, and integrate into the host society. Some of these studies call for increased sensitivity, but the underlying assumption is that host institutions are impartial and without fault. Few studies consider how institutions and individuals may purposefully or inadvertently marginalise international students.[42]

CROSS-CULTURAL ENCOUNTERS

The clumping of local and international students into separate groups points to the continuing power of the local–international distinction. It can be modified by cultural identity. Local citizen students who share cultural backgrounds with internationals are a source of friends for them (chapter 13); however, in the dynamics of student separation the local–international distinction also becomes reinforced by other differences: generic cultural distinctions such as Western–non-Western, and distinctions based on physical appearance (race) such as white–non-white.[43] The local–international distinction becomes locked into a process of difference-making as Othering, which tends to subordinate and isolate international students.

Difference-making as Othering is layered and complex. Reifying distinctions are first enforced by stereotyping, which may or may not entail judgements about superior–inferior but always blocks sympathetic and nuanced engagement. Many internationals experience

42 *ibid*, 388.

43 These distinctions, like the local–international distinction, are not natural but human creations. For Collins '"racialization" is the constitution of a racial category through "the process of *investing* skin colour with meaning" (Ahmed)': Collins, 2006, 221–2; Ahmed, 2002.

discrimination, prejudicial encounters and abuse in which difference-making is exclusion and domination. Discrimination is legitimised post hoc by more stereotyping. Together, stereotyping, discrimination and abuse feed group separation and segregation, which shape the cross-cultural landscape. 'Separation' means little people contact between groups. 'Segregation' means separation is imposed by one group regardless of and probably against the will of the other. Stereotyping is discussed first, then discrimination and abuse.

STEREOTYPING

Spencer-Rogers defines stereotyping as follows:

> Stereotypic representations have been broadly defined as cognitive structures that contain a perceiver's knowledge, beliefs, and expectancies about a social group . . . An important defining feature of cultural stereotypes is their consensual nature: there must be agreement among members of one group about the characteristics of another group before an attribute can be included as part of a social stereotype.[44]

Church notes that 'ethnocentric attitudes and stereotypes' inhibit 'positive social interaction' between international students and locals.[45] For Olson and Kroeger, stereotyping produces Othering by creating barriers. 'The individual . . . seeks to create distance from others who are different from them so that they can remain comfortably in denial . . . [This includes] the common tendency to relegate others who are different to a subhuman status.'[46] Stereotyping protects a defensive local identity while evading cultural encounters. Even when contact occurs, intimacy and understanding are decisively limited. Research suggests that most (not all) international students want their cultural identity to be acknowledged, but they resist stereotyped descriptors and the distance-making that is entailed. Unlike discrimination or abuse, stereotyping does not require cross-cultural contact. Low contact helps to sustain the pristine reified form of the stereotype. This encourages more low contact forming a self-reproducing

44 Spencer-Rodgers, 2001, 642.

45 Church, 1982, 551.

46 Olson and Kroeger, 2001, 120.

system. Stereotyping is much more likely to be carried out by locals than internationals, the latter of whom need openness and contact so as to survive and learn. Many arrive with the explicit desire to engage.

Spencer-Rodgers studied 100 American college student nationals' consensual stereotype of international students.[47] Although internationals are 'extremely diverse in terms of race, ethnicity, and nationality, and religious, linguistic, political, and socioeconomic background',[48] the local students had 'substantial' agreement about their alleged positive and negative qualities.[49] Their foreign or outsider status, the one feature common to all internationals, enabled local students to picture a homogenous group. 'Social categorisation . . . is a necessary precursor to stereotyping.'[50] The most common positive stereotypes were intelligent (58 per cent of respondents), adventurous (41 per cent), hard working (23 per cent), determined (22 per cent), learning about a new culture (21 per cent) and friendly (20 per cent). Main negative stereotypes were foreign/different (30 per cent), socially and culturally maladjusted (29 per cent) and poor English (23 per cent).[51] The level of agreement was high.[52] Spencer-Rodgers also found that 'international students are perceived as handicapped, deficient, bewildered, and psychologically distressed' and 'socially and culturally maladjusted' – asynchronous, with descriptors such as 'out of place', 'don't fit in', 'don't know how to act', 'lonely, anxious, and frightened' and 'naïve'.[53] The stereotypic beliefs held by individual local students 'were significantly correlated with attitudes and behaviours' to internationals. Holding strong negative stereotypes was closely correlated to 'prejudicial attitudes and social avoidance'.[54]

In a UK study of international students from China Stephens questions the stereotypes of Chinese students as 'Asian learners' with limiting characteristics[55], such as inability to think critically or

47 Spencer-Rodgers, 2001, 639.
48 *ibid*, 642.
49 *ibid*, 639.
50 *ibid*, 650.
51 *ibid*, 647.
52 *ibid*, 650.
53 *ibid*, 651.
54 *ibid*, 639.
55 Stephens, 1997.

initiate verbally. Difficulties with language and unfamiliarity with educational conventions are attributed to intellectual deficits and generalised across whole student populations. Ninnes[56] uses empirical analysis of Indian postgraduate student learning to deconstruct the Asian learners stereotype, while observing the actual strengths and weaknesses of the group.

Stereotypes are not overcome simply by increasing cross-cultural contact.[57] Leong and Ward noted that while 'it is generally accepted that intercultural contact can promote good will and understanding', some researchers note that 'intercultural contact may also result in negative experiences', especially when discriminatory behaviours are the norm.[58] Likewise Otten notes that in some instances contact heightens tensions and reinforces stereotyping. However, contact can break down simplified stereotypes. Volet and Ang find 'negative stereotypes and ethnocentric views were . . . major stumbling blocks in the formation of culturally mixed groups' in class. Both internationals and locals had 'stereotyped perceptions of each other'.[59] Some students came to understand that they held stereotypes and others had stereotyped views of them.[60] One stated that 'With opportunities to work together, perceptions change',[61] though this change in immediate perceptions did not in itself create ongoing relationships.[62]

DISCRIMINATION, PREJUDICE AND ABUSE

International students' experiences of discriminatory treatment, prejudice and abuse are a difficult topic for research. The first problem is to confine observation to genuine cases of discrimination, meaning evaluations or behaviours determined by category membership rather than merit.[63] Also, perceptions of discrimination have a subjective

56 Ninnes, 1999.

57 Pritchard and Skinner, 2002, 324; see also Spencer-Rodgers and McGovern, 2002, 624–5. Nesdale and Todd, 2000, reviewed the then literature on the contact hypothesis, the notion that contact improves cross-cultural relations and reduces negative stereotyping.

58 Leong and Ward, 2000, 766.

59 Volet and Ang, 1998, 14.

60 *ibid*, 15.

61 *ibid*, 16.

62 *ibid*, 16.

63 Nasrin, 2001, 43, comments on this.

aspect,[64] and discrimination, prejudice and abuse are under-reported in studies of international education by governments and universities concerned to maintain a positive image, especially in the commercially minded nations. The UK survey by Li and Kaye focuses on financial issues, language, homesickness and relations with locals.[65] It did not ask about discrimination. Nor did the 2006 Australian Education International survey. As Otten remarks, 'Asymmetric power structures usually are not expressed frankly'.[66]

This is not to dispute the existence of discrimination, which is repeatedly reported in other studies. It is the darkest side of international education. Students who suffer discrimination are trapped by distinctive attributes of their being they cannot readily alter, such as appearance, language, voice and religion. Boyer and Sedlacek state that 'Understanding and ability to deal with racism' is a variable predictive of academic success.[67] That might appear to provide a Darwinian legitimation for racism on the grounds of meritocracy, as a kind of tempering test that prepares non-white students for the struggles of the world beyond the university. If so it is a test that white students do not have to face. It is cruel and utterly unjust.

USA

Hayes and Lin note the 'prejudices that members of the host culture may hold for the various international students they encounter' tend to block cross-cultural networking.[68] Perrucci and Hu found that 'language skill, exposure/contact with Americans, and discrimination/ negative attitudes' are strongly correlated with international graduate student satisfaction'.[69] Language competence, self-esteem, interaction with locals and absence of discrimination are mutually supportive.[70] There is discrimination and Othering in the criticism of foreign graduate teaching assistants by local students, as well as

64 Lee and Rice, 2007, 391–2.
65 Li and Kaye, 1998, 48.
66 Otten, 2003, 16.
67 Boyer and Sedlacek, 1989, 405.
68 Hayes and Lin, 1994, 5.
69 Perrucci and Hu, 1995, 502.
70 *ibid*, 506.

communication issues.[71] In Nasrin's study of non-European students in the deep south of the USA, all reported discriminatory experiences by lecturers, fellow students and others. Some saw this as inevitable.[72] As discussed in chapter 9 the 2003 statement by the Harvard Civil Rights Project indicates that discriminatory and abusive actions towards internationals worsened after the 2001 attack on the World Trade Center.

Numerous studies show discrimination and abuse vary according to national and/or cultural background. Non-white students fare poorly compared to students from English-speaking and European nations. Hanassah and Tidwell surveyed 640 international students at the University of California Los Angeles.[73] African students expressed the strongest concerns about stereotypes and discrimination. 'One Irish student wrote, "When people look at me, they take me for an American so I don't suffer any discrimination".'[74] Problems of discrimination were most severe off campus, particularly for Middle Eastern students.[75] Constantine and colleagues found that African students 'generally indicated prejudicial or discriminatory treatment... they were called names and racial slurs by White Americans'.[76] The researchers noted that 'much' medical literature 'documenting the strong link between perceived racist events and negative health-related and psychological outcomes such as hypertension, cardiovascular reactivity, depression, general psychological distress, eating problems, and substance abuse'.[77] Solberg and colleagues remark that Asian students are sometimes seen as a 'model minority' who have less academic difficulties than students from Africa or Latin America, but this conceals both student problems and the major variations within the category 'Asian'.[78]

Lee surveyed 501 international students at a southwest public research university. Student experiences varied according to national-cultural origin and physical appearance. Students from Japan, a nation

71 Mori, 2000, 138–9; Spencer-Rodgers, 2001; Spencer-Rodgers and McGovern, 2002, 610–11.
72 Nasrin, 2001, 44.
73 Hanassah and Tidwell, 2002.
74 Hanassah, 2006, 163.
75 Hanassah and Tidwell, 2002; Hanassah, 2006.
76 Constantine et al., 2005a, 60.
77 *ibid*, 62
78 Solberg et al., 1994, 275; Wan, 2001, 34.

Table 15.1 Comparison of experience of international students from predominantly white regions with students from predominantly non-white regions, one university, USA

	Predominantly white region	**Predominantly non-white region**
Difficulty in social adjustment	7.38	9.73
Treated equally and fairly	8.91	8.19
Physical and financial security	10.52	10.06
Satisfaction with institutional services	13.58	13.00
Satisfaction with non-academic resources	10.43	9.89
Difficulty in college and living expenses	5.26	5.67

Note: Higher number signifies greater agreement with the survey statement.
Source: Lee, 2005, 10.

with western European living standards, were 'subject to discrimination in ways more similar to students from Africa, the Middle East and other Asian countries' than students from Europe, Canada and Australasia.[79] In all areas of enquiry, students from predominantly non-white regions reported less satisfaction and greater difficulties (table 15.1).[80]

Lee uses the term 'neo-racism' for 'discrimination based on national order or culture'. She argues that non-white appearance operates as a trigger or proxy for discrimination based on cultural essentialism.[81] Neoracism maintains the power and identity of dominant groups using mechanisms of cultural intolerance.

> Neo-racism finds refuge in popular understandings of 'human nature' and appeals to 'common sense' nationalist instincts, but ultimately gives new energy to principles of exclusion and nationalism. Discrimination becomes, seemingly, justified by cultural difference or national origin rather than by physical characteristics alone and can thus disarm the fight against racism by appealing to 'natural' tendencies to preserve group cultural identity – in this case the dominant group. Underlying neo-racism are notions of cultural or national superiority and an increasing rationale for marginalising or assimilating groups in a globalising world. Neoracism does

79 Lee, 2005, 13.
80 *ibid*, 11–12.
81 *ibid*, 6; Spears, 1999.

> not replace biological racism but rather masks it by encouraging exclusion based on the cultural attributes or national origin of the oppressed.[82]

Neoracism is associated with 'barriers to forming interpersonal relationships in the host society'.[83] Lee and Rice interviewed 24 internationals from 15 countries. Non-white students reported many 'instances of discrimination related to students' race, culture, or status as foreign residents . . . [in] . . . campus social interactions, interactions with faculty and administration, denial of funding or job opportunities, and in off-campus interactions such as housing and shopping'.[84]

> Students from Asia, India, Latin America, and the Middle East reported considerable discrimination while students from Europe, Canada, and New Zealand did not report any direct negative experiences related to their race or culture . . . Many international students were confronted with discrimination early upon entering the U.S. and it became a difficult reality for those who have never experienced it in their home country. A woman from the Gulf region explained that 'The most difficult thing for me personally was the race issue. I wasn't that conscious of my race because of where I come from. Race issues do exist but it's more social class. American students would ask me why I spoke like a White person [and] I didn't get it. I had no clue what they were talking about.'[85]

Spencer-Rodgers and McGovern examine the impact of cross-cultural communication barriers as a casual factor for discrimination and prejudice.[86] 'Intercultural communication emotions (negative affect associated with perceived linguistic and cultural barriers) . . . [are] strongly and uniquely related to prejudice toward . . . foreign students.'[87] Some host nationals saw international students as 'illegitimate competitors'.[88] Male graduate students

82 Lee and Rice, 2007, 389–90.
83 *ibid*, 389–90.
84 *ibid*, 391, 393.
85 *ibid*, 393, 395.
86 Spencer-Rodgers and McGovern, 2002, 610.
87 *ibid*, 609.
88 *ibid*, 621.

reported greater prejudice than did females.[89] 'Unfavorable relations with host nationals have serious consequences for the psychological wellbeing of international students.'[90]

UK and New Zealand

In the UK, Bradley's study reported that some international students 'gave examples of racism in the form of threats and abuse'.[91] In the 2004 UKCOSA survey just 46 per cent of internationals agreed that 'the UK is a welcoming and tolerant society'; 19 per cent disagreed. The other 35 per cent were ambivalent or did not answer.[92] In New Zealand, Anderson reported the experiences of three female internationals. Two of them stated that they were targets of overt racism, mostly at school.[93] Focus groups interviewed by McGrath and Hooker stated that 'rudeness, unfriendliness, and racist remarks' were barriers to intercultural relations.[94] Collins discusses media stereotyping of northeast Asian students in Auckland.[95]

Australia

In Australia Schweitzer's survey of 446 internationals at one university, 9.9 per cent reported discrimination.[96] Robertson and colleagues surveyed 408 undergraduate internationals at one Australian university, together with 121 staff: 20 students mentioned 46 separate incidents of racial discrimination on campus. Outside the university 'racist remarks or actions' was the third most frequently mentioned problem after 'difficulty making friends with locals' and 'difficulty understanding slang, idioms, colloquial language'.[97] Incidents mostly occurred in

89 *ibid*, 620.
90 Spencer-Rodgers and McGovern, 2002, 613.
91 Bradley, 2000, 425.
92 UKCISA, 2004, 57, 70.
93 Anderson, 2006, 1.
94 McGrath and Hooker, 2006, 7–8.
95 Collins, 2006.
96 Schweitzer, 1996, 5.
97 Robertson et al., 2000, 93.

Table 15.2 Incidence of abuse, international students at the University of Melbourne, 2006

	Proportion of students experiencing abuse	
	Men %	**Women** %
Physical abuse	1.2	3.9
Verbal abuse	32.9	26.7
Sexual harassment	1.9	12.1
Exclusion	29.8	34.0

Source: Rosenthal, et al., 2008a, 57.

the street, when shopping or on public transport.[98] Staff did not see discrimination as a major issue.[99]

A 2004 report from the University of Melbourne noted that many academic staff 'spoke of an underlying prejudice towards Asian students among colleagues, who perceive them as problematic'. Further, many staff had low awareness of 'the cultural differences between students from Asia', and between internationals and Asian born locals.[100] In 2006 Rosenthal and colleagues asked internationals if they had experienced physical and/or verbal abuse, sexual harassment and exclusion. Verbal abuse and exclusion were each reported by nearly one-third (table 15.2).[101]

In all four areas women students reported higher average emotional distress than men. Men were more often affected by verbal abuse, women by exclusion. Malaysian and Singaporean students had higher than expected rates of both.[102] Students were also asked whether 'people treat me differently because of my cultural background'. Most did: 23.1 per cent ticked 'Very much' or 'Considerably' and 40.9 per cent 'To some degree'. Only 36.0 per cent recorded outright 'No'.[103] Students who said they had experienced abuse had significantly

98 *ibid*, 96.
99 *ibid*, 99.
100 University of Melbourne, 2004.
101 Rosenthal et al., 2008a, 57.
102 Rosenthal. et al., 2006, 42.
103 *ibid*, 28.

Table 15.3 Respect and courtesy from different social groups, local and international students in higher education, Australia, 2006

Whether students are treated with respect and courtesy, by	International students %	Local students %
Teaching staff at educational institution	89	92
Administrative and support staff at educational institution	85	88
People in the Australian community	77	89
Local students	76	91
International students	93	80

Source: AEI, 2007b, 30.

stronger perceptions that 'people treat me differently because of my cultural background'.[104]

The 2006 AEI survey asked international students whether they were treated with respect and courtesy by different groups within Australia. There was a parallel survey of domestic students. The largest difference between local and internationals concerned relations with each other (below). International students rated the respect and courtesy they received from all groups, except other international students, at a lower level than did local students (table 15.3). As in other studies internationals had more respect inside than outside campuses. Just 77 per cent felt respected in the community compared to 89 per cent of local students.[105] The study also found only 24 per cent of internationals had satisfactory access to work experience in their fields.[106]

Students were also asked whether they had close friends in Australia among different groups of people. Of the internationals, 68 per cent had close friends among workmates and 39 per cent in local Australian community, cultural or religious groups. Among locals, 89 per cent had workplace friends and 74 per cent had friends in the community.[107] Among internationals 'Australian attitudes' to them were among the strongest influences on overall stay

104 *ibid*, 57.
105 AEI, 2007b, 30.
106 *ibid*, 26. The local student figure was 46 per cent.
107 *ibid*, 33.

Table 15.4 International student satisfaction with Australian attitudes towards them, by region or nation of origin, Australia, 2006

Region or nation of origin	Number of students in study	Satisfaction rating
Europe	353	8.54
North and South America	297	8.27
Africa	132	7.74
Other	134	7.64
India	245	7.63
Other south and central Asia	112	7.48
Other southeast Asia	772	7.44
Indonesia	213	7.36
China, incl. Hong Kong China	1006	7.31
Other northeast Asia	106	7.23
Thailand	104	6.98
Japan and Korea	111	6.86

Note: The higher the number the higher the level of satisfaction with Australian attitudes.
Source: AEI, 2007b, 46.

satisfaction,[108] especially whether 'Australians are welcoming to international students'.[109] There is sharp variation between nations concerning student satisfaction with Australian attitudes to them (table 15.4). The lowest satisfaction was among students from north-east Asia and Thailand, followed by Indonesia. As in the USA white students are happier than non-white students about the attitudes of Australians to them.

RELATIONS BETWEEN INTERNATIONAL AND LOCAL STUDENTS

Empirical investigation of cross-cultural relations between international and local students is also challenging. The many different forms and qualities of intimacy do not always lend themselves to linear scaling and in qualitative research students have varied expectations about relationships and terminology for describing them. Some want close cross-cultural relations, some useful networks, some friendly acquaintances to brush up their English language skills with. All might be described as friends. Despite the difficulties, relations between local

108 *ibid*, 40.
109 *ibid*, 43.

and international students are often researched.[110] Most studies find these relations are undeveloped or deficient.[111] 'Cultural diversity and internationalisation do not automatically lead to intercultural contacts and intercultural learning experiences', states Otten.[112]

Not all cross-cultural failure can be ascribed to locals. Internationals need to set aside politeness regimes in which hosts are expected to make the first approach to them as guests. Inhibitions based on different values and lifestyles can block initiative. Same-culture enclosures can be so engaging as to reduce cross-cultural contact and English immersion time. As the interview data will show internationals are aware of these issues.

USA

Many studies find cross-cultural contact is correlated to the psychological adjustment, social adjustment and educational achievement of international (and sometimes local) students and can improve intercultural understanding. Sometimes these conclusions are premises,[113] sometimes they are established in research. Perrucci and Hu concluded that among international graduate students 'contact with US students' is primary for academic satisfaction and significant in relation to social satisfaction.[114] Language skill is also correlated to satisfaction. The virtuous effects of cross-cultural relations may be mediated by communicative competence. But Hayes and Lin state that 'host students neither make themselves available nor make an effort great enough to create a bridge for international friendship'. Though host nationals know international students have language difficulties they 'are often insensitive' to internationals need for conversation.[115] Li and Gasser found that cross-cultural contact with host nationals is positively related to the sociocultural adjustment of Asian students and positively related with student self-efficacy. 'The effect of cross-cultural

110 Church, 1982, 552–3, summarises the discussion to that point.

111 In addition to those discussed Constantine et al., 2005b, 164; Hayes and Lin, 1994, 5; Lee et al., 2006, 552; UKCISA, 2004, 67–8.

112 Otten, 2003, 14.

113 Hanassah and Tidwell, 2002, 319.

114 Perrucci and Hu, 1995, 491.

115 Hayes and Lin, 1994, 5; see also Spencer-Rodgers, 2001, 654; Spencer-Rodgers and McGovern, 2002, 610, 624.

self-efficacy on sociocultural adjustment was partially mediated by contact with the hosts.'[116]

UK

In the UK Li and Kaye found that the greatest difficulties facing internationals are financial problems and mixing with UK students. There is a strong association between problems with English language mixing problems.[117] The association is circular (see chapter 12). Students with language problems have difficulties mixing with UK students, while students who do not so mix have fewer opportunities to communicate in English, which tends to perpetuate their language problems.[118] The 2004 UKCOSA survey found that 59 per cent of international students had most of their friendships with co-nationals or other internationals, one-third (32 per cent) a mixture of internationals and UK students and 7 per cent mainly UK students.[119] This was not their preference. Less than one-quarter 'preferred to mix with people from their own country and culture'.[120] Students from east and southeast Asia were least likely to have UK friends. Only 15 per cent of Chinese students had UK friends.[121] Again language was salient. So was the behaviour of local students: 43 per cent of internationals stated that UK students were hard to get to know. In answering a different question, just 60 per cent stated that UK students were friendly once one got to know them.[122]

Australia

Rosenthal and colleagues confirm that most students mix socially with people whose cultural background is seen as similar to their own: 67.4 per cent within the university and 76.7 per cent outside it.[123] Of all respondents, 29.6 per cent have no social contact with

116 Li and Gasser, 2005, 569–71.
117 Li and Kaye, 1998, 44–7.
118 *ibid*, 48; see also Spencer-Rodgers and McGovern, 2002, 610.
119 UKCISA, 2004, 67.
120 *ibid*, 68.
121 *ibid*, 67.
122 *ibid*, 68.
123 Rosenthal et al., 2006, 23.

Table 15.5 Social mixing on and off campus, University of Melbourne, 2006

Who the respondent mixes with socially	Very much %	Considerable degree %	To some degree %	Not at all %
At university: people of similar cultural background to self	27.3	40.1	22.8	9.7
At university: other international students	27.9	32.0	36.2	4.0
At university: Australians	4.2	17.2	49.0	29.6
Outside university: people of similar cultural background to self	44.0	32.7	18.2	5.1
Outside university: Australians	5.8	15.0	39.8	39.4

Source: Rosenthal, et al., 2008, 57.

Australians[124] on campus and 39.4 per cent have no contact outside the university setting. Only one-fifth of respondents have 'very much' or 'considerable' social contact with Australians in either setting[125] (table 15.5).

'Asian students mix more with those of similar cultural background than non-Asian students', and less with Australians than non-Asians. Asian networking correlates with the patterns of those not speaking English at home.[126] On and off campus the highest rate of same-culture networking was among students from Malaysia, Hong Kong China, Indonesia, China and Singapore. The lowest was India, other south Asian and European students. Students from the English-speaking countries, India, south Asia and Europe mix most with Australians. Those from Hong Kong China, China and Indonesia did this least at university; those from Hong Kong China, Indonesia and Malaysia did it least off campus.[127] Older students and graduate research students were more likely to mix with Australians. Females mixed more with co-culturals' and less with Australians on campus. Students who found their academic progress better than expected mixed with Australians more. Same-culture networking had no implication for perceived academic progress.[128]

124 Again, the category 'Australian' does not distinguish same-culture and other-culture people.
125 Rosenthal et al., 2006, 23.
126 *ibid*, 24.
127 *ibid*, 24; large groupings only.
128 *ibid*, 24.

The 2006 Australian Education International survey contains much on cross-cultural relations. Table 15.3 shows that internationals were more likely to think they were treated with respect and courtesy by other internationals (93 per cent) than by Australian students (76 per cent). Australian respondents were more likely to think they were treated with respect and courtesy by other Australians (91 per cent) than internationals (80 per cent), though the difference was less.[129] The proportion of internationals who perceived that they were treated with 'respect and courtesy' was lowest for those from Korea, Thailand and Japan. Answers to the question about whether the respondent had Australian student close friends were also culturally stratified, with the lowest proportions for Thailand (54 per cent) and China and Hong Kong China together (56 per cent). In total 68 per cent of internationals had close friends among Australian students. Perceived barriers to such friendships included lack of interest among Australians in having international friends, the belief among some international students that Australians should make the first move and lack of English language skills.[130] Table 15.6 has those data.

The two groups had sharply different views about cross-cultural friendship. The vast majority of internationals, 81 per cent, wanted more Australian friends. In all 67 per cent of internationals tried actively to make such friends, with the highest proportions for India, North and Latin America. But only 46 per cent of Australian students wanted more international friends and only 37 per cent made the effort. Not surprisingly, almost half the internationals (48 per cent) thought Australians were not interested in having international friends. Only 24 per cent disagreed.[131] Just 58 per cent stated that Australian students were 'friendly' towards internationals. One-quarter of the internationals (26 per cent) believed that their lack of communicative competence in English was a barrier; China and other northeast Asian countries were over-represented.[132] Notably also, almost half the international students believed that 'Australian students should take the first steps to make friends with international

129 AEI, 2007a, 6, 65; AEI, 2007b, 51.
130 AEI, 2007a, 6, 65.
131 AEI, 2007b, 51.
132 *ibid*, 31; however, 53 per cent of all internationals were sure language was not a handicap in making friends.

Table 15.6 Relations between international students and Australian students in higher education, as perceived by international students, by region or nation of origin, 2006

Region or nation of origin	Treated with respect or courtesy by Australian students %	Many or some close friends among Australian students %
Europe	95	83
North America	90	84
South America	88	75
Pacific	77	80
Malaysia and Singapore	76	72
Indonesia	73	68
India	73	67
Other southeast Asia	70	69
China and Hong Kong China	70	56
Other north Asia	69	61
Japan	61	71
Thailand	58	54
Korea	57	80
Other	79	71
Total	76	68

Source: AEI, 2007a, 66–7.

students',[133] but only 9 per cent of the Australians agreed. No wonder so many international students were disappointed in the outcomes (table 15.7).

Local students were more ambivalent. Almost half (48 per cent) were unsure whether they wanted more international students friends, though only 5 per cent were clearly opposed. Over half (51 per cent) were unsure whether they made the effort. Only 5 per cent considered international students not interested in local friends – a contrast with the 48 per cent of internationals who thought Australians were not interested – but over one-third of locals were unsure. Half (50 per cent) were unsure about whether internationals should take the first steps.[134]

A high proportion (89 per cent) of international students had 'close friends' (not defined) from their country of residence or other

133 AEI, 2007a, 68.
134 AEI, 2007b, 32.

Table 15.7 Attitudes to cross-cultural friendship, international and Australian students in higher education, 2006

International student perception	International students agree %	Australian student perception	Australian students agree %
I would like to have more Australian students as friends	81	I would like to have more international students as friends	46
I make an effort to have Australian students as friends	67	I make an effort to have international students as friends	37
My English ability stops me from making friends with Australian students	26	n/a	n/a
Australian students are friendly towards international students	58	International students are friendly towards Australian students	60
Australian students do not seem interested in having international students as friends	48	International students do not seem interested in having Australian students as friends	22
Australian students should take the first steps to make friends with international students	44	International students should take the first steps to make friends with Australian students	9

Source: AEI, 2007a, 68.

international students, 68 per cent had Australian students as close friends and 65 per cent studied with Australians. Among Australian students 93 per cent had Australian close friends and 64 per cent had international student close friends. While 74 per cent of Australian students had close friends in the local Australian community only 39 per cent of international students said this. Many internationals felt that 'Australian students lacked the maturity, patience and interest in forming friendships with students from overseas, particularly those from non-English-speaking countries'. As one put it, 'They're nice, but they don't really want to know you'.[135]

135 *ibid*, 32–3.

Questions about intercultural relations

As outlined in chapter 13 interviewees were asked several questions related to friends and networks, including these.

- Have you been able to make friends with people from other cultures while here: (1) other international students, (2) local students and others? If so, how close are these relationships?
- Are there significant barriers in making friends across cultures?
- Have you experienced hostility or prejudice[136] while in Australia? From other students? From local people? In relation to nationality, religion, dress or other matters?

Most material in this chapter is from answers to these questions. Data from some other interview questions are also included.

CROSS-CULTURAL FRIENDSHIPS

The locals: 'They just can't step out of culture'

The style of local Australians often caught international students by surprise. One student from Spain, who also studied in Japan and the USA, found the Australian approach to foreigners different: more direct and honest but less engaging, with neither Japanese politeness nor the sometimes hypocritical friendliness encountered in the USA.

> Maybe they are a bit more sincere here. Australian people are more honest, they don't intend to be politically correct all the time. If they feel good and they feel like being kind, they are talkative; if they don't they are [indecipherable phrase follows] . . . [at first] I was expecting 'Good morning. How are you? Can I help you? Blah, blah, blah' . . . I thought there was something I was doing wrong. After three years in Tokyo I probably had become too localised to the Japanese system, where the politeness is extreme. I was shocked . . . [Eventually] I realised that Australian people, they tend not to explain everything. If you don't ask, they don't tell you. If you want them to give you information you have to ask.
>
> ~ male, 33, PhD in medicine, Spain

136 For the first 45 interviews the words 'discrimination or bad treatment' were used, not hostility or prejudice'. The wording was changed because 'bad treatment' was too open-ended, in that it invoked non-cultural incidents such as assessment disputes, and 'discrimination' invoked definitional problems.

One student said that 'We always have different kind of people coming to Brunei', but many Australians could not deal effectively with this kind of diversity.

> Some people they just can't step out of culture.
>
> ~ female, 35, ceramics, Brunei

Being cosmopolitan: 'Come here with an open mind'

There was a near consensus that it was much easier to relate to other internationals. Compared to local encounters, many internationals had a superior capacity in other-cultural encounters. They were more experienced, more able to open themselves and more motivated. The key was to respect other cultures while engaging with all. Students were asked if they had made many new friendships in Australia.

> Oh, tell me about it. A whole new world! . . . But not many local students . . . I've had some really bad experiences.
>
> ~ male, 21, business, Pakistan

> That's my advice . . . come here with an open mind to learn, to learn new experiences, to meet new people.
>
> ~ female, 40, PhD in gender studies, PNG

> [T]alk as much as you can. And go outside, look with your own eyes. Don't always stay inside.
>
> ~ female, 26, PhD in science, China

> Make friends as many as possible. Get to know more people other than your own nationalities. It's also better if you have your own communities. Try to mingle with the Australian people and culture. Try to adjust as much as possible rather than trying to get people adjust to you.
>
> ~ male, 27, computing, Indonesia

Opening to the locals: 'We can adjust ourselves to suit into them'

Many international students saw it as essential to synchronise with the locals. Some talked about the need to dissolve cultural differences. Several focused on the need to prepare local knowledge.

> You shouldn't come here with a mental block. Even in the official publications for overseas students, you get the idea that international students see themselves as something different from the locals . . . I think it's the kind of prejudice it would be the best to lay aside.
>
> ~ female, 19, arts, India

> Students coming in should do their research into the country, the people and the lifestyle.
>
> ~ female, 22, business, Zimbabwe

> If we can get used to their culture and adjust ourselves to suit into them it's not that difficult.
>
> ~ female, 22, science, Malaysia

A significant minority of interviewees from various national and cultural backgrounds said there were no barriers to cross-cultural relations. A Muslim from Sri Lanka who grew up in Bahrain and was studying medicine stated that he preferred friendships with local students, though this response was unusual.

> I think most of my friends are local students. Very few are international students.
>
> ~ male, 21, medicine, Sri Lanka

Others declared 'close' or 'very close' local friends, though 'close' was undefined. But it was tough 'adjusting' locally when the odds were against you. Students were asked if there were significant barriers in making friends across cultures.

> Partly. There were in the beginning when I was in school. That was largely because I didn't understand any of the slang . . . the Australian humour is very different. I was also one of two Asian kids in the entire school, which was a bit daunting. The other one went to parties and drank with the others; I didn't really fit in there. But I learnt very quickly that to fit in you have to not be an achiever. I tried very hard to be mediocre, to try not to stand out. You already stand out physically, and everyone expects an Asian to be hardworking. I get it in hospitals all the time. Well, the reason why we're here is our parents are really struggling to make ends meet to keep us here, so we can't afford to slacken off. I used to study in the toilet in the middle of the night so nobody knew I

> was doing work, which probably didn't help because they thought I was naturally a freak, which was not quite true. It was actually quite difficult in the beginning and if I could go back now, I would do a lot of things differently.
>
> ~ female, 25, medicine, Malaysia

Sport played a more minor role for internationals than for local students but was one venue for bridging. Soccer was the most popular sport, followed by basketball. Cultural activities and religious activities were each mentioned about the same number of times as sport. Several students attended dance clubs.

Taking the initiative: 'We have to approach them'

One student said Australians were approachable but rarely initiated friendship. International students had to make the first moves. Many internationals found this hard. It seemed to breach politeness regimes in which locals welcome guests.

> I guess it's a question of creating the opportunity to meet them. If you're a new student you obviously come with your own mind-set and your stereotypes. You're coming from Asia, you don't go out and actively engage with people, you don't go and meet people just for the heck of meeting them. We wait for an opportunity to present. But that's a problem. And, I guess, with the locals . . . maybe it just doesn't occur to them. They have their own circle of friends.
>
> ~ male, 29, economics, India

> Asians not really as easy going as locals here, they don't dare to make the first move. While Australians, OK, they are usually easy going, but we have to approach them in the first place.
>
> ~ female, 20, business, Indonesia

Better intercultural relations were in reach if international students took more initiatives, said some. Only then could shared ground be discovered. The logical corollary was that success in cross-cultural encounters was seen as a function of personality. 'You have to go beyond being polite within an Indian culture', said one female student, despite the risk of being branded 'strong' and 'aggressive'.

Students were asked if there were significant barriers in making friends across cultures.

> I don't think there are significant barriers. Of course that depends on one personality. If one is shy and is withdrawn to himself or herself then he or she would not go out to make friends with people. But the only barrier for me right now is time.
>
> ~ female, 40, gender studies, Papua New Guinea

> I've got a friend in each country, culture or nationality and I suppose I've been lucky that way, but I suppose it's something to do with your personality.
>
> ~ female, 22, business, Zimbabwe

Dynamics of separation: 'It's much more difficult than I imagined'

Many students found that their unaided efforts, while necessary, were not always sufficient. Forming friendships with local students had proven harder than expected. This is one of the strongest findings in the study.

> When I was [still] living in China I thought that it would be difficult to make friends with the locals [in Australia]. But provided that I am talking – I have an active attitude and I'm an outgoing and friendly person – I will be able to make local friends. But it was much more difficult than I imagined.
>
> ~ female, 25, business, China

> I don't think they like us or we cannot make them happy. I don't know why . . . Some are really good, some are completely adverse.
>
> ~ male, 36, business, Bangladesh

Many also commented on how local and international students steered separate courses. They often had cosmopolitan relationships with people from various backgrounds (chapter 13) but few ties to locals. With other internationals they had the international education experience itself in common, including the desire for intercultural encounters and experience of dealing with locals. Another strong finding was that many internationals saw the student body as broadly divided into two groups. Some saw the two groups as local (white or Anglo) Australians, and 'Asians'. Others saw them as locals and

European heritage internationals ('Westerners'), and non-white internationals. It was not always clear where local non-European students fitted in these dichotomies or whether the main distinction was local–foreigner or white–non-white but it was clear that 'Asian' and 'local Australian' were each imagined as large generic groups.

> It's very much an Asian and Caucasian thing.
>
> ~ female, 22, arts, Singapore

> If you take Australians or those with white skin, I generally feel that they don't usually mix up with our Asian students. It happens both ways, we also don't mix up with them . . . I feel more comfortable with other students from Asian countries.
>
> ~ female, 34, business, Sri Lanka

> When you enter the university you find that most of the students around you are from the same-culture background . . . My close friends they are all from China. We speak the same language . . . It's very hard to make friends with the outside community. It's very hard to enter the Australia group . . . You don't know their jokes. You don't know why they are laughing. The sense of humour is different and you don't know their culture, what they are talking about. Although you know every word, you don't really understand the true meaning of the sentence.
>
> ~ female, 24, business, China

One student from Singapore noted that while there was free culture exchange in his residential college and he was 'very happy' there, a local–Asian dichotomy was apparent. Students had different degrees of closeness with the two broad groups. Those in the international student group bonded across national and cultural lines. There was a gap with the locals.

> Two hundred and forty students live together . . . from all over the world. That's the great thing about living there, you get to meet a lot of people from different backgrounds. You also assimilate very fast into the local culture because there are so many Australians there; you don't just meet them for class. You live with these people, you talk to them every day, you get to see them when you go for supper . . . Basically in my college there are two [groups] . . . there is a relatively big Asian community. It is a little bit segregated from

> the Australian community but within ourselves we are quite united and close . . . They are my close buddies, most of the time, so I go to them when I have problems. We are like brothers and sisters.
>
> ~ male, 24, arts, Singapore

A US student identified three broad groupings: local students, European-Americans, perhaps including Latin Americans and Asian students.

> There is not a strong tradition within Australia of moving to different cities to go to university. Most of the people who go to university here are already fairly entrenched in their social circle, and it's generally only people that are maybe feeling disenchanted or trapped, that are seeking out new friends from other places. So most of my friends here are from different [non-local] countries. A wide array – but mostly European countries, South American countries or North American . . . I do have a few friends from southeast Asia or Asia but most of them are people that I know through my scholarship program, that's how we have been introduced to each other. When I've been in classes, even with the high mix of international students, basically you see almost two divisions, students from Asia and then students from North America and Europe, and I think Latin Americans tend to coalesce.
>
> ~ male, 24, business, USA

The locals don't care: 'They stay separate'

Outside favoured zones such as residential colleges, local–international separation was more complete. Many (but not all) interviewees emphasised that the dynamics of this separation were driven primarily by the locals, who did not want to mix. The separate groupings took the form of segregation.

> There are already cliques, comfort zones, with the Australian students. They have the cliques from school . . . then they come to college, so they have their own support groups already established. They are comfortable. They don't need to got out and make friends. They are not really keen on getting to know you other than just as an international student.
>
> ~ female, 29, PhD in education, India

> Aussie students are a little bit separate. They stay separate too.
>
> ~ female, 33, environmental science, Bangladesh

> Local students . . . well, I don't have a problem communicating with them but it's very hard to talk to them . . . [people who were] classmates from last semester, this semester when I see them they don't even recognise who you are. Maybe it's what they all say: Asians look all the same to them. I don't really know. I just feel it.
>
> ~ male, 21, business, Malaysia

> Yeah, you don't call it discrimination . . . just segregation.
>
> ~ male, 20, medicine, Japan

There were few opportunities to befriend locals. One student was sad that she had never been invited into a local Australian home, though other internationals had shared Christmas.

> You're curious, you want to know about them . . . their traditions, how they are celebrated, their relationship with their families, and you want to join them. You want to laugh at the same jokes and share the culture things. There's just so little chance to get you there.
>
> ~ female, 25, economics, China

> I'm quite a sociable person but we don't have a lot of chance to meet new people. Actually, the Australian students are not really keen on talking and speaking to [people from] other countries, especially of Asian background.
>
> ~ female, 32, PhD in education, Vietnam

This contrasted with those who argued there were no intercultural barriers, that it was a matter of personality.

Levels of intimacy: 'They're friendly, but . . . '

A significant number of interviewees remarked that while local students could be polite, and even warm, and were not abusive as were some in the outside community, it was another matter to achieve a real conversation, let alone become friends.

> I make quite a number of friends, not necessarily with Australians but with other international students . . . [With local students], I

> don't know why, it tends to be performative; it just doesn't seem to last. We just doesn't seem to have things in common.
>
> ~ female, 29, PhD in architecture, Indonesia

> They're friendly but I don't think they really want to make friends with us sometimes.
>
> ~ female, 23, nursing, Hong Kong China

> Just say 'Hi' and 'Goodbye'.
>
> ~ female, 32, psychology, Hong Kong China

Where cross-cultural relationships did develop there were often clear limits.

> My friends are from Indonesia, Malaysia, Singapore. I do [have local friends], but I am not very close to them. They have a different lifestyle. Our thinking is different as well. But they are very nice to talk with. Mostly, they are friends from my course. Yeah, sometimes we met in school. We talk together but we never hang out together outside.
>
> ~ female, 21, business, Indonesia

> I lived with a local Australian person but we didn't get along well with each other. He didn't like me to cook Chinese vegetables. He doesn't like to smell them . . . So I moved out . . . Now I live with two Chinese friends . . . We feel very happy.
>
> ~ male, 25, computing, China

As one student who shared accommodation with two local girls put it this way.

> I think we are good friends. Just some limits. Yes, like we are good for each other but we don't interfere in each other. How do you say it . . . ? [Interviewer: 'Just mind your own business?'] Yes. But if you have some trouble or you know if you're homesick and you want somebody to talk, yes, they are there for you.
>
> ~ female, 25, computing, China

International groupings: 'We always ask each other'

Some internationals commented that international same-culture groupings contributed to the separation from the locals.

> I'm having difficulties in getting to know the Australians. There seems to be a group and they're not allowing us in . . . and, well, what I can see is Asian people that don't want to try to get into the Australians anyway.
>
> ~ male, 20, business, Indonesia

> With the Asian students it's easier. In this program we have many Asian students, like Vietnamese. We have trouble in understanding assignment sometimes and we always ask each other. We don't ask Australian people, we ask each other.
>
> ~ female, 33, education, China

Students were asked if there were significant barriers to making friends across cultures.

> Yes. Asian people are really close between them. This is like a circle, this is like a team.
>
> ~ female, 28, business, Colombia

> In the case of Latin America, [if] more students start to come here . . . in the future [we could] start to have communities like that here.
>
> ~ male, 27, science, Mexico

Even so, many wanted both types of relationships. One 19 year old business student from Pakistan tried to spend time with local students but in the end focused mostly on 'people from my country'. Differences of values had emerged; some locals were more 'materialist' than him, and there had been some 'really bad experiences'. He felt freer, more himself in same-culture settings.

Opportunity barriers: 'Not many in the class'

Cultural differences were compounded by other barriers. Lack of time was a real problem for some, particularly those with families in Australia. Older internationals found it more difficult to reach young locals. Some male internationals found it hard to talk to local females. The temporary nature of student life inhibited depth of friendship. 'People come and go', said one student from Malaysia.

Internationals in some institutions lived with same-culture friends, studied in classes in business often largely composed of internationals and worked hard; they had few other activities in their lives. There might be few structured opportunities to mix with locals. Meanwhile a world of internationals was accessible.

> Perhaps there are more overseas students than local students here.
>
> ~ male, 37, PhD in mathematics, Indonesia

> Melbourne is just full of people, especially Asian. It's crowded with Chinese and Indian people, from everywhere in the world. Sometimes I think I am in India. Yes, most of my friends are Asian. Even in my class there are lots of Asians . . . You don't really have a chance to mingle with them [locals] because not many of them in the class, about four.
>
> ~ female, 25, business, Malaysia

Communication barriers: 'Different cultures have different topics'

Communication barriers were key (see chapter 12). It was not simply a problem of grammar and vocabulary but also one of shared cultural references and meanings. To conduct a deeper conversation, let alone an ongoing friendship, it was necessary to have a shared imaginary with some agreement about what was emotionally significant. It helped to know about local sport and the television programs that local students were watching. These were often the diet of conversations.

> International students were asked if they had close friends.

> Yes, mostly Asian, like Japanese, Taiwanese, Chinese. Sometimes I find it so difficult to communicate with the ones with blond(e) hair. They just ignore you or don't want to do work with you because they think that you're English is poor.
>
> ~ female, 26, design, Hong Kong China

> Mainly is the language . . . the culture is quite important too. People from different cultures have different topics. Sometimes it's quite hard to really make close friends with people from other cultures.
>
> ~ female, 23, nursing, Hong Kong China

Thus just to enter local homes did not necessarily establish common ground. On campus students had their study in common. Off campus it could be harder.

> With the Australian students it's so difficult. Every time I say 'Hi. How are you?', [then it's] 'Fine, thank you', and no more. What else to talk about? One day my classmate was so friendly, he invited us to his house. He is married with many children. At the table with his wife, me, [it's] 'How are you?', 'What are you doing?', 'Where do you come from?' Then that's it. No more conversation. We didn't know what to say, and they didn't want to talk to us any more, because it was boring.
>
> ~ female, 33, education, China

Lifestyle barriers: 'Here it's nightclubs, girls, alcohol'

An ongoing problem for some international students was differences in values and lifestyle. One student in 10 said they did not share local party lifestyles, alcohol, smoking and other substance use, or sex outside marriage. This confirms findings in the research literature, particularly on sex and alcohol.

> A lot of them [internationals] are culturally not prepared to live in an area like Newtown, which has a huge gay population. Particularly southeast Asian students who say, 'I've seen this. What's this about? What am I supposed to do about that?' . . . And also there's the drinking culture over here. I came from England, I'm fine with it. A lot of them find it very confronting that all of this . . . [is normal for] the average Australian person.
>
> ~ female, 24, law, UK

> Over here in Australia there is no social life. What I mean to say is if you want to have fun it's nightclubs, girls, alcohol. If I told you how I spend most of the time with my friends in India, all talking and stuff, you wouldn't understand what kind of enjoyment I have. But here you have to have alcohol or drugs, girls, you know in the bedroom, in the bed – that's fun.
>
> ~ male, 23, business, India

> Here to mix up with the culture, you have to go clubbing . . . entertainment is not the same like back home, which is

> family get together, friends get together . . . because I'm Muslim, I don't drink. Here when you get together, people start drinking, and I sort of feel isolated.
>
> ~ male, 27, computing, Sri Lanka

CROSS-CULTURAL PATHOLOGIES: DISCRIMINATION AND ABUSE

In total 99 of 200 interviewees (49.5 per cent) said 'Yes' to the question 'Have you experienced hostility or prejudice while in Australia?' (see table 15.8).

This might seem to refer to any instance of hostility but it immediately followed the enquiry about cross-cultural friendships and barriers, and the responses of interviewees show they interpreted the question as being about intercultural tensions. The rate of 'Yes' replies was broadly similar in each age group but slightly higher for 35 years and above. More women were affected (56 per cent) than men (42 per cent).

Of the large national groupings 67 per cent from Malaysia and 72 per cent from Singapore reported instances of hostility or prejudice. The rate was above average for China (55 per cent), Hong Kong China and India (52 per cent) and below for Indonesia (45 per cent) and other south Asian nations (32 per cent). Some students answered 'No' to the question on hostility or prejudice but provided data on discriminatory experiences, which suggests that some saw hostility or prejudice as a high threshold of discrimination and that table 15.8 is thus a conservative estimate.

Being positive: 'I can be what I want'

Among the interviewees who stated they had not experienced hostility or prejudice were many non-white students.

> Australia is one country in the world that has no religion or social life discrimination. I can be what I want.
>
> ~ male, 28, business, Indonesia

> There are not some issues that you have in America. Racism is not such an issue here. Things are more cool and relaxed.
>
> ~ male, 33 PhD in medicine, Spain

Table 15.8 Instances of self-reported hostility or prejudice by national origin and gender

Nation of origin	Women from this nation	Women saying 'Yes'	%	Men from this nation	Men saying 'Yes'	%	People from this nation	People saying 'Yes'	%
China	22	11	50	6	4	67	28	15	54
Hong Kong China	5	3	60	0	0	0	5	3	60
Other east Asia*	3	3	100	6	1	17	9	4	44
Malaysia	13	8	62	5	4	80	18	12	67
Singapore	7	6	86	4	2	50	11	8	72
Indonesia	22	10	45	27	12	44	49	22	45
Indochina**	3	2	67	3	1	33	6	3	50
Southeast Asia and Pacific nei***	5	3	60	1	1	100	6	4	67
India	4	4	100	17	7	41	21	11	52
Other South Asia****	5	2	40	14	4	29	19	6	32
Middle East and North Africa	2	1	50	5	0	0	7	1	14
Other Africa	3	3	100	4	2	50	7	5	71
Latin America	2	0	0	1	0	0	3	0	0
Europe	2	1	50	4	3	75	6	4	67
Canada/ USA/UK	3	0	0	2	1	50	5	1	20
Total	101	57	56	99	42	42	200	99	50

Note: nei = not elsewhere included
* Korea, Japan, Taiwan, Macau
** Laos, Cambodia, Vietnam
*** Brunei, Thailand, PNG
**** Sri Lanka, Nepal, Bangladesh, Pakistan

It was often difficult to read incidents. Bad experiences could have more than one explanation. Was it just the Australian lack of politeness? Some students also wanted to put the best face on things and refrain from criticising the host nation.

> Maybe it's a case of bad service. You wouldn't really know whether it's discrimination, or they just don't care or can't be bothered.
> ~ male, 25, social sciences, Singapore

> Drunkards, they're not in their senses, so you would exclude them.
> ~ male, 19, business, Pakistan

Intercultural tensions: 'You just feel it'

But the marketing of Australia as cosmopolitan, tolerant and friendly had set benchmarks. Expectations were often high and experience failed to meet them. When asked what were the barriers to making friends across cultures, there were many anecdotes concerning discrimination and abuse.

> I guess language is the most important. And I feel this racism going on here. It's racism towards Asians most of the time . . .
>
> ~ female, 20, business, Indonesia

Students were also asked if they had experienced hostility or prejudice while in Australia.

> Yes, yes, many times.
>
> ~ male, 37, PhD in mathematics, Indonesia

Several students stated that the essential problem was not overt conflict or incidences of discrimination but the segregation of international students from local people. Nevertheless, the tensions evaded, protected and fostered by segregation could surface in encounters with locals. Interviewees made statements such as 'I felt uncomfortable' and 'It's just a feeling' to describe these half expressed tensions.

> Sometimes you feel a little bit of discrimination. You just feel it. But you cannot speak out.
>
> ~ male, 26, computing, China

Alongside local signals of exclusion or hostility was ignorance from locals unable to imagine cultural difference. Sometimes it hurt but it could be laughed off.

> When I was in Year 12, I was in a tram and a drunk man told me to go home. He didn't mean to school . . . People have preconceptions when they see me. That's why I wear make-up, partly, because if I didn't wear make-up, I'd look like every other Asian person. And they immediately stereotype . . . Often white people are surprised when I open my mouth and start speaking English to them. They can't believe I can speak English and I say to them, 'Do you believe I just got here six months ago?'. [laughs] They are actually gullible, some of them. I'm very quick . . . so yeah, do get

> some discriminatory remarks but they're not always said with a malicious intent.
>
> ~ female, 26, medicine, Malaysia

> Experiences constantly varied.

> Sometimes when you are in the supermarket they are very kind to you. When you have some problem they are willing to help you very much; they lead you to some place that you don't know. That's amazing. Sometimes when you ask somebody they say 'I don't know', and you think they are surprised. [There's] a little bit of dislike, they don't want to help you. Some days they hate you. You can feel that.
>
> ~ male, 41, PhD in computing, China

There were also intercultural tensions among international students.

> Making friends with those Chinese people, we have to be very careful, because they're quite cunning some of them.
>
> ~ female, 21, business, Malaysia

> [The] student union is run by an Indian, so so many Indians there, you cannot, you are Chinese . . . I went to a meeting and there are always all Indians talking talking.
>
> ~ female, 33, education, China

Appearance and voice: 'I mean, it's my first language'

Discriminatory incidents were most readily triggered by non-white appearance or perceived foreign accent. Students doing telephone work dealt with customers offended by their voice tones. It was worse when appearance was also involved. Some locals turned off and made no effort to engage, concluding before anything was said that a non-Anglo was not going to speak English competently. It was tough for second language speakers trying to communicate in English. They felt native speakers should respect their efforts and respond reciprocally.

> They just assume that you don't know English. You say something and they don't understand. I don't know, I just got the feeling that they think you are dumb.
>
> ~ female, 22, business, Africa

Others were more annoyed by the turn off because they were fluent:

> When I went for treatment at the general clinic . . . they acted as though I would not understand English. In the referral letter they gave, it was stated that I might not be able to communicate properly, that I might have some language problems. 'Would the doctor at the hospital please keep the explanation simple and straightforward', which was very insulting. I mean, it is my first language.
>
> ~ female, 19, arts, India

On being Muslim: 'Honestly, we feel threatened'

Muslim students had the most problems. The wellsprings were not religious intolerance per se but the community stereotype of Muslims as terrorists and the polarising effect of US military intervention in Iraq and Afghanistan. One student from Iran referred to the 'tension between our countries'. Indonesian students often faced difficulties.

> Most of Aussie people you know look at Indonesians as terrorists.
>
> ~ female, 19, computing, Indonesia

> The relationship between Australia and Indonesia at the moment is not really good. We feel the threat from the local people. Honestly, we feel threatened.
>
> ~ male, 24, business, Indonesia

> I am afraid that I wouldn't be able to come back home because of the dispute between Indonesia and Australia. I am very aware about political things. The terrorism issue . . . moreover my wife is wearing the scarf. Sometimes when we are walking people stare at us. From their eyes we can see and feel that's they don't like us.
>
> ~ male, 45, PhD in education, Indonesia

Wearing a headscarf was no simple matter for Muslim women, especially in provincial towns with less cultural diversity and tolerance (see chapter 9). Some took off the scarf when anti-Muslim tendencies heightened after the Bali bombing and in the early stages of the second Gulf War; others did not.

> When September 11 happened, because I was wearing scarves everybody looked at me. I could feel this tension going on . . . but nobody actually harassed me or did anything to me. Most of the

> crowd here are very, very open minded, but you know the minority where you can see that look.
>
> ~ female, 21, business, Bahrain

Sikh men encountered an equivalent problem when they wore a turban.

> I decided on coming to Australia because it was after September 9/11 had happened. A lot of Sikhs in America and UK were being targeted because people were not aware that we're not Muslims.

When asked if they had experienced hostility or prejudice while in Australia, this same student replied:

> No . . . just a couple of things of concern. I might be travelling on the train and a group of people might come in and start calling me Osama bin Laden. Things like that.
>
> ~ male, 30, dentistry, India

International conflict could be a problem for American students too.

> When I first came here the war in Iraq was starting and I did find there was a lot of anti-American feeling, especially in the schools. I was very conscious that every time I opened my mouth and was speaking, people knew I was American. Some people were not nice because of that.
>
> ~ male, 39, PhD in computing, USA

> I felt a really strong anti-American sentiment when I first arrived, during the first semester. [It made] . . . me uncomfortable, I wanted to go home. A lot of it can be traced to the war in Iraq. I didn't even support it, but at the same time it felt like I was being blamed for it, especially in political science classes, and even in social settings. I'd be introduced and as soon as somebody found out that I wasn't Canadian, I felt there was a kind of dislike. I think it has lessened.
>
> ~ male, 24, business, USA

Inside the university: 'They are used to international students'

There were fewer cultural tensions on campus than outside. Local students and staff sometimes reacted negatively to skin colour or accent, or to Muslim identity. Sometimes classmates said hurtful things. One student recounted an incident in which her friend had talked about 'you and your stupid Muslim brothers' when criticising polygamy. This had shocked her, and cruelled their relationship. One student believed that, though he was a good actor, he was consistently excluded from prominent parts in university plays because of his appearance. One student had been abused by a uniformed member of the university service staff.

> It happened just two days after September 11 . . . He just yelled at me with very rude words, and said 'Fucking Muslims', and 'Go back to your country'. I reported the incident to security and they made a formal report.
>
> ~ female, 30, science, Indonesia

Nonetheless, many interviewees said staff and other students were pleasant and helpful. They had no complaints on cultural grounds. One student praised his university's policy.

> Very recently they provided special protection for international students, especially from the harassment and discrimination. They provide a line for us to call any time. It's very good for us.
>
> ~ male, 29, humanities, Indonesia

> I think they are quite used to international students.
>
> ~ female, 26, PhD in science, China

Overall, the favourable comments balanced the unfavourable, which was in contrast to the discussion of cultural tensions outside universities.

In the community: 'The people here don't like me'

A large number of non-white student interviewees had been abused in the street, with epithets such as 'Go home', 'Yellow Asian', 'Yellow monkey', 'Ching Ching'. 'You nigger' was often directed at south Asian students (see the discussion of hate crimes in chapter 9). Some students mentally blocked out these incidents to prevent them from having an emotional impact. Several who lived in Sydney and Melbourne said the fact there were so many Asian students took the edge off the abuse. But for some others nasty incidents were hard to forget.

> I was in the first week, two years ago. Really scared. Everything was new. I was walking home one afternoon and approached a traffic light along the route. A car went past, with no top. There were four Australians inside, high school kids, shouting at me, 'Hey, hey, Chinese', and calling me many things. 'Hey, go back to your country!' I thought, Oh, it's terrible; the people here don't like me. They want me to go back, and I've just arrived here. What am I going to do? I am living here for three years. You're alone and you're really scared, in the middle of broad daylight. As the car approached the red light it stopped. I was thinking, should I turn and run or should I walk up to them and see what's going to happen. I decided to do the latter and walked slowly towards the traffic light. Luckily, when I was near the traffic light turned green and they sped off. I would now think that these are just high school students wanting to have a bit of fun, immature people. I would ignore it.
>
> ~ male, 24, arts, Singapore

One student from Sri Lanka had been refused entry to a nightclub with the remark 'It isn't rhythm and blues night, sorry'. There were a dozen stories of discourtesy in shops and queue breaking at automatic teller machines.

> I went to a supermarket with my daughter. In the line in front of me there was a European person and the cashier was very nice to him. 'Hello sir, how are you?' But when it came to my turn, the cashier didn't say anything. Her face was just so rude.
>
> ~ male, 36, PhD in business, Indonesia

> A group of us were at Mt Buller and it was very obvious in the restaurant itself . . . although we were standing there, they let everyone behind us go ahead. They ignored us, and when we finally got their attention, they very grudgingly showed us a place and just threw the menu at us. It was not very nice and it was obviously not happening to every one else. They were very nice and very warm to everyone [else].
>
> ~ female, 22, arts, Singapore

Bad incidents could be compartmentalised, but a more instrumental problem was difficulties in the private rental market (chapter 7). One Indonesian student said that he and his friends had been consistently refused accommodation, whereas other students had succeeded. In a seller's market landlords could pick and choose. Some students talked of discrimination at work and in job selection (see chapter 6); others in Melbourne pointed to the refusal of the state government to grant the same transport concessions to international as local students.

CONCLUSIONS

International education is a process of self-formation in which students and their families invest in learning and personal change. The term 'self-formation' highlights the role of self-directed and reflexive agency. Elements external to the student help to shape international education, including institutions, teachers, cultural groupings and networks, but self-determination is central to the experience. This is an important corrective to theorisations that imagine the international student as a weak, deficient or conflicted agent largely shaped by forces outside the self.

In the process of self-formation internationals fashion themselves using identity resources they bring to the country of education, and identity resources they find there. This process can scarcely be glimpsed by large survey samples and regression equations. Kettle's study of a single Thai student captures indepth the evolution of self-developing agency,[137] indicating the potential of intensive qualitative work.

Self-formation takes two main forms. We can call them 'multiplicity' and 'hybridity'.[138] It entails multiplicity because the temporary immigrant is more than one person and lives more than one kind of life. In the case of hybridity the sojourner synthesises different cultural and relational elements into a combination self. Many employ elements of both strategies. With continuing relations back home, same-culture networks, cosmopolitan friendships with other internationals and relations with locals, the possibilities are broad and open. But the choices are constrained in some respects. For most international students, engagement with local society and language is as important as the study program and the diploma. Many gain much from that engagement. But the limitations, disappointments and

137 Kettle, 2005.
138 Marginson, 2009; Marginson and Sawir, forthcoming.

cross-cultural pathologies also stand out strongly. Three findings from the present study stand out:

1 nearly all internationals want to make friends with local people on and off campus
2 most internationals find this hard to achieve
3 cross-cultural relations are riven by division that often takes the form of segregation.

Most of the locals exclude international students[139] by refusing to engage at all or by engaging only superficially. A small but potent minority denigrates or abuses the visitors, while some people impose stereotyping and discrimination on them, regardless of how they behave. Once imposed, this segregation between the groups enables the bulk of locals to remain unchanged and certain of the superiority of their lives. Thus they thereby evade the challenges and the benefits of intercultural relations. For their part, most international students have little choice but to follow the path of separation, which at least allows them to avoid frustration and humiliation. The wall between the groups limits mutual cultural transformation and the scope for local students to become globally competent. It also restricts the capacity of international students to improve their language, understand the nation of education and draw on its cultural resources in evolving their identities.

As yet there is no consensus and little clarity on how to improve intercultural relations. The empirical findings of this study and our reading of other research suggest that the keys to the international student experience, including student security, are communicative competence and self-effective agency, which operate as mutually reinforcing mediations across the range of activity. Hence we would normally expect to find correlation effects between each and all of the communicative competence of internationals, their self-determining agency, however modelled, the quantity of cross-cultural relations and the quality and intensity of intercultural relations. But up to now most of the discussion has been about changing international student behaviour to enhance adjustment, which in practice means bringing them into line with local values and behaviours. Some would like to reduce the role of same-culture networks, despite these networks'

139 Olson and Kroeger, 2001, 120–1.

crucial functions in student security, as if that would trigger a more individualist local-like agency that is more willing to engage with local friends.[140] Dismantling same-culture support systems would be counterproductive and misplaced. Most internationals, who undergo personal transformations in the period of study, are open to change. There is no consistent evidence to show that same-culture networks weaken effective agency or block friendships with locals, and the notion that internationals must shed their chosen values is repugnant. Where the zero sum argument comes into play is in relation to time of immersion in English language settings. It is essential that internationals embrace plural language use during their stay and that institutions better facilitate this by supporting foundation English (chapter 12).

We believe that the way forward is to enhance the capacity for multiple and hybrid experience by strengthening the resources of self-formation and the opportunities for local engagement. If this occurs, then the local also needs to change. An asymmetrical focus on internationals in the context of an unchanging local environment is unlikely to get to the roots of local disengagement. Bringing local students into intercultural education is *the* unsolved problem of international education. The solution lies partly in changes in teaching and learning. Though this takes us some way beyond the terms of this study and book, we will make some remarks.

STRATEGIES FOR INTERCULTURAL RELATIONS

Wide and deep intercultural engagement would enrich the educational experience of all students. It would also markedly contribute to international student security. It would accelerate language development, augment confidence and encourage initiative. It would speed the socialisation of internationals into local practices, broaden networks and expand work and housing opportunities. It would create better local understanding of internationals and enable reduction in stereotyping, discrimination and abuse. These pathologies are worse outside campus than in, but division and disengagement between internationals and locals sustain them on campus also; stronger local student

140 For example the business studies professors who criticised same-culture networks and the lack of class participation; Andrade, 2006, 131.

friendships would strengthen the protective integration of internationals into Australian society.

Oncampus strategies can be divided into three broad groups. First, structured mixing arrangements through early arrival programs, accommodation, service delivery, teaching and learning to encourage cooperation, networks, friendship and mutual learning. Second, altering the competences and sensibilities of internationals to assist them to learn quickly and integrate locally by, for example, providing data, augmenting communication skills and flexibility and building confidence. Third, changing the sensibilities of local teachers and students.

In institutions the first step is to secure collective responsibility[141] across the whole of teaching and service delivery (see chapter 11 for a discussion of structured programs). Buddy systems involving host culture nationals and mentoring by locals or same-culture seniors are used in many Australian institutions,[142] though their impact is normally limited in time; only a minority of students have access to them – the AEI survey found that only 17 per cent of the international students had used a friendship program, mentoring program, buddy or access program – and satisfaction with them is lower than in relation to most other services.[143]

A strong finding of the present study is that cross-cultural student residences can be a favourable and secure setting for cross-cultural friendship. They can augment interaction in several spheres: day-to-day living, including shared eating, recreation and study. They are accessible to social rule setting. Nesdale and Todd noted that 'The effectiveness of intercultural contact is dependent on the extent to which individuals' intercultural knowledge and openness are enhanced'.[144] Cross-cultural residences provide relatively favourable conditions in this regard, but the cost places residential accommodation out of the reach of many or most international and local students. Most Australian universities do not subsidise accommodation and nor do governments. The preferred approach has been to partner commercial operators charging market rents (chapter 7). Again, we found

141 Lee and Rice, 2007; Volet and Tan-Quigley, 1999; Bretag et al., 2002.

142 Bradley, 2000, 430; see also the literature reviewed by Lee and Rice, 2007, 388.

143 AEI, 2007b, 21–2.

144 Nesdale and Todd, 2000, 357.

that a fully commercial industry limits the potential for intercultural education and student security.

Within the classroom, the tendency of students to separate spontaneously into groups makes structured mixing essential at times.[145] Many researchers also emphasise the need for educators to be more culturally aware.[146] Otten urges that 'The individual and collective experience of people from other cultures'[147] should be brought into the learning program. Several researchers emphasised the need to understand students' prior formation, including home curricula and assessment, and styles of learning and class participation.[148] 'Where there is a willingness . . . to learn about the backgrounds of students from other countries, a process of intercultural learning can begin.'[149] The harder question is how to motivate in local students curiosity about internationals. One argument often used is the career-building potential of global learning. This works better with internationals, who are already practising it, than it works with locals. Another argument is the need to welcome visitors. Perhaps students would be more touched by an appeal to their kindness and generosity than by yet another appeal to their self-interest, which they will tend to resist because such appeals are the staple of commercial culture.

Here is one key to the puzzle. We know most internationals expect locals to make the first move to welcome them. This is the politeness regime they know. Hosts welcome guests throughout most of east and southeast Asia, Africa and Latin America. We also know this is not how things work in Australia, New Zealand and the UK, though it has some standing in the USA. So unless guest international students take the initiative and approach host locals, little will happen. The AEI survey brings out the contrasting expectations, and to us suggests two tactics. One is that internationals should be encouraged to approach locals from day one and to self-manage the slights and indifference that result. Above all, persist. The second is that locals should be taught a host–guest welcome regime. If each set of counterintuitive behaviours developed at scale, more favourable conditions would emerge.

145 Volet and Ang, 1998; Ramburuth and McCormick, 2001; Pritchard and Skinner, 2002.

146 See the literature on cosmopolitanism; Purdie et al., 1998.

147 Otten, 2003, 15.

148 Teekens, 2003, 117; see also Wan, 2001, 28; Savicki et al., 2004, 313, and in Australia the contributions of Ninnes et al., 1999; Prescott and Hellsten, 2005; Leask, 2004, 4; Dunn and Wallace, 2006, 362.

149 Robertson et al., 2000, 89; see also Volet and Ang, 1998.

Off campus there is scope for redesign of buildings, public and semipublic urban precincts and services to facilitate the interactions of resident international students with local communities. Research by Fincher and colleagues at the University of Melbourne, released as this book was being completed, discusses the creation of common interactive spaces and forms of housing to encourage greater cultural mixing. The Fincher team points out that half of the residential population of the city of Melbourne are students, many of them internationals. There is scope here for a brilliant 'university quarter' in which security would be achieved less by locking society out and more through supportive community.[150]

The most difficult cross-cultural issue is that of offcampus hate crimes. Internationals need better backup. The ESOS Act does not acknowledge either the specific provision of safety, or the right to freedom from discrimination. It does not require institutions to redress discrimination on campus and it fails to mandate specific police protection by state and territory governments. Ostensibly, international students are here in the same position as citizens, but they are more vulnerable because from time to time they are specifically targeted and because they have less legal standing than citizens. The cross-cultural element in much of the abuse of international students suggests the need for special legal and police provision and for community education that could begin to wind back the violence and abuse perpetuated by some locals, and render local communities as a whole more understanding and supportive.

These and other overarching issues are discussed in the final chapter.

150 Fincher et al., 2009.

PART 4 PROTECTION AND EMPOWERMENT

16 FINAL THOUGHTS

There's no point in coming here if the government is not helping international students. They are charging us double the amount they are charging Australian students... If they are charging us more, then they should give us something for that. They should give attention to our problems.

~ male, 22, business, India

INTRODUCTION: INSECURITY IN THE MARKETPLACE

Though the sanitised report of the Victorian taskforce on international students largely sidestepped the safety issue (chapter 9), six months after its publication the state government had still not responded. Politicians and police still denied racism was an issue.[1] But it was too late. Either the bashings of south Asian students were more frequent or reported more often, which, in policy terms, was the same. By late May 2009 each attack was front page news in Australia, India and around the world.

On Saturday, 23 May 2009, at a party in Melbourne's north four Indian students were attacked with a screwdriver by gate-crashers shouting racist epithets. One student was treated in intensive care. A witness to the assault said, 'We are not safe in this country. They are taking so many fees and taxes from international students, but they are not protecting us'. On 25 May another Indian student was stabbed while walking home. The chief executive of Universities Australia, which represents the vice-chancellors, said, 'We are certainly worried about the impression this may

1 Gilling, 2009.

create among potential students and their parents'. Foreign Minister Stephen Smith said, 'Australia takes very seriously its reputation as a safe destination for Indian students'.[2] On 26 May Minister for Education and Deputy Prime Minister Julia Gillard told parliament that 'International students enrich our society . . . They help us to provide a diverse and rich education experience for Australians'. Nothing was said about enriching the economy, as distinct from society, but the minister had this in mind. 'To remain competitive' Australia would need to 'improve . . . students' living experiences and safety'. Gillard announced that in 2010–11 the ESOS Act would be reviewed, creating the potential to change the regulatory framework.[3] The government also set up a cross-departmental taskforce to manage its political response and a consultative international student taskforce to manage the student critics.

But each effort to regain the status quo was being destabilised by more targeted assaults, more publicity and more fury in India where Prime Minister Kevin Rudd was being burnt in effigy at rallies. India called in the Australian ambassador in Delhi on 29 May. Rudd told Indian Prime Minister Manmohan Singh that everything possible was being done.[4] Stories of attacks on students in Sydney began to surface. On 31 May, a rally organised in Melbourne by the Federation of Indian Students of Australia attracted 2000 demonstrators, some of whom subsequently broke from the march and blockaded a busy Melbourne intersection;18 were arrested.[5] On 4 June conservative columnist Greg Sheridan, under the headline 'Blind eye to racism', blasted Victorian inaction: 'The recent spate of bashings of Indian students in Melbourne is an appalling episode in this nation's history. It is a serious social, educational, diplomatic and probably economic crisis that no one is taking seriously enough', he wrote. 'It is infinitely more important to deal with the problem than try to deal with the perception. Solve the problem and the spin will deal with itself.'[6] Left wing columnist Guy Rundle was in furious agreement:

2 Wade and Das, 2009, 1.
3 Gillard, 2009a.
4 Wade, 2009.
5 May, 2009.
6 Sheridan, 2009, 14.

> Just about the first thing many people worried about during the recent Indian demonstrations was how this would affect our global 'image' and our education 'market' – vile and anti-human sentiments. Whatever the basis we put our immigration policy on, the very worst is to treat people as cash cows to be shipped in, milked and treated with indifference and lack of respect . . . The first and last thing is to stand in solidarity with the Indian students and their demands to be treated as full human beings. Anything else would be, in the face of evil, utter passivity.[7]

For Rundle the underlying issue was 'how globalisation sets mobile people against those who are stuck'. The attackers were victims too. 'All an increasingly marooned white working class' could see, he said, 'was that Chinese and Indians were getting into uni and they weren't'.[8] The Victorian government ordered a token increase in police presence at railway stations in Melbourne's west. The assaults continued. Under 'Bashings undermine image blitz', the *Age* reported on 8 June that, 'as part of the plan to dispel negative perceptions, AEI will distribute 600 000 copies of a *Study in Australia* booklet through Indian newspapers'.[9] The same day Indian students retaliated by stabbing a man who racially abused them, the first reported instance of retaliation.[10] On 12 June the federal minister announced a 'student hotline' to field anonymous complaints and safety tips, and that the review of the ESOS Act would begin earlier, in 2009–10.[11] A Chinese government official expressed concern about the safety of Chinese students. He hoped the Australian government would provide better protection 'to ensure their legitimate rights in Australia'.[12] There were calls for a parliamentary inquiry into the industry.[13]

International student security was now a mainstream political issue, but no remedies were in the offing. There had been no change in the policy settings of an industry that had long swept the issue out of sight. Prospects for change had risen because of south Asian student mobilisation, Indian government pressure and action by other export

7 Rundle, 2009.
8 *ibid.*
9 Flitton et al., 2009, 1.
10 Jackson, 2009.
11 Gillard, 2009b.
12 Maslen, 2009.
13 Connelly, 2009.

nations on safety. It remained to be seen whether the commercial approach would be modified sufficiently to put student security first or whether the marketing machine and its continuous claims about Australia as ever-safe would outlast research, media, protesters and home governments.

ISSUES DISTINCTIVE TO INTERNATIONAL STUDENTS

Cross-border education has many benefits, as the deputy prime minister pointed out in her speech to parliament. It enhances global educational capacity, especially in nations where student growth exceeds the number of places in good institutions. It brings local and global together in export and import nations. It has intercultural potentials.[14] Commercial international education in the UK, Australia and New Zealand contributes to these benefits though they are incidental to its bottom line, especially capacity building. Commercial providers expand quickly.[15] For export nations education export also generates revenues. These larger benefits and costs of international education rightly enter the policy equation. However, they are often marginal to student security and are not interrogated in this book except to the extent that they affect human security. Correspondingly, the book argues that policy and practice should be modified so as to bring security to the fore.

International students are not a weak vulnerable population lacking agency and rights. That is not the connotation intended by the use of the term 'security'.[16] Many internationals perform miracles of rapid complex learning, cultural suturing and personal growth. They want to be free to maintain their traditions and linkages, while adjusting and innovating in their own lives as they choose and fulfilling the requirements of families and education institutions. They find many different ways of doing so.

Students were asked what they would advise other students coming to Australia about the risks and problems of studying and living here.

14 Marginson and Sawir, forthcoming.

15 Vincent-Lancrin, 2007.

16 Thanks to Jenny Lee for underlining this point.

> Come with an open mind. Be willing to adapt and accept the local culture for what it is... You're going to have to change your understanding of what you've grown up with to fit into the culture. You can still have people from your background. You can socialise with them. It's not impossible. But it's important to try and adapt. If you don't, you're the one who will end up losing.
>
> ~ male, 21, medicine, Sri Lanka

> Mainly, to maintain their values in life.
>
> ~ male, 34, business, Sri Lanka

Just as do others, international students need both protection and empowerment. Policy should combine these human needs without one undermining the other (chapter 4). The Anglo-American policy world has lurched from a paternalistic welfare regime to a regime of deregulated markets. Social protection has worn thin; it is less protective today than it was. It provides poor support for those without the private capacity to finance and manage their own security. Meanwhile, individuals have gained more freedom to shape their lives only if they had the financial means, knowledge and communicative capacity to act. Interviews in the present study suggest that few international students have all three. The key to moving forward on security is to rebalance economic markets and human needs so as to enhance both protection and empowerment. This rebalancing is also key to safeguarding the global market position of export nations such as Australia and the UK.

The twin concerns of protection and empowerment suggest the need for better support systems, including a safety net for isolated students and those in crisis, and the more effective empowerment of students to manage their lives and pilot their own course. In both respects international students have similar objectives to locals, but in key areas meeting international student needs invokes distinctive problems and requires tailored policies and support. The legislative framework should address that which is distinctive to internationals. So should oncampus provision. Some universities have taken the mainstreaming of international student services too far. Combining international and local student services makes sense when requirements are common but not when it dissolves staff capacity to accumulate knowledge of and respond to issues specific to internationals.[17]

What are the core issues distinctive to international students? Chapters 12 and 15 argued that the conjunction of communicative competence and effective agency is core to the capacity to cope and relate. Self-determining agency and communicability advance the protective and proactive aspects of security in dealings with authorities, institutions, services and educational processes. The language experiences of most internationals in English-speaking countries are very different to those of locals. This language–agency coupling has recurred through the pages of *International Student Security*. There are also other issues distinctive to international students.

Four groups of questions triggered extensive and passionate responses from interviewees in the present study. The topics were all sensitive, difficult, unresolved and problematic in the international student world: dealing with the immigration department, experiences of isolation and loneliness, crime and safety, which affect a relatively small number, and discrimination and abuse, which affected a larger number. In all these areas the issues for internationals were quite different from those facing locals. Below is some discussion of each area. International students also faced distinctive problems in domains such as housing, work, finance and dealing with universities. We will not take these further here but note that issues of communication, safety and discrimination arose in these areas.

This final chapter focuses on Australia but the larger issues apply in other export nations. It covers three areas. First, the overarching regulatory framework and culture of the education export industry, and the support systems and agencies that could strengthen the legal framework, including student self-organising. We also consider student security where it is weakest, in the broader community beyond education institutions where the legislation, dependent on a government, provider or student nexus, does not effectively reach. Second, the chapter discusses the abovementioned hot topics: language and communication, immigration, loneliness, safety, abuse and discrimination. Third, the chapter suggests a new approach to framing

17 Forbes-Mewett, 2008.

and regulating the international education product. The chapter closes with thoughts on global level regulation.

REREGULATING STUDENT SECURITY

The *2008 Review of Australian Higher Education*[18] found that the quantity and quality of domestic tertiary education in Australia is too dependent on international student revenues (chapter 3). This has driven a volume maximising and minimum cost–service approach. Provider institutions have cut corners on security and other general and academic services with no resultant commercial pay off. The national review said public money sufficient to reduce this dependence is crucial to broadening the approach to international education. Wise words.

More public money is essential to reform of international education, and reform is certainly needed. Our overall finding is that a radical change in the culture and regulation of the Australian industry is essential if security is to be effectively addressed. Regulation has been captured by provider institutions.

The ESOS Act reflects the genesis of the industry in the high time of deregulation and privatisation policy in the 1980s. Minimal requirements were placed on education suppliers to maximise enterprise flexibility, profitability and growth. The present Act still manifests these characteristics and needs to be subjected to the regulation revolution that began in the late 1990s. Deregulation enabled many firms to secure enhanced profit from monopolies or oligopolies secured in the carve-up of public assets. Governments have found it necessary to increase the scale and scope of regulation to control the resultant distortions. In the education sector the leading providers enjoy a natural oligopoly that is historically stable and immune from direct economic sanctions such as bankruptcy. International education has been closely nurtured by the state to protect the global flows of export earnings and skilled human capital. The regulatory state has been captured by producer institutions in the sense warned of by Stigler of the Economics Department at the University of Chicago in the early 1970s.[19] AEI and other institutions have been one voice on all essential

18 Bradley, 2008, 87–107.

19 Stigler, 1971.

matters. The capture has been informal and formal. Formally speaking, AEI has been the regulatory supervisor of the industry as well as the agency chiefly responsible for promoting it at home and abroad. The 2009 government decision to separate the marketing and regulatory functions was right but there is further to go. The regulator must be freed to achieve critical distance from industry interests and the Act amended to ensure that regulation cannot be captured again.

We will not attempt to spell out all the possible inclusions in a new Act, which is a local discussion; changes in some sections were proposed in parts 2 and 3.

While the legal framework is overhauled it will be equally essential to secure a different culture in the industry. In debate about student safety often the reflex first response of industry and government was concern for Australia's market position. The focus was not student harm but on reputation harm, the possibility of Australia being stigmatised as an unsafe place for study and its global profits put at risk. The instinct was to downplay or deny the severity of the problem and deflect attention from student safety and care. This is repugnant on moral grounds. It also makes little commercial sense because it blatantly positions the industry against its clients.

By moving from denial strategy to assurance strategy government and industry can find a way out of this trap without abandoning profitability or market share.

> An assurance strategy . . . attempts to regain trust and confidence by assuring audiences that the crisis was an isolated event that will not reoccur . . . For example, tourist police patrols are stepped up in areas frequented by tourists after crime-related events . . . medical personnel screen arriving passengers at airports following outbreaks of disease. From an impression management perspective, these displays have two interrelated functions: they try to redress the past and extend a promise of a more desirable state in the future.[20]

An assurance strategy includes allocation of resources sufficient to address the problem. This is better understood in UK government circles than elsewhere. In the USA it is understood in education but

20 Nelsen, 2005, 4.

contested in national security circles. Australia has been slower than other countries to abandon denial (chapter 9).

Support structures

To support the framework of a reregulated industry while keeping the providers honest, the government should mandate a body to monitor and advise on the Act from a perspective outside government. This would include representatives of international students, and governments whose nations are major suppliers of students; it could be expected to be strongly student centred. This body would be a check against regulatory capture, provided it operates independently.

Australian institutions are effective in staff development; a professional development program that trains state and institutional staff to meet the human security needs of internationals would make a difference. The program would necessarily emphasise cross-cultural relations (chapter 15). Another support structure for regulation is research on student security issues. We believe that our own work shows the potential of independent research to contribute constructively to the reflexive evolution of the industry. The Australian industry needs to move beyond seeing bearers of uncomfortable news as an enemy to be contained. The UK and the USA better understand the constructive potentials of research.

These support structures would not satisfy all unmet needs. As noted in chapter 11 a difficulty for many students is that when issues arise in their dealings with immigration or the universities they have no point of appeal beyond them. These authorities are terminal. Students cannot secure assistance from authorities that are themselves the problem. International students need places where they can receive understanding and sympathetic support. As one interviewee said:

> There should be some kind of organisation where we can go and just talk it out with somebody. When I was three months here all alone and I was very sad, I really didn't know where to go . . . I didn't want to come to my university.
>
> ~ female, 25, media and communication, India

The need for an independent point of reference and support can be met by two structures. First is a fully resourced national ombudsperson. The ombudsperson for international students in Western

Australia has shown the way. The fact that there is no such national position points to the extent of industry capture. An ombudsperson cannot solve all problems but over time will encourage more user friendly, effective and transparent systems. There may also be a case for the creation of a tagged ombudsperson or helpline in areas where students are isolated from other support systems, for example in relation to exploitation and abuse at work.

The other structure is self-organisation by international students.

Student self-organisation

International student organisations have an indispensable role to play in building and systematising knowledge of student needs and problems, advocating for internationals and building their collective and individual agency. At best they sustain and resource intensive networking on a large scale, bridging between different national and cultural groupings and making issues public.

Relations between international student and general student bodies are a concern. General student unions in Australia often neglect the international students, who constitute one-fifth of all onshore students. When general student unions do include an international office, there are alternating tendencies to marginalise it or attempt to take it over. A more nuanced relationship based on mutual respect and partial autonomy seems hard to secure. General student unions should take more responsibility for building intercultural relations and lifting the global horizons of local students. In Australia in 2009 the National Union of Students (NUS) became more focused when dissatisfied Chinese and Indian international students increasingly operated outside established NUS structures.

National and cultural organisations of international students are desirable and inevitable, but we underline the potential of cosmopolitan organisations that represent all international students at national, regional or local level. When such an organisation is captured by particular groupings and run exclusively in their interests this subtracts from the common social capital. During most of the life of our study the National Liaison Committee (NLC), until 2009 a body affiliated with and funded by NUS, played a constructive role. The NLC was established in the late 1980s in response to Australia's decision to commercialise international education. Initially, its leaders sought to shape the emerging regime by arguing that Australia as a developed country had a moral responsibility to provide education as aid to its developing country neighbours. When this approach failed to secure traction NLC leaders began to emphasise the rights of students as consumers, a message that resonated with some full-fee paying students.

Yet the capacity of NLC leaders to influence education institutions and the state remained constrained because their arguments were primarily underpinned by appeals to morality and fairness at a time when generating economic revenue was the primary driver of international education. While an industrial union can function in such an environment by pressuring employers and governments by threatening to withdraw its members' labour, which puts the accumulation of profits at risk, student unions cannot exert influence in this manner. Even so the analogy with the capital–labour relationship does have some substance in international education markets. Marx observed that the accumulation process led capitalism to create an industrial environment in which the working class grew in size and gained a highly strategic position within the production process. In turn, this development enabled workers to create trade unions, organisers of discontent that became the voice of labour and could help workers win reforms that improved the security of the class. Similarly, the pursuit of profit has induced Australian education providers and their supporters in government to increase the number of international students and position them within an education industry in which they can plausibly threaten the profitability of the sector. These students cannot withdraw from the education system. Once in the host country they are effectively locked in. What they can do is to attack the customer base of their host by convincing or threatening to convince their own governments and/or home communities that the country of education is an undesirable place for study. As a former international student leader says:

> [The] capacity for overseas student leadership to potentially exercise influence on future students' choice of study destination by generating bad publicity, for example, by questioning the inadequacies of quality education and support services offered by Australian institutions, or raising issues such as prevalent racism, cannot be underestimated.[21]

21 Sebastien, 2009, 20.

In 2003 in New Zealand and in 2009 in Australia, Chinese and Indian students and others willing to voice student discontent exercised this power with effect. These developments suggest that when so called on, the export industry anywhere in the world must now address student demands to preserve its market position. This development is of fundamental importance. It is likely to radically transform the dynamics of global student markets and the attention and resources that are accorded to international student security. In Australia international students' direct political action has also driven NUS to re-evaluate how international students are represented and how their capacity to impose costs on the education sector can be mobilised to strengthen the student position more generally. Concomitantly, the leaders and regulators of higher education are striving to develop the structures and practices needed to manage international students' newfound power.

Beyond the campus

International Student Security has repeatedly emphasised the limited capacity of regulation to redress problems beyond the campus. Chapter 4 and the introduction to part 3 raised that problem; it was also discussed in relation to work (chapter 6), housing (chapter 7), safety (chapter 9) and cross-cultural relations (chapter 15). Some issues of health (chapter 8), language (chapter 12) and student isolation (chapter 14) also play out in the general community. It was in the community beyond the campus that all the incidents recounted at the opening of chapter 1 took place. The community also houses part of the support networks of students (chapter 13), though relations with oncampus peers are more important.

Any regulatory framework that works primarily through provider institutions faces this limitation. Even if institutions made a concerted attempt to monitor and track all students when they are off campus they would be limited in what they could observe and do. It is crucial to improve coordination between the universities and other public agencies, especially police, local government and state officials handling housing or tenancy and health services. It is also possible to deploy non-university public agencies and support systems in a more explicit and systematic way. The fact that, under the ESOS Act, the states and territories are agents of the federal government suggests they could be mandated to provide better support in security matters. The states and territories could, for example, be made explicitly responsible for the safety of international students on streets and public transport (chapter 9) by providing more police and transport staff. Whether or not this happens, a key issue in student security remains the need for a substantial increase in resources for police and other agencies to enable them to create permanent divisions that provide for international student needs and build expertise over time.

Another possible regulatory innovation is the creation in the ESOS Act of ombudspersons at state and territory level as well as or instead of national level.

HOT TOPICS

Language

Problems with language and the resultant inhibition of cross-cultural relations and local connectivity create barriers to developing and realising individual capacities. To date there have been two sides in this debate. One is those who argue that no special English language assistance should be provided, that international students should be treated the same as other students and their fitness guaranteed by raising the level of English required at entry. The other is those who tolerate English learning on the job, supported by a mix of foundation or ongoing support programs. As chapter 12 noted practice falls between the two and has the virtues of neither. The provision of support English (especially foundation programs) is inadequate. Advocates of test standards are undermined by the market in which entry standards are often varied downwards to sustain numbers and revenue.

When research found that some graduates were not well versed in English, reforms to immigration requirements in 2007 instituted a mandatory period of work experience and/or further English testing of graduates prior to decisions on permanent residence. However, the debate about English support and the reforms to immigration are yet to address the threshold question. Should competence in English language expression and communication be a formal requirement for degree status? In a tertiary education system that services domestic students this did not arise. In the public debate it is mostly taken for granted that graduates should be fully competent in English. But this is not part of the formal requirement (except in the study of English itself) and is not explicitly taught or resourced. Few tertiary teachers are trained in English language teaching. Academic practice varies. Many insist on native-level quality in students' written work and oral expression. Many others vary the standard of English to fit the students, crediting international students if their progress in the knowledge content of the discipline is good, even if their English expression is not. In this context it is unsurprising many graduates in, for example, technical fields such as accounting, complete their programs without good English language skills, especially the oral skills, which are mostly weaker than written work when the student first arrives.

It is odd to introduce administratively intensive and corruptible systems that demand proof of work experience and English standard after graduation, rather than directly tackle English standards in programs. Mandatory English language standards within degree and diploma programs would improve graduate quality and would meet the expectations of students and their families, for whom preparation in English is often as important as preparation in the discipline or occupation. Because language and communication are central to human security, mandatory English standards would substantially advance the protection and empowerment of international students. On the other hand, to mandate these standards would add to the cost of providing programs and implies a major commitment to academic staff development. On balance we favour such a change. We also recognise that if mandatory English standards were widely implemented the number of international students would fall. Not all providers would want to embrace the change.

Immigration

Despite the Senate committee report (see chapter 10) and a change of government the draconian immigration regime has continued. In the three years to the end of March 2009, 299 international students were detained at Villawood in Sydney and Maribyrnong in Melbourne, the majority (207) for overstaying their visas, some for trivial reasons such as missing relevant correspondence from immigration because of a mix-up over addresses. Most were deported. In early June 2009, five people were in detention. As before some students were held for lengthy periods. The main changes since the Senate committee report was that in 2006–9 only one student was detained for breach of the 20 hours a week work rule.[22]

Detention underscores the routine unpleasantness faced by students when dealing with the immigration department. Australia is the only nation that detains international fee-paying students for breaches of the immigration laws. It does so at scale. Tourism overstays are also subject to investigation, but it is inconceivable that paying customers of the Australian tourist industry would be subject to a general regime based on intimidation and fear. There is something strange at work here, especially given that many students are prospective candidates for immigration status. A large proportion of graduate applicants are accepted by this same immigration department. It is almost as if the immigration department wants to perpetuate the founding transportation regime begun with the British settlement of Australia, in which future citizens endured a period of purgatory before entering the promised land. Detention should be abolished. All would gain if the processing of appeals against visa cancellation was sped up.

Loneliness

Routine reliance on networks for student support is right in principle. Civil supports are better than bureaucratic systems. But it is wrong and does not work to the extent that civil supports are asked to carry full responsibility for student security. This suggests that the optimum student support system deploys professional institutional support as a backup targeted to needs rather than universally. The best solution to the problem of vulnerable isolated students without adequate networks is to conduct network audits (chapter 14) and provide monitoring and pastoral care as required on a one-to-one basis. For the most part existing provision is well short of this but it is routinely provided to students reckoned to be of high value, such as graduate research students. It is provided to some but not all students who come to the attention of university authorities as being at high risk.

22 Healy, 2008.

If an international education program enrolled 10 000 students and appointed full-time staff members who each had mentoring and monitoring responsibilities for 100 students, 100 such staff would be required each year. In practice they would focus most of their time on the small group of students reckoned to be most at risk. If each staff member cost A$100 000 in salary and other costs each year, the approximate cost of employing the monitoring staff would be $10 million, or $1000 per student. Depending on the level of tuition charged, this expenditure would constitute about 5–7 per cent of gross revenues from student fees. Many parents would gladly pay a $1000 premium on top of the existing fee to secure one-to-one pastoral care. But not all parents or all students would want to pay that money, and some students might resent the surveillance.

A cheaper variation of this approach that might reduce resistance to surveillance but might be harder to manage would be to use graduate students in the mentoring and monitoring roles. This would also have the advantage of providing employment for international students on campus at lower cost than if staff were employed in these roles. It would contribute to student safety and student financial security. Another variation would be to increase the number of issues managed in this manner. Financial problems, work issues, housing, health, perhaps language difficulties and problems of academic progress, for example, could be initially tackled this way, though would reduce the number of cases that each staff member could handle and increase total costs.

Safety

Government sponsored international students, such as those entering Australia with AusAID scholarships, have good predeparture information, ongoing briefings and information, as well as ongoing backup services. Private students do not receive this level of support. Their safety would be better protected if they did. At the least all students should be provided with a sustained program of education in relation to safety issues, including full information on the level of risk to their security and what they might do to contain such risk (chapter 9).

Some government and institution-provided predeparture information and education programs have been cut back, which has created an increased reliance on websites and DVDs. But these cannot replace structured educational programs and face-to-face contact. Another problem is that predeparture information flow is often managed by agents. It is well known that agents do not always pass on to their clients all officially mandated information. However, even if the information flow improves new arrival instruction in safety and harm minimisation is needed.

Student housing in the private rental market should be subject to a mandatory university register of landlords and a mandatory register of premises, based on inspection by university housing officers or municipal authorities. Safety and health standards should be implemented on a consistent basis (chapter 7).

Discrimination

Discrimination is hard to address because much of it occurs outside the territory of responsibility of the education providers, and it is difficult to regulate publicly (chapter 15). That said, activation of antidiscrimination legislation for non-citizen international students would be a good start.

There is a primary need for public education campaigns on the benefits of and the need to foster community relationships with international students. This is crucial in Sydney and Melbourne, cities that house the largest numbers of international students. Campaigns need to move beyond vapid feel-good marketing to confront community attitudes in hard areas, such as safety, violence, discrimination and abuse, if they are to add value to international student security. In this and other areas there is potential for an expanded role for municipal authority.

In the long run a lasting improvement in the situation requires the emergence of a more active cosmopolitan outlook in the community. Tolerance at a distance on the basis of separated plural groups has failed to shift racist attitudes among that part of local communities disconnected from globalising culture. Here the universities can lead a more active cosmopolitanism[23] but need to deepen their approach to intercultural learning.

23 Hannerz, 1990.

POSSIBLE FUTURE DIRECTIONS

Product definition and differentiation

At present all Australia institutions formally provide the same product to their international student customers – education or training services as a degree or diploma program. There is no differentiation on the basis of product definition: the product is a one size fits all standard commodity. There is differentiation only on the basis of year length and tuition cost. It is true that there is informal differentiation on the basis of provider status, but the top end market providers (the leading research universities) do not maintain their market position by providing a superior service or education package. They merely leverage their positional advantage in the status market, which is confirmed by university rankings. There are no incentives to develop high quality products. If the top end providers created a superior product this could exercise a gravitational effect by lifting market standards as a whole.

The uniformity of product definition means the market underprovides for need. Most students and their families would support the mandating of English standards as part of the objectives of programs and for it to be included in standard provision (see above). Many if not most students and their families would welcome a comprehensive system of monitoring and back-up pastoral care (see above). Neither need is met. Institutional marketing merely feints in those directions. In practice assessment systems rarely incorporate English standards as an explicit objective. No institution formally contracts to provide or provides one-to-one pastoral coverage for tertiary students. The monoproduct form, together with a universal focus on the minimisation of net costs, precludes provision of these additional services in the commercial market. This is the case not only in Australia but also in the UK and New Zealand.

These services should be made available as part of a set of differentiated products with varying prices. Not one but several standard commodities should be offered. If they were, then providers would have the choice of which product or products they would offer. Buyers would have a larger set of product and price options from which to choose. Product definition and provision could be managed

Table 16.1 Possible range of products in the cross-border education market

Product	Inclusions Discipline and/or vocational program	Guaranteed standard English	One-to-one pastoral care	Tuition cost
ALL PRESENT PROGRAMS	✓			
Type A The full package	✓	✓	✓	More expensive than other options
Type B Language focus	✓	✓		Middle level in cost
Type C Pastoral care focus	✓		✓	Middle level in cost
Type D Program only	✓			Cheaper than other options

by a system of standards setting and regular audit through quality assurance.

If these suggestions were implemented, the portfolio of available products might look like this (table 16.1).

Global regulation

Chapter 4 argued that to treat international students solely as market consumers does not provide for their rights as human beings or students. In Australia these students pay consumption taxes and income tax when their annual income is sufficiently high to trigger the first tax threshold. But they are excluded from social citizenship on grounds that national policy makers have never satisfactorily explained. National governments often retain an interest in the students but they are too far away, which suggests there is a potential role here for global agencies and protections.

At present no global agency or international NGO supports international students or monitors their position. The International Labour Organization (ILO) is interested in immigrants but does not address the needs of international students as workers. The International Organization for Migration ignores them also.

This may change. One possible scenario is the evolution of integrated global and local approaches to issues affecting cross-border populations. Archibugi and Held argue the protection of those who cross borders is increasingly a matter for the world community. They suggest a cosmopolitan transnational organisational model 'in which citizens, wherever they are located in the world, have a voice, input and political representation in international affairs, in parallel with and independently of their own governments'.[24] Our analysis suggests the need for governments and global institutions to accept international students as citizens along such lines instead of treating them just as fee-paying transnational consumers.[25] A standardised set of rights and protections could be devised. Students would have a global point of appeal in relation to problems connected with mobility that arose in jurisdictions other than their national one. While there would be formidable obstacles to overcome before this approach became multilateral it seems likely that international students will enter global governance in future.

Signing off

There are no human ends that we can see. Life goes on. But single projects have an end. In signing off on *International Student Security* we are more convinced than we were at the beginning of the project of the value of this kind of work. Research and the dissemination of knowledge that is linked to public discussion can make a difference, more so when research asks difficult embarrassing questions and foregrounds subaltern voices. The task of critical social research is to rip the mask from comfortable common sense and discover what is really going on. At best such research helps to foster social openness, movement and reflexive change. There is still far to go on the student security issue. Let the discussion become broader, deeper and sharper.

It remains to again thank all who brought us to where we stand, at the finish of the first book from this long project, and to wish our readers well.

Melbourne and Hiroshima
18 September 2009

24 Archibugi and Held, 1995, 5.

25 Thanks to Gaby Ramia for this argument.

REFERENCES

Abbott, M. & Ali, E. (2005). The impact of exchange rate variations and university reputation on the choice of destinations of international students. *Working Paper Series*, No. 13. School of International Studies AIS, St Helens, New Zealand.

Abu-Ein, M. (1995). A Study of the Adjustment Problems of International Students at Texas Southern University. *Dissertation Abstracts International*, 55 (8-A).

Adler, P. (1977). Beyond cultural identity: Reflections upon cultural and multicultural man. In R. Brislin (ed.), *Culture Learning: Concepts, applications and research*. Honolulu: University of Hawai'i Press.

Agron, J. (1996). Seeking shelter. *American School and University*, 68(June), 36–40.

Agron, J. (2006). High life. *American School and University*, 78(June), 41–4.

Ahmed, S. (2002). Racialized bodies. In M. Evans and E. Lee (eds), *Real Bodies: A sociological introduction*, 46–62. New York: Palgrave.

Alexander, H. (2007). Unis open to students who fail English. *Sydney Morning Herald*, 30 January.

Allan, M. (2003). Frontier crossings: Cultural dissonance, intercultural learning and the multicultural personality. *Journal of Research in International Education*, 2(1), 83–110.

Allen, F. & Cole, J. (1987). Foreign student syndrome: Fact or fable?. *Journal of American College Health, 35*, 182–6.

Al-Shehry, A. (1989). *An Investigation of the Financial and Academic Problems Perceived by Saudi Graduate Students While they are Studying in the United States*. PhD, Oregon State University.

Altbach, P. (2004). Higher education crosses borders. *Change*, March–April. Accessed 28 January 2008 at www.bc.edu/bc_org/avp/soe/cihe/publications/pub_pdf/Student%20_flows.

Anderson, P. (2008a). Man bashed just 500m from home. *Herald Sun*, 4 February.

Anderson, P. (2008b). Dr Zhongjun Cao's widow and the love that won't die. *Herald Sun*, 4 February.

Anderson, P., Lawton, L., Rexeisen, R. & Hubbard, A. (2006). Short-term study abroad and intercultural sensitivity: A pilot study. *International Journal of Intercultural Relations*, 30(4), 457–69.

Anderson, V. (2006). Who's Not Integrating? International women speak about New Zealand students. Paper presented at the ISANA International Education Conference, Educate, Advocate, Empower, University of New South Wales, Sydney, 5–8 December.

Andrade, M. (2006). International students in English-speaking universities. *Journal of Research in International Education*, 5(2), 131–54.

Andre, R. (1991). *Positive Solitude: A practical program for mastering loneliness and achieving self-fulfillment*. New York: Harper Collins.

Appadurai, A. (1996). *Modernity at Large: Cultural dimensions of globalization*. Minneapolis: University of Minnesota Press.

Arambewela, R. (2003). *Post-choice Satisfaction of International Postgraduate Students from Asia Studying in Victorian Universities*. PhD, Victoria University, Melbourne.

Archer, W. & Disbury, A. (2008). Perspectives for Students in China, India, Pakistan, Malaysia and Indonesia: Which Countries are Most Attractive for International Study? Results from the 2008 Student Pulse Research Programme. Paper presented to the Australian International Education Conference, Brisbane, 7–10 October.

Archibugi, D. & Held, D. (1995). Editors' introduction. In D. Archibugi and D. Held (eds), *Cosmopolitan Democracy: An agenda for a new world order*, 1–16. Cambridge: Polity Press.

Ari, R. & Hamarta, E. (2000). Investigation of social skills and loneliness level of university students with respect to their personal characteristics. *Selcuk University Journal of Faculty of Education*, 10, 121–34.

Armitage, C. (2008). Chinese students 'deserve better'. *Australian*, 1 October.

Arthur, N. (2004). *Counseling International Students*. New York: Kluwer.

Arup, C., Gahan, P., Howe, J., Johnstone, R., Mitchell, R. & O'Donnell, A. (2006). *Labour Law and Labour Market Regulation*. Sydney: The Federation Press.

Asmar, C. (1999). Scholarship, experience or both?: A developer's approach to cross-cultural teaching. *International Journal for Academic Development*, 4(1), 18–27.

Asmar, C. (2005). Internationalising students: Reassessing diasporic and local student differences. *Studies in Higher Education*, 30(3), 291–309.

Auditor-General (2002). *International Students in Victorian Universities*. Melbourne: Government Printer for the State of Victoria.

Australian Broadcasting Corporation, ABC Radio, *PM* (2005), 27 July.

Australian Bureau of Statistics (ABS) (2009). *International Trade in Goods and Services*, Australia, December 2008. ABS catalogue number 5368.0. Canberra: ABS.

Australian Education International (AEI) (2007a). *2006 International Student Survey: Higher education summary report*. Canberra: AEI.

Australian Education International (2007b). *2006 International Student Survey: Report of the consolidated results from the four education sectors in Australia*. Canberra: AEI.

Australian Education International (2008a). Statistical data on international education. Accessed 31 December 2008 at http://aei.gov.au/AEI/PublicationsAndResearch/Default.htm

Australian Education International (2008b). *2007 Follow-up International Student Survey*. Canberra: AEI.

Australian Federal Police (2005). Murdered university student identified – police pursue suspect. ACT Policing media release, 7 March. Accessed 21 October 2005 at www.afp.gov.au/afp/page/Media/ACTMedia/2005/07032005_078.pdf.

Australian Government, Attorney-General's Department (2005). *Australia's National Framework for Human Rights: National action plan*. Canberra: Commonwealth of Australia.

Australian International Education Foundation, AIEF (1998). *1997 Survey of International Students Studying in Australia*. Canberra: Australian Government Publishing Service (AGPS).

Australian Universities Quality Authority (AUQA) (2007). Accessed 5 March 2007 at www.auqa.edu.au.

Australian Vice-Chancellors' Committee (AVCC) (1994). *Code of Ethical Practice in the Provision of Education of International Students by Australian Higher Education Institutions*. Canberra: AVCC.

Australian Vice-Chancellors' Committee (2005). *Provision of Education to International Students: Code of practice and guidelines for Australian universities*. Canberra: AVCC.

Australian Vice-Chancellors' Committee (2007). *Australian University Student Finances 2006*. Canberra: AVCC.

Baker, M., Roberson, F., Taylor, A. & Doube, L. (1996). *The Labour Market Effects of Overseas Students*. Canberra: AGPS.

Baker, R. & Siryk, B. (1986). Exploratory intervention with scale measuring adjusting to college. *Journal of Counseling Psychology*, 33(1), 31–8.

Baldwin, D. (1997). The concept of security. *Review of International Studies*, 23(1), 5–26.

Baldwin, R. & Cave, M. (1999). Regulatory strategies. In R. Baldwin and M. Cave (eds), *Understanding Regulation: Theory, strategy and practice*. Oxford: Oxford University Press.

Baloglu, M. (2000). Expectations of international students from counselling services. Paper presented at the annual conference of the American Psychological Association, 4–8 August, Washington, DC. ERIC Document, ED 447 372.

Barakat, H. (1988). *A Study of the Problems Facing Foreign Students Attending Michigan State University in 1988*. PhD. East Lansing: Michigan State University.

Barbaret, R., Fisher, B. & Taylor, H. (2004). *University Student Safety in the East Midlands*, Home Office *Online Report* 61/04, London.

Barron, P., Baum, T. & Conway, F. (2007). The learning, living and working issues of international postgraduate students at a Scottish university. *Journal of Hospitality and Tourism Management*, 14(2), 85–101.

Bartram, B. (2007). The sociocultural needs of international students in higher education: A comparison of staff and student views. *Journal of Studies in International Education*, 11(2), 205–14.

Basaran, T. (2008). Security, law, borders: Spaces of exclusion. *International Political Sociology*, 2(4), 339–54.

Bashir, S. (2007). Trends in international trade in education: Implications and options for developing countries. *Education Working Paper Series*, No. 6. Washington, DC: World Bank.

Baumeister, R. & Leary, M. (1995). The need to belong: Desire for interpersonal attachments as a fundamental human motivation. *Psychological Bulletin*, 117(3), 497–529.

Bayliss, D. & Raymond, P. (2004). The link between academic success and L2 proficiency in the context of two professional programs. *Canadian Modern Language Review*, 61(1), 29–51.

BBC *News Monday* (2008). Students suffer in poor housing. Accessed 29 October 2008 at http://news.bbc.co.uk/2/hi/uk_news/education/1625201.stm.

Bebbington, W. (2008). Migration is the Key to our Future. *Australian*, 15 October.

Bekurs, G. (2007). Outsourcing student housing in American community colleges: Problems and prospects. *Community College Journal of Research and Practice*, 31(8), 621–36.

Benabou, R. & Tirole, J. (2005). Belief in a just world and redistributive politics. *NBER Working Paper Series*. Cambridge: National Bureau of Economic Research.

Bennett, M. (1993). Towards ethnorelativism: A developmental model of intercultural sensitivity. In R. Paige (ed.), *Education for the Intercultural Experience*. Yarmouth: Intercultural Press.

Bernstein, N. (2003). Crime database misused for civil issues, suit says. *New York Times*, 17 December.

Berry, J. (1974). Psychological aspects of cultural pluralism. In R. Brislin (ed.), *Topics in Cultural Learning*, 2: 17–22. Honolulu: East–West Centre, Hawai'i University.

Berry, J. (1984). Cultural relations in plural societies. In N. Miller and M. Brewer (eds), *Groups in Contact*, 11–27. San Diego: Academic Press.

Berry, J. (1997). Immigration, acculturation and adaptation. *Applied Psychology*, 46(1), 5–34.

Berry, J., Kim, U., Power, S., Young, M. & Bujaki, M. (1989). Acculturation attitudes in plural societies. *Applied Psychology*, 38(2), 185–206.

Bexley, E., Devlin, M., James, R. & Marginson, S. (2007). Australian University Student Finances 2006. Centre for the Study of Higher Education, University of Melbourne, Australian Vice-Chancellors' Committee.

Bexley, E., Marginson, S. & Wheelahan, L. (2004). *Social Capital in Theory and Practice: The contribution of Victorian tertiary education in the 'new economy' disciplines of business studies and IT*, draft report. Centre for the Study of Higher Education, University of Melbourne, Melbourne.

Bigelow, H. & Kerstjens, M. (2006). Prevention is better than cure: Timely provision of strategies for success to RMIT Business Portfolio students. Paper presented at the ISANA International Education Conference, Educate, Advocate, Empower. University of New South Wales, Sydney, 5–8 December.

Birrell, B. (2006) Implications of low English standards among overseas students at Australian universities. *People and Place*, 14(4), December.

Blakey, M. (1994). Student accommodation. In S. Hazelgrove (ed.), *The Student Experience*. Buckingham: SRHE/Open University Press.

Bochner, S. (1972). Problems in culture learning. In S. Bochner & P. Wicks (eds), *Overseas Students in Australia*. Sydney: UNSW Press.

Bochner, S. (1977). The mediating man and cultural diversity. In R. Brislin (ed.), *Culture Learning: Concepts, applications and research*. Honolulu: University of Hawai'i Press.

Borjas, G. (2002). Rethinking foreign students: A question of the national interest. *National Review*, June 2002. Accessed 28 January 2008 at http://opendoors.iienetwork.org/?p=29516.

Borjas, G. (2006). Immigration in high-skill labor markets: The impact of foreign students on the earnings of doctorates. *NBER Working Paper Series*, Working Paper 12085, National Bureau of Economic Research, Cambridge, Massachusetts.

Borland, H. & Pearce, A. (2002). Identifying key dimensions of language and cultural disadvantage at university. *Australian Review of Applied Linguistics*, 25(2), 101–27.

Borys, S. & Perlman, D. (1985). Gender differences in loneliness. *Personality and Social Psychology Bulletin*, 11(1), 63–74.

Bourdieu, P. (1984). *Distinction: A social critique of the judgment of taste*. London Routledge & Kegan Paul.

Bourdieu, P. (1986). The forms of capital. In J. Richardson (ed.), *Handbook of Theory and Research for the Sociology of Education*, 241–58. Ithaca: Greenwood Press.

Boyer, S. & Sedlacek, W. (1989). Noncognitive predictors of counseling center use by international students. *Journal of Counseling and Development*, 67(7), 404–7.

Bozick, R. (2007). Making it through the first year of college: The role of students' economic resources, employment, and living arrangements. *Sociology of Education*, 80(3), 261–85.

Bradley, D., Chair of Panel (2008). *Review of Australian Higher Education: Final report*. Canberra: Australian Government. Accessed 10 January 2008 at www.deewr.gov.au/HigherEducation/Review/Pages/ReviewofAustralianHigherEducationReport.aspx

Bradley, G. (2000). Responding effectively to the mental health needs of international students. *Higher Education*, 39(3), 417–33.

Brennan, T. (1982). Loneliness at adolescent. In L. Peplau & D. Perlman (eds), *Loneliness: A sourcebook of current theory research and therapy*, 269–90. New York: Wiley-Interscience.

Bretag, T., Horrocks, S. & Smith, J. (2002). Developing classroom practices to support NESB students in information system courses: Some preliminary findings. *International Education Journal*, 3(4), 57–69.

Brinkley, W. (2005). *The Clery Act: An examination of the Clery Act and the influence of the Clery Act on crime statistics reported by four year colleges and universities*. PhD, Central Missouri State University.

Brislin, R. & Yoshida, T. (1994). *Intercultural Communication Training: An introduction*. Thousand Oaks: Sage.

British Council (2006). *Safety First: A personal safety guide for international students.* Accessed 30 September 2008 at www.britishcouncil.org/eumd.

British Council (2007). *Creating Confidence, International student safety survey.* Accessed 30 September 2008 at www.britishcouncil.org/eumd.

Brody, L. (1996). Gender, emotional expression, and parent-child boundaries. In R. Kavanaugh, B. Zimmerberg and S. Fein (eds), *Emotion: Interdisciplinary perspectives*, 139–70. Mahwah: Lawrence Erlbaum.

Brody, L. & Hall, J. (2000). Gender, emotional expression. In M. Lewis and J. Haviland-Jones (eds), *Handbook of Emotions* (2nd edn), 338–49. New York: Guilford.

Brown, R. (2006). International students talk about healthcare and health insurance in the United States. *Student Health Spectrum*, April, 17–23.

Buffington, F. (2008). The third phase of international education; Maintaining the lead. Paper presented at the Australian International Education Conference, Brisbane, 7–10 October.

Bureau of Justice Statistics (2004). *Cross-National Studies in Crime and Justice.* National Criminal Justice Reference Service. Washington, DC: Bureau of Justice.

Burgess, J., Henderson, L. & Strachan, G. (2007). 'I just juggle': Work and family balance in Australian organisations. *Hecate*, 33(1), 94–115.

Burke, G. (1988). How large are the cuts in operating grants per student? *Australian Universities Review*, 31(2).

Butcher, A. & McGrath, T. (2004). International students in New Zealand: Needs and responses. *International Education Journal*, 5(4), 540–51.

Cadieux, R. & Wehrly, B. (1986). Advising and counselling the international student. *New Directions for Student Services*, 36 (Winter), 51–63.

Carr, J., Koyama, M. & Thiagarajan, M. (2003). A women's support group for Asian international students. *Journal of American College Health*, 52(3), 131–4.

Carroll, J. (2005) Lightening the load. Teaching in English, learning in English. In J. Carroll & J. Ryan (eds), *Teaching International Students*, 35–42. London: Routledge.

Carstensen, L. (1995). Evidence for a life-span theory of socio-emotional selectivity. *Current Directions in Psychological Science*, 4(5), 151–6.

Casrnir, F. (1999). Foundations for the study of intercultural communication based on a third-culture building model. *International Journal of Intercultural Relations*, 23(1), 91–116.

Chamberlain, G. (2003). Mandatory Counseling Appears to Reduce Suicide Rate by Half. *Inside Illinois*, 23(3), 333.

Chang, T. & Chang, R. (2004). Counseling and the internet: Asian American and Asian international college students' attitudes towards seeking online professional psychological help. *Journal of College Counselling*, 7, 140–49.

Charbonneau, P., Johnson, L. & Andrey, J. (2006). Characteristics of University student housing and implications for urban redevelopment in mid-sized cities. *Canadian Journal of Urban Research*, 15(2), 278–301.

Chen, C.-H. (2003). *Marketing International Higher Education in Taiwan International Higher Education: Reaching the Taiwanese market*. PhD, Griffith University, Brisbane.

Cheng, E. (1999). *A Study of International Students' Adjustment Problems at the University of South Dakota*. PhD, University of South Dakota, Vermillion.

Chirkov, V., Vansteenkiste, M., Tao, R. & Lynch, M. (2007). The role of self-determined motivation and goals for study abroad in the adaptation of international students. *International Journal of Intercultural Relations*, 31(2), 199–222.

Christie, H., Munro, M. & Rettig, H. (2002). Accommodating Students. *Journal of Youth Studies*, 5(2), 209–35.

Christie, N. & Dinham, S. (1991). Institutional and external influences on social integration in the freshman year. *Journal of Higher Education*, 62(4), 412–36.

Church, A. (1982). Sojourner adjustment. *Psychological Bulletin*, 91(3), 540–72.

City of Melbourne (2006). *International Students Perception Survey – Data Report*. Melbourne: Evaluation Solutions.

Clements, K. (1990). Toward a sociology of security. *Conflict Research Consortium Working Paper*, 90–4. Colorado: University of Colorado.

Cole, J., Allen, F. & Green, J. (1980). Survey of health problems of overseas students. *Social Science & Medicine. Part A: Medical Psychology & Medical Sociology*, 14 (6), 627–31.

Coleman, J. (1988). Social capital in the creation of human capital. *American Journal of Sociology*, 94/Supplement, S95–S120.

Coley, M. (1999). The English language entry requirements of Australian universities for students of non-English-speaking background. *Higher Education Research and Development*, 18(1), 7–17.

College & University Business Officers (CUBO) (2008). *Enhancing the Student Experience*. Nottinghamshire: Masterpoint. Accessed 24 February 2009 at www.cubo.org.uk/publications/.

Collins, F. (2006). Making Asian students, making students Asian: The racialisation of export education in Auckland, New Zealand. *Asia Pacific Viewpoint*, 47(2), 217–34.

Committee on the Health and Safety Implications of Child Labor (CHSICL), National Research Council of Medicine (1998). *Protecting youth at work; Health, safety and development of working children and adolescents in the United States*. Washington, DC: National Academy Press.

Commonwealth of Australia (2009). *Transforming Australia's Higher Education System*. Federal budget statement, 2009–10. Canberra: Commonwealth of Australia.

Connelly, S. (2009). *IEAA calls for Senate Inquiry into the International Education Industry*. 12 June. Melbourne: International Education Association of Australia.

Constantine, M., Anderson, G., Berkel, L., Caldwell, L. & Utsey, S. (2005a). Examining the cultural adjustment experiences of African international college students: A qualitative analysis. *Journal of Counseling Psychology*, 52(1), 57–66.

Constantine, M., Kindaichi, M., Okazaki, S., Gainor, K. & Baden, A. (2005b). A qualitative investigation of the cultural adjustment experiences of Asian international college women. *Cultural Diversity and Ethnic Minority Psychology*, 11(2), 162–75.

Coston, C. (2004). Worries about crime among foreign students studying in the United States. In C. Coston (ed.), *Victimizing Vulnerable Groups. Images of uniquely high-risk crime targets*, 173–93. Westport: Praeger.

Cowling, S., LaJeunesse, R., Mitchell, W. & Watts, M. (2006). Work Choices: The low productivity road to an underclass. *Australian Journal of Social Issues*, 42(2), 221–34.

Cox, J., Babiker, I. & Miller, P. (1981). Psychiatric problems and first year examinations in overseas students at Edinburgh University. *Journal of Adolescence*, 4(3), 261–70.

Crystal, D. (2003). *English as a Global Language*, 2nd edn. Cambridge: Cambridge University Press.

Cullen, M. (2006). Cullen: Future directions for international education. Speech, New Zealand government. *Scoop Independent News*. Accessed 28 January 2008 at www.scoop.co.nz/stories/PA0608/S00544.htm.

Curtis, S. (2000). Undergraduates are now filling the McJobs. *Professional Manager*, May, 44–6.

Curtis, S. & Lucas, R. (2001). A coincidence of needs?: Employers and full-time students. *Employee Relations*, 23(1), 38–54.

Curtis, S. & Williams, J. (2002). The reluctant workforce: Undergraduates' part-time employment. *Education and Training*, 44(1), 5–10.

Cutrona, C. (1982). Transition to college: Loneliness and the process of social adjustment. In L. Peplau and D. Perlman (eds), *Loneliness: A sourcebook of current theory, research and therapy*, 291–309. New York: John Wiley and Sons.

Crump, S. & Slee, R. (2005). Robbing public to pay private? Two cases of refining education infrastructure in Australia. *Journal of Education Policy*, 20(2), 243–58.

Dadfar, S. & Friedlander, M. (1982). Differential attitudes of international students toward seeking professional psychological help. *Journal of Counseling Psychology*, 29(3), 335–8.

Danna, K. & Griffin, R. (1999). Health and wellbeing in the workplace: A review and synthesis of the literature. *Journal of Management*, 25(3), 357–84.

Daroesman, S., Looi, K. & Butler, D. (2005). *Survey of final year international students on their experience of the University of Melbourne*. Melbourne: University Planning Office, University of Melbourne.

Das, S. (2008a). The dollars and the scholars, *Age, Insight*, 26 July.

Das, S. (2008b). Taking it to the Streets, *Age*, 2 May.

Das, S. (2008c). Blitz on 24-hour shop pay levels, *Age*, 16 August.

Davidson, M. (2008). The global market in education is changing beyond recognition. *Guardian*, 4 December.

Day, C. (2006). More homes for students. *Messenger – The City*, Adelaide, 20 December.

Deardorff, D. (2006). Identification and assessment of intercultural competence as a student outcome of internationalization. *Journal of Studies in International Education*, 10(3), 241–66.

Demir, A. & Tarhan, N. (2001). Loneliness and social dissatisfaction in Turkish adolescents. *Journal of Psychology*, 135(1), 113–23.

Deniz, M. (2005). An investigation of social skills and loneliness level of university students with respects to their attachment styles in a sample of Turkish students. *Social Behaviour and Personality*, 1(1). Accessed 6 July at www.findarticles.com/p/articles/mi_qa3852/is_200501/ai_9520806/print

Department of Education, Employment and Workplace Relations (DEEWR) (2007). *National Code of Practice for Registration Authorities and Providers of Education and Training to Overseas Students*, Australian Government. Accessed 5 February 2008 at http://aei.dest.gov.au/AEI/ESOS/NationalCodeOfPractice2007/Default.htm.

Department of Education, Employment and Workplace Relations (DEEWR) (formerly Department of Education, Science and Training) (DEST) (2007, 2009). Selected Higher Education Statistics. Accessed 10 January 2009 at www.dest.gov.au/sectors/higher_education/publications_resources/profiles/students_2005_selected_higher_education_statistics.htm.

Department of Immigration and Citizenship (DIAC) (formerly Department of Immigration, Multicultural and Indigenous Affairs) (DIMIA) (2008). *Conditions for Working While Studying*. Accessed 14 February 2008 at www.immi.gov.au/students/students/working_while_studying/conditions.htm.

Department of Immigration, Multicultural and Indigenous Affairs (DIMIA) (2005). *Migration Series Instruction*, related to the Migration Act 1958 and Migration Regulations 1994 and other related legislation. Canberra: DIMIA.

Depken, C. II (1998). College Demand and the Campus Security Act of 1990, *Atlantic Economic Journal*, 26(3), 326.

Devos, A. (2003). Academic standards, internationalization, and the discursive construction of 'the international student'. *Higher Education Research and Development*, 22(2), 155–66.

de Witt, H. (2008). The dynamics of international student circulation in a global context. Paper presented at the Australian International Education Conference, Brisbane, 7–10 October.

Dex, S. & McCulloch, A. (1995). *Flexible Employment in Britain: A statistical analysis*. Manchester: Equal Opportunities Commission.

Diener, E., Suh, E., Lucas, R. & Smith, H. (1999). Subjective wellbeing: Three decades of progress. *Psychological Bulletin*, 125(2), 276–302.

DiTommaso, E. & Spinner, B. (1997). Social and emotional loneliness: A re-examination of Weiss' typology of loneliness. *Personality and individual differences*, 22(30), 417–27.

Doherty, C. & Singh, P. (2005). How the West is done: Simulating Western pedagogy in a curriculum for Asian international students. In P. Ninnes and M. Hellsten (eds), *Internationalising Higher Education: Critical explorations of pedagogy and policy*, 53–74. Dordrecht: Springer.

Dooey, P. (1999). An investigation into the predictive validity of the IELTS Test as an indicator of future academic success. In K. Martin, N. Stanley and N. Davison (eds), *Teaching in the Disciplines/Learning in Context*, 114–18. Proceedings of the 8th Annual Teaching Learning Forum, University of Western Australia, February 1999.

Dorough, C. (2006). *An Evaluation of Academic and Social Needs of Foreign-born Students at a University and School of Nursing*. PhD, Nova Southeastern University, Florida.

Drill, S. (2006). Students' lives 'at risk'. *Waverley Gazette* (Melbourne), 5 December.

Dunn, J. (2006). *Academic Adjustment of Chinese Graduate Students in U.S. Institutions of Higher Education*. PhD, University of Minnesota.

Dunn, L. & Wallace, M. (2006). Australian academics and transnational teaching: An exploratory study of their preparedness and experiences. *Education Research and Development*, 25(4), 357–69.

Dunn, M. & Sikora, N. (2008). The big squeeze. *Herald Sun*, 17 May.

Education New Zealand (2007). Statistical data on international education. Wellington: Government of New Zealand. Accessed 10 January 2009 at www.educationnz.org.nz/policy.html

Eggens, L., Van Der Werf, M. & Bosker, R. (2008). The influence of personal networks and study support on study attainment of students in university education. *Higher Education*, 55(5), 553–73.

Ehrenberg, I. (2008). Some international student experiences in Australia. Paper presented at the Australian International Education Conference, Brisbane, 7–10 October.

Elder, C. (1993). Language proficiency as a predictor of performance in teacher education. *Melbourne Papers in Language Testing*, 2(1), 68–78.

Ewart, H. (2007). Unis 'demanding' foreign students be passed, Australian Broadcasting Corporation, television program transcript, *7.30 Report*, accessed on 26 February 2007 at www.abc.net.au/7.30/content/2007/s1852629.htm.

Faccenda, J., Watt, B. & Leitch, A. (1994). Pulmonary tuberculosis in overseas students of higher education is increasing in Edinburgh. *Respiratory Medicine*, 88(9), 669–70.

Fallon, F. & Barbara D. (2005). Are our international students using the health system effectively? Paper presented at the ISANA International Education Association 16th International Conference, Internationalisation – Practical Solutions: A trans-Tasman work-out. Christchurch, New Zealand, 29 November–2 December.

Fatima, N. (2001). International female graduate students' perceptions of their adjustment experiences and coping strategies at an urban research university. Paper presented at the American Educational Research Association. Seattle, 10–14 April.

Feast, V. (2002). The impact of IELTS scores on performance at university. *International Education Journal*, 3(4), 70–85.

Feizi, K. (1990). *The Correlation Between Academic Success and Problems Perceived by Graduate International Students*. PhD, University of California, San Francisco.

Fenwick, C. (2006). How low can you go? Minimum working conditions under Australian's new labour laws. *Economic and Labour Relations Review*, 16(2), 85–126.

Fincher, R., Carter, P., Tombesi, P., Shaw, K. & Martel, A. (2009). *Transnational and Temporary: Students, community and place-making in central Melbourne. Final Report.* Melbourne: University of Melbourne.

Finn, P. (2007). Russian medical school imposes curfew for Hitler's birthday. *Washington Post Foreign Service*, 21 April.

Fisher, B. (1995). Crime and fear on campus. *Annals of the American Academy of Political and Social Science*, 539(1), 85–101.

Fisher, B. & Wilkes, A. (2003). A tale of two ivory towers. A comparative analysis of victimization rates and risks between university students in the United States and England. *British Journal of Criminology*, 43(3), 526–45.

Flitton, D., Jackson, A., & Harrison, D. (2009). Bashings undermine image blitz. *Age*, 8 June.

Forbes-Mewett, H. (2008). *Understanding and Managing International Student Security Needs in Australia: The case of Monash University*. PhD, Monash University, Melbourne.

Forbes-Mewett, H., Marginson, S., Nyland, C., Ramia, G. & Sawir, E. (2009). Australian university international student finances *Higher Education Policy*, 22(2), 141–61.

Forbes-Mewett, H. & Nyland, C. (2008). Cultural diversity, relocation, and the security of international students at an internationalised university. *Journal of Studies in International Education*, 12(2), 181–203.

Forde, P. (2000). *Employer Expectations for Business Graduate Communication and Thinking: An investigation conducted in Singapore and Perth*. PhD, Curtin University of Technology, Perth.

Foucault, M. (1986). *The Care of the Self. The history of sexuality, Volume 3*. R. Hurley (trans.). London: Allen Lane.

Foucault, M. (1991). Governmentality. In G. Burchell, C. Gordon and P. Miller (eds), *The Foucault Effect: Studies in governmentality*, 87–104. Hemel Hempstead: Harvester Wheatsheaf.

Furnham, A. & Bochner, S. (1986). *Culture Shock: Psychological reactions to unfamiliar environments*. London: Methuen.

Furnham, A. & Tresize, L. (1983). The mental health of foreign students. *Social Science and Medicine, 17*(6), 365–370.

Guardian (2008) Obama victory 'could affect UK student intake'. *Guardian* (comments from Dominic Scott). Accessed 4 February 2009 at www.e4s.co.uk/news/articles/view/987/job-news-and-information/graduate/Obama-victory-could-affect-UK-student-intake.

Gardner, G. (1962). Cross-cultural communication. *Journal of Social Psychology*, 58(2), 241–56.

Gatfield, T. Barker, M. & Graham, P. (1999). Measuring student quality variables and the implications for management practices in higher education institutions: An Australian and international student perspectives. *Journal of Higher Education Policy and Management*, 21(2), 239–52.

Giddens, A. (1990). *The Consequences of Modernity*. Cambridge: Polity Press.

Gillard, J., Deputy Prime Minister of Australia (2009a). International Education – It's Contribution to Australia. Statement to the Australian Parliament, 26 May. Canberra: DEEWR.

Gillard, J., Deputy Prime Minister of Australia (2009b). International Student Safety and Welfare. Media release, 12 June. Canberra: DEEWR.

Gilling, J. (2009). Violence against Indian students not racially motivated: Victoria Police. *Campus Review*, 25 May.

Ghobrial, S. (2006). The Safety of our International Students – A proactive approach. Paper presented at the ISANA International Education Conference, Educate, Advocate, Empower. University of New South Wales, Sydney, 5–8 December.

Gollust, S., Eisenberg, D. & Golberstein, E. (2008). Prevalence and correlates of self-injury among university students. *Journal of American College Health*, 56(5), 491–9.

Gonzalez, H. (2001) A cross-cultural study of the influence of value orientation, network support and adjustment stresses in help-seeking behaviour. *Journal of the Australian and New Zealand Student Services Association*, 17 (April), 4–18.

Gonzalez, V., Chen, C. & Sanchez, C. (2001). Cultural thinking and discourse organisational patterns influencing writing skills in a Chinese English-as-a-Foreign-Language (EFL) learner. *Bilingual Research Journal*, 25(4), 417–42.

Gooch, L. (2008). The Big Business of Global Education: International students performing well despite struggles. *South China Morning Post*, 11 October.

Gordon, S. (2003). Reaching out to Students. *University Affairs*, 44(10), 22–5.

Gough, D. (2004). Students and 'hard-timers' fill new ghettos – housing crisis. *Age*, 13 November.

Gough, D. (2006). Student housing money snare. *Sunday Age*, 25 June.

Government of Victoria (2008). *Report of the Overseas Student Education Experience taskforce (Victoria)*. Melbourne: Victorian Government.

Grant, B. (2009). Between cents and sensibility. *Age*, 24 August.

Grayson, J. (2005). Language problems of international and domestic ESL students at UBC, York, McGill and Dalhousie, and academic achievement. Paper presented to the 2005 Annual Meeting of the Canadian Society for the Study of Education, London, Ontario.

Green, J. (2002). *Health and Wellness*. Washington, DC: NAFSA, Association of International Educators.

Green, J. (2006). *Insurance: Not just a good idea*. Washington, DC: NAFSA, Association of International Educators.

Green, L., Richardson, D., Lago, T. & Schatten-Jones, E. (2001). Network correlates of social and emotional loneliness in young and older adults. *Personality and Social Psychology Bulletin*, 27(3), 281–8.

Green, S. & Rood, D. (2005). Slipping through the safety net. *Age*, 23 May. Accessed 1 August 2009 at http://infoweb.newsbank.com.ezproxy.lib.monash.edu.au/iw-search/we/InfoWeb?p_product=AUNB&p_theme=aggregated5&p_action=doc&p_docid=10A4297F7A707A89&p_docnum=32&p_queryname=4.

Grinberg, L. & Grinberg, R. (1989). *Psychoanalytic Perspectives on Migration and Exile*. New Haven: Yale University Press.

Gunesch, K. (2004). Education for cosmopolitanism? Cosmopolitanism as a personal cultural identity model for and within international education. *Journal of Research in International Education*, 3(3), 251–75.

Gunningham, N., Kagan, R. & Thornton, D. (2004). Social Licence and Environmental Protection: Why do businesses go beyond compliance. *Law and Social Inquiry*, Spring, 1–25.

Haas, A., Hendin, H. & Mann, J. (2003). Suicide in College Students. *American Behavioural Scientist*, 46(9), 1224–40.

Haas, D. (1979). *Interaction in the Thai Bureaucracy: Structure, culture and social exchange*. Colorado: Westview Press.

Habermas, J. (1987). *The Theory of Communicative Action*. Boston: Beacon Press.

Haley-Lock, A. & Ford Shah, M. (2007). Protecting vulnerable workers: A framework for understanding how public policy and private employers shape the contemporary low-wage work experience. *Families in Society*, 88(3), 485–95.

Hall, S. (2002). Political belonging in a world of multiple identities. In S. Vertovec and R. Cohen (eds), *Conceiving Cosmopolitanism: Theory, context and practice*. Oxford: Oxford University Press.

Hanassah, S. (2006). Diversity, international students and perceived discrimination: Implications for educators and counsellors. *Journal of Studies in International Education*, 10(2), 157–72.

Hanassah, S. & Tidwell, R. (2002). International students in higher education: Identification of needs and implications for policy and practice. *Journal of Studies in International Education*, 6(4), 305–22.

Hannerz, U. (1990). Cosmopolitans and locals in world culture. In M. Featherstone (ed.), *Global Culture: Nationalism, globalisation and modernity*, 237–51. London: Sage.

Harding, L. (2007). Moscow foreign students told to stay in as racist attacks rise over Hitler's birthday. *Guardian*, 20 April.

Harju, B., Long, T., & Allred, L. (1998). Cross-cultural reactions of international students to US health care. *College Student Journal*, 32(1), 112–21.

Harman, G. (2005). Internationalisation of Australian higher education: A critical review of literature and research. In P. Ninnes and M. Hellsten, *Internationalising Higher Education: Critical explorations of pedagogy and policy*, 119–40. Dordrecht: Springer.

Harrison Properties: Student Housing Solutions (2009). Accessed 18 August 2009 at www.harrison-properties.net/hpstudenthousing/.

Harvard Civil Rights Program (2003). *Know Your Rights on Campus: A guide on racial profiling, and hate crime for international students in the United States*, Cambridge. Accessed 2 September 2008 at www.eric.ed.gov/ERICDocs/data/ericdocs2sql/content_storage_01/0000019b/80/1b/15/b8.pdf.

Hayes, G. (2004). *Identifying the Needs of New International Students, at the University of the Cariboo, to Minimise the Risk of Suicide During Transition.* MA, Royal Roads University, Victoria.

Hayes, R. & Lin, H.-R. (1994). Coming to America: Developing social support systems for international students, *Journal of Multicultural Counselling and Development*, 22(1), 7–16.

Head, M. (2005). Making a choice. *New Zealand Listener*, 3402.199. Accessed 14 January 2008 at www.listener.co.nz/issue/3402/features/4385/making_a_choice.html.

Healy, G. (2008). Overseas students held like terrorists. *Australian*, 28 August, 6.

Hegel, G. (2008 [1820]). *Outlines of the Philosophy of Right*. Trans. T.M. Knox, S. Houlgate (ed.). Oxford: Oxford University Press.

Hellsten, M. & Prescott, A. (2004). Learning at university: The international student experience. *International Education Journal*, 5(3), 344–51.

Hill, K., Storch, N. & Lynch, B. (1999). A comparison of IETS and TOEFL as predictors of academic success. In R. Tulloh (ed.), *International English Language Testing System Research Reports*, vol. 2. Canberra: IELTS Australia.

Hodginson, A. & Markey, R. (2007). Industrial Relations Change in the Illawarra Region of NSW: An insight into responses to the Workplace Relations Act. *Australian Bulletin of Labour*, 33(1), 32–60.

Hoffman, D. (2003). Internationalization at home from the inside: Non-native faculty and transformation. *Journal of Studies in International Education*, 7(1), 77–93.

Hofman, W. & Steijn, A. (2003). Students or lower-skilled workers? 'Displacement' at the bottom of the labour market. *Higher Education*, 45(1), 127–46.

Hofstede, G. (1980). *Culture's consequences: International differences in work-related values.* Beverly Hills: Sage.

Hofstede, G. (1998). Think locally, act globally: Cultural constraints in personal management. *Management International Review*, 38(2), 7–26.

Hojat, M. (1982). Psychometric Characteristics of the UCLA Loneliness Scale. *Educational and Psychological Measurement*, 42(3), 917–25.

Holdsworth, C. (2006). Don't you think you're missing out living at home? Student experiences and residential transitions. *Sociological Review*, 54(3), 495–519.

Home Office (2004). *Crimes Against Students: Emerging lessons for reducing student victimization.* Home Office Development and Practice Report. London: Home Office.

Home Office (2007). *University Student Safety*. Accessed 26 January 2009 at www.homeoffice.gov.uk/rds/pdfs2/r194.pdf.

Houston, C. (2003). Rise in overseas students drives building activity. *Age*, 1 June.

Hughes S., White, R. & Hertz, G. (2008). A new technique for mitigating risk on US college campuses. *Journal of Higher Education Policy and Management*, 30(3), 309–18.

Hullett, C. & Witte, K. (2001). Predicting intercultural adaptation and isolation: Using the extended parallel process model to test anxiety/uncertainty management theory. *International Journal of Intercultural Relations*, 25(2), 125–39.

Humfrey, C. (2008). *Towards a New UK Quality Standard for International Student Services: Executive Summary*. Accessed 10 January 2009 at www.ukcisa.org.uk/about/material_media/reports_papers_reviews.php.

Humphrey, R. & McCarthy, P. (1997). High debt and poor housing: A taxing life for contemporary students. *Youth and Policy*, 56, 55–64.

Huntington, S. (1996). *The Clash of Civilizations and the Remaking of World Order*. New York: Simon & Schuster.

Husserl, E. (1936 [1970]). *The Crisis of the European Sciences*. Evanston: Northwestern University Press.

i-Graduate (2008). Perspectives for students in China, India, Pakistan, Malaysia and Indonesia: Which countries are most attractive for international study? Results from the 2008 Student Pulse Research Programme. Paper presented at the Australian International Education Conference, Global Citizens Global Impact, Brisbane Conference and Exhibition Centre. Queensland, 7–10 October.

Illing, D. (2005). The murder that nobody noticed. *Australian*, 16 March.

Industry Commission (1991). *Exports of Education Services*. Canberra: Australian Government Publishing Service.

Institute for International Education (IIE) (2007). Data on international education in the United States. Accessed 12 January 2007 at www.iie.org/.

International Development Program Australia, IDP Education Australia (2007). *Overseas Student Health Cover*. Accessed 26 January 2007 http://students.idp.com/english/essentials/article30.asp.

International Development Program Australia, IDP Education Australia (2008). Interview with representative.

Jackson, A. (2009). Indians 'retaliate' after new attacks. *Age*, 9 June.

Jackson, J. (2005). Regulation of international education: Australia and New Zealand. *Australia & New Zealand Journal of Law and Education*, 10/11(1), 67–82.

Jacob, E. & Greggo, J. (2001). Using counselor training and collaborative programming strategies in working with international students. *Journal of Multicultural Counseling and Development*, 29(1), 73–88.

Janosik, S. & Gregory, D. (2002). The Clery Act and the Views of Campus Law Enforcement Officers. EPI Policy Paper Number 12, Blacksburg, VA: Virginia Polytechnic Institute and State University (Virginia Tech).

Janosik, S. & Plummer, E. (2005). The Clery Act, Campus Safety and the Views of Assault Victim Advocates. *College Student Affairs Journal*, 25(1), 116–31.

Jiang, X. (2005). Globalisation, Internationalisation and the Knowledge Economy in Higher Education: A case study of China and New Zealand. PhD, University of Auckland, Auckland.

Joffe, P. (2008). Personal communication, 15 January.

Johnson, V. (2004). Immigration policy and international students: A threat to national security. *St. John's Journal of Legal Commentary*, 19(1), 25–31.

Jones, P. (2006). *Understanding the International Students' Innovation Decision Process with Particular Reference to International Higher Education Service in Australia and in Thailand*. PhD, Victoria University, Melbourne.

Jong, E. (2006). Health concerns of international students. *Student Health Spectrum*, April, 10–13.

Joyce, S. & Thomson, I. (1999). Earning a Social License to Operate: Social Acceptability and Resource Development in Latin America. *Mining Journal*, 11 June, 441.

Kashima, E. & Loh, E. (2006). International students' acculturation: Effects of international, conational, and local ties and need for closure. *International Journal of Intercultural Relations*, 30(4), 471–85.

Kenyon, E. & Heath, S. (2001). Choosing this life: Narratives of choice among house sharers. *Housing Studies*, 16(5), 619–35.

Kerbaj, R. (2008). Overseas students flout work rules, *Australian*, 11 August.

Kerstjens, M. & Nery, C. (2000). Predictive validity in the IELTS test: A study of the relationship between IELTS scores and students' subsequent academic performance. In R. Tulloh (ed.), *International English Language Testing System Research Reports*, 3, 85–108. Canberra: IELTS Australia.

Kettle, M. (2005). Agency as discursive practice: From 'nobody' to 'somebody' as an international student in Australia. *Asia–Pacific Journal of Education*, 25(1), 45–60.

Kichigina, L. (2008). *Student Perceptions Abroad of the United States*. Accessed 19 July at www.nafsa.org/knowledge_community_network.sec/international_student_3/campus_and_community/practice_resources_16/cultural_programs/student.

Kilinc, A. & Granello, P. (2003). Overall life satisfaction and help seeking attitudes of Turkish college students in the United States: Implications for college counsellors. *Journal of College Counselling*, 6 (March), 56–68.

Kim, Y. (2007). Difficulties in quality doctoral academic advising. *Journal of Research in International Education*, 6(2), 171–93.

Kirkpatrick, L. & Shaver, P. (1992). An attachment-theoretical approach to romantic love and religious beliefs. *Personality and Social Psychology Bulletin*, 18(3), 266–75.

Knight, S. (2001). NUS says students' living conditions are 'second class'. *StudentBMJ*, December, 448.

Knox, H., Savage, M. & Harvey, P. (2006). Social networks and the study of relations: Networks as method, metaphor and form. *Economy and Society*, 35(1), 113–40.

Kramer, A., Prufer-Kramer, L., Stock, C. & Tshiananga, J. (2004). Differences in health determinants between international and domestic students at a German university. *Journal of American College Health*, 53(3), 127–32.

Krause, K-L., Hartley, R., James, R. & McInnis, C. (2005). *The First Year Experience in Australian Universities: Findings from a decade of national studies, Final Report*. Canberra: Department of Education, Science and Training.

Larsen, M. (2008). North American insecurities, fears and anxieties: Educational implications. *Comparative Education*, 44(3), 265–78.

Latour, B. (1999). On recalling actor-network theory. In J. Law and J. Hassard (eds), *Actor Network Theory and After*. Oxford: Blackwell, 15–25.

Leask, B. (2004). *Transnational education and intercultural learning: Reconstructing the off-shore teaching team to enhance internationalisation*. Australian Universities' Quality Agency (AUQA) Occasional Paper. Melbourne: AUQA.

Lebihan, R. (2007). Cash Strapped Unis Offer Land for Digs. *Auskor Australasia*. Accessed 23 March 2088 at www.auskor.net/Student_Accommodation_Industry_Expert_November%2007.

Leder, G. & Forgasz, H. (2004). Australian and international mature students: The daily challenges. *Higher Education Research and Development*, 23(2), 183–98.

Lee, J. (2005). The influence of international student experiences on recommending study in the U.S., Draft paper. Center for the Study of Higher Education, University of Arizona, Tucson.

Lee, J. (2009). Personal communication.

Lee, J., Koeske, G., & Sales, E. (2004). Social support buffering of acculturative stress: A study of mental health symptoms among Korean international students. *International Journal of Intercultural Relations*, 28(5), 399–414.

Lee, J., Maldonado-Maldonado, A. & Rhoades, G. (2006). The political economy of international student flows: Patterns, ideas and propositions. In J. Smart (ed.), *Higher Education: Handbook of theory and research, Volume XXI*, 545–90. Dordrecht: Springer.

Lee, J. & Rice, C. (2007). Welcome to America? International student perceptions of discrimination. *Higher Education*, 53(3), 381–409.

Le Grand, J. & Bartlett, W. (1993). *Quasi-Markets and Social Policy*. London: Macmillan.

Leonard, D., Pelletier, C. & Morley, L. (2003). *The Experiences of International Students in UK Higher Education: A review of unpublished research*. London: UKCOSA.

Leong, C.-H. & Ward, C. (2000). Identity conflict in sojourners. *International Journal of intercultural Relations*, 24(6), 763–76.

Leong, F. & Sedlacek, W. (1986). A comparison of international students and U.S. students' preference for help sources. *Journal of College Personal*, 27, 426–30.

Leung, C.-H. (2001). The psychosocial adaptation of overseas and migrant students in Australia. *International Journal of Psychology*, 36(4), 251–9.

Levett, C. (2008). Lesson in fear: Chinese students plagued by crime. *Sydney Morning Herald*, 8 August.

Leviyeva, E. (2005). The changing face of the Russian democracy: Racism and xenophobia in Russia – foreign students under attack in Russia and the U.S. *Rutgers Race & The Law Review*, 7, 229–88.

Lewis, N. (2005). Code of Practice for the pastoral care of international students: Making a globalising industry in New Zealand. *Globalisation, Societies and Education*, 3(1), 5–47.

Li, A. & Gasser, M. (2005). Predicting Asian international students' sociocultural adjustment: A test of two mediation models. *International Journal of intercultural Relations*, 29(5), 561–76.

Li, M. (2007). The Impact of the Media on the New Zealand Export Education Industry. Paper presented at the International Business in the Asia–Pacific Regions: Challenges, opportunities and strategies for research and practice, University of International Business and Economics, Beijing, 22–4 September.

Li, M. (2008). Keeping them safe: A review of Chinese students' safety issues in New Zealand. Paper presented at the ANZCA08 Conference, Power and Place. *Wellington*, July.

Li, M., Baker, T. & Marshall, K. (2002). Mismatched expectations: A case study of Asian students in New Zealand. *New Zealand Journal of Applied Business Research*, 1(1), 1–23.

Li, R. & Kaye, M. (1998). Understanding overseas students' concerns and problems. *Journal of Higher Education Policy and Management*, 20(1), 41–50.

Lin, J. & Yi, J. (1997). Asian international students' adjustment: Issues and program suggestions. *College Student Journal*, 31(4), 473–80.

Lindsey, T. (2009). Learn the lingo to earn from Asia. *Australian*, 26 August.

Lipsett, A. (2009). University lecturers may boycott immigration 'snooper' rules on foreign students. *Guardian*, 25 May. Accessed 28 May at www.guardian.co.uk.

Long, M. & Hayden, M. (2001). *Paying Their Way – A survey of Australian undergraduate university student finances, 2000*. Australian Vice-Chancellors' Committee, Council of Australia's University Presidents, Canberra.

Loughborough University Careers Service (2004). Recruiting International Students and Graduates: Survey of employers project report. Accessed on 11 August 2009 at www.careers.iboro.ac.uk/pdf/internationalsurvey2004.pdf.

Lucas, R. (1997). Youth, gender and part-time work – students in the labour process. *Work, Employment and Society*, 11(4), 595–614.

Lunt, P.(1991). The perceived causal structure of loneliness. *Journal of Personality and Social Psychology*, 61(1), 26–34.

MacIntyre, P., Clément, R., Dörnyei, Z. & Noels, K. (1998). Conceptualizing willingness to communicate in a L2: A situational model of L2 confidence and affiliation. *Modern Language Journal*, 82, 545–62.

MacWilliams, B. (2006). Dangerous Times in Russia. *Chronicle of Higher Education*, 52(44). Accessed 10 January 2009 at http://chronicle.com/weekly/v52/i44/44a04001.htm.

Madsen, C. (2006). *Crime Rates Around the World*. Nation Master. Accessed 14 September 2008 at www.nationmaster.com/article/Crime-Rates-Around-the-World.

Malcolm, I. & McGregor, A. (1995). *Worlds apart. An investigation of linguistic and cultural factors affecting communication between NESB and Edith Cowan University Staff*. Western Australia: Centre for Applied Language Research, Edith Cowan University.

Malkin, M. (2004). *Invasion: How America still welcomes terrorists, criminals, and other foreign menaces to our shores*. Washington, DC: Regnery Publishing.

Manthei, R. & Gilmore, A. (2005). The effect of paid employment on university students' lives. *Education & Training*, 47(2/3), 202–15.

Marginson, S. (1997). *Markets in Education*. Sydney: Allen & Unwin.

Marginson, S. (2007). Global position and position-taking: The case of Australia. *Journal of Studies in International Education*, 11(1), 5–32.

Marginson, S. (2009). Student sojourners and creative cosmopolitans. In M. Peters, S. Marginson and P. Murphy, *Creativity in the Global Knowledge Economy*, 217–55. New York: Peter Lang.

Marginson, S. & Considine, M. (2000). *The Enterprise University: Power, governance and reinvention in Australia*. Cambridge: Cambridge University press.

Marginson, S. & Eijkman, H. (2007). *International Education: Financial and organisational impacts in Australian universities*. Report prepared for the Monash Institute for the Study of Global Movements. Melbourne: Monash University. Accessed 1 January 2008 at www.cshe.unimelb.edu.au/people/staff_pages/Marginson/Marginson.html.

Marginson, S., Murphy, P. & Peters, M. (2010). *Global Creation: Space, mobility and synchrony in the age of the knowledge economy*. New York: Peter Lang.

Marginson, S. & Sawir, E. (forthcoming). *Intercultural Education and Self-Formation*.

Marginson, S. & Van der Wende, M. (2009). The new global landscape of nations and institutions. In Organization for Economic Cooperation and Development, Center for Educational Research and Innovation, *Higher Education to 2030. Volume 2: Globalization*, 17–62. Paris: OECD.

Maris, R., Berman, A. & Silverman, M. (2000). *Comprehensive textbook of suicidology*. New York: Guildford Press.

Marshall, M. (2007). Slum-type housing springs up. *Preston Post Times* and *Northcote Leader*, 5 December.

Maslen, G. (2009). Australia: Racial attacks hit billion dollar industry. *University World News*, 7 June. Accessed 8 June at www.universityworldnews.com.

Mathews, G. (2006). No Choices. *Multinational Monitor*, 27(4), 10–16.

Matsumoto, D., LeRoux, J., Bernhard, R. & Gray, H. (2004). Unraveling the psychological correlates of intercultural adjustment potential. *International Journal of Intercultural Relations*, 28(3–4), 281–309.

May, A. (2009). Roundtable proposed as India calls Australian racist. *Campus Review*, 1 June.

Mazzarol, T. (1997). *An Examination of the Factors Critical to the Establishment and Maintenance of Competitive Advantage for Education Services Enterprises within International Markets*. PhD, Curtin University of Technology, Perth.

Mazzarol, T. & Soutar, G. (2001). *The Global Market for Higher Education*. Cheltenham: Edward Elgar.

Mazzarol, T. & Soutar, G. (2002). 'Push–pull' factors influencing international student destination choice. *International Journal of Educational Management*, 16(2), 82–90.

Mazzarol, T., Soutar, G., Smart, D. & Choo, S. (2001). *Perceptions, information and choice: Understanding how Chinese students select a country for overseas study*. Canberra: Australian Education International, Commonwealth of Australia.

McCarthy, J. (2007). Powers to raid sought – Crackdown likely on boarding houses. *Courier-Mail*, November 24.

McCluskey-Titus, P. & Oliver, R. (2001). The relationship between community development and academic achievement of undergraduate students in residence halls. *College Student Affairs Journal*, 20(2), 12–21.

McDonald, P., Bailey, J., Oliver, D. & Pini, B. (2007). Compounding vulnerability? Young workers' employment concerns and the anticipated impact of the WorkChoices Act. *Australian Bulletin of Labour*, 33(1), 60–89.

McGrath, T., Beaven, S., Chong, J. & Eriquez, R. (2008). Connecting international students, domestic students and community people in campus, classroom and community situations. Paper presented to The 19th ISANA International Education Conference, Auckland, 2–5 December.

McGrath, T. & Hooker, S. (2006). International students in New Zealand: Responses and barriers to intercultural interaction opportunities. Paper presented at the ISANA International Education Conference – Educate, Advocate, Empower, University of New South Wales, Sydney, 5–8 December.

McInnis, C. & Hartley, R. (2002). *Managing Study and Work, The impact of full-time study and paid work on the undergraduate experience in Australian Universities*. Canberra: Evaluations and Investigations Programme, Commonwealth Department of Science, Education and Training.

McLean, P. & Ransom, L. (2005). Building intercultural competence. In J. Carroll and J. Ryan (eds), *Teaching International Students*, 45–62. London: Routledge.

McNeal, L. (2007). Clery Act: Road to compliance. *Journal of Personal Evaluation in Education*, 19(2), 105–13.

McRae, C. (2007). *Report on Issues Affecting International Students*. Melbourne: Cambridge International College.

Medew, J. (2008). Neighbour: 'We just couldn't help him'. *Age*, 4 January.

Megarrity, L. (2007a). Regional goodwill, sensibly priced: Commonwealth policies towards Colombo Plan scholars and private overseas students, 1945–72. *Australian Historical Studies*, 38(129), 88–105.

Megarrity, L. (2007b). A highly regulated 'free market': Commonwealth policies on private overseas students from 1974 to 2005. *Australian Journal of Education*, 51 (1), 39–53.

Meiras, S. (2004). International education in Australian universities: Understandings, dimensions and problems. *Journal of Higher Education Policy and Management*, 26(3), 371–80.

Melbourne Institute of Applied Economic and Social Research (MIAESR) (2006). Poverty Lines: Australia. March Quarter 2006. Accessed 1 March 2009 at www.melbourneinstitute.com/labour/inequality/poverty/Poverty%20lines%20Australia%20March%202008.pdfa.

Merrick, B. (2007). Preparation for success: Key themes in the Prime Minister's Initiative for International Education (UK). Paper presented at the 2007 ISANA International Conference – Student success in international education, Stamford Grand, Adelaide, 27–30 November.

Mill, J.S. (1947). *On Liberty*. New York: Appleton-Century-Crofts.

Miller, A. (2007). Students caught in 'death traps'. *Waverley Gazette*, Melbourne, 3 April.

Miller, D. (1987). International students: Their effect on college health education. *Journal of Health Education*, 18(2), 26–8.

Mische, A. & White, H. (1998). Between conversation and situation: Public switching dynamics across network domains. *Social Research*, 65, 695–724.

Misra, R. & Castillo, L. (2004). Academic stress among college students: Comparison of American and international students. *International Journal of Stress Management*, 11(2), 132–48.

Misra, S. (1999). Cross-cultural variation in loneliness: Implications for marketing. CCRS Proceedings, 1999. Accessed 19 August 2005 at http://marketing.byu.edu/htmlpages/ccrs/proceedings99/misra 1.htm.

Mitchell, W., Juniper, J. & Myers, J. (2006). The dynamics of job creation and job destruction in Australia. *Australian Journal of Social Issues*, 41(2), 247–61.

Moore, J. & Constantine, M. (2005). Development and initial validation of the collectivist coping styles measure with African, Asian, and Latin American international students. *Journal of Mental Health Counseling*, 27(4), 329–47.

Morgan, D. & McDowell, L. (1979). *Patterns of Residence: Costs and options in student housing*. Guilford: The Society for Research into Higher Education.

Mori, S. (2000). Addressing the mental health concerns of international students. *Journal of Counseling and Development*, 78(2), 137–44.

Moroi, K. (1986). Loneliness induced by situational changes in live of freshmen. *Japanese Journal of Experimental Social Psychology*, 25, 115–25.

Moynihan, S. (2003). Green Thumbs Up to Escaping a Criminal Record. *Sunday Age*, 9 November.

Murphy, P. (forthcoming). The world circumference. In S. Marginson, P. Murphy and M. Peters (forthcoming), *Global Creation: Space, mobility and synchrony in the age of the knowledge economy*. New York: Peter Lang.

Murphy-Shigematsu, S. (2002). Psychological barriers for international students in Japan. *International Journal for the Advancement of Counselling*, 24(1), 19–30.

Naidoo, R. & Jamieson, I. (2005). Knowledge in the marketplace: The global commodification of teaching and learning in higher education. In P. Ninnes and M. Hellsten (eds), *Internationalising Higher Education: Critical explorations of pedagogy and policy*, 37–52. Dordrecht: Springer.

Naidoo, V. (2006). International education: A tertiary-level industry update. *Journal of Research in International Education*, 5(3), 323–45.

Nasrin, F. (2001). International female graduate students' perceptions of their adjustment experiences and coping strategies at an urban research university. Eric Document, ED 452 336.

National Association of Foreign Student Advisors (NAFSA): Association of International Educators (2006). *Could Foreign Student Numbers Be Headed for a Rebound?* Accessed 14 March 2009 at www.nafsa.org/press_releases.sec/press_releases.pg/06enrollsurveyre.

National Association of Foreign Student Advisors (NAFSA): Association of International Educators (2008) NAFSA Letter Urges 2008 Presidential Candidates to Leverage International Education to Meet Public Diplomacy and Foreign Policy Challenges. Accessed 14 March 2009 at www.prnewswire.com/cgi-bin/stories.pl?ACCT=104&STORY=/www/story/11–09–2007/0004701911&EDATE=.

National Liaison Committee (NLC) (2004). *Submission for the ESOS Act Evaluation*. Melbourne: NLC. Obtained by writing to research@nlc.edu.au. Not posted on NLC website but other and related documents can be accessed at www.nlc.edu.au/main/nlc_submissions.html [9 February 2008].

National Union of Students/Unipol (2007). *Accommodation Costs Survey 2006/07*. London: National Union of Students.

Neill, N., Mulholland, G., Ross, V. & Leckey, J. (2004). The influence of part-time work on student placement. *Journal of Further and Higher Education*, 28(2), 123–37.

Nelson, B. (2005). Using Theories of Stigma Management and Impression Management to Understand and Repair Destination Image Following Tourism Crises. *Best Education Network Think Tank on Managing Risk and Crisis for Sustainable Tourism: Research and Innovation*, University of the West Indies, Kingston, 6–19 June.

Nesadurai, H. (2005). *Conceptualizing Economic Security in an Era of Globalization: What does the East Asian experience reveal?* Coventry: Centre for the Study of Globalization and Regionalization, University of Warwick.

Nesdale, D. & Todd, P. (2000). Effect of contact on intercultural acceptance: a field study. *International Journal of Intercultural Relations*, 24(3), 341–60.

Ninnes, P. (2005). Higher education engaging with the 'developing' world: The case of the virtual Colombo Plan. In P. Ninnes and M. Hellsten (eds), *Internationalising Higher Education: Critical explorations of pedagogy and policy*, 141–58. Dordrecht: Springer.

Ninnes, P., Aitchison, C. & Kalos, S. (1999). Challenges to stereotypes of international students' prior education experience: Undergraduate education in India. *Higher Education Research and Development*, 18(3), 323–42.

Norton, D. (2000). Tuberculosis screening for international students. *Journal of American College Health*, 48(4), 187.

Nurmi, J., Toivonen, S., Salmera-Aro, K. & Eronen, A. (1997). Social strategies and loneliness. *Journal of Social Psychology*, 137(6), 764–78.

Nyland, C. (2008). Don't treat them like cash cows. *Herald Sun*, 16 June.

Nyland, C., Forbes-Mewett, H., Marginson, S., Ramia, G., Sawir, L. & Smith, S. (2009). International Student Workers in Australia: A new vulnerable workforce. *Journal of Education and Work*, 22(1), 1–14.

Ogunyieka, G. (1983). *Self Perceived Problems of Nigerian Students at Southeastern University*. PhD, George Washington University, Washington, DC.

Olson, C. & Kroeger, K. (2001). Global competency and intercultural sensitivity. *Journal of Studies in International Education*, 5(2), 116–37.

Ong, D. (2006). *Study–work–life Balance of International Students, The case of Monash University*. Honours thesis, Monash University, Melbourne.

Organisation for Economic Cooperation and Development (OECD) (2001) *The Well-being of Nations: The role of human and social capital*. Paris: OECD.

Organisation for Economic Cooperation and Development, OECD (2004). *Internationalisation and Trade in Higher Education*. Paris: OECD.

Organisation for Economic Cooperation and Development (OECD) (2005, 2006, 2007a, 2008a). *Education at a Glance*. Paris: OECD.

Organisation for Economic Cooperation and Development (OECD) (2007b). *Science and Technology Indicators*. Paris: OECD.

Organisation for Economic Cooperation and Development (OECD) (2008b). *Tertiary Education for the Knowledge Society: OECD thematic review of tertiary education*. Paris: OECD.

Organisation for Economic Cooperation and Development (OECD) and World Bank (2007). *Cross-border Tertiary Education: A way towards capacity development* Paris: OECD.

Osterman, K. (2001). Students' need for belonging in the school community. *Review of Educational Research*, 70(3), 323–67.

Otten, M. (2003). Intercultural learning and diversity in higher education. *Journal of Studies in International Education*, 7(1), 12–26.

Overseas Student Health Cover Forum (OSHC) Forum (2006). *OHSC – Best Practice and Practical Solutions*. Record of a meeting held in Canberra, 31 August, co-hosted by the Australian Department of Health and Ageing, Department of Immigration and Multicultural Affairs, Department of Education, Science and Training, and the Australian Vice-Chancellors' Committee.

Paladino, D. (2008). Comprehensive college student suicide assessment: Application of the basic ID. *Journal of American College Health*, 56(6), 643–50.

Paloutzian, R. & Ellison, C. (1982). Loneliness, spiritual wellbeing and the quality of life. In L. Peplau and D. Perlman (eds), *Loneliness: A sourcebook of current theory*, research and therapy, 224–37. New York: John Wiley and Sons.

Pantelidis, U. (1999). Meeting the language needs of tertiary NESB students. *Australian Journal of Language and Literacy*, 22(1), 60–76.

Parker, C., Scott, C., Lacey, N. & Braithwaite, J. (2004). Introduction, in C. Parker, C. Scott, N. Lacey and J. Braithwaite (eds), *Regulating Law*. Oxford: Oxford University Press.

Patiniotis, J. & Holdsworth, C. (2005). Seize that chance! Leaving home and transitions to higher education. *Journal of Youth Studies*, 8(1), 81–95.

Pedersen, P. (1991). Counselling international students. *Counseling Psychologist*, 19(10), 10–58.

Peplau, L. & Perlman, D. (1982). Perspectives on loneliness. In L. Peplau and D. Perlman (eds), *Loneliness: A sourcebook of current theory, research and therapy*, 1–20. New York: John Wiley and Sons.

Pergament, K. (1990). God help me: Toward a theoretical framework of coping for the psychology of religion. *Research in Social Scientific Study of Religion, 2*, 195–224.

Perkins, M. (2008). Indian students die in house fire, *Age*, 3 January.

Perrucci, R. & Hu, H. (1995). Satisfaction with social and educational experiences among international graduate students. *Research in Higher Education*, 36(4), 491–508.

Petersen, R., Moracco, K., Goldstein, K. & Andersen Clark, K. (2004). Moving Beyond Disclosure: Women's perspectives on barriers and motivators to seeking assistance for intimate partner violence. *Women & Health*, 40(3), 65–80.

Pinkerton, M. (2006) *U.S. Public Image: A study of the perceptions of international students from predominantly Muslim nations*. PhD, University of Texas, Arlington.

Pocock, B. & Masterman-Smith, H. (2005). WorkChoices and women workers. *Journal of Australian Political Economy*, 56 (December). Accessed 27 January 2009 at www.jape.org.

Polanyi, K. (1944). *The Great Transformation: The political and economic origins of our time*. Boston: Beacon Press.

Poole, D. (2000). *The Strategic Management of International Entrepreneurial Activities at Australian Universities*. PhD, University of Technology, Sydney.

Powell, M. (2007). *Understanding the Mixed Economy of Welfare*. Bristol: The Policy Press.

Power, C. & McKenna, T. (2005). International student housing. More than just a market. In R. Adams and K. White (eds), *Internationalising Education: Risks and returns, proceedings of 2003 Victoria University/UCLA Conference, 216–27*. Melbourne: Victoria University.

Poyrazli, S., Arbona, C., Bullington, R. & Pisecco, S. (2001). Adjustment issues of Turkish college students studying in the United States. *College Student Journal*, 35(1), 52–62.

Poyrazli, S. & Grahame, K. (2007). Barriers to adjustment: Needs of international students within a semi-urban campus community. *Journal of Instructional Psychology*, 34(1), 28–45.

Prescott, A. & Hellstén, M. (2005). Hanging together with non-native speakers: The international student transition experience. In P. Ninnes and M. Hellsten (eds), *Internationalizing Higher Education: Critical explorations of pedagogy and policy*, 75–95. Dordrecht: Springer.

Pritchard, R. & Skinner, B. (2002). Cross-cultural partnerships between home and international students. *Journal of Studies in International Education*, 6(4), 323–54.

Productivity Commission (2003). Social Capital: Reviewing the concept and its policy implications. Research Paper, AusInfo, Canberra.

Purdie, N., O'Donoghue, T. & da Silva, R. (1998). Goals and coping behaviours: The development of a model for international students. *Queensland Journal of Educational Research*, 14(2), 29–56.

Putnam, R. (2000). *Bowling Alone: The collapse of American community*. New York: Simon & Schuster.

Quidington, P. (2008). Come together: An Asian Bologna? *Campus Review*, 18(46), 8–9.

Rahman, O. & Rollock, D. (2004). Acculturation, competence, and mental health among South Asian students in the United States. *Journal of Multicultural Counseling and Development*, 32(3), 130–42.

Ramburuth, P. & McCormick, J. (2001). Learning diversity in higher education: A comparative study of Asian international and Australian students. *Higher Education*, 42(3), 333–50.

Ramsay, S., Barker, M. & Jones, E. (1999). Academic adjustment and learning processes: A comparison of international and local students in first-year university. *Higher Education Research and Development*, 18(1), 129–44.

Redmond, M. (2000). Cultural distance as a mediating factor between stress and intercultural competence. *International Journal of Intercultural Relations*, 24(1), 151–9.

Reeves, S. & Henry, C. (2000). Dietary change, energy balance and body weight regulation among migrating students. *International Journal of Food Sciences & Nutrition*, 51(6), 429–39.

Rennie, R. (2008). Killers sentenced over 'curry bashing'. *Herald Sun*, 22 December.

Reserve Bank of Australia (2008). Australia's exports of education services. *Reserve Bank Bulletin*, June.

Rivera, L. (2008). Managing 'Spoiled' National Identity: War, tourism, and memory in Croatia. *American Sociological Review*, 73(4), 613–34.

Rizvi, F. (2005). Identity, culture and cosmopolitan futures. *Higher Education Policy*, 18, 331–9.

Rizvi, F. (2008). Epistemic virtues and cosmopolitan learning. *Australian Educational Researcher*, 35(1), 17–35.

Robertson, M., Line, M., Jones, S. & Thomas, S. (2000). International students, learning environments and perceptions: A case study using the Delphi technique. *Higher Education Research and Development*, 19(1), 89–102.

Rogers, J. & Larsen, D. (2002). *Optimizing Health Care*. Washington, DC: NAFSA, Association of International Educators.

Rokach, A. (1988). The experience of loneliness: A tri-level model. *Journal of Psychology*, 122(6), 531–44.

Rokach, A. (1989). Antecedents of loneliness: A factorial analysis. *Journal of Psychology*, 123(4), 369–84.

Rokach, A. (1990). Surviving and coping with loneliness. *Journal of Psychology*, 124(1), 39–54.

Rokach, A. (1999). Cultural background and coping with loneliness. *Journal of Psychology*, 133(2), 217–29.

Rokach, A. & Brock, H. (1998). Coping with loneliness. *Journal of Psychology*, 132(1), 107–27.

Rose, N. (1999). *Powers of Freedom: Reframing political thought.* Cambridge: Cambridge University Press.

Rosenberg, M., Schooler, C., Schoenabch, C. & Rosenberg, F. (1995). Global self-esteem and specific self-esteem: Different concepts, different outcomes. *American Sociological Review*, 60(1), 141–56.

Rosenthal, D., Russell, J. & Thomson, G. (2006). *A Growing Experience: The health and the wealth-being of international students at the University of Melbourne*. Melbourne: University of Melbourne.

Rosenthal, D., Russell, J. & Thomson, G. (2008a). The health and wellbeing of international students at an Australian university, *Higher Education*, 55(1), 51–67.

Rosenthal, D., Russell, J. & Thomson, G. (2008b). International student use of university health and counselling services. *Higher Education*, 56(1), 59–75.

Ross, J. (2008). International students: Shield them or yield them. *Campus Review*, 18(25), 1, 4.

Ross, N. (2008). Two teenagers jailed for bashing death of Dr Zhongjun Cao. *Herald Sun*, 22 December.

Rosser, V., Hermsen, J., Mamiseishvili, K. & Wood, M. (2007). A national study examining the impact of SEVIS on international student and scholar advisers. *Higher Education*, 54(4), 525–42.

Rost, M. (2005). Submission to Senate Legal and Constitutional References Committee Inquiry into the Administration and Operation of the Migration Act 1958. Accessed 12 February 2008 at www.aph.gov.au/Senate/committee/legcon_ctte/migration/submissions/sublist.htm.

Rout, M. (2008a). Senseless death of a kind, gentle academic. *Australian*, 19 January.

Rout, M. (2008b). Education trumps tourism. *Australian*, 6 February.

Rubenstein, C. & Shaver, P. (1982). The experience of loneliness. In L. Peplau and D. Perlman (eds), *Loneliness: A sourcebook of current theory, research and therapy*, 206–23. New York: John Wiley and Sons.

Rugg, J., Rhodes, D. & Jones, A. (2000). *The Nature and Impact of Student Demand on Housing Markets*. London: Joseph Rowntree Foundation.

Rundle, G. (2009). Indians passive by nature? Don't add insult to injury. *Age*, 7 June.

Russell, D., Cutrona, D., Rose, J. & Yurko, K. (1984). Social and emotional loneliness: An examination of Weiss's typology of loneliness. *Journal of Personality and Social Psychology*, 46(6), 1313–21.

Ryan, J. & Carroll, J. (2005). Canaries in the coalmine. International students in Western universities. In J. Carroll and J. Ryan (eds), *Teaching International Students*, 1–10. London: Routledge.

Ryan, M. (2003). Contemporary issues in student housing finance. *New Directions for Student Services*, 103 (Fall), 59–71.

Sable, M., Danis, F., Mauzy, D. & Gallagher, S. (2006). Barriers to reporting sexual assault for women and men: Perspectives of college students. *Journal of American College Health*, 55(3), 157–62.

Samuelson, P. (1954). The Pure Theory of Public Expenditure. *Review of Economics and Statistics*, 36(4), 387–9.

Sarason, B., Sarason, I. & Gurung, R. (1997). Close personal relationships and health outcomes: A key to the role of social support. In S. Duck (ed.), *Handbook of Personal Relationships: Theory, research, and intervention* (2nd edn), 547–73. Chichester: Wiley.

Savicki, V., Downing-Burnette, R., Heller, L., Binder, F. & Suntinger, W. (2004). Contrasts, changes and correlates in actual and potential intercultural adjustment. *International Journal of Intercultural Relations*, 28(3–4), 311–29.

Savin-Williams, R. & Berndt, T. (1990). Friendship and peer relations. In S. Feldman and G. Elliot (eds), *At the Threshold: The developing adolescent*, 277–302. Cambridge, MA: Harvard University Press.

Sawir, E. (2005). Language difficulties of international students in Australia: The effects of prior learning experience. *International Education Journal*, 6(5), 567–80.

Schneiders, B. & Lucus, C. (2008). Cabbies' boilover ends in victory – Assault abuse fare evasion 12-hour shifts poor security all this for $8 an hour. *Age*, 1 May.

Schwartz, A. & Whitaker, C. (1990). Suicide among college students: Assessment, treatment and intervention. In S. Blumenthal (ed.), *Suicide Over the Life Cycle*, 303–40. Washington, DC: American Psychiatric Press.

Schweitzer, R. (1996). Problems and awareness of support services among students at an urban Australian university. *Journal of American College Health*, 45(2), 73–81.

Scott, S. (1999). The academic as service provider: Is the customer always right? *Journal of Higher Education Policy and Management*, 21(2), 193–202.

Segal, P. (1994). As they see us and as we see them: American students view foreigners and foreign-born students view Americans. *Migration World Magazine*, 22(2–3), 17–21.

Selvadurai, R. (1991). Adequacy of selected services to international students in an urban college. *Urban Review*, 23(4), 271–85.

Sen, A. (1985). Well-being, agency and freedom: The Dewey Lectures 1984. *Journal of Philosophy* 82(4), 169–221.

Sen, A. (1992). *Inequality Reexamined*. Cambridge, MA: Harvard University Press.

Sen, A. (1999). Global justice: Beyond international equity. In I. Kaul, I. Grunberg and M. Stern (eds), *Global Public Goods: International cooperation in the 21st century*, 116–25. New York: Oxford University Press.

Sen, A. (2000). *Development as Freedom*. New York: Anchor Books.

Senate Legal and Constitutional References Committee (2005). *Questions Taken on Notice*, Immigration and Multicultural and Indigenous Affairs Portfolio. Inquiry into the Administration and Operation of the Migration Act 1958, 11 October.

Senate Legal and Constitutional References Committee (2006). *Administration and Operation of the Migration Act 1958 Report*, March. Canberra: Parliament of Australia. Accessed 14 February 2008 at www.aph.gov.au/Senate/committee/legcon_ctte/migration/report/index.htm.

Shanghai Jiao Tong University Institute of Higher Education (SJTUIHE) (2008). *Academic Ranking of World Universities*. Accessed 28 August 2008 at www.arwu.org/.

Sharif, B. (1998). The forgotten world on campus: Acculturation and health issues of international students. *Abstract. Health Educator*, 30(1), 11–18.

Sheridan, G. (2009). Blind eye to racism. *Australian*, 4 June.

Sherry, C., Bhat, R., Beaver, B. & Ling, A. (2004). Students' as customers: The expectations and perceptions of local and international students. Paper presented at the Herdsa Conference, *Sarawak*, 4–7 July.

Sidhu, R. (2006). *Universities and Globalisation: To market, to market*. London: Lawrence Erlbaum.

Silverman, M. (2002). Suicide Assessment, Intervention and Prevention, *The Doctor will See You Now*. Accessed 20 March 2009 at www.thedoctorwillseeyounow.com/articles/behavior/suicide_13/.

Silverman, M., Meyer, P., Sloane, F., Raffel, M. & Pratt, D. (1997). The big ten student suicide study: A 10-year study of suicides on Midwestern University campuses. *Suicide & Life-Threatening Behavior*, 27(3), 285–303.

Singh, M. (2005). Enabling translational learning communities: Policies, pedagogies and politics of educational power. In P. Ninnes and M. Hellsten (eds), *Internationalising Higher Education: Critical explorations of pedagogy and policy*, 9–36. Dordrecht: Springer.

Si-Tayeb, S. (1982). *Nature and Distribution of Problems Encountered by Foreign Students at the University of Alabama*. PhD, University of Alabama, Tuscaloosa.

Skelton, M. (2008). Cited by Sonja, R. *The revolution will not be Anglicised: international students and the Australian student movement*. Accessed 2 May 2008 at http://jura.org.au/files/jura/Mutiny%2030%20-%20WEB.pdf.

Skinner, K. (2007). *International Student Access: The regulatory dilemma of American higher education*. DEd, Peabody College for Teachers of Vanderbilt University, Nashville.

Slattery, L. (2008). Australian universities fear a dangerous dependence. *Chronicle of Higher Education*, August.

Smith, G., Lambert, S., Knox, G., Morey, A. & Foster, C. (2000). *Looking Behind the Numbers: How international students evaluate their Australian experience, a survey of international students who finished a course of study in 1999*. Canberra: Commonwealth Department of Education, Training and Youth Affairs.

Smith, G., Morey, A. & Teece, M. (2002). *How International Students Evaluate Their Australian Experience*. Canberra: Australian Education International.

Smith, M. & Fossey, R. (1995) *Crime on Campus: Legal issues and Campus Administration*. Phoenix: Oryx Press.

Smith, S. (2007). National Liaison Committee for International Students in Australia, Submission to Residential Accommodation Issues Paper, Consumer Affairs Victoria. Accessed 31 July 2009 at www.nlc.edu.au/research%20files/nlc_cav_housingpaper.pdf.

Smolentseva, A. (2004). International students in Russia. *International Higher Education*, Summer. Accessed 19 September 2000 at www.bc.edu/bc_org/avp/soe/cihe/newsletter/News36/text011.htm.

Snider, P. (2001). Counselling for international students in Western universities: A cross-cultural examination of counselling expectations and services. *International Education Journal*, 2(5), 61–85.

Solano, C. & Koester, N. (1989). Loneliness and communication problems: Subjective anxiety or objective skills? *Personality and Social Psychology Bulletin*, 15(1), 126–33.

Solberg, V., Ritsma, S., Davis, B., Tata, S. & Jolly, A. (1994). Asian-American students' severity of problems and willingness to seek help from university counselling centres: Role of previous counselling experience, gender and ethnicity. *Journal of Counseling Psychology*, 41(3), 275–9.

Song, A., Richters, J., Crawford, J. & Kippax, S. (2005). HIV and sexual health knowledge and sexual experience among Australian-born and overseas-born students in Sydney. *Journal of Adolescent Health*, 37(3), 243.e249–243.e214.

Spack, R. (1997). The acquisition of academic literacy in a second language: A longitudinal case study. *Written Communication*, 14(1), 3–62.

Spears, A. (1999). Race and ideology: An introduction. In A. Spears (ed.), *Race and Ideology: Language, symbolism and popular culture*, 11–59. Detroit: Wayne State Press.

Spencer, S., Ruhs, M., Anderson, B. & Rogaly, B. (2007). *Migrants' lives beyond the workplace: The experiences of Central and East European migrants in the UK*. Report funded by the Joseph Rowntree Foundation, London.

Spencer-Rodgers, J. (2001). Consensual and individual stereotypic beliefs about international students among American host nationals. *International Journal of Intercultural Relations*, 25, 639–57.

Spencer-Rodgers, J. & McGovern, T. (2002). Attitudes towards the culturally different: The role of intercultural communication barriers, affective responses, consensual stereotypes, and perceived threats. *International Journal of Intercultural Relations*, 26(6), 609–31.

Stephens, K. (1997). Cultural stereotyping and intercultural communication: Working with students from the People's Republic of China in the UK. *Language and Education*, 11(2), 113–24.

Stephenson, J., Belesis, M. & Balliet, W. (2005). Variability in college student suicide: Age, gender, and race. *Journal of College Student Psychotherapy*, 19(4), 5–33.

Stewart, A. (2006). Work Choices in Overview: Big bang or slow burn? *Economic and Labour Relations Review*, 16(2), 25–60.

Stigler, G. (1971). The Theory of Economic Regulation. *Bell Journal of Economics*, The RAND Corporation, 2(1), 3–21.

Stokes, J. (1985). The relation of social network and individual difference variables to loneliness. *Journal of Personality and Social Psychology*, 48(4), 981–90.

Stokes, J. & Levin, I. (1986). Gender differences in predicting loneliness from social network characteristics. *Journal of Personality and Social Psychology*, 51(5), 1069–74.

Stone, N. (2006). Internationalising the student learning experience: Possible indicators. *Journal of Studies in International Education*, 10(4), 409–13.

Stoynoff, S. (1997). Factors associated with international students' academic achievement. *Journal of Instructional Psychology*, 24(1), 56–69.

Study Melbourne (2008). *Overseas Student Experience Taskforce Terms of Reference*. Melbourne: Victorian Government.

Stuewe-Portnoff, G. (1988). Loneliness: Lost in the landscape of meaning. *Journal of Psychology*, 122(6), 545–55.

Sugimoto, Y. (2009). 'Japanese culture': An overview. In Y. Sugimoto (ed.), *The Cambridge Companion to Modern Japanese Culture*, 1–20. Melbourne: Cambridge University Press.

Sundeen, R. (1984). Explaining the fear of crime among international students from developing countries: A revised model. *Criminal Justice Review*, 9(2), 7–13.

Suren, G. (2008). *China–Australia Workshop: Managing international students*. Accessed 4 November at http://suren.totuba.com/2008/10/27/china-australia-workshop-managing-international-students/#commentarea 2008.

Takeda, K. (2005). The excruciating job hunt. *Global: The magazine of the overseas students' association*, September, University of Adelaide.

Tam, O. & Morrison, K. (2005). Undergraduate students in part time employment in China. *Educational Studies*, 31(2), 169–80.

Tan, W. & Simpson, K. (2008). Overseas educational experience of Chinese students. *Journal of Research in International Education*, 7(1), 93–112.

Tatar, S. (2005). Classroom participation by international students: The case of Turkish graduate students. *Journal of Studies in International Education*, 9(4), 337–55.

Taylor, C. (1988). *Sources of the Self: The making of modern identity*. Cambridge: Harvard University Press.

Teekens, H. (2003). The requirement to develop specific skills for teaching in an intercultural setting. *Journal of Studies in International Education*, 7(1), 108–19.

Thomas, K., & Althen, G. (1989). Counseling foreign students. In J. Pedersen and J. Lonner (eds), *Counseling across cultures* (3rd edition) 205–41. Honolulu: University of Hawai'i Press.

Thompson, A. (2006). *Entrepreneurship and Business Innovation*. PhD, Murdoch University, Perth.

Thompson, J., Samiratedu, V. & Rafter, J. (1993). The effects of on-campus residence on first-time college students. *NASPA Journal*, 31(1), 41–7.

Thune, T. (2007). University-industry collaboration: The network embeddedness approach. *Science and Public Policy*, 34(3), 158–68.

Tibbits, A. & Robinson, G. (2008). Balcony victim's desperate call. *Sydney Morning Herald*, 4 November. Accessed 23 January 2009 at www.smh.com.au/news/national/balcony-victim-calls-000/2008/11/03/1225560738032.html.

Times (2008). World university rankings. *Times Higher Education Supplement*. Accessed on 30 March at www.thes.co.uk (subscription required).

Todd, B. (2007). Hooliganism or violent intolerance? A comparative look at the problem of hate crime in Russia and the United States. *School of Russian and Asian Studies*. Accessed 15 August 2008 at www.sras.org/hate_crime_in_russia.

Tolbert, V. (2006). From hard waiver to mandatory: Ensuring a coverage for international students. *Spectrum*, April, 14–16.

Trades Union Congress (TUC) (2009). *TUC Commission on Vulnerable Employment, Hard Work Hidden Lives*. Accessed 11 August at www.vulnerableworkers.org.uk/cove-report/full-report/.

Tran, L. (2006). Different shades of the collective way of thinking: Vietnamese and Chinese international students' reflection on academic writing. *Journal of Asia TEFL*, 3(3), 121–41.

Tremblay, K. (2005). Academic mobility and immigration. *Journal of Studies in International Education*, 9 (3), 196–228.

Trestrail, C. (2005). *Full-fee Paying International Students at Murdoch University 1985–1991: A policy case study*. PhD, Curtin University, Perth.

Triandis, H. (1989). Cross-cultural studies of individualism and collectivism. In J. Berman (ed.), *Nebraska Symposium on Motivation*, 41–133. Lincoln: University of Nebraska Press.

Triandis, H., Bontempo, R, Villareal, M., Asai, M. & Lucca, N. (1988). Individualism and collectivism: Cross-cultural perspectives on self-ingroup relationships. *Journal of Personality and Social Psychology*, 54(2), 323–38.

Tseng, W. & Newton, F. (2002). International students' strategies for wellbeing. *College Student Journal*, 36(4), 591–7.

Tulloch, C. (2007). Vulnerable Groups. Presentation to the Student welfare Reference Committee, June 2007. Canberra: Commonwealth Department of Immigration and Citizenship.

UK Council for International Education (UKCISA) (2004). *International Students in UK Universities and Colleges, Broadening our Horizons – Report of the UKCISA survey*. London: UKCISA.

UK Council for International Education (UKCISA) (2006). *New Horizons. The Experiences of International Students in UK Further Education Colleges – Report of the UKCISA survey, 2006*. London: UKCISA.

UK Council for International Education (UKCISA) (2007). *Benchmarking the Provision of Services for International Students in Higher Education Institutions*. London: UKCISA.

UNITE (Student Accommodation) & UKCISA (2006). *The International Student Experience Report 2006*. London: UNITE/UKCISA.

UNITE & UKCISA (2006). National Readership Survey 2006. Classification of social classes in UK. Accessed 8 March 2009 at www.businessballs.com/demographicsclassifications.htm.

United Nations (1948). *Universal Declaration of Human Rights*. Adopted 10 December, General Assembly Resolution 217A (III), UN GAOR, 3rd session. (Resolutions, Part 1, at 71, UN Doc. A/810, 1948).

United Nations Development Program (UNDP) (1994). *Human Development Report*. New York: United Nations Development Program.

Universities Australia (UA) (2008). *Provision of Education to International Students: Code of practice and guidelines for Australian universities*. Accessed 2 April at www.universitiesaustralia.edu.au/documents/publications/CodeOfPracticeAndGuidelines2005.pdf (9 February 2008).

University of Melbourne (2004). *Students from Asia: Issues in learning and teaching*. Melbourne: Faculty of Education and Asialink, University of Melbourne.

University of Queensland Social Research Centre (UQSRC) (2005). *Final Report of the Survey of International Students' Spending in Australia*. Prepared for Australian Education International (AEI), Department of Education, Science and Training (DEST). Revised 28 July 2005 by M. Western, P. Boreham, W. Laffan, M. Haynes, J. Chesters, M. Tighe and Dionne Arts.

Urias, D. (2005). Empowering the Disenfranchised: Supporting spouses of international students and scholars. *International Educator*, 14(2), 42–7.

Urias, D. & Yeakey, C. (in press). Analysis of the U.S. student visa system: Misperceptions, barriers, and consequences. *Journal of Studies in International Education*.

Vaughan-Williams, N. (2008). Borders, territory, law. *International Political Sociology*, 4(2), 322–38.

Vera, E. & Schupp, T. (2006). Network analysis in comparative social sciences. *Comparative Education*, 42(3), 405–29.

Verbik, L. & Lasanowski, V. (2007). *International Student Mobility: Patterns and trends*. London: Observatory on Borderless Higher Education (OBHE).

Vincent-Lancrin, S. (2007). Developing capacity through cross-border tertiary education. In Organization for Economic Cooperation and Development (OECD) and the World Bank, *Cross-Border Tertiary Education: A way towards capacity development, 47–108*. Paris: OECD.

Volet, S. & Ang, G. (1998). Culturally mixed groups on international campus: An opportunity for intercultural learning. *Higher Education Research & Development*, 17(1), 5–24.

Volet, S. & Tan-Quigley, A. (1999). Interactions of Southeast Asian students and administrative staff at university in Australia: The significance of reciprocal understanding. *Journal of Higher Education Policy and Management*, 21(1), 95–115.

Volkwein, J., Szelest, B. & Lizotte, A. (1995). The relationship of campus crime to campus and student characteristics. *Research in Higher Education*, 36(6), 647–69.

Wade, M. (2009). Rudd steps in as fury builds over assaults on Indian students. *Sydney Morning Herald*, 30 May.

Wade, M. & Das, S. (2009). India fury on student bashings. *Age*, 29 May.

Wan, G. (2001). The learning experience of Chinese students in American universities: A cross-cultural perspective. *College Student Journal*, March, 28–44.

Wang, J. (2004). *A Study of the Adjustment of International Graduate Students at American Universities, Including Both Resilience Characteristics and Traditional Background Factors*. PhD, Florida State University, Tallahassee.

Ward, C. (2005). Comments during plenary session, 'Internationalisation III'. Paper presented at the annual of ISANA, International Education Association Inc., 2 December. Reported in V. Anderson (2006), 4.

Ward, C. (2008). Thinking outside the Berry boxes: New perspective on identity, acculturation and intercultural relations. *International Journal of Intercultural Relations*, 32(2), 105–14.

Ward, C. & Chang, W. (1997). 'Cultural fit': A new perspective on personality and sojourner adjustment. *International Journal of Intercultural Relations*, 21(4), 525–33.

Ward, C. & Kennedy, A. (1994). Acculturation strategies, psychological adjustment and sociocultural competence during cross-cultural transitions. *International Journal of Intercultural Relations*, 18(3), 329–43.

Ward, C., Leong, C.-H. & Low, M. (2004). Personality and sojourner adjustment: An exploration of the Big Five and the cultural fit proposition. *Journal of Cross-Cultural Psychology*, 35(2), 137–51.

Ward, C. & Masgoret, A.-M. (2004). *The Experiences of International Students in New Zealand: Report on the results of the national survey*. Wellington: New Zealand Ministry of Education.

Ward, C., Okura, Y., Kennedy, A. & Kojima, T. (1998). The U-curve on trial: A longitudinal study of psychological and sociocultural adjustment during cross-cultural transition. *International Journal of Intercultural Relations*, 22(3), 277–91.

Weiss, R. (1973). *Loneliness: The experience of emotional and social isolation*. Cambridge, MA: MIT Press.

Weiss, R. (1974). The provisions of social relationships. In Z. Rubin (ed.), *Doing unto Others*. New Jersey: Prentice Hall.

Wesley, M. (2009). *Building an Asia-literate Australia*. Griffith Asia Institute. Brisbane: Griffith University.

Whitlock, J., Eckenrode, J. & Silverman, D. (2006). Self-injurious behaviours in a college population. *Pediatrics*, 117(6), 1939–48.

Wilkinson, L. & Kavan, H. (2003). Dialogues with dragons: Helping Chinese students' academic achievement. *ATLAANZ Conference proceedings*, 119–31, Waikato: University of Waikato, ATLAANZ.

Woolcock, M. (2000). The place of social capital in understanding social and economic outcomes. In J. Helliwell (ed.), *The Contribution of Human and Social Capital to Sustained Economic Growth and Well-Being*. Ottawa: Human Resource Development Canada and OECD.

World Bank (2009). *Data and Statistics*. Accessed 18 September 2009 at http://web.worldbank.org/WBSITE/EXTERNAL/DATASTATISTICS/0,,contentMDK:20399244~menuPK:1390200~pagePK:64133150~piPK:64133175~theSitePK:239419~isCURL:Y,00.html.

Xi, M. & Ning, G. (2006). *Christmas in Summer: Chinese students in New Zealand*. Shenzhen: Haitian Publisher.

Xia, Z.-H. (1991). *Asian students' adjustment problems at the University of Wisconsin-Madison*. PhD, University of Wisconsin-Madison, Madison.

Yang, E., Wong, S., Hwang, M. & Heppner, M. (2002). Widening our global view: The development of career counseling services for international students. *Journal of Career Development*, 28(3), 203–13.

Yang, R., Noels, K. & Saumure, K. (2006). Multiple routes to cross-cultural adaptation for international students: Mapping the paths between self-construals, English language confidence, and adjustment. *International Journal of Intercultural Relations*, 30(4), 487–506.

Yang, Y. (2008). *Chinese International Students' Perceptions of their Learning and Social Experiences in New Zealand*. MMgt thesis, Massey University, Wellington.

Zhang, N. & Dixon, D. (2003). Acculturation and attitudes of Asian international students toward seeking psychological help. *Multicultural Counselling and Development*, 31(3), 205–22.

Zhu, W. (2004). Faculty views on the importance of writing, the nature of academic writing, and teaching and responding to writing in the disciplines. *Journal of Second Language Writing*, 13(8), 29–48.

Zimmerman, D. (2003). Peer effects in academic outcomes: Evidence from a natural experiment. *Review of economics and statistics*, 85(1), 9–23.

INDEX